Social Class on British
and American Screens

Social Class on British and American Screens

Essays on Cinema and Television

Edited by NICOLE CLOAREC,
DAVID HAIGRON *and*
DELPHINE LETORT

McFarland & Company, Inc., Publishers
Jefferson, North Carolina

Acknowledgments

We would like to thank all the people and institutions who have contributed to make this volume possible, in particular Rennes 2 University and its research group ACE (EA 1796) which, in partnership with 3L.AM (EA 4335) at the University of Le Mans (Université du Maine), hosted the conference which inspired most of the essays.

We would also like to thank the research groups LIDILE (Rennes), HCTI (Université de Bretagne Occidentale), ERIBIA (Caen), ESO (Rennes 2), the SERCIA association, the Institut des Amériques and the Institut franco-américain for their support.

LIBRARY OF CONGRESS CATALOGUING-IN-PUBLICATION DATA

Names: Cloarec, Nicole, editor. | Haigron, David, editor. | Letort, Delphine, editor.
Title: Social class on British and American screens : essays on cinema and television / edited by Nicole Cloarec, David Haigron and Delphine Letort.
Description: Jefferson, North Carolina : McFarland & Company, Inc., Publishers, 2016 | Includes bibliographical references and index.
Identifiers: LCCN 2015048996 | ISBN 9781476662343 (softcover : acid free paper) ∞
Subjects: LCSH: Social classes in motion pictures. | Motion pictures—Social aspects—Great Britain. | Television broadcasting—Social aspects—Great Britain. | England—In motion pictures. | Motion pictures—Social aspects—United States. | Television broadcasting—Social aspects—United States. | United States—In motion pictures.
Classification: LCC PN1995.9.S6 S6215 2016 | DDC 791.43/6552—dc23
LC record available at http://lccn.loc.gov/2015048996

BRITISH LIBRARY CATALOGUING DATA ARE AVAILABLE

ISBN (print) 978-1-4766-6234-3
ISBN (ebook) 78-1-4766-2312-2

© 2016 Nicole Cloarec, David Haigron and Delphine Letort. All rights reserved

No part of this book may be reproduced or transmitted in any form or by any means, electronic or mechanical, including photocopying or recording, or by any information storage and retrieval system, without permission in writing from the publisher.

On the cover: Demond Wilson and Redd Foxx from *Sanford and Son*, 1972–1977 (NBC/Photofest)

Printed in the United States of America

McFarland & Company, Inc., Publishers
    Box 611, Jefferson, North Carolina 28640
    www.mcfarlandpub.com

Table of Contents

Acknowledgments   iv

Introduction   NICOLE CLOAREC   1

Part One. The Persistence of Stereotypes: Social Class in TV Sitcoms and Series

Six Decades of Social Class in American Sitcoms   RICHARD BUTSCH   18

Social Class and Class Distinctions in "Britcoms" (1950s–2000s)   RENÉE DICKASON   34

Authenticity and Performance of Class in British Factual TV Series   JONATHAN BIGNELL   58

Part Two. Going Beyond Stereotypes? Social Class in Documentaries and Docudramas

"The only way is UP": Social Mobility in Michael Apted's *UP* Documentary Series   SABINE HILLEN   76

Race and Class in Luisa Dantas's *Land of Opportunity*   DELPHINE LETORT   89

"Gizza job! I can do that!" The Unmaking of the British Working Class in Alan Bleasdale's *Boys from the Blackstuff*   CARYS LEWIS   101

From Documentary to Docudrama: Post-War British Television and the Social Issues of the Lower Classes   GEORGES FOURNIER   115

Part Three. Representing Class Divisions in Films

The Representation of Strike in British Cinema Since 1956: From
    Class to Gender and Ethnicity   ANNE-LISE MARIN-LAMELLET   134

In Praise of the Working Poor: Archeology of Class Struggle through
    the Arts of Representation in *Comrades* and *The Fool*
    NICOLE CLOAREC   153

Ken Loach and the Geographies of Class   WENDY EVERETT   167

Part Four. Social Class through a Gender Perspective

Vanishing Act: The Sexualization of the Workplace and
    Disappearance of Class in American Television Dramas
    (1990s–2010s)   AVA BARON   184

The Gender and Class Politics of Social Realism in *The Wire*
    T. ANN KENNEDY   204

Striking Women: *Salt of the Earth*, *Norma Rae* and *Bread and Roses*
    PENNY STARFIELD   218

Art and the Reversal of Hierarchies: Representing Women in
    Domestic Service in *Upstairs, Downstairs*
    DELPHINE LEMONNIER-TEXIER   234

About the Contributors   249

Index   251

Introduction

NICOLE CLOAREC

Shortly before becoming prime minister in 1990, John Major famously promised to build a "genuinely classless society."¹ Far from referring to a kind of Marxist utopia, the "classless society" Margaret Thatcher's successor envisaged was rather a meritocracy tightly controlled by a "responsible" elite, in keeping with his predecessor's vision of society made up of individuals governed first and foremost by self-interests,² and in which the very concept of class was something of the past.³ Nonetheless, the fact that after a grocer's daughter, the Brixton-grown, state-school educated son of a circus performer could become prime minister was nothing but a very inspiring example of upward mobility.

More than 20 years later, in a speech to Tory constituents, John Major declared he found "truly shocking" that "in every single sphere of British influence, the upper echelons of power in 2013 are held overwhelmingly by the privately educated or the affluent middle class."⁴ After the advent of David Cameron and Nick Clegg at the head of the government was dubbed the "return of the toffs" in the media, the perceived collapse in social mobility has been amply commented upon by many—including scholars and politicians such as the government's social mobility adviser and former Labour Cabinet member Alan Milburn who declared:

> The shocking lack of social mobility is entrenched in British society. There is a glass ceiling in British society—and more and more people are hitting it. Whether it is law or medicine or journalism or politics, the upper echelons of Britain are dominated by a social elite. [...] One-third of MPs, half of senior doctors and over two-thirds of high court judges all hail from the private schools that educate just 7% of our country's children. The data is so stark, the story so consistent, that it has all the hallmarks of social engineering. Sir John Major is right to be shocked.⁵

More surprisingly, similar cries of alarm have recently been sounded across the Atlantic, in a nation which has supposedly built itself by rejecting the rigidity of the British class system in favor of a truly "classless" society in which the American dream holds the promise of equal opportunities for all to rise socially. In his 2014 state-of-the-union address, President Barack Obama deplored the increasing social inequalities that compromise the American dream[6] and would render success stories such as his own or House Speaker John Boehner's no longer possible.[7] *New Yorker* financial journalist John Cassidy humorously commented: "It's not often these days that you hear any progressive politician use the term 'class,' but the President, to his credit, didn't shy away from the 'c' word."[8] In her book *Hard Choices*, Hillary Clinton goes as far as talking about "the cancer of inequality" that must be stopped in order "to give people in our country the ladders of opportunity that have always been a hallmark of the United States and the American Dream."[9]

Despite Lady Thatcher's endeavor to erase the term from the British political scene, the notion of social class has come back in the national debate—with a vengeance. The large media coverage and popular success of "The Great British Class Survey" bear witness to the enduring fascination British people have with questions of social distinction. Through that survey, which draws on Pierre Bourdieu's notion of "cultural capital" and examines the respondents' cultural and social life as much as their economic standing, a group of sociologists claims to identify a new model composed of seven classes,[10] which has triggered a number of academic debates in addition to the media buzz. A new vocabulary has even emerged in Britain around the word "chav" which has been popularized as a term of abuse for loud, aggressive working class youth. *The Guardian*'s columnist Owen Jones analyzed its routine demonization in the media[11] in his acclaimed book *Chavs: The Demonization of the Working Class* (2011), which exposes class hatred in modern Britain, raising the nagging question: "How did the salt of the earth come to be viewed as the scum of the earth?"

If such media coverage might not seem so surprising in Great Britain where "class, like the weather and the monarchy, is a peculiarly and particularly British preoccupation,"[12] class-bound debates are not the sole province of class-obsessed Britain. Consider the recent popular success of French economist Thomas Piketty in the United States: his latest book *Capital in the Twenty-First Century* (2014), which denounces growing inequalities in Western countries and in the U.S. in particular where, he argues, "the egalitarian pioneer ideal has faded into oblivion," jumped onto the *New York Times* best-seller list in February 2014.[13]

Ironically, the definition of class itself has increasingly been the subject of much debating among scholars. If until the mid–1970s class analysis provided "the grandest and most masterly narrative available,"[14] the Marxist idea that social history was the result of class structure and class struggle has repeatedly been questioned since then. After long-lasting quarrels opposing different models of class structures and class formations[15]—class as identity and class as relationship—class has ceased to be the ultimate conceptual framework that historians and sociologists use to analyze modern societies and their economic, social and political evolutions. Traditional Marxist-based models of clear-cut, homogeneous and self-conscious classes have thus been dismissed as oversimplified, overlooking the actual diversity of social life.[16] Most specifically, cultural perspectives, feminist and postcolonial studies have challenged class as the prevailing category of social analysis, foregrounding instead a conception of identities as decentered and motile, the products of conflicting cultural forces and interpersonal relationships.

What emerges from this ongoing debate is a significant shift from analyzing society through the concept of class to analyzing the very concept of class as a discursive and representational construct determined by historical context and discourse. In other words, the new class paradigms are as much conceptual models constructed to analyze society as the subjects of analysis themselves.[17] From this perspective, the part that collective and personal representations play in "class making," conceived as a continuous process of classification and social positioning,[18] becomes critical. Now cinema and television have long proved to be powerful popular media that contribute to building up, strengthening or, on the contrary, challenging collective and stereotypical representations of social groups.

Many recent studies have documented the part that Hollywood and American films in general have played in bolstering and sustaining the American dream. Studies on early American cinema have shown how cinema gained its popularity by appealing primarily to working class audiences in industrial cities and quickly became one of the means for integrating newcomers into the values and customs of their new country. Very soon, though, the film industry, while originally "receiving their principal support from the lowest and most invisible classes in American society,"[19] geared production toward the "broader, more affluent white-collar trade"[20] and its consensual middle class ideology. As Robert Sklar aptly observes, notwithstanding the fact that "as a business and as a social phenomenon, the motion pictures came to life in the United States when they made contact with working-class needs and desires," movies also soon "became a major factor in the reorientation of traditional values. [...] For no matter how despised they were by defenders of traditional middle class culture, movies were, after all, made by men deeply committed to the capitalist values, attitudes and ambitions that were part of the dominant social order."[21] Despite some notable early exceptions—Charlie Chaplin's films and his popular tramp character, or D.W. Griffith's melodramas pitting the deserving poor against depraved rich villains—film scholar Steven J. Ross has shown that early movies urged many Americans to conceive of themselves as being "middle class."[22] Hollywood in particular has long nourished the myth of an open society where the "cross class fantasies" emphasize class harmony while eschewing any realistic representation of working class living conditions. Images of the middle class have prevailed along with racial and political discourses that contribute to marginalizing other classes—be they the ruling dynasties or the underclass. Likewise, television dramas more often than not mirror the mainstream ideology by extolling the virtues of the middle class, their social aspirations and their conservative values.

In the United Kingdom, portrayals of class and class differences in the media have proved enduringly popular: from the lasting success of television series such as *Upstairs, Downstairs* (LWT, 1971–75, updated in 2010 by the BBC) or the multi-award-winning, critically-acclaimed *Downton Abbey* (ITV, 2010–) to the character of Vicky Pollard in *Little Britain* (BBC, 2003–06), from the nostalgic indulgence of heritage films to the scathing criticisms of Ken Loach's social realist films, television and cinema have both shaped and challenged stereotypes that articulate the ideological discourse on class.

Caught in the dialectic movement of documenting social realities while also contributing to changing them, films have therefore been battlegrounds for public understandings of labor, capital, and class. But the notion of class not only helps shed a critical light on the content of film representations, it also raises questions of aesthetic strategies and genres. Class therefore proves a useful concept as it raises aesthetic and ideological questions that underpin the analyses of genres, influencing conventions and characterization. The concept of class representation has thus been a major critical tool in a number of academic works about British cinema,[23] its specificity as "British" or "English," its generic and aesthetics classifications: film critic John Hill argues that social realism has permitted "the making visible of the working class"[24] within Great Britain whereas the heritage film and its romance have been associated with the upper classes. Sue Harper contends that British costume dramas from the 1930s to the 1950s build up a discourse of class that embodies an "aristocratic/proletarian alliance."[25] John Hill relates the tradition of realist and documentary aesthetics to class:

> Within the British cinematic tradition, [cinematic realism] has generally involved the working class. In so far as the working class is neither more nor less "real" than other social groups, the idea that realism is linked to the representation of the working class derives in part from context, and specifically the perceived absence of (adequate) representation of this group within the dominant discursive regimes.[26]

More recently, a new trend of horror films and thrillers dubbed "hoodie horrors" has been cashing in on the so-called latter-day British "underclass" whom Johnny Walker identifies as the source of terror in the genre:

> The impoverished and economically deprived milieu of the "chav," the new British "underclass"—a social stratum which is the subject of considerable negative mythologizing and stereotyping and which is blamed by many in authority for the latest phase of Britain's alleged moral decline—has functioned as a potent allegorical backdrop against which the most interesting, and most controversial, British horror films have recently emerged.[27]

In light of such considerations, the present collection of essays intends to explore the notion of class through fiction and nonfiction films made in the UK and in the U.S. Contributors were invited to consider cinema through the prism of class and to focus on the dialectical relationship between films that document a social reality that in return seeps into their narrative and help elaborate or distort collective myths that involve stereotypical representations of social groups.[28] The focus on two distinct cultural areas allows comparative and complementary views to be implemented on two societies which to a large extent have come to define themselves in relation to each other. Both diachronic and synchronic perspectives have been adopted to highlight the legacy and persistence of class as a concept that affects so many other aspects of the social and cultural life in these societies.

In so doing, the present collection does not aim at analyzing films to give a thorough account of the social fabric of American and British societies (which would be far too presumptuous a task) or even the experience of a specific class. Rather, it intends to question the very relationship between class and film discourse. In other words, not only how films shape visions of class while relying heavily on social stereotypes or on the contrary challenging and subverting them, but also how the notion of class can highlight questions of aesthetic, discursive and representational strategies.

Media scholar Richard Butsch's essay opens the first part dedicated to the genres of television sitcoms and series. His study encompasses an impressively comprehensive research on six decades of American television situations comedies that, he argues, reproduce and reinforce stereotypes of social classes. Focusing on the domestic sitcoms that have been the mainstay, the bread and butter, of prime-time television over the last six decades, he demonstrates that social class predetermines the representation of family life in the genre. Considering characters' appearances and narrative formulae as signifiers of class, Butsch reveals pervasive and persistent images that crystallize as cultural types. As popular television programs with high audience rates, sitcoms illustrate the power of dominant culture to shape perceptions of gender and social class through the codified representation of working class and middle class males and females. While the traditional nuclear family has given way to a much broader picture that includes new character types and situations (including the gay parents, the single-parent family unit, etc.), the stock character of the ineffectual, stout, even grotesque man has persisted as the dominant image of the working class. Middle class men may shy away from assuming patriarchal control, but they "still retain self-respect, while the working class do not." Butsch ironically notes that *"plus ça change, plus c'est la même chose"*: major upheavals in American society and culture have reverberated through the television spectrum, yet they have not dislodged the patterns of class representation that are replicated through more than three hundred domestic sitcoms comprised in the everyday programs of American television.

Likewise in Great Britain, social representations have been central to many popular British television series. Renée Dickason's comprehensive analysis focuses on how social classes have been depicted in British sitcoms from the 1950s to the 2000s. She questions the reliability of the different social markers such as language and manners, examines how they have evolved through counter currents of deference and disdain and how workplaces in urban and rural settings are used to create a contrasted yet distorted representation of contemporary British society. If Britcoms make abundant use of stereotypes, they also provide vibrant examples of social discrepancies and (mis)understandings of social matters along with their political implications. Dickason thus argues that the "us and them" syndrome is much palpable in sitcoms depicting microcosms where a mythically "fair" and "civilized" society is pitted against differences leading to jealousies and the rejection of the "Others."

British television scholar Jonathan Bignell examines a fairly recent trend of British television called "factual television" and notices that its emphasis on character, storyline and performance undermines its claim to "class authenticity." Drawing on documentaries and soap operas that "have their own traditions and conventions for representing social class," factual television puts forth a claim to articulate "the representation of ordinary people and ordinary events." However, a major shift can be observed: while documentaries aim to present genuine representatives of the working class and soap operas pay particular attention to notions of genuineness and authenticity in the diegetic representation of class, reality television programs rely on "narratives of personal improvement and aspiration" and make "a spectacle of differences in social power and class," turning social authenticity into a performance so as to achieve an entertaining "emotional realism." Bignell contends that reality television programs do not challenge conservative representations of social class, for the "performance of identity and the testing of its authenticity and effectiveness have become ways of disciplining and stigmatizing class identities."

The second part focuses on the tradition of social documentary and docudramas, which have long been associated with social commitment. In the 1950s, technical developments of synchronized sound and light-weight cameras not only permitted on location interviews, but they prompted filmmakers to investigate the experience of their subjects in their direct social environment, empowering the speech of ordinary people. The first two essays deal with two outstanding examples of what Bill Nichols has termed the participatory documentary mode, whereby filmmakers "seek to represent their own direct encounter with their surrounding world,"[29] using interviews and compilation footage to tackle the minorities. The other two essays examine some British TV fiction films designed to be read as documentaries.

Sabine Hillen analyzes the renowned British documentary series *7UP*, which follows the lives of fourteen children from the age of seven every seven years. The series is rightly presented as an experiment that started in 1964 to test the initial assumption that a child's social background and education will determine his/her future. While underlining the originality of the film's endeavor and the long-term commitment on the part of its directors, Hillen considers the sociological limitations of the program is related to the format of the film apparatus itself since the focus on individual interviews foregrounds private lives and relationship rather than public issues.

Delphine Letort examines a lesser known but no less challenging documentary. Comprised of a documentary film and an Internet multi-platform project, Luisa Dantas's *Land of Opportunity* highlights the social consequences of reconstruction in the five-year time span since Hurricane Katrina wreaked havoc on the Mississippi Gulf Coast. Based on a series of interviews that construct "a criss-cross portrayal of the city," the documentary questions the economic debates that determined urban policies, revealing "the silent salience of class" which underlies those debates. While endeavoring to provide a detailed picture of reconstruction processes, the film captures "the implicit class distinctions that permeated the rationale for devising a series of priorities—affecting land use and home maintenance." Ultimately, it offers a platform to concerned citizens who are willing to make themselves heard.

Carys Lewis focuses on Alan Bleasdale's five-part television drama *Boys from the Blackstuff* (1982) which soon established itself as "the TV drama event of the eighties." Quoting E.P. Thompson's celebrated study on *The Making of the English Working Class*, Lewis argues that the series represents the "unmaking of the British working-class." Set in the grim landscape of the decaying Liverpool of the time, it follows the story of five men faced with chronic unemployment and subsequent loss of identity. She underlines the specificity of the series's production context, which made use of the innovative technique of the Light Mobile Control Room that provided a documentary-like feel to the film that contrasted with the screenwriter's Brechtian distancing devices. Lewis then explores how the representation of working-class men mobilizes a collective structure of feeling around notions of working class culture and what sociologist Raymond Williams has dubbed a "knowable community" of working class solidarity. In particular, she examines how *Boys from the Blackstuff* "succeeded at once in confusing and sharpening the viewer's identification with an understanding of the characters' plight in what many have deemed to be an elegy for a working class culture."

Georges Fournier offers a wide-ranging study of significant broadcasts in the history of British television that fitted in the ideal of television as a tool for the promotion of social democracy. Filmic testimonies on the state of the country abounded in postwar years, fueling debates and controversies about crucial social issues like housing and poverty. In the 1960s, in the wake of the British documentary tradition as well as factual radio programs like the radio ballads, a new generation of filmmakers was given the opportunity to explore the limits of the documentary model within the television media. Public broadcasting thus offered a unique environment that could accommodate unprecedented ambitious programs which managed to tackle political and social issues while using innovative techniques mixing fiction and documentary. Most specifically, these programs, focusing on the social issues of the lower classes, aimed at a greater understanding and acceptance of the difficulties the most disadvantaged classes encountered.

Paradoxically enough, if class, perceived to be so intrinsically constitutive of British society, has long been a pervasive motif in British cinema, representations of class conflicts have been much less frequent in mainstream films. The third part tackles the issue of representing class conflicts through three different perspectives: first through a diachronic perspective with the study of British films dealing with the representation of strikes since the mid–1950s, then through the analysis of two historical films set in the 19th century which both use self-reflexive *mise en scène* to question the "natural" social order of the time, lastly through a fresh approach to the cinema of Britain's longest-established and most consistent and committed social realist director Ken Loach, using the problematic of place and space in film and their relationship to social experience.

Anne-Lise Marin-Lamellet points out the paradox of a British cinema that has rarely represented labor disputes despite its long-lasting interest in the working class. However, she contends that the somewhat limited corpus of films produced since the mid–1950s provides good indications on the political and ideological debates that prevailed over the time. Her analysis reveals that despite noticeable evolution, most of the films have adopted an overwhelmingly critical view. Until the end of the 1970s, films were mainly satires, highly critical of the trade unions deemed responsible for the fragmentation of society. From the 1980s onwards and the watershed of the Thatcher years that set the neoliberal trend and caused the destruction of manufacturing industry while undermining working class identity, the portrayal of workers has become more complex. But workers' organizations such as trade unions are now being blamed for their absence, or even their share of responsibility in the fragmentation and depolitization of the British working class. Through a general evolution of generic conventions from comic satires to chronicles focusing on the plight of individuals, the strike films clearly follow a shift from a class to a post-class perspective that reflects the economic and social changes brought about by deindustrialization and deregulation, resulting in the systematic undermining of the working class's clout and culture. Marin-Lamellet concludes by examining other emerging forms of resistance and solidarity that accompany the shift in the representation of strikes from illustrating working class fights to depicting the struggles of women and minorities against the established white male order.

In the next essay, Nicole Cloarec analyzes two art-house films from the late 1980s which both eschew the distressing grittiness of social realism as well as the more comfortable nostalgic outlook of the costume drama that prevailed in British film productions of that period. While based on historical records that give voice to the dispossessed and downtrodden, Bill Douglas's *Comrades* and Christine Edzard's *The Fool* articulate a powerful denunciation of the social inequalities and injustices in 19th-century Britain. But to this effect, the two films use a highly self-reflexive *mise en scène* which highlights the artificiality of the arts of representation—be it pre-cinema optical devices or the stage— to expose the arbitrariness of the "natural" social order. In so doing, both films also provide an indirect scathing commentary on their own production time, when unions' power was systematically undermined and financial deregulation reigned supreme.

As Wendy Everett aptly remarks: "Just as it is impossible to think about British society without reference to class divisions, so too it is impossible to consider contemporary British cinema without reference to the films of Ken Loach, all of which are concerned with giving a voice to those who have traditionally been ignored, demeaned, or exploited, predominantly, of course, the working class or its post–Thatcher incarnation as 'underclass' or 'post-working class.'" Her essay offers a fresh approach to Loach's cinema through adopting a geographical, "horizontal" perspective to his films rather than the more traditional "vertical" approach positing "a direct correlation between historical event (as cause) and filmic production (as effect)." After examining the problematic of place and space in film and their relationship to social experience, Wendy Everett argues that not only are Loach's chosen locations particularly significant to each narrative, offering a "geography of class" which literally maps out what can be identified as the shrunken actualities of working-class life, but ultimately, it is through the tension inherent in the complex articulation of place that Loach is able to overcome the perceived limitations of cinema as regards the representation of social phenomena and of social class in particular. In other words, Loach's use of location proves to be the primary strategy to make the spectator aware of the wider structural problems that underlie the personal struggles of his protagonists, to make us aware of the invisible historical, social and political forces that shape out social reality.

As was mentioned above, debates about social classes have been challenged by feminist theories from the 1970s onwards. Feminist historians have rightfully observed that traditional Marxist theories more often than not overlooked more than half of humanity, even though they are still referred to as a "minority." They have insisted that, in many ways, women often experienced working life and class relations in a very different way from their white male counterparts and that tensions and conflicts between the sexes revealed competing claims of class and gender. As a result, they have contended that social identity could not be fully apprehended through the single perspective of class. Conversely, analyses of class structures and relations have thus been complexified by taking into account gender (and racial) perspectives. The last part offers remarkable illustrations of these theoretical developments in film studies.

Ava Baron's essay presents a very comprehensive sociological approach to the representation of women in relation to their workplace in American television dramas from the 1990s to the 2010s. Providing some historical background information from the 1970s, she draws attention to issues of sexuality in the workplace and their narrative treatment on television. While these dramas have offered women prominent roles in highly professional jobs such as lawyers, doctors, and police detectives, this increased visibility has ironically been accompanied by discursive and representational strategies that have downplayed issues related to hierarchy and power relationships between genders. Whereas sexual difference was first minimized by presenting women workers as looking and behaving like men, today's television dramas readily depict sexuality as normal and unproblematic in the workplace. Baron emphasizes the nagging issues of gender inequality and sexual harassment that are unheard of, thus appearing irrelevant or non-existent. The scholar argues that the legal and social realities of persistent gender inequalities and conflicts at work have been masked by television depiction of the workplace as "a space where power is irrelevant, hierarchical relations are portrayed as natural and reasonable and conflicts [...] as based solely on individual disagreements."

T. Ann Kennedy's essay is about one of the recent most critically acclaimed American television series—David Simon's *The Wire*. While observing the series's creator endeavored to provide much of the interpretative framework, which Simon claims is "about class," Kennedy questions his statement that season 2 (2005) is "a meditation on the death of work and the betrayal of the American working class." Indeed, the author contends the director's claim to "systemic social critique" is misleading as regards gender. Women are consistently depicted as a threat to "capitalist domesticity": foreign girls are associated with endangering the American domestic space and economy whereas black mothers are assimilated to a "culture of poverty." Analyzing the structural opposition between the "masculine space of the docks" in relation to "women's place in global economics," she demonstrates that *The Wire* "contributes to the mythologizing of its primary symbol: the industrial white male," making "a choice to avoid telling the story of U.S. working class women's displacement." Her harsh conclusion offers a radically new outlook on this celebrated series: "In the end *The Wire* uses poor women to realign the working class with masculinity and to align American morality with patrolling the borders of a 'good' nationalist capitalist domesticity."

Based on three films in which women play a leading role in industrial conflict, Penny Starfield's essay addresses the issue of class struggle through a gender perspective. After providing some useful insights into the history of American strike films and the questions they raise in terms of film aesthetics and the issue of "realism," she examines more closely the role of women in this subgenre. The three films she analyses, although produced in rather distant historical contexts and fairly different styles, prove to be highly significant case studies that detail the women's difficult path to political awareness. Filmed in a semi-documentary style at the height of the McCarthy era by blacklisted director Herbert J. Biberman, *Salt of the Earth* relates a Mexican American miners' strike in the South of the United States from the point of view of one of the miners' wife and how the women eventually come to take over the strike. The other two films, *Norma Rae* and *Bread and Roses*, while adopting more mainstream fictional modes, are concerned with the right of workers to unionize and similarly describe how women workers are gradually led into the struggle to defend their rights. The three films foreground women's role in industrial conflict and highlight not just issues of class but also of gender and ethnicity. Female activism may still be partly judged in terms of masculinity, with men being the guiding force in *Norma Rae* and *Bread and Roses*. However, women's involvement is shown to be instrumental in bringing the strikers' demands to a more or less happy conclusion, although their own fate remains open-ended. Full empowerment is achieved when they are no longer "surrogate strikers," but acting for themselves. Yet in each film the different path to empowerment is as much a personal struggle as a collective movement.

Lastly, Delphine Lemonnier-Texier recalls how before becoming a catchphrase for the representation of the spatial and social dichotomy that governs masters and servants in television period dramas, *Upstairs, Downstairs* (1971) was a radically new project both in terms of content and of aesthetics strategies. The series was indeed the brainchild of Jean Marsh and Eileen Atkins, two actresses hailing from working class families, who were concerned to document a historical dimension so far largely ignored in television shows, the parts of servants being then akin to "mobile props." Focusing on the second episode of season 1, in which the artist commissioned to paint her Ladyship's portrait decides to paint—and exhibit—another canvas representing the two maids, Lemonnier-Texier analyzes how the differential filmic treatment of both paintings reflects "the ambition of the series to create a specific filmic/artistic space for the representation of maids." Through minute filmic micro-analyses of the process of creation, she shows how the use of narrative suspense, dramatic irony, as well as the choice of shot scales and camera angles not only gradually dislodges Lady Marjorie from her apparently central position but ends up establishing a new social hierarchy through the painter's subversion of pictorial genres: "the artist deliberately subverts the hierarchy of genres as much as the hierarchy of class, just as the episode scripts the making of 'Lady Marjorie' portrait as an anti-climax whereas the picture of Sarah is turned into a suspenseful of revelations [...], displacing the filmic and narrative focus of the episode onto the maid(s)." For the author, this subversion is very much emblematic of the whole series.

Notes

1. "We will have to make changes so that across the whole country we have a genuinely classless society so that people, according to their ability or good fortune, can rise to whatever position": http://articles.baltimoresun.com/1990-11-24/news/1990328012_1_classless-society-thatcher-hurd. See also the article the then-chancellor of the exchequer published in *Today* on 24 November 1990: "In the next ten years, we will have to continue to make changes which will make the whole of this country a genuinely classless society." Quoted in David and Gareth Butler, *Twentieth-Century British Political Facts, 1900–2000*, Basingstoke: Palgrave Macmillan, 2000, 296.

2. See John Major's first speech as Conservative Party leader in 1991: "Labour fosters those divisions. It thrives on them. Our task is to end them for good. I spoke of a classless society. I don't shrink from that phrase. I don't mean a society in which everyone is the same, or thinks the same, or earns the same. But a tapestry of talents in which everyone from child to adult respects achieve-

ment; where every promotion, every certificate is respected; and each person's contribution is valued. And where the greatest respect is reserved for the law." http://www.britishpoliticalspeech.org/speech-archive.htm?speech=137.

3. "Class is a Communist concept. It groups people as bundles, and sets them against one another." Margaret Thatcher, "Don't Undo My Work [No Such Thing as Majorism]," *Newsweek*, 27 April 1992: http://www.margaretthatcher.org/document/111359.

4. Christopher Hope, "Sir John Major's Attack on Britain's Privileged Governing Class: Edited Speech Transcript," *The Daily Telegraph*, 11 November 2013: http://www.telegraph.co.uk/news/politics/conservative/10441029/Sir-John-Major-attack-on-Britains-privileged-governing-class-the-speech-transcript.html.

5. Patrick Wintour, "UK's Lack of Social Mobility Is Due to Entrenched Elitism, Says Alan Milburn," *The Guardian*, 13 November 2013: http://www.theguardian.com/society/2013/nov/13/uk-social-mobility-elitism-alan-milburn. Alan Milburn is currently chair of the Social Mobility and Child Poverty Commission.

6. "Today, after four years of economic growth, corporate profits and stock prices have rarely been higher, and those at the top have never done better. But average wages have barely budged. Inequality has deepened. Upward mobility has stalled. [...] [We] know our opportunity agenda won't be complete—and too many young people entering the workforce today will see the American Dream as an empty promise—unless we do more to make sure our economy honors the dignity of work, and hard work pays off for every single American." http://www.whitehouse.gov/the-press-office/2014/01/28/president-barack-obamas-state-union-address.

7. "It's [...] how the son of a barkeeper is Speaker of the House; how the son of a single mom can be President of the greatest nation on Earth." *Ibid.*

8. John Cassidy, "Is Obama Getting Serious About Inequality?" *New Yorker*, 4 December 2013: http://www.newyorker.com/online/blogs/johncassidy/2013/12/is-obama-getting-serious-about-inequality.html.

9. "We Must Stop the 'Cancer of Inequality,'" http://www.realclearpolitics.com/video/2014/05/28/hillary_clinton_we_must_stop_the_cancer_of_inequality.html.

10. See "The Great British Class Survey—Results," BBC, 3 April 2013: http://www.bbc.co.uk/science/0/21970879.

11. For an analysis of this demonization in the media, see Keith Hayward and Majid Yar, "The 'Chav' Phenomenon: Consumption, Media and the Construction of a New Underclass," *Crime, Media, Culture*, vol. 2, no. 1, 2006, 9–28.

12. David Cannadine, *Class in Britain*, London: Penguin, 2000, 1.

13. Sam Tanenhaus, "Hey Big Thinker: Thomas Piketty, the Economist Behind 'Capital in the Twenty-First Century,' Is the Latest Overnight Intellectual Sensation," *New York Times*, 25 April 2014: http://www.nytimes.com/2014/04/27/fashion/Thomas-Piketty-the-Economist-Behind-Capital-in-the-Twenty-First-Century-sensation.html.

14. Cannadine, *Class in Britain*, 12.

15. "Since the Second World War, therefore, we can trace the emergence of a distinctive sociological strand of 'class analysis.' [...] Following from Bendix and Lipset's appropriation of Marx's distinction between a class 'in itself' and 'for itself,' class structure and class action are regarded as analytically separable." Rosemary Crompton, *Class and Stratification: An Introduction to Current Debates*, Cambridge: Polity Press, 1993, 41. For a comprehensive account of how historians and sociologists have debated the concept of class, see Patrick Joyce (ed.), *Class*, Oxford: Oxford University Press, 1995.

16. "Today, scholars are much more inclined to stress [...] the general absence of clear-cut classes and clear-cut class conflict, and the way in which different social groupings and identities merged easily and imperceptibly into one another in the seamless web of the social fabric. [...] With so many fluctuating and sometimes contradictory senses of identity, which constantly cut across each other, there no longer seems any justification for privileging class identity—or class analysis." David Cannadine, *Class in Britain*, 15–16.

17. In *Class in Britain* for example, David Cannadine intends to analyze the history of different competing systems of social classification, claiming that "changes in popular perceptions of British society have been at least as important as changes in British society itself, and it is in the evolving relationship between these social perceptions and social structures that the history of class is properly to be found and to be studied." *Ibid.*, 23.

18. See for instance Beverly Skeggs's account of "class making" in *Class, Self and Culture*, London: Routledge, 2005, 3.

19. Robert Sklar, *Movie-Made America: A Cultural History of American Movies*, New York: Vintage, 1994 [revised and updated], 3.

20. Russell Merritt, "Nickelodeon Theaters, 1905–1914: Building an Audience for the Movies," in Tino Balio (ed.), *The American Film Industry*, Madison: University of Wisconsin Press, 1985 [2nd revised edition], 85. Russell Merritt contends that the major social change of theatres' audiences occurred as soon as the years between 1905 and 1912. "The five-cent theater may have been widely regarded as the working man's pastime, but the less frequently reported fact was that the theater catered to him though necessity, not though choice. The blue collar worker and is family may have supported the nickelodeon—the scandal was that no one connected with the movies much wanted his support—least of all the immigrant film exhibitors who were working their way out of the slums with their theaters—the exhibitors' abiding complaint against nickelodeon audiences was that moviegoers as a group lacked 'class.'" *Ibid.*, 89.

21. Sklar, *Movie-Made America: A Cultural History of American Movies*, 16, 90.

22. Steven J. Ross, *Working-Class Hollywood: Silent Film and the Shaping of Class in America*, Princeton: Princeton University Press, 1998.

23. To quote a few recent telling titles: John Hill's "From the New Wave to 'Brit-Grit': Continuity and Difference in Working Class Realism" (in Justine Ashby and Andrew Higson, eds., *British Cinema, Past and Present*, London: Routledge, 2000, 249–260) and "Failure and Utopianism: Representations of the Working Class in British Cinema of the 1990s" (in Robert Murphy, ed., *British Cinema of the 90s*, London: BFI, 2000); Julia Hallam's "Film, Class and National Identity" (in Justine Ashby and Andrew Higson, eds., *British Cinema, Past and Present*, London: Routledge, 2000, 261–273); Claire Monk's "Underbelly UK: The 1990s Underclass Film, Masculinity and the Ideologies of 'New' Britain" (in Justine Ashby and Andrew Higson, eds., *British Cinema, Past and Present*, London: Routledge, 2000, 274–287); Cora Kaplan's "The Death of the Working Class Hero" (*New Formations*, vol. 52, Summer 2004, 94–110); Mike Wayne's "The Performing Northern Working Class in British Cinema: Cultural Representation and Its Political Economy" (*Quarterly Review of Film and Video*, vol. 23, no. 4, 2006, 287–297); Huw Beynon and Sheila Rowbotham's *Looking at Class: Film, Television and the Working Class in Britain* (London: Rivers Oram Press, 2001); Paul Dave's *Visions of England: Class and Culture in Contemporary Cinema* (Oxford: Berg, 2006) in which the author is concerned with exploring "the ways in which changes in the experiences of class have worked their way into contemporary British films" (xiii).

24. John Hill, *British Cinema in the 1980s*, Oxford: Oxford University Press, 1999, 135.

25. Sue Harper, *Picturing the Past: The Rise and Fall of the British Costume Film*, London: BFI, 1994, 183.

26. John Hill, "From the New Wave to 'Brit-Grit': Continuity and Difference in Working Class Realism" in Justine Ashby and Andrew Higson (eds.), *British Cinema, Past and Present*, 250.

27. Johnny Walker, "A Wilderness of Horrors? British Horror Cinema in the New Millennium," *Journal of British Cinema and Television*, vol. 9, no. 3, 2012, 447.

28. The articles come from a selection of papers delivered at the international conference "Representing Social Classes in Films on Television and in Cinema in English-speaking Countries" held at Rennes 2 University on 10–11 October 2013 and organized by the research group ACE (EA 1796) in partnership with 3L.AM (EA 4335): http://classesinfilms.sciencesconf.org/.

29. Bill Nichols, *Introduction to Documentary*, Bloomington: Indiana University Press, 2010 [2nd ed.], 187.

Works Cited

Beynon, Huw, and Sheila Rowbotham. *Looking at Class: Film, Television and the Working Class in Britain*. London: Rivers Oram Press, 2001.

Butler, David, and Gareth Butler. *Twentieth-Century British Political Facts, 1900–2000*. Basingstoke: Palgrave Macmillan, 2000.

Cannadine, David. *Class in Britain*. London: Penguin, 2000.

Cassidy, John. "Is Obama Getting Serious About Inequality?" *New Yorker*, 4 December 2013: http://www.newyorker.com/online/blogs/johncassidy/2013/12/is-obama-getting-serious-about-inequality.html, accessed 10 August 2014.
Clinton, Hilary. "We Must Stop the 'Cancer of Inequality.'" http://www.realclearpolitics.com/video/2014/05/28/hillary_clinton_we_must_stop_the_cancer_of_inequality.html, accessed 10 August 2014.
Crompton, Rosemary. *Class and Stratification: An Introduction to Current Debates*. Cambridge: Polity Press, 1993.
Dave, Paul. *Visions of England: Class and Culture in Contemporary Cinema*. Oxford: Berg, 2006.
"The Great British Class Survey—Results." *BBC*, 3 April 2013: http://www.bbc.co.uk/science/0/21970879, accessed 9 August 2014.
Hallam, Julia. "Film, Class and National identity" in Justine Ashby and Andrew Higson (eds.), *British Cinema, Past and Present*. London: Routledge, 2000, 261–273.
Harper, Sue. *Picturing the Past: The Rise and Fall of the British Costume Film*. London: BFI, 1994.
Hayward, Keith, and Majid Yar. "The 'Chav' Phenomenon: Consumption, Media and the Construction of a New Underclass." *Crime, Media, Culture*, vol. 2, no. 1, 2006, 9–28.
Hill, John. *British Cinema in the 1980s*. Oxford: Oxford University Press, 1999.
Hill, John. "Failure and Utopianism: Representations of the Working Class in British Cinema of the 1990s" in Robert Murphy (ed.), *British Cinema of the 90s*. London: BFI, 2000, 178–187.
Hill, John. "From the New Wave to 'Brit-Grit': Continuity and Difference in Working Class Realism" in Justine Ashby and Andrew Higson (eds.), *British Cinema, Past and Present*. London: Routledge, 2000, 249–260.
Hope, Christopher. "Sir John Major's Attack on Britain's Privileged Governing Class: Edited Speech Transcript." *The Daily Telegraph*, 11 November 2013: http://www.telegraph.co.uk/news/politics/conservative/10441029/Sir-John-Major-attack-on-Britains-privileged-governing-class-the-speech-transcript.html, accessed 9 August 2014.
Jones, Owen. *Chavs: The Demonization of the Working Class*. London: Verso, 2011.
Joyce, Patrick (ed.). *Class*. Oxford: Oxford University Press, 1995.
Kaplan, Cora. "The Death of the Working Class Hero." *New Formations*, vol. 52, Summer 2004, 94–110.
Major, John. http://articles.baltimoresun.com/1990-11-24/news/1990328012_1_classless-society-thatcher-hurd, accessed 9 August 2014.
Major, John. http://www.britishpoliticalspeech.org/speech-archive.htm?speech=137, accessed 9 August 2014.
Monk, Claire. "Underbelly UK: The 1990s Underclass Film, Masculinity and the Ideologies of 'New' Britain" in Justine Ashby and Andrew Higson (eds.), *British Cinema, Past and Present*. London: Routledge, 2000, 274–287.
Nichols Bill. *Introduction to Documentary*. Bloomington: Indiana University Press, 2010 [2nd ed.].
Obama, Barack. http://www.whitehouse.gov/the-press-office/2014/01/28/president-barack-obamas-state-union-address, accessed 10 August 2014.
Piketty, Thomas. *Capital in the Twenty-First Century*. Cambridge: Harvard University Press, 2014.
Ross, Steven J. *Working-Class Hollywood: Silent Film and the Shaping of Class in America*. Princeton, New Jersey: Princeton University Press, 1998.
Skeggs, Beverly. *Class, Self and Culture*. London: Routledge, 2005.
Sklar, Robert. *Movie-Made America: A Cultural History of American Movies*. New York: Vintage, 1994 [revised and updated].
Tanenhaus, Sam. "Hey Big Thinker: Thomas Piketty, the Economist Behind 'Capital in the

Twenty-First Century,' Is the Latest Overnight Intellectual Sensation." *New York Times*, 25 April 2014.
Thatcher, Margaret. "Don't Undo My Work [No Such Thing as Majorism]." *Newsweek*, 27 April 1992: http://www.margaretthatcher.org/document/111359, accessed 9 August 2014.
Thompson, Edward P. *The Making of the English Working Class*. London: Penguin, 1991 [1966].
Walker, Johnny. "A Wilderness of Horrors? British Horror Cinema in the New Millennium." *Journal of British Cinema and Television*, vol. 9, no. 3, 2012, 436–456.
Wayne, Mike. "The Performing Northern Working Class in British Cinema: Cultural representation and Its Political Economy." *Quarterly Review of Film and Video*, vol. 23, no. 4, 2006, 287–297.
Wintour, Patrick. "UK's Lack of Social Mobility Is Due to Entrenched Elitism, Says Alan Milburn." *The Guardian*, 13 November 2013: http://www.theguardian.com/society/2013/nov/13/uk-social-mobility-elitism-alan-milburn, accessed 9 August 2014.

Films, Series and Documentaries Cited

Boys from the Blackstuff (1982): Written and directed by Alan Bleasdale, BBC.
Bread and Roses (2000): Directed by Ken Loach, screenplay by Paul Laverty, Parallax Pictures and coproduction.
Comrades (1986): Written and directed by Bill Douglas, SKREBA Films and coproduction.
Downton Abbey (2010–): Created by Julian Fellows, ITV.
The Fool (1990): Directed by Christine Edzard, written by Christine Edzard and Olivier Stockman, Sands Films.
Land of Opportunity (2010): Directed by Luisa Dantas.
Little Britain (2003–2006): Created by Kevin Cecil, Matt Lucas, Andy Riley and David Walliams, BBC.
Norma Rae (1979): Directed by Martin Ritt, written by Irving Ravetch and Harriet Frank, Jr., Twentieth Century Fox Film Corporation.
Salt of the Earth (1954): Directed by Herbert J. Biberman, written by Michael Wilson, Independent Production Company.
7 UP (1964–): Written and directed by Michael Apted, Granada Television.
Upstairs, Downstairs (1971–1975): Created by Jean Marsh and Eileen Atkins, LWT.
Upstairs, Downstairs (2010–): Created by Heidi Thomas, BBC.
The Wire (2002–2008): Created by David Simon, HBO.

Part One

The Persistence of Stereotypes:
Social Class in TV Sitcoms
and Series

Six Decades of Social Class in American Sitcoms

RICHARD BUTSCH

In the United States today, manual labor is devalued although it is still essential to the operation of the society, not only in manufacturing and construction, but also in essential services such as sanitation, first responders, maintenance and operation of transportation systems and of all forms of machinery upon which our economy depends. Yet, over the past 40 years, due to de-industrialization, drastic weakening of labor unions and labor laws, median wages and benefits, adjusted for inflation, unskilled and semi-skilled manual labor has dropped substantially. Shrunken apprenticeship programs and vocational education have limited paths for training in skilled manual work. After World War II, apprenticeship training in manual occupations shriveled, while colleges expanded.[1]

All of this has been made to seem appropriate by a widespread cultural disregard and disrespect for manual labor that began in the post-war era and intensified since then. Stereotypes of manual workers, overwhelmingly represented as male, have depicted them as dumb, lazy, immature, irresponsible—and not even muscular. American education and the predominant concept of intelligence built into standardized testing have reinforced these prejudices. The values underpinning the American educational system have erased any support for manual training and any recognition of its importance to the society.[2] For example, it was initiated to distinguish middle-class from working-class occupations, and it was built upon an artificial separation of mental and manual skills that presumed manual skill is devoid of mental skills and that reduced education and intelligence exclusively to academic mental skills. Finally, post-war secondary education constructed a prestige hierarchy both organizationally and culturally in which schools were layered in tracks for college prep at the top and vocational technical at the bottom, and labeled those in vo-tech as too dumb for anything else. Economist Robert Lerman said, "The

United States lacked a well-structured approach to education and training, especially for the 'forgotten half' of young people not pursuing a college education," most of whom are manual workers, because of "the nearly exclusive emphasis in public policy and in public funding is on academic skills."[3] Every parent was and is urged to provide their children with college educations as the only avenue to a good job with decent income. Sociologist James Rosenbaum said that many high schools tell students that "college is the only respectable goal and is easily attainable by all."[4] In effect manual laborers were the educational waste.

This has not always been the case. Through the nineteenth and into the mid-twentieth centuries, manual labor retained respectability, such that a son could be proud to follow in his father's footsteps into a trade or a factory, in which he could make a decent, "honest" living. Through this century or more, with periods of reversal and mostly with the efforts of unions, wages and other compensations improved for manual work. At its peak in the post-war era, an unskilled factory worker could buy a home, a car, and send his children to college on his sole wage.

From the late 19th century, images of manual labor in public spaces celebrated the value of manual work and dedication of the workers.[5] A fairly common theme before the Great Depression was a narrative of national progress and glory, from pioneering, agriculture and industrialization as the pinnacle. Each of these was depicted through manual labor and muscle. This seems to have been from the turn of the century and peaked in the 1920s—perhaps an architectural extension of the international exhibitions of the second half of the 19th century that glorified industrialization and by extension manual labor that became an iconic representation of industrialization, man and machine together. Another was the cooperation of manual and mental labor. A number of murals and friezes depict both in the same tableau, e.g., an architect or engineer along with construction workers, a factory owner or manager along with manual workers at machinery.[6] These narratives were not confined to murals, but also appeared in the pageantry movement as part of local civic boosterism,[7] and in books and magazines that told stories of city progress through industry.

This culminated in the Federal Writers Project series of books on American cities, and the Federal Arts projects in thousands of sculptures, murals and architectural decorations depicted manual labor and muscle in positive, even heroic terms.[8] Many of these showed heavily muscled, often bare armed and chested men using their strength and tools to build or make things. Two iconic sculptures capture the spirit of these works and these times. Even before the Federal Project, a 1927 Max Kalish sculpture, "New Power,"[9] presents a powerful, bare chested man with upright posture and broad shoulders, muscled chest and arms, and tight stomach looking straight ahead while he uses a jack hammer. This celebrates not skill so much (the air powered hammer requires no great skill), but the common manual worker's mastery over his tools and materials. The posture expresses self-respect and pride in one's work. The second are identical twin sculptures placed at the apex of the Federal Trade Commission building at its completion in 1942. These sculptures too present a bare-chested and heavily muscled man, this time leaning back and heels dug in to restrain a large and powerful work horse. It is titled "Man Controlling Trade," apropos the Trade Commission's responsibility to control trade by prohibiting competitive practices that restrain trade and undermine competitive markets—although it might as easily be interpreted as "man controlling capitalism" especially as, at the time, the Depression was widely blamed on capitalism. These are merely two striking examples of a far larger federal project of thousands of decorative arts in federal buildings, including numerous post offices in small towns, throughout the nation.

All of this demonstrates that manual labor was publicly represented and included as part of these stories of national pride—until the post-war era. Its visibility before then makes its absence after seem all the more remarkable. After the war the most widespread imagery was that which television delivered every night into nearly every living room of the U.S. Television representation reached a larger portion of the population than any other before it and during its ascendance. Even today, the numbers of viewers for a show with average broadcast network ratings still make it a mass medium. The most widely consumed medium, television seldom features manual labor, and when it does, often presents manual workers in unflattering ways. This article documents the scarcity and negative representations of male manual workers throughout the history of television in the U.S., in prime-time domestic situation comedies.

Aesthetics of a cultural work, a pleasure of the mind, can be enjoyed and understood at the level of individual works. But to ascertain the social importance for a society requires more than inquiry into individual works. Representations become social when they are sufficiently pervasive and persistent so that they sediment into the culture and thus become naturalized and enduring, and are reproduced through further representations and everyday discourse.

Images of Working Class and Middle Class in American Sitcoms

In my research I have been concerned with how images of class support class inequality in American society. My purpose is not to provide a deep analysis of a particular text, but rather to document the representation of the working class across the broad television landscape, to reveal how American television sitcoms, watched by tens of millions every night, reproduce and reinforce stereotypes of social class. They have presented repeatedly the same image of working-class men which have become taken for granted as real and dovetail with similar assumptions about class in other institutions and discourses to "discipline and punish," and which comfort higher classes, who thus can be smug in their superiority, and shame lower classes for their inadequacy and failures. It is for this principle of repetition that I have researched nearly 400 prime-time American domestic situation comedies, 65 years of television from 1948 to 2013 that reveal durable patterns despite significant industry and audience changes.

I chose domestic situation comedies, or sitcoms, because, first, they are the most numerous programs in prime-time entertainment television. Other genres come and go, but domestic sitcoms have been the most reliable moneymakers for television networks for six decades. This longevity has had the advantage of tracking the history without shifting genres. Second, their focus on family life does not pre-determine the social class represented, unlike law or medical dramas for example, so producers can choose any class, sex or age characters. This openness of choice then reveals that the representations are not due to individual prejudices, but rather due to how industry structure and culture shape representations, and shows why stereotypes keep getting reproduced. As an additional and unplanned bonus, the domestic setting captures gender and age relations, as facets used to reinforce class representations.

I found that sitcoms depicting working-class families were relatively scarce, only about ten percent of all domestic sitcoms, while upper middle-class sitcoms were far most numerous. Gerbner and Gross call this absence a form of symbolic annihilation.[10] Their invisibility implies that such people are not worthy of representation, uninteresting, boring, etc. In the few series that depicted working-class families, there is a striking consistency especially in representing white working-class men. They are buffoons or bunglers, often well-meaning and warm-hearted, but incompetent, immature, ignorant, irresponsible. They are opposites of models for their children to emulate or be proud of. The comedy of the shows is based on laughing at them.

The nature of humor differs depending on the class characterized in the sitcom. There are three types of comic characters found in drama history: the Innocent, the Fool and the Scoundrel.[11] We are expected to sympathize with the Innocent, to smile amusedly but protectively about their mistakes. We are expected to laugh with the Scoundrel as he outsmarts Authority. We are expected to laugh at the Fool, so the Fool is diminished. Scoundrels rarely appeared in American sitcoms. One notable example is *The Phil Silvers Show* in the 1950s. An Army sergeant outwitted his superiors for fun and profit and his schemes always worked. Privates and corporals under his command admired and aided his taking down authority. Many middle-class domestic sitcoms focused on innocent children. Their mistakes are amusing as the parents, who are models of parenting, working as a team, gently guide and teach them. A few middle-class sitcoms feature a fool, but it is almost always the woman, usually a housewife. In almost all working-class sitcoms, however, comedy centers on a fool, and he is almost always the male breadwinner, who defines the social class of the family and represents his social class too. He is contrasted to his wife and children, who typically are more sensible, competent, mature and intelligent. The children will not follow his footsteps into a manual labor job, but will go to college and rise into the professional/managerial upper middle class.

The contrasting portrayal of working class and middle class is strikingly evident in the visual appearance, the figure, posture and dress of the characters. The lead male characters of working-class domestic sitcoms from the 1950s into the 2010s are consistently overweight, have a beer belly and little muscle tone. The animated characters are slump shouldered and the two most famous, Fred Flintstone and Homer Simpson, are perpetually unshaved. Their dress is sloppy casual. It is the consistency over decade that is so striking. The flabbiness and slumped stance of the sitcom working-class men contrast to the workers' powerful muscles taming the physical world and their posture expressing pride in one's work and oneself as represented in sculptures, bas reliefs, and murals from the 1880s through the 1940s. Numerous public art works demonstrate that these are a continuing theme in these decades, granting respectability to manual labor and laborers that is wholly lacking in the television sitcoms of the next sixty years. The contrast to the lead males in upper-middle-class sitcoms is also striking. Sampling the most successful series, the husbands/fathers are slim, flat stomachs with upright posture and shoulders back. While style changes over the decades from formal to casual, all the middle-class male characters are well dressed.

The greater similarity of the physical appearance of wives across classes is remarkable. Working-class and middle-class wives are intermixed in this figure. Yet it is difficult distinguish the differences between the two classes of women. Regardless of class and over six decades, working-class wives are depicted much as are middle-class wives. Both have slim and trim figures with a narrow waist, shoulders straight and erect posture as with the middle-class men. They are dressed neatly at home, usually with a freshly press dress and often a necklace or other jewelry even at home. The similarity implies that the working-class women identify and express middle-class values rather than their own husband's working-class status—which is often thematized in the stories as wives aspire to the prestige and privilege of middle-class occupations and culture. The physical appearance of the working-class women thus stands as a contrast and a chastisement to their men, while the middle-class wives' appearance affirms the success and pride/respect of the middle-class men.

These physical characteristics stereotype the appearance of working-class and middle-class men. But it is the personal character associated with these body types that affirms and elucidates contrasting valuations of class, so that physique becomes a symbol of the personal character and can be assumed about such men in real life. I now turn to those associated characterizations. I have selected the most successful domestic sitcoms of each decade to illustrate the point. But similar themes appear in many more, less well known sitcoms through these years.

The 1950s and 1960s: Establishing the Formulas

The 1950s were notable for a small cluster of very successful working-class sitcoms, *The Life of Riley, I Remember Mama, The Honeymooners,* and *The Goldbergs.* The Honeymooners and Goldbergs lived in New York City tenements; the families of Riley and Mama (set in the early 20th century) had their own homes. The lead characters in *Riley* and *Honey* were the husbands; for *Mama* and *Goldbergs,* it was the wife who overshadowed the husband. In all four sitcoms, the men were ineffectual. *Riley, Mama* and *Goldbergs* were derivatives of radio and theater in the 1930s and 1940s. *The Honeymooners* was concocted by comedian Jackie Gleason, at least partly from his own childhood.

Chester Riley was a riveter in an aircraft factory, yet could afford a postwar suburban home. The recurring situation was Chester concocting some hair-brained scheme, usually to help his family, such as helping his daughter win an election at high school. The scheme invariably backfires, and he ends the show looking into the camera and exclaiming, "What a revoltin' development this is!" more perplexed than angry. It is however no surprise to his wife and children, each of whom are more sensible than he. Nevertheless his wife Peg remains calm, sensible and reassuring and is very tolerant of Chester, and his teen son and daughter, somewhat embarrassed by him, ultimately care for their father too.

The childless *Honeymooners* lasted only one season (1955–56) as a sitcom, but ran for several years as a sketch act in Jackie Gleason's various variety shows through the 1950s. Ralph Kramden was a New York City bus driver. The childless couple however have a meager income and live in a humble, poorly furnished apartment in Brooklyn. Ralph too was always concocting schemes, often to get rich quick so that he could buy whatever his wife desired. But this is a comedy with a good deal of anger. The financial stress and Ralph's inappropriate attempts to resolve it lead to bitter arguments between husband and wife, Alice telling Ralph, "I told you so," when his scheme fails and he, at a loss for a retort, explodes and threatens, "One of these days, Alice, pow, right to the moon!" The show expresses little warmth and much anger between the two. She is always right and he is always wrong, and a fool to not see that in advance.

Through the decade of the 1960s there was only one working-class sitcom on television, *The Flintstones* (1960–65), and that before the turmoil of the decade burst on to television. It was integral to the nation's 1950s era. Father Fred was modeled on Chester and Ralph, engaging in schemes that always fail, this time often in order to have some fun with his buddy Barney while hiding it from his wife Wilma. Fred is not only dumb; he is also childish and irresponsible. Despite the fact that he is a father and husband, he wants to skip work in order to play, and to avoid his wife's objections by lying, not unlike a child with his hand caught in the cookie jar. In contrast Wilma is smart, sensible, mature and gently scolds him as a caring mother would. Fred is happy-go-lucky, miraculously his schemes result in no serious consequences, and his wife always manages to repair whatever mess he creates.

There was a version of this same formula in a small percent of middle-class sitcoms, e.g., *Burns and Allen, I Love Lucy* (1951–57). The character of fool however was played by the wife, while the husband was successful in his career and sensible and mature at home. Lucy of course was by far the most famous and longest running. The Ricardo family lived in a posh Upper East Side Manhattan apartment building. Husband Ricky was a successful bandleader. Lucy, like the working-class men, concocts schemes that backfire. Ricky, like the wives in working-class shows, rescues and chastises her. The shows are not about sex, but rather about class, as the characterizations of sex are reversed from class to class. These shows taken together construct a picture in which sex is used to undercut the working-class breadwinner and affirm the status and respect of the upper-middle-class breadwinner.

Most middle-class sitcoms of this era, however, depict couples in which the father and mother are presented as the ideal parents working as a team to teach their children. The shows are little homilies to American viewers in the post-war, baby boom era of large families. The title of *Father Knows Best* (1954–60) captures the message of these shows, especially when broadcast in the same years as *I Remember Mama* is announcing that mother knows best in the working-class home. Father Jim Anderson is a successful insurance man. The family live in an American classic small town home with a white picket fence. Opening and closing stills and publicity shots of the show present wife Margaret and the children dotingly and admiringly looking up at the father. In each episode, a child finds themselves caught in some situation. Father arrives home to resolve the problem and to explain to the children, and to the audience, the lesson to be learned from this. Quite the contrast to the working-class fathers discussed above.

My Three Sons (1960–72) presented the preeminent father of 1960s television. Steve, a single father of three sons, is a successful engineer with his own firm. The surrogate housewife is the grandfather, who is less wise and to agree plays the part of a mild fool. As with *Father Knows Best* the sons admire their father and eagerly listen and follow his advice. These "super-parent" shows provided stark contrasts to the working-class shows in which the man is a failure as a man, as husband, father and sometimes as breadwinner. The sitcom landscape of these two decades leaves an impression that working-class men are inadequate while upper-middle-class men are successful at home as well as in business, and to be admired and respected.

The 1970s and 1980s: A Mix of Reality and Pollyanna[12]

These decades began with the winding down of the Vietnam War and the strife of the 1960s. Television's response to this was to finally include some of these issues in sitcoms. The principal author of this more realistic approach was independent producer Norman Lear who created several successful series of the era. Yet, despite the progressive messages of these shows, male leads representing subordinate groups continued the television stereotypes of the 1950s. The most well-known of these sitcoms is *All in the Family* (1970–79). The Bunker family lives in a modest Queens semi-detached house. The father, Archie, was a loading dock worker, who was loud, angry and most of all, prejudiced. His prejudice substitutes for the schemes of earlier shows. His wife Edith was not as bright and middle-class as most wives, but she is skeptical of Archie's claims and tries to calm him and moderate his prejudices. Daughter Sally and son-in-law Mike on the other hand challenge Archie and chastise him for his prejudice. Archie, unable to win arguments with them with words, ends by shouting at and name calling his son-in-law.

Sanford and Son (1972–77) was a black family spinoff of *All in the Family*. Fred Sanford was a junk yard owner operator, a distinctly lower-class small businessman who lives on-site with his son Lamont. Fred is loud mouthed and prejudiced, just as is Archie. Like Archie's daughter and son-in-law, Lamont chastises his father for his prejudice and ill-manners, and seeks respectability and upward mobility. A third in this series, another black family sitcom, *The Jeffersons* (1975–85), features a successful businessman, affluent enough to afford a luxury apartment on the Upper East Side of Manhattan, New York City. However George Jefferson is black and behaves as Archie and Fred in his loud-mouthed, angry and prejudiced manner. His wife, Louise, a latter-day Alice, is sensible and sarcastic about her husband. While appearing at first to contradict the class pattern (upper-middle-class man as buffoon), this show instead applies the formula to race (black man as buffoon).

While, in these shows, real social problems breach the walls of television entertainment, other sitcoms continued the tradition of the idealized middle-class family. In the same era, *The Brady Bunch* (1969–74) upheld the tradition of *Father Knows Best* (1954–63) and *My Three Sons* (1960–72). Mike Brady, widowed with three boys, marries Carol with her three girls. The kids provide a steady supply of problems, which husband and wife together solve and use to teach their children well. *Happy Days* (1974–84) offered a slight diversion from this. The show's focus is mostly on a group of teens set in the 1950s. But the father of the male teen lead is hardware store owner, who regularly offers wise advice to all the teens who respect him. Even the working-class biker character, Arthur Fonzarelli (the Fonz), whom the boys admire, urges them to listen to the father. The wife on the other hand is a bit ditzy, a toned-down version of Gracie Allen from *The George Burns and Gracie Allen Show* (1950–58).

Two more shows carried the middle-class super-parent formula through the 1980s. *The Cosby Show* (1984–92) reversed the black sitcoms of the 1970s, presenting instead ideal parents skillfully helping their children through modern difficulties of growing up. Bill Cosby created the shows explicitly for the didactic purpose of educating American parents. Cosby played Cliff Huxtable, a medical doctor and father who had ample time for his children. His wife is also a professional, a successful lawyer. Husband and wife sometimes debate issues but ultimately work as a team. Cliff clowns around with his children, but always makes clear that he is the father. Complementing the Huxtables in the same years was *Growing Pains* (1985–92), about the Seavers, a white middle-class family with a father who is a psychologist and a mother who is a journalist. Nonetheless, their professional careers never interfere with their parenting and family.

Yet in this same era, some shows express the first doubts about upper-middle-class perfection and authority. A handful of middle-class sitcoms depicted professional and executive men as dumb and incompetent: a doctor in *Maude* (1972–78); a therapist, a dentist and an airline pilot in *Newhart*

(1972–78); and a governor in *Benson* (1979–86). The shows seem a remnant of the 1960s critiques of authority that originated in revelations about Vietnam and ended with Watergate, as well as a reflection of 1970s recessions that produced unusually high levels of professional and managerial unemployment. Nevertheless the working-class male stereotype remained firm.

The 1990s: Some New Twists, and Yet...

Roseanne (1988–97) is unique in its contradiction of the traditional representations in working-class family sitcoms. The show realistically depicts the lifestyle and difficulties of the de-industrialized American working class. Husband and wife hold various jobs and are intermittently employed, and struggle to pay the bills, have the usual battles with their teen daughter. But they are content with and unapologetic about their working-class tastes and lifestyle. What is different is that it is the wife, Roseanne, the lead character, who is sarcastic, volatile and angry like Ralph, Archie and Fred, the lead male characters in earlier working-class sitcoms. The father, Dan, in the supporting role, is sensible and solid, when Roseanne explodes. He's unlike the typical working-class sitcom father and more like the steady wife, Wilma Flintstone or the father in *Happy Days*, even while at times he has rollicking fun with Roseanne, and relishes his motorbike and other working-class pleasures.

"Content and unapologetic about his working class lifestyle": John Goodman (as Dan Conner) in *Roseanne* (1988–97) (© ABC/Photofest).

The explanation for this is equally unique: Roseanne Barr, the working-class stand-up comedian who created and starred in the show, played the same sharp-tongued and brash woman who was the essence of her comedy act. Why such a working-class woman persona was such a success in this era is the real question. A few other entertainments about this time also turned working-class voices into hits, such as Bruce Springsteen who became a superstar in the mid–1980s. It seems that working-class audiences pummeled by factory closings that dismantled their communities and lives welcomed media figures who talked back on their behalf.

Yet, the old familiar survived in the animated sitcom *The Simpsons* (1989–present), the longest running prime-time series in American television history. It repeats the old working-class stereotypes. The father, Homer, is a carbon copy of Fred Flintstone, beard, beer belly and all. Wife Marge is ditzy but relatively the sensible one, reminiscent of Edith Bunker. As in several working-class sitcoms over the decades, the children are smarter than their father. They regularly best him in arguments and other contests such as video games, leaving him fuming and speechless.

Step by Step (1991–98) clearly uses the super-parent formula, and seems to offer the rare case of a working-class show featuring ideal parents helping their children in a blended family through troubles. Also, the father, Frank Lambert, physically fits the middle-class model, slim, tight stomach and straight posture. But it also confuses class. Frank owns a small construction company; wife Carol Foster owns a beauty salon, typical working-class occupations, although self-employed. They do not require college education and offer relatively limited and uncertain income. But episodes variously depict Frank and his business as a small home renovation operation, and at other times, he wins a multi-million dollar contract to build a new office building, is invited by another contractor to join an exclusive club, and is elected as an officer of another club. Continuity of characters' social class is never a top priority for television; in this show, writers seem to wander back and forth across class borders.

Home Improvement (1991–99) introduced a new twist on the middle-class man, but not a contradiction to the pattern. Husband Tim Taylor is the star of his own home improvement television show, establishing his success. He jokes around on the show as well as at home. However, he is not a buffoon: we are not meant to laugh *at* him, but rather *with* him. He is a variant on the scoundrel, although less about undercutting authority. Rather he is willfully adolescent and macho. He is a smarter, more successful version of Fred Flintstone. He is played against his wife, Jill who is the serious, sensible and responsible one in the family. His wife is not his better; she is frustrated with him, but does not chastise, as did Alice Kramden and Wilma Flintstone.

The husband in *Everybody Loves Raymond* (1996–2005), is part Tim and part Fred Flintstone. Raymond Barone is a successful sports writer, but is intimidated by his wife Debra and his own parents. He wants to have fun with his friends, like Tim and Fred, but unlike Tim and more like Fred, he is worried that his wife will be cross with him for it. Similarly, he is unable to stand up to his parents. While Raymond is occupationally upper middle class, his father (occupation unspecified), loud mouthed and angry with poor posture and muscle tone, is the standard stereotype from earlier working-class sitcoms.

The 2000s: More of the Same, and Different

Yet the old stereotype remained alive and thriving in the 2000s. In the animated *Family Guy* (1999–present), Peter Griffin holds a miscellany of unskilled jobs and is Fred Flintstone all over again with wacky schemes to have fun. His wife Lois is a new Wilma, patient and tolerant with Peter. The *King of Queens* (1998–2007) too is a revival of the Flintstones with a dash of annoyed wife. Doug is a uniformed IPS truck driver, and seems content enough not to strive for more. He's overweight and schlumpy like Fred. He wants his wide screen television and other toys and to relax with his buddies. He concocts schemes to do that and often to hide it from his wife. His wife Carrie is an unspecified office worker and has hopes for upward mobility. She is not satisfied, a slight echo of Alice Kramden.

Also in the old tradition but a half-step beyond is *According to Jim* (2001–09); Jim (Belushi, overweight too) has a vaguely implied small scale construction business, as in *Step by Step*, so his class is a bit blurred. But his appearance and characterization are much the same as Doug in *The King of Queens*.

Two and Half Men (2003–2015) features another fun loving guy, but without the wife. This show is a modern twist on *Bachelor Father* (1957–62) and *Courtship of Eddie's Father* (1969–72). The situation is a playboy who has family life foisted on him in the form of care of a child, creating a clash between his lifestyle and his new family responsibilities. In this genre, then and now, the men are highly successful and affluent if not wealthy. In this sitcom, Charlie Harper is a very successful jingle writer with a Malibu beach house, and women flock to him. The humor arises from his cluelessness about raising and even talking to a child, his brother's, who have moved in with him. The stiff brother, a failure with women, fills the role of disapproving wife. The sentiment tends to favor the fun Charlie and to turn his brother into an unattractive scold. Further the boy tends to mimic Charlie rather than his father. So here we have a case where the upper-middle-class male lead, is slim and trim, successful, but not responsible and wise, as is Rickie Ricardo, Mike Brady or Cliff Huxtable. Instead he is another of this recent cross-class pattern of fun seeking, responsibility avoiding adult men.

At the same time, the middle-class super-parent formula too is alive and well. One is *Seventh Heaven* (1996–2007), not strictly a sitcom, but one of small genre of saccharine, hour-long family dramas that occasionally appeared, like *Eight Is Enough* (1977–81) and *The Waltons* (1971–81). As if to make clear the goodness of the father, Eric Camden is cast as a minister, and to assure his position he has seven children. Further, his wife Annie does not have a job, as in most sitcoms by this time, but is a housewife devoted to her husband and seven children. A true half-hour sitcom, *My Wife and Kids* (2001–05) was black comedian Damon Wayon's homage to *Cosby Show*. The father Michael Kyle is a self-made business success, who works at home in a plush Connecticut suburb. Wife Janet is a housewife who also "works" at home, day trading stocks. As in the *Cosby Show*, they are ideal parents.

Through the 1990s and 2000s shows continue the traditional class formulas, but are increasingly accompanied by some shows that diverge. In some cases, class lines are blurred. Another new development is that of the fun seeking husband/father, in opposition to or escaping a more responsible and sober wife. In *Home Improvement, Everybody Loves Raymond, Family Guy, The King of Queens* and *Two and Half Men* we find a new cross-class commonality among sitcom men. However, the class difference remains that the fun-loving middle-class men are successful, affluent, slim, trim and attractive models, while the working-class fun lovers continue to be getting by only, overweight, flabby and apologetic to their wives when they get caught. As in past decades, the working-class men are denied respect and dignity, in contrast to those public sculptures before the television era.

The 2010s: The Traditional Nuclear Family Outnumbered

From the fall 2009 to fall 2013, there were more single-parent sitcoms (14) than married couples. Households became extremely complicated, with a proliferation of ex-spouses, multiple relatives moving in, couples living with parents, and gay couples. Occupational class became increasingly confused, blurring lower middle, worker or manager, mixed class occupations. And notably, only three new sitcoms survived the four years to fall 2013.

Modern Family (2009–present) has been a big success, featuring an extended family living in three households, but spending all their time together. Patriarch Jay Pritchett advises everyone and often makes a philosophical statement about families and relationships directly to the camera at the end of the episode. Jay is a retired successful businessman, now with a younger sexy Hispanic housewife, Gloria, and her son. Jay's son Mitchell is gay and married to Cameron with their adopted East Asian daughter. Daughter Clair is a controlling, competitive and attractive housewife to Phil Dunphy, a real estate agent.

Lest we lose our traditions, *The Cleveland Show* (2009–present), another animated spinoff from *Family Guy*, continued the old working-class stereotype again. Cleveland Brown is variously a cable installer and a cold-call salesman. His wife, Donna, is an assistant to a school principal, a waitress, and an airport ground crew member. He engages in the usual inept schemes, à la Fred Flintstone, while she is the sensible one, another Wilma, but a bit more annoyed and judgmental, reminiscent of Louise Jefferson.

And to muddy class representations, in *The Middle* (2009–present), the dad, Mike Heck, works at a rock quarry, apparently as a supervisor or manager, but it is unclear. The mom, Frankie, is alternately a used car salesperson and a dental assistant, suggesting marginally working-class ambitions. She is wound a bit too tight and is easily upset. Mike is the calm, sensible one. The two are a bit like the pairing of Dan and Roseanne of *Roseanne* in the 1990s. Their preadolescent boy and teen girl are smart, mature and reflective, the ones who do the voice-over commentaries.

By the fall 2013 crop of sitcoms, the middle-class, happy family has been deconstructed, replaced by unconventional ones, and social class is more mixed or murky. For example, *The Fosters* (2013) are a lesbian couple with a biological child of one, an adopted child and a foster child, and of varied ethnicities. Stef Foster is a white policewoman, and Lena Adams is a black school administrator, mixing classes. They are openly affectionate and sexual with each other. They have various issues and arguments but in the end they are good parents.

Clearly we see change with the times over these six decades. In some sitcoms, characters become more three-dimensional and more complicated. The traditional nuclear family gives way to widows, divorcees, blended families, single parents, black families, and, eventually, gay couples. Middle-class men range more in character, are less perfect, do not always know best. In the latter decades, some middle-class as well as working-class men seek fun and avoid responsibility, although the middle-class men are successful and still retain self-respect, while the working-class men do not.

Yet, despite all these changes, some things persist. The formulas found in the 1950s sitcoms, of the working-class man as fool, but the middle-class woman as fool, and the middle class super-parent ideals, appear decade after decade, less universally and with other sitcoms that diverge from these formulae, but nevertheless still a substantial portion, especially among the most long-lasting sitcoms. *Plus ça change, plus c'est la même chose.*

Notes

1. Ben Olinsky and Sarah Ayres, "Training for Success: A Policy to Expand Apprenticeships in the United States," Center for American Progress, November 2013.
2. James P. Smith and Finis Welch, "No Time to Be Young: The Economic Prospects for Large Cohorts in the United States," *Population and Development Review*, vol. 7, no. 1, March 1981, 71–83.
3. Robert Lerman, "Are Skills the Problem? Reforming the Education and Training System in the United States" in Timothy Bartik and Susan Houseman (eds.), *A Future of Good Jobs*, Kalamzoo, MI: Upjohn Institute for Employment Research, 2008, 17–80; Harold Howe, *The Forgotten Half*, New York: William T. Grant Foundation, 1988, 18, 28.
4. James Rosenbaum, *Beyond College for All: Career Paths for the Forgotten Half*, New York: Russell Sage Foundation, 2001, 56.
5. Melissa Dabakis, *Visualizing Labor in American Sculpture: Monuments, Manliness, and the Work Ethic, 1880–1935*, Cambridge: Cambridge University Press, 2011; Janet Marstine, "Working History: Images of Labor and Industry in American Mural Painting 1893–1903," PhD Pittsburgh, 1993.
6. Dottie Lewis (ed.), *Cincinnati Union Terminal and the Artistry of Winold Reiss*, Cincinnati: The Cincinnati Historical Society, 1993.
7. David Glassberg, *Sense of History: The Place of the Past in American Life*, Amherst: University of Massachusetts Press, 2001, 65–71; Naima Prevots, *American Pageantry: A Movement for Art and Democracy*, Ann Arbor: UMI Research Press, 1990.
8. Marlene Park and Gerald E. Markowitz, *Democratic Vistas: Post Offices and Public Art in the New Deal*, Philadelphia: Temple University Press, 1984; Barbara Melosh, *Engendering Culture: Manhood and Womanhood in New Deal Public Art and Theater*, Washington, D.C.: Smithsonian Institution Press, 1991.
9. Reproduced in Dabakis, *Visualizing Labor in American Sculpture: Monuments, Manliness, and the Work Ethic, 1880–1935*.
10. George Gerbner and Larry Gross, "Living with Television: The Violence Profile," *Journal of Communication*, vol. 26, no. 2, June 1976, 172–194.
11. David Grote, *The End of Comedy: The Sitcom and the Comedic Tradition*, Hamden, CT: Shoe String Press, 1983.
12. Pollyanna is the title character of a best-selling 1913 novel by Eleanor H. Porter. Her name has come to depict an inborn optimistic outlook, however dire the circumstances, thus celebrating social passivity and upholding the status quo.

Works Cited

Dabakis, Melissa. *Visualizing Labor in American Sculpture: Monuments, Manliness, and the Work Ethic, 1880–1935*. Cambridge: Cambridge University Press 2011.
Gerbner, George, and Larry Gross. "Living with Television: The Violence Profile." *Journal of Communication*, vol. 26, no. 2, June 1976, 172–194.
Glassberg, David. *Sense of History: The Place of the Past in American Life*. Amherst: University of Massachusetts Press, 2001.
Grote, David. *The End of Comedy: The Sitcom and the Comedic Tradition*. Hamden, CT: Shoe String Press, 1983.
Lewis, Dottie (ed.). *Cincinnati Union Terminal and the Artistry of Winold Reiss*. Cincinnati: The Cincinnati Historical Society, 1993.
Howe, Harold. *The Forgotten Half*. New York: William T. Grant Foundation, 1988.
Lerman, Robert. "Are Skills the Problem? Reforming the Education and Training System in the United States" in Timothy Bartik and Susan Houseman (eds.), *A Future of Good Jobs*. Kalamzoo, MI: Upjohn Institute for Employment Research, 2008.
Marstine, Janet. "Working History: Images of Labor and Industry in American Mural Painting 1893–1903." PhD Pittsburgh, 1993.

Melosh, Barbara. *Engendering Culture: Manhood and Womanhood in New Deal Public Art and Theater*. Washington, D.C.: Smithsonian Institution Press, 1991.

Olinsky, Ben, and Sarah Ayres. "Training for Success: A Policy to Expand Apprenticeships in the United States." Center for American Progress, November 2013.

Park, Marlene, and Gerald E Markowitz. *Democratic Vistas: Post Offices and Public Art in the New Deal*. Philadelphia: Temple University Press, 1984.

Prevots, Naima. *American Pageantry: A Movement for Art and Democracy*. Ann Arbor: UMI Research Press, 1990.

Rosenbaum, James. *Beyond College for All: Career Paths for the Forgotten Half*. New York: Russell Sage Foundation, 2001.

Smith, James P., and Finis Welch. "No Time to Be Young: The Economic Prospects for Large Cohorts in the United States." *Population and Development Review*, vol. 7, no. 1, March 1981, 71–83.

Social Class and Class Distinctions in "Britcoms" (1950s–2000s)

RENÉE DICKASON

The situation comedy (sitcom) originated, like the soap opera, another staple of TV schedules, on radio in the United States after the First World War. It first appeared on British television with American import *I Love Lucy* (1955), a year before the broadcast of the first truly British sitcom (Britcom), *Hancock's Half Hour*. British television has regularly transmitted and sometimes reflected the influence of American sitcoms (from *The Phil Silvers Show*, 1957–1960, to today's *How I Met Your Mother* and *Big Bang Theory*), while an admittedly smaller but still considerable number of British productions (e.g., *Absolutely Fabulous, Are You Being Served?, Fawlty Towers, The Office, Steptoe and Son, Till Death Us Do Part*, etc.) have crossed the Atlantic in the opposite direction or been transmitted in original or modified form elsewhere in the English-speaking world or beyond.

Nevertheless, if comedy can travel, especially when there are no linguistic barriers, the impact of national, or even local, social or cultural factors has meant that a substantial majority of the sitcoms on British television have been home grown. From this it follows that the situations in Britcoms are firmly anchored in British society, reflecting an evolving variety of everyday concerns, characteristics and preoccupations, one of the most abiding of which is the issue of social class. Over what is now almost 60 years of the existence of the genre, the country has changed radically. The solidarity of the Welfare State and the age of full employment have given way to the "me-generation" and the economic liberalism of the Thatcher era, and led on to the tensions inherent in a post-industrial society buffeted by globalization. The period has also seen other trends: the desire for greater equality, at least of opportunity, the liberalizing of moral attitudes and demographic changes due to immigration and greater life expectancy, all of which have had an impact on the social fabric.

Attitudes to social class have evolved too, and so has their treatment in

Britcoms, but before exploring this development in detail, this article proposes to place the subject in context by examining some of the prevailing visions of class distinctions in later 20th century Britain and by suggesting that the conventional nature of the sitcom has sometimes limited how society is represented. It then moves on to explore three recurrent but evolving themes in the Britcom. It considers the (un)reliable markers of class, familiar or trivial details that may help the audience to identify, with varying degrees of certainty, the social status of the fictional characters on screen. Next, it explores the contrasted and ever-changing depiction of British society, and of the interactions between classes, in living and working environments in rural and urban settings. Finally, it reflects on the example of misfits, characters who attempt to escape the constraints of social class by challenging their place in the social structure, and on their (in)ability to resolve their situation.

When the Britcom was born, class awareness was not just alive and well, but bordered on a national obsession, as George Orwell had implied when referring to England as "the most class-ridden country under the sun."[1] At least until the end of the 20th century, it seemed that little had changed for in the 1995 revised edition of *Change in British Society*, sociologist A. H. Halsey quoted Orwell's epithet and additionally used the term "class-ridden prosperity" in the title of his critical assessment of the Thatcher years. Of course, both Orwell and Halsey had a political agenda, arguing that inequality and injustice within the social structure were sustained by fascination with class and by an accompanying ingrained attitude of deference. This does little, however, to explain the details of what it means to be a member of a given social class at a specific time. For most of the 20th century, the notion was generally equated, either officially in the Registrar General's Social Class classification or for commercial or political purposes,[2] with socio-economic categories based on employment which may be simply summarized as follows:

A—Higher managerial, administrative or professional
B—Intermediate managerial, administrative or professional
C1—Supervisory or clerical and junior managerial, administrative or professional
C2—Skilled manual
D—Semi-skilled and unskilled
E—State pensioners, casual or lowest grade workers

However, these categories can only represent part of what is meant by class. Quite apart from the omissions (those who do not work, have never worked, have never needed to or simply cannot, apparently have no place), such rigid and arbitrary classification raises the question of who may be qualified to judge the value or status of the work of another.[3] More importantly, as Bourdieu argued, other major factors which he termed "cultural capital" and "social capital" combine with wealth and income ("economic capital") in order to produce a more complex and accurate model of class. "Cultural capital" includes the ability to appreciate and engage with cultural goods, and other benefits of education such as knowledge, analytical/critical capacity, acquaintance with a range of ideas and values, and facility of expression. "Social capital" is represented by contacts and connections which allow people to interact successfully with others and to draw on their social networks, thereby achieving contacts with those of similar interests.[4] In addition, the multi-faceted, overarching composite notion of class may be broadened to include such innate or acquired factors as aspiration, behavior, language and upbringing which enable individuals to place themselves, and others to place them, within the class structure. This self-evaluation was demonstrated succinctly but in a manner which is entirely appropriate to this study in a famous television sketch, broadcast in April 1966, in *The Frost Report*.[5] With the primary purpose of satirizing the absurdities of the notion of class, this one-minute sequence presents three men of different physical sizes (John Cleese, 6'5," Ronnie Barker, 5'8" and Ronnie Corbett, 5'1"), dressed as archetypal representatives of the upper, middle and working class respectively, speaking in accents befitting their station, indicating which category they represent and how they view themselves and others:

> **Cleese:** *(in bowler hat, black jacket and pinstriped trousers)* I look down on him *(Barker)* because I am upper-class.
> **Barker:** *(in trilby hat and raincoat)* I look up to him *(Cleese)* because he is upper-class; but I look down on him *(Corbett)* because he is lower-class. I am middle-class.
> **Corbett:** *(in cloth cap and muffler)* I know my place. I look up to them both. But I don't look up to him *(Barker)* as much as I look up to him *(Cleese)*, because he has got innate breeding.

Innate breeding marred by poverty (Cleese), wealth marred by vulgarity (Barker), and vulgarity alone (Corbett) complete this stereotyped picture of social prejudice and self-assessment.

This brief extract demonstrates that depicting class distinctions can be a suitable vehicle for achieving comic effect, which is especially relevant to the sitcom whose primary purpose is to produce pleasure and amusement. Indeed, the viewer is expected to laugh at (or with) the characters presented and, in order to encourage this reaction, most Britcoms have been recorded, and in the early years were simply performed live, before a studio audience. Humor can be achieved through the full range of comic devices, from broad farce and slapstick to caricature, role reversal, wordplay and wit, which of course enables a program to appeal to a wide range of tastes. But sitcom can also be regarded as comedy in its original sense. Its subject matter is not the important thoughts, decisions and deeds of the great and the good, for these are the stuff of tragedy, but rather the minor tribulations of ordinary people, like the viewers, whose trivial problems are resolved, using the classic narrative structure for comedy. Each episode has a happy ending or, at least, finishes with the restoration of order[6] which can then be disrupted once more in the next episode thereby starting the whole process all over again.

If such is the comedy in Britcoms, then we may reasonably wonder, what is the situation? That this blanket term may cover a particular limited spatial area or relate to a wider field of social interaction is acknowledged by the customary division into domestic situation comedies ("domcoms") and situation comedies set in the workplace or similar institutions ("workcoms"). Nevertheless, this distinction is by no means rigid. Indeed, Ray Galton and Alan Simpson, the writers of the seminal *Hancock's Half Hour* (and its successor, named simply *Hancock*) rapidly saw the comic potential of moving the central figure out of his restricted home environment in order for the limits of his lower-middle-class character to be exposed by contact with people of different backgrounds and horizons, and many subsequent Britcoms have adopted the same approach.

In fact, the genre as a whole suffers from "[a surprising] comparative dearth of critical analysis."[7] Most often, it is defined in terms of its form (a series of self-contained episodes rather than a developing serial), its length (between 23 and 28 minutes to fit a 30-minute time slot, with or without advertising breaks), its narrative structure or its potential for repetition. We might also add that its need to achieve high viewing figures in a competitive market frequently leads to the reliance on tried and tested formulae. Consequently, as Cornell, Day and Topping indicate,

> Sitcom is normally considered to be television's most reactionary genre [...] conservative and middle class from the outset, but the genre is, in theory, no more constrained than any other. What has tended to happen is that popular sitcom success will automatically produce imitation and thus, logically, stagnation.[8]

With this stance, it is natural that the Britcom should only rarely take on comedy's "assumed social role as a questioner of norms and [...] licence to say the unsayable,"[9] and thus seldom cast doubt on the norms of society. Allusions to contemporary events may give a certain topical spice to episodes, satirical sitcoms such as *Drop the Dead Donkey* and *The New Statesman* may show contempt for specific groups in society, and worker/management frictions may illustrate class differences. However, in the period under study, only one Britcom (*Citizen Smith*) carries echoes of the class war, but then merely to ridicule the revolutionary pretensions of the six members of the self-styled Tooting Popular Front. More abrasive were, however, the anarchic alternative comedy series (the first being *The Young Ones*, 1982–84) which used the techniques of culture shock primarily to shatter the comfortable predictability which dominated many of the bland domcoms in the 1970s and 1980s. They also, indirectly, attacked the conformist, respectable vision of society that emanated from them in Margaret Thatcher's Britain. With hindsight, alternative Britcoms can be seen as a striking, perhaps necessary, but transient phenomenon which nevertheless served as a reminder that comedy can come in different guises and thereby appeal in different ways, at different times to different audiences.

While maintaining that the issue of class distinctions, whether foregrounded or underlying, is a motif common to most if not all Britcoms, which makes it a convenient lens through which to view the huge variety the genre has offered and still does, it should not be forgotten that the treatment of the theme is first and foremost designed to be comic and intended for consumption within the comfort of the home environment. This may explain why so many domcoms center on what writer Barry Took has called "comic traps," namely situations in which trivial incidents, sibling rivalry, generation gaps and petty jealousies are bound to arise and can be exploited for comic effect, but always with the reassuring premise that:

> Nothing that has happened in the narrative of the previous week must destroy or even complicate the way the situation is grounded. [...] Events from the outside [...] have to be dealt with in such a way that the parameters of the situation are ultimately unaffected [...] so that the situation can be maintained or taken up again the following week.[10]

The other silver lining for the audience is that they may realize that, as the domestic problems they see on screen are similar to their own, they are not alone in having to cope with such difficulties.

(Un)Reliable Markers of Class

After the above examination of how class may be defined and the conclusion that what is often most important for the individual is a personal assessment of his/her position within the social structure, this section considers some of the more or less conclusive ways in which status can be suggested in Britcoms. Most series contain more or less clear markers which help viewers to readily identify the status of characters and to judge whether they themselves are higher or lower on the social spectrum than the fictional creations. These indicators may be minimalist or overdetermined, but can never be wholly conclusive as the attributes of class change over time, as regional and local variations may contradict as well as confirm the basic perceptions and as individuality should never be ruled out. Moreover, as series dealing with solely the upper class or nobility are non-existent and those featuring exclusively the working class are comparatively rare, the characters which most Britcoms depict are, by default, middle-class, a category so broad as to defy precise definition, even for members of an audience keen to estimate their own status as accurately as possible.

Nevertheless, there are markers that are reasonably reliable, the most prominent of them being housing. Large-scale owner occupation in Britain, reinforced by the belief that "the Englishman's home is his castle," makes the place where people live a matter of pride and the ultimate potential status symbol. As Linsey Hanley, author of *Estates: An Intimate History*, pointed out in a recent radio broadcast, differences are easy to spot: "You can map social class in Britain simply by walking around, by straying from a middle-class area to a working-class area [...] into an area of private housing, into an area of council housing."[11] The opening title sequences of some Britcoms establish expectations in just this way. In the early episodes of *Till Death Us Do Part*, the camera moves downriver and downmarket from the Houses of Parliament to a terraced house in Wapping in the East End of London to reach the home of the working-class Garnetts, while the house occupied by the large Boswell family (*Bread*) is in another typical working-class area, an ungentrified Victorian terraced street running down to the Mersey in Liverpool, with only a door and no garden to separate the living room from the pavement. These homes contrast with the large detached house occupied by the well-established Leadbetters in *The Good Life*, or with less opulent but still semi-detached and patio equipped "home sweet home" of the more modest middle-class Terry and June Medford (*Terry and June*). In some series, the address or mere name of the area is sufficient indication for the viewer who knows the middle-class pretensions of Surbiton (*The Good Life*), the respectability of Tooting (*Citizen Smith*), or the working-class implications of Peckham (*Only Fools and Horses*). Hancock's fictional address, 23 Railway Cuttings, East Cheam is more subtle: by combining the poshness of Cheam with the inglorious proximity of the railway, it acts as an objective correlative of the character's lower-middle-class uncertainties and snobbishness.

Significant too is the space within the house and the way it is used. Working-class homes are typified by the crowding of characters into a single room, the kitchen for the five Boswell children and their mother (*Bread*), and for Mrs. Butler, her son, her daughter and her daughter's husband (*On the Buses*), or the living room cluttered with furniture in the *Royle Family* (habitually occupied by grandmother, parents, two children, future son-in-law and visited by assorted neighbors). This promiscuity contrasts with the comfort offered to middle-class couples, many of whom are childless (e.g., the Goods and the Leadbetters in *The Good Life*) or empty nesters (the Perrins and the Medfords). In fact, the intergenerational family is a recurrent working-class marker, but one with positive overtones, as the Boswell children care for their grandfather who lives next door, and the Trotter brothers (*Only Fools and Horses*) share their high-rise flat with their grandfather, and after the latter's demise with their great uncle.

On the other hand, matters like clothes, décor and furnishings are more likely to reflect individual taste or contemporary fashion and period than anything else. For example, the wall in the Garnetts' living room is graced with a set of flying china ducks, an adornment typical of homes across the social spectrum in the 1960s, but what is revealing about Alf Garnett is the accompanying oversized picture of Winston Churchill which clearly typifies him as that particular British anomaly, a working-class Conservative, more than ready to cross swords with his equally working-class but firmly Socialist son-in-law. Different social activities can be class-determined too, but in Britcoms they are mentioned rather than shown as integral to the life of the characters, and amount to little more than window-dressing or name-dropping. Modes of transport too may not be as indicative as they might seem. It is clear that their reliance on, at best, public transport, or, at worst, Shanks's pony is a serious hindrance to the working-class Bob and Terry's attempts at seducing the opposite sex (*The Likely Lads*). Similarly, the clapped-out motorcycle and sidecar used by Arthur Rudge in *On the Buses* in 1969 stresses his working-class credentials, for most of the middle classes would have avoided this uncomfortable, dirty and noisy mode of transport like the plague. However, when a similar vehicle reappears a few years later, ridden by George Roper in *George and Mildred*, a series that was launched in 1976, we may wonder if class distinction is all that it conveys or whether it is not there primarily as a comic device. In the case of the three-wheeled Reliant van emblazoned "Trotters Independent Trading Co. New York Paris Peckham" in *Only Fools and Horses*, there is no possible room for doubt. The model is so incongruous as to be simply a joke on wheels, raising laughter by its mere appearance.[12] Enigmatic too is the classic Jaguar driven by Nellie Boswell's eldest son Joey (*Bread*). This expensive model, along with the character's smart leather clothing, leads to the suspicion that his night-time job, about which even his family is kept in the dark, may be more than lucrative as well as of dubious legality. Nevertheless, this extravagance seems to be more a personal whim to stand out than a declaration of class difference, for he continues to live happily in the cramped family home along with his sister and three brothers.

Finally, we are left with potentially the most striking, but actually the most complex class marker of all, language. As it can reflect a level of education and is integral to Bourdieu's notion of cultural capital, its potential for social differentiation is considerable. In Britcoms, a strong local accent often suggests a lower level of education and a lack of contact with others from outside the same geographical area or social stratum, and helps typecast, for example, the Boswells, the Royles, the Garnetts, the Steptoes and the Likely Lads.[13] Similarly, ungrammatical expressions and errors of pronunciation, including the dreaded dropped or stray aitches, are typical of many working-class Britcom characters who are also more likely to use colloquialisms and taboo expressions. Back in the 1960s, Mary Whitehouse, a tireless campaigner for the improvement of the moral standards of television, was appalled by a single episode of *Till Death Us Do Part*, in which Alf Garnett uttered the word "bloody" no less than 78 times. At the time the word was a strong expletive,[14] but from today's perspective, its offensiveness pales into insignificance, when compared to the same character's regular use of "coons" for people of color or "silly moo" to refer to his long-suffering wife. More recently, swearing has become commonplace in Britcoms, across the social spectrum: even the highly respectable, middle-class pensioner Victor Meldrew (*One Foot in the Grave*, 1990–95) sprinkles his curmudgeonly utterances with "bloodies," albeit in a finely modulated Scots accent. Nevertheless, Jim Royle's opening gambit "It's good to talk. My Arse!" in the very first episode of the *Royle Family* (1998), his reference to his son as a "sausage-jockey" (homosexual) or his remark that it is "time for an Eartha Kitt" when heading for the toilet suggest that the Britcom working class has lost little of its penchant for earthiness. Any such general conclusion remains, however, questionable. The vernacular of the Trotters in *Only Fools and Horses* manages, while eschewing coarseness, to be both indicative of their status and an expression of individuality. Many of their expressions are simply popular colloquialisms or mispronounced variants of standard words ("pukka"—perfect, "luvverly"—terrific, "woofter"—homosexual) but others ("twonk"—idiot, "brassic"—broke, "pony"—£25) do indeed smack of the idiolect of a micro culture impenetrable to the uninitiated.

Higher up the social ladder, offensiveness may diminish, but sometimes at the expense of clarity of thought or expression, which leads us to suspect that context as well as class may play a significant role in how ideas are formulated. In *The Office*, manager David Brent speaks in rambling, incomplete sentences, clichés and mixed metaphors which serve to make his thoughts and intentions incomprehensible to his employees, less out of lower-middle-class diffidence than out of a desire to create uncertainty among them and thereby maintain his superiority. Reginald Perrin's upper-middle-class boss, the supremely self-confident company owner CJ, in *The Fall and Rise of Reginald Perrin*, deals unhesitatingly in would-be aphorisms beginning "I didn't get where I am today by..." while Perrin's army officer brother-in-law offers explanations starting with the mildly offensive "bit of a cock up on the ... front" before continuing the argument in incomplete sentences as if unable to rid himself of the techniques of signals code.[15] Pride of place nevertheless goes to Gus Hedges of *Drop the Dead Donkey* who takes meaningless vacuity to new levels with such management speech gems as "We've got to downsize our sloppiness overload. Am I making myself clear?"

Contrasted and Ever-Changing Representations of British Society in Living and Working Environments in Rural and Urban Settings

After considering some of the building blocks that help in the construction of class identity, let us now examine the evolving and contrasted representations of society as a whole, in situations where different classes, or sometimes characters of very similar status, meet and interact in rural and urban settings. As with the markers of class distinction discussed above, the representation of this theme is in constant evolution, with the more subtle differences evoked in some Britcoms taking the place of the rigid hierarchy which prevails in others.

As most inhabitants of Great Britain live and work in an urban environment, it is no surprise that rural sitcoms are particularly thin on the ground or that they should give a view of life that is at once stereotyped, ill-informed and surprisingly rose-tinted. It is true that British broadcasting's longest-running program is a rural (radio) soap opera, *The Archers*, which dates from 1951. Originally subtitled "an everyday story of country folk," it is still a relatively reliable source of information about trends in agriculture, but it gives a socially conservative vision of country life with different groups and classes coexisting in relative harmony. This seems to have influenced two of the Britcoms broadcast in the period studied (*To the Manor Born* and *The Vicar of Dibley*). The third, *The Last of the Summer Wine*, is free from class consciousness. It relates the minor adventures of three elderly men who have never really grown up and who just happen to live in a particularly picturesque corner of the Pennines.[16]

To the Manor Born offers the epitome of a feudal hierarchical structure, in a community where everyone knows and accepts their appointed place, or at least until the moment when the local Lord of the Manor dies, leaving his widow, Audrey fforbes-Hamilton, with huge unpaid debts. This opens the way for an outsider, rich urban businessman Richard DeVere, to buy up the Grantleigh Estate and the Manor House, thereby disturbing the established *status quo*. In this rural idyll, hierarchy and class closely coincide, and the virtually penniless Mrs. fforbes-Hamilton (the "ff" being a sign of aristocratic lineage) exploits her acquired influence over her former employees on the estate and over other inhabitants of the area who live or depend on it. Thus, when she is obliged to leave the Manor House and occupy the nearby conveniently vacant Old Lodge, she continues to employ as domestic servant her former butler, Brabinger, a well-spoken middle-class retainer in the Jeeves mold, and as gardener, a working-class former estate laborer, Ned. The petty class rivalry between the two disappears in the presence of "Mrs. fforbes" to whom they both show due deference. The status of other local inhabitants is equally clear, although Audrey fforbes-Hamilton is superior to all of them: the local shopkeeper who gives her credit, the vicar whose living depends on the estate, her old school friend, wealthy spinster Marjorie Frobisher, almost, but not quite, from the same social bracket and the established superior middle-class retired military man, Brigadier Lemington OBE. Within this strictly structured environment, class friction appears only between Audrey and Richard, a self-made millionaire of Czechoslovakian origin and director of Cavendish Foods whom she snobbishly dubs "the grocer." For her, the invariably charming and well-mannered DeVere can never bridge the class gap and must remain an uncultured "*parvenu*," at least until she marries him.

The Vicar of Dibley offers a somewhat similar picture. Like Grantleigh, the fictional Dibley has a clear hereditary leader, David Horton, a Conservative millionaire from the established local landowning family who chairs the parish council. David is not only wealthy but has considerable social capital, which allows him to arrange for a diocesan bishop, an acquaintance from their schooldays, to baptize his granddaughter, and for a wealthy business contact to pay for the replacement of the church's storm-damaged west window. The other figure whose status is clear is the vicar Geraldine Granger.[17] She is educated, middle-class, unpretentious and assiduous in her pastoral duties, but a maverick in her private life: she drinks to excess, has a torrid and very public affair with Horton's brother and tells the verger, Alice Tinker, scurrilous jokes which the latter is never bright enough to understand. Alice, of humble origins, ignorant and deferent to a fault nevertheless ends up marrying Horton's son Hugo, not out of hopes of social advancement, but out of love. The two are well-matched for Hugo is living proof that wealth and class do not necessarily mean brains. The status of the other recurrent characters remains somewhat enigmatic: farmer Owen Newitt may be a landowner or a tenant, but his language and preoccupation with bodily functions, his own and his animals,' suggest lowly origins; Letitia Cropley, Frank Pickle and Jim Trott are all retired. It would seem that Mr. Pickle, Dibley's parish clerk, worked as a middle-class pen-pusher, but language is the only indication that Mrs. Cropley is of a higher status than the singularly inarticulate and presumably working-class Mr. Trott. In any case, social friction does not exist in Dibley and this unlikely bunch of eccentrics unites whenever the good of the community is threatened.

Another (increasingly) outdated[18] evocation of social classes is offered in *Are You Being Served?*, a workcom set in an old-fashioned, up-market department store so crowded with staff and devoid of customers that it is perplexing that it could ever have made a profit. The business is marked by a rigid hierarchical structure. At the top of the pecking order is the owner, young Mr. Grace, an octogenarian gentleman who seems bemused by what he encounters on his occasional forays from his top-floor office to the sales areas below. Next come the permanently harassed middle-manager Cuthbert Rumbold, the officious floor walker Stephen Peacock, who, like some military types, is sufficiently obsessed by his status to wish to be addressed by his former army rank (merely captain), and the elderly, well-spoken and evidently respectable department head Mr. Grainger. The junior sales personnel include Mr. Lucas, with his sharp tongue and eye for the ladies, Mrs. Slocombe, with ideas above her station and an accent to prove it, and Miss Brahms, the victim of most of Mr. Lucas's sexist remarks. At the bottom of the ladder is Mr. Harmen, working-class and proud of it, who distinguishes himself from the others by a total absence of deference. With the exception of Peacock and Rumbold in private, staff never offend protocol by using first names to address one another. There would be nothing remarkable about this stereotypical group of characters, were it not for the presence of the outrageously camp senior sales assistant Mr. Humphries, whose excessive mannerisms significantly hardly cause his colleagues to raise an eyebrow. In this regard, when compared with other Britcom characters of the 1970s, such as Alf Garnett or Rupert Rigsby (*Rising Damp*), the staff of Grace Brothers do at least distinguish themselves by this example of tolerance.[19]

Such behavior as Mr. Humphries's would have been totally inadmissible in a differently structured environment, such as that presented in the military sitcoms broadcast from the late 1950s to the early 1980s and familiar to members of the viewing audience who were about to do two years' national service, had already done so, or knew someone who had.[20] From the point of view of social class, the premise of these series was simple: the ordinary conscripts might be from mixed backgrounds, but the majority were working-class, and in any case they all united to flout authority when they could. The officers were distant, mostly upper-middle-class figures as some of their names suggest (e.g., Major Upshot-Bagley, Captain Gervaise Duckworth), and were content to leave discipline and training to NCOs, typically of working-class origins, who were separated from their men by their knowledge and authority and from the officers by their lower social status and much greater competence in military matters.[21]

In comparison, the position of the intermediate figure of the foreman in the two workplace Britcoms of the same period is much less secure. Reg in *The Rag Trade* has divided loyalties, to his own working class personified by the seamstresses of Fenner's clothing factory and to his boss who has promoted him, and finally survives by simply not committing himself. In any case, shop floor power was extremely strong throughout British industry in the 1950s–1970s, and, in this Britcom, the workers, led by a particularly aggressive female shop steward, Paddy, wielding the strike weapon, invariably win any argument with the management. Unlike Reg, Inspector Blake in *On the Buses* does try to exercise responsibility. The problem is that despite demanding to be addressed by his title rather than his first name, which is never revealed, he too is working-class and has no management backing in any stand he takes against the recalcitrant drivers in his depot. His petty-minded attempts to catch them out invariably fail, making him a comic figure, with no more than anger and empty threats to console him.

As the 20th century drew on, manufacturing industry declined, and the scene in British workcoms shifted from the factory or the workshop to the office where the different declensions of the middle class could be observed in all their splendor and where business practices could be satirized. Sunshine Desserts, a failing company where the luckless Reginald Perrin spends his day is a good example. As a manager, of sorts, for much of his working time is spent ogling his attractive secretary, Joan, or visiting the incompetent company doctor who has similar preoccupations, Perrin is uncomfortably placed in a status gap between his boss, CJ, and his assistants, David Harris-Jones and Tony Webster. The first is an autocrat, the founder of the company whose bluff exterior conceals a steadfast belief in his own infallibility. CJ has little but contempt for his staff, calling them to meetings at the most inconvenient times, debasing them by making them sit on chairs equipped with whoopee cushions and laughing at the vulgar noise that invariably follows when they stand up to leave. Perrin's juniors are a pair of sycophantic yes-men, of different temperament certainly

(David is hesitant and nervous, while Tony is supremely self-confident), but indistinguishable by either class, status or competence. To Perrin's chagrin, they receive each new instruction that he reluctantly transmits to them with an enthusiastic "Super" (David)/"Great" (Tony) which leaves him no choice but to carry on with the latest hare-brained sales-boosting project that CJ has devised.

Sunshine Desserts is what might be called a challenging place to work, but it is at least free from the personal conflicts that afflict staff at Globelink News TV (*Drop the Dead Donkey*). The business is owned by self-made millionaire Sir Royston Merchant, whose initials suggest similarities with the two biggest British media tycoons of the moment, Robert Maxwell and Rupert Murdoch, and who directs the business at arm's length, leaving the day-to-day running of the newsroom where the action takes place, to the immaculately dressed Gus Hedges whose management-speak jargon does nothing to mask his lack of humanity. When faced with Hedges, the news editor and only (conceivably) sympathetic character, George Dent, is unable to make constructive decisions and his weak leadership ensures a toxic working environment in which it is every man/woman for himself/herself, which apparently suits them well. The staff are generously paid, even the most junior of them drives a Porsche, egotistical and jealous (sexually as well as financially), and employ most of their undoubted talent making jokes at one another's expense and plotting to further their own careers. It is no surprise that none of them is happily married.

This overtly abrasive depiction of the middle-class at work is a far cry from the polite and verbally exquisite portrayal offered in *Yes Minister*,[22] one that fully exploits the subtler nuances of class distinction. The newly-appointed minister, Jim Hacker, a graduate of the thoroughly meritocratic London School of Economics, finds himself confronted by a top Whitehall mandarin, his department's (ministry's) permanent secretary, Humphrey Appleby KCB, MVO, MA (Oxon.), very definitely from socio-economic group A. Both consider themselves superior to the other, but only Sir Humphrey is proven right. Hacker is a minister of the crown, with a popular mandate to bring sweeping and long-overdue improvements to the running of his department, but Sir Humphrey has weightier advantages. As an Oxford graduate, a servant who actually is cleverer than his master and speaks administrative jargon fluently, he can joke with other like-minded permanent secretaries at their gentlemen's club that when Hacker joined the cabinet he increased its average age but diminished its average IQ. Moreover, he knows from long experience how a ministry works, and, more importantly how to prevent it from working, but his trump card is what, at a lower class level, would be called job security, namely that he cannot be dismissed from his post whereas ministers, Hacker included, may come and go, depending on electoral fortunes or the whims of the prime minister. With all this social and cultural capital, Sir Humphrey cannot lose, and without it, as the series demonstrates time and again, Hacker cannot win.

Living away from home and sharing rented accommodation with others and staying or eating out at a hotel are familiar social situations which do not immediately prompt expectations of unpleasantness and rivalry. However, in two iconic Britcoms, *Rising Damp* and *Fawlty Towers*, this is exactly the fate that awaits those unlucky enough to find themselves under the roof of, respectively, Rupert Rigsby and Basil Fawlty. The former, the miserly owner of a boarding house in an unnamed northern town, rents out bedsits as his only source of income. In principle, beggars not being choosers, he provides accommodation to anyone able to pay, but his regular tenants are all from the local university, lovelorn, eye-fluttering administrator Miss Jones, on whom Rigsby has unrequited amorous/lustful designs, first-year medical student Alan Moore and the more mature Philip Smith who is studying town planning. With her education, delicacy and rewarding job, Miss Jones has the refinement of the middle class and so, by their education and open-mindedness, are the other two. Worse still from Rigsby's point of view, the three lodgers are on first name terms, which excites his jealousy and leads him to spy on them with scant respect for their privacy. Both of the young men have attributes that excite Rigsby's scarcely concealed prejudices. Alan is young, long-haired and free thinking; Rigsby is a frustrated, middle-aged bigot who cannot tolerate sexual liberation. With Philip, things are worse still: he is black but speaks impeccably modulated English, and has little difficulty in warding off Rigsby's racist barbs, once he has convinced the gullible landlord that he is the son of a tribal chief and therefore a person to be reckoned with in his own country. Rigsby's lack of social graces, meanness and unrelentingly scruffy appearance belie his status as landlord, making it easy for the others to mock him and outmaneuver him on almost every occasion.

Basil Fawlty is a different type. With his physique, accent and veneer of culture, he finds it easy to impress the guests at his relatively prosperous hotel, provided, that is, he considers them as equals, for his overriding characteristic is his snobbery. Himself middle-class, he treats those he meets according to his often flawed assessment of their merit and status: he shows his permanent residents, Miss Tibbs, Miss Gatsby and Major Gowen some consideration, has a certain respect for waitress/maid Polly who is helpful in the running of the hotel, but is unfailingly rude and aggressive to the waiter Manuel, a mere foreigner from Barcelona, whom he bullies mercilessly. Where his talent for snobbishness reaches its peak is in his behavior towards his passing guests. He fawns upon those he judges superior, is rude to all those he views as not meeting his standards for politeness or good manners, despite the fact that he can be intolerably rude himself, despises foreigners who can only be his inferiors and ignores or insults those he considers beneath his station. The hotel with its regularly changing guests should be a perfect vehicle for interaction between diverse social classes, but, in fact, this Britcom focuses not on the customers, but almost exclusively on the egocentric Fawlty, giving him full rein to display his prejudices and to demonstrate the fallibility of his judgment, and leaving him to suffer the chastisement of laughter.

Misfits, Failures and Survivors: Questioning the Social Status Quo and Its Limits

In what we have seen so far, the vast majority of Britcom characters are relatively at home with their social status, but this study would be incomplete if it did not consider those who are not, or no longer, fully satisfied with the limits their social class seems to impose upon them, either through peer or family pressure or the need to keep up appearances, or again because of personal ambition or idealism. The reasons for these expressions of discontent have evolved over the years, reflecting contemporary attitudes and aspirations, and a further development has been the emergence in Britcoms of groups whose grievance is not with the class in which they find themselves, but rather with society as a whole which seems indifferent to their fate, leaving them to survive by their own initiative and on their own terms.

Of all these cases, the most frequently found is the desire to move up the social ladder to a position of greater comfort and prestige, although, in Britcoms, the way characters attempt this and their degree of success vary according to the period considered, strongly suggesting that in such a conservative genre the questioning of the social *status quo* has its limits. The first two series to broach this theme were the nearly contemporaneous *Steptoe and Son* (1962–74) and *The Likely Lads* (1964–66) and its sequel *Whatever Happened to the Likely Lads* (1973–74). In both cases the characters with aspirations are working-class, and the comedy is tinged with pathos, but there the similarities end. Harold Steptoe is a London rag and bone man who does his rounds by horse and cart[23] and lives with this father in a house adjoining their scrap yard in Oil Drum Lane, Shepherd's Bush. Although the two men are partners, 40-year-old Harold does all the work and would like to be upwardly mobile, by transforming the rag and bone activity into a respectable antiques business.

He fails completely, partly because of the lack of education frequently betrayed by his cockney accent and convoluted and ungrammatical speech, but mainly because his father thwarts his ambitions at every turn and even drives away the few girlfriends he is foolish enough to bring home. The two men are completely different: Harold is hard-working, ambitious and likeable, while Albert is mean, rude, lazy and usually unwashed. Albert is a working-class Conservative, while Harold is an equally staunch Socialist. In the end, however, in an interesting insight into the insecurity of those who try to climb the social ladder, blood is thicker than water and family loyalty prevents Harold from ever quite bringing himself to take the ruthless step of abandoning Albert in order to further his own interests. The Likely Lads, Bob Ferris and Terry Collier, initially show no more than moderate dissatisfaction with their lives as electricians in Newcastle. It is not until the last episode of the final series that Bob, inspired by the experiences of an old friend, decides to join the army, to see the world (as the recruitment poster has it), to enjoy life and to improve his job prospects by acquiring new skills in the REME (Royal Electrical and Mechanical Engineers). Terry belatedly feels the urge to join him in the adventure and also signs on for three years, but as the young men are likely (i.e. likeable) rather than lucky, Terry reaches the REME depot just in time to exchange a few words with Bob who has been medically discharged because he has flat feet. When they meet again eight years later, in *Whatever Happened to the Likely Lads*, things have changed for Bob. He has made the break with the past and now has an office job, a house on a new suburban estate, a car and is about to marry his boss's daughter, an old flame named Thelma. In short, he has left the working class behind him. On the other hand, Terry has no such pretensions and remains loyal to his roots and to his old, lazy and heavy-drinking ways which, although he does not know it, may make him unemployable in the harder realities of the 1970s. For Bob, he is an unholy cross between a Banquo's ghost, haunting him with the thought that he is a traitor to his class (and to their former friendship), and a Mephistopheles trying to tempt him back to his old ways, but in the end he narrowly fails, and Bob and Thelma seem set to tread their new path together.

The 1980s Britcoms *To the Manor Born* and the *New Statesman* deal with a different class and in different circumstances. In the former, millionaire Richard DeVere successfully achieves his ultimate goal, and his mother's, namely to reach the highest social status in his adopted country, the UK, even if only through marriage. That he does so without harming others is entirely to his credit, for he is generous and respects both those less well placed than himself and the sensitivities of the community he lives in. Later in this "me-decade," as Alan B'stard demonstrates in *The New Statesman*, any such restraint is an unnecessary waste of time. Indeed, the series begins with a car crash that

B'stard himself has arranged, which kills off both his political opponents and ensures his election to Parliament. This appropriately named right-wing Conservative politician ruthlessly exploits his more conformist, socially-superior party colleagues, notably the singularly dense Piers Fletcher-Dervish, and is interested only in himself, his career and his wealth. His marriage to a rich Yorkshire heiress is a sham, for she only agreed to marry him for his money and despises him as a *nouveau riche* upstart. Both are unfaithful. B'stard's large majority (the biggest in Parliament, he claims, not without a certain sexual innuendo) helps him to have several quick-fire affairs while his wife stays at home, on occasion, in bed with his (female) constituency agent, unless she can find a couple of men to sleep with, preferably both at the same time. That the *New Statesman* has a clear political message is unquestionable, but B'stard's ability, exaggerated though it is, to succeed by riding roughshod over anyone who gets in his way says much about changing attitudes to the nature of society itself in the later years of Mrs. Thatcher's Britain.

Keeping Up Appearances is less disturbing, perhaps because its principal character, another would-be social climber Hyacinth Bucket is lower-middle-class and thus close in status to the viewing audience, perhaps because her attempts to impress those better placed than herself always fail horribly, or perhaps merely because it is pleasant to see such an odious snob getting her comic come-uppance. Hyacinth Bucket is keen not just to pursue the middle-class suburban game of "keeping up with the Joneses," but to outdo them. She pronounces her name Bouquet, has an acquired cultured accent which buckles under stress, talks loudly and often about her sister Violet who has a house with a sauna and swimming pool and forces her husband and neighbors to attend social events designed to improve her own social status. Worst of all, she does all she can to ignore the existence of her father and two other sisters, who live on a nearby council estate, but who turn up unbidden at moments which cause her a maximum of embarrassment. In short, she gets her just deserts, and is a relatively rare example of a wholly unsympathetic weak Britcom character that the audience can only delight in laughing at and not with.

The forced respectability and conformity of middle-class life, at home, at work or both, occasionally leads to feelings of discontent or even thoughts of rebellion in Britcoms. Anticipating the worst when he and his wife move to a new suburban townhouse, working-class George Roper of *George and Mildred* is steadfast in his determination to resist his wife's social ambitions, but in *The Good Life*, Tom Good is more radical. Reaching the age of 40 and tiring of his work as a draughtsman, he decides that it is time to leave the rat race and adopt a self-sufficient life style, growing his own vegetables and keeping animals in the garden of his house in Surbiton. Not without serious misgivings, his wife

"Dropping out of the rat race": Felicity Kendal and Richard Briers (as Barbara and Tom Good) in *The Good Life* (1975) (© BBC/Photofest).

Barbara agrees to join him in this ecological endeavor, and becomes an even greater enthusiast than her husband. The venture is fraught with risks: they know nothing about agriculture, and their posh neighbors, Jerry and Margo Leadbetter, from the superior end of the middle class, are aghast at the idea that can only damage the standing of the avenue where both couples live. Much of the humor derives from the inevitable clash of interests that ensues, but, in an ultimate happy ending and against all the odds, the Goods are successful and Jerry and Margo, by stages appalled, indignant, resigned and amused come to accept, support and even envy their neighbors. If *The Good Life* stretches the limits of plausibility, *The Fall and Rise of Reginald Perrin* goes far beyond.[24] The initial premise is just tenable. The middle-class, middle-manager Perrin, in a mid-life crisis at 46 and utterly fed up with the boredom of his daily life both at home and the office, feels the need to revolt. He develops a vivid imagination, seeing his mother-in-law as a hippopotamus and fantasizing about making love in the open air to his secretary, Joan. What follows develops into a full-blown satire of business life and middle-class propriety. Perrin stages his own suicide, leaving his clothes on a Dorset beach, only to return in very inadequate disguise and attend his own funeral. He then remarries his wife, who had recognized him at once, finds himself unemployed, sets up, at her suggestion, a company called Grot that is a runaway success selling worthless goods at excessive prices, thus becoming a business tycoon, employing his former colleagues and boss. It is at this point that he realizes that he has returned to just the routine which he sought to escape, "commits suicide" again, this time with his wife, using the same technique as before, and returns to found a very visible community designed to make the middle-aged and middle-class "better people." The project is so class-ridden that it attracts the anger of local thugs and has to close, but Perrin finds a job with his former boss's brother. Once again he finds himself trapped in the same humdrum existence, and the series ends with him heading once more for Dorset. If *The Good Life* is excessively cheerful and the *Fall and Rise of Reginald Perrin* is caustic, melancholy is the dominant mood of *Butterflies*, another (quietly) dissatisfied Britcom set in the 1970s. Approaching middle age, Lia Parkinson is unfulfilled by her daily lot. She is a typical middle-class housewife, with no job, for her husband Ben's dental practice is sufficiently prosperous to support them very comfortably, and with a limited role as the more strenuous household tasks are handled by a cleaning lady. Her two teenage sons are growing up too quickly for her liking and Ben is too distant to rein them in, or indeed to take much pleasure in life with her. The only thing that the boys and their father have in common is their negative appreciation of Lia's hopeless cooking. All in all, she has the impression that she has achieved nothing and that life is passing her by. The remedy, of course, would be an affair, and Lia duly encounters a smooth-talking would-be lover, a business man whose wife has left him, but she is too shy to ever quite bring herself to consummate the relationship, settling for her husband and middle-class conformity, which does nothing to mitigate her feeling of failure.

Disrespect for society as a whole is a more recent Britcom phenomenon. The characters, in the alternative comedy of the 1980s and 1990s, had nothing to say about class, but were united in their derision for propriety, good manners or anything approaching civilized behavior.[25] Other sitcoms appearing at much the same time, and with much greater longevity, have adopted a different approach, portraying groups distancing themselves from the conventions of society simply in order to survive. As one might expect, the characters are resolutely working-class, displaying many of the stereotypical markers that were examined earlier, but, most importantly, taken as a whole, they are sympathetic characters who remain faithful to their own values. The title of the first of these Britcoms, *Only Fools and Horses*, sets the tone for them all. It is an incomplete version of the cockney saying "only fools and horses work," but this simple assertion does not do justice to the resilience of the Trotters in this series, or indeed of the Boswells in *Bread* and the eponymous Royle Family. In fact, the Trotters feel no debt to society, for their credo is that, since the government gives them nothing, they owe nothing in return, *"no income tax, no VAT"* as the theme song puts it, their occupation of a council flat being virtually their only contact with officialdom. On the other hand, they do all they can to ensure that they are not a burden to the state. They are always active, small-time market traders running their "business" as best they can, no more honest with their customers than is strictly necessary, but touchingly convinced that, no matter how many times their ill-conceived schemes to make quick money fail, one day their dream will come true and they will finally make their fortunes. In the meantime, they survive. The two brothers are very different, Derek (Del), the elder, is street-wise, self-assured and flashy, Rodney is worried and hesitant, but what binds them together and makes them likeable rogues rather than mere losers is their unshakeable sense of family loyalty and their determination never to give up.

The Boswells in Liverpool have a similar positive attitude to their kith and kin. The money the four brothers and one sister earn individually goes into a common fund on which they can all draw, with no questions asked as to the source of the cash, not even by the devoutly Catholic head of the family, Nellie, whose husband has walked out. Moreover, the boys are very protective towards their sister. In fact, one son (christened James, but preferred name Adrian) does have what he calls a "proper job," in an estate agent's office, until he is made redundant, which is no real surprise for Merseyside has long been an area of high unemployment. Of the other brothers, the eldest, Joey, has a mysterious night job, the two others, Jack and Billy, deal, rather like the Trotters, in whatever comes their way. The survival instinct is ingrained in all of them. Among their regular ports of call is the local Social Security office in the hope of receiving further allowances (to which they are not entitled), but this is nothing compared to their long-term and very successful scam: the family has exchanged houses with their granddad who lives next door, entitling both him and them to claim housing benefit on rents they do not pay. The Royles do not even have this lifeline. They occupy a council house in Manchester and apparently depend almost exclusively on benefits, although Mrs. Royle does serve part-time in a bakery. Father Jim, mother Barbara and daughter Denise spend most of their time smoking, watching television, complaining about what they see and arguing with one another. In this, they are joined by their daughter's boyfriend and future husband, Dave, and Barbara's elderly mother. Their days are "lightened" by the frequent visits of their neighbors, the Carrolls, and their daughter who is friends with Denise. Jim is constantly irritated by their arrival, as by much else, but they, like the other regular caller, a bulky man known ironically as "Twiggy" who brings cheap clothes and other goods that have conveniently "fallen off the back of a lorry," are the Royles' contacts with the outside world and suggest the working-class solidarity that enables life to go on in communities where work is scarce and prospects are limited.

Marc Duguid's study on the family sitcom in the British Film Institute's *Screen on Line* is subtitled "half a century of social change played for laughs." Of course, any such simple description cannot do full justice to a genre which has been a pillar of popular entertainment, attracting, sometimes huge, mass audiences,[26] and which survives comfortably in today's market-orientated television environment. There are several reasons for the continuing success of the Britcom such as the quality of the dialogues (e.g., *Fawlty Towers, Yes Minister*) or of the acting (e.g., Leonard Rossiter as Rupert Rigsby and Reginald Perrin, Penelope Keith as Audrey fforbes-Hamilton, Dawn French as Geraldine Granger). The genre has equally been notable more recently for its capacity for innovation with, for example, the increasingly significant role played by female characters or with the appearance of series offering the non-white population's comic perspective on life in Britain (e.g., *The Fosters*, 1976–77; *Desmond's*, 1998–94; *Citizen Khan*, 2012–). Nevertheless, as this article has sought to demonstrate, Duguid's designation is fundamentally true. The Britcom has succeeded in striking a chord with the everyday experience of the viewer, and in keeping abreast of developments in society, for, with their variations, evolutions and nuances, the ingredients which fuel the situations of television comedies are rich living archives that give an insight into the complexities of contemporary British society. Moreover, the genre has consistently exploited the British penchant for self-mockery and the sense of the absurd, one of the more salient features of which is social class in its multifarious representations.

Notes

1. Orwell's observation is taken from *The Lion and the Unicorn* (1941). His reference to England is entirely correct for the subject of this article. For most of its existence, British television has been heavily English-biased and none of the Britcoms mentioned in this article were produced or set elsewhere in the United Kingdom.

2. As seems most appropriate, the categories quoted here are those of the Broadcasters' Audience Research Board (BARB) whose task was and is to define the audience viewing a particular television channel at a given moment for the purpose of pricing advertising time on commercial television stations. For political parties, the C2 category is considered the most important, as the votes of skilled manual workers are thought the most likely to determine the results of a general election. The Registrar General's classification (renamed Social Class based on Occupation in 1990) used figures instead of letters but remains broadly similar: **I**—Professional (etc.) occupations; **II**—Managerial and technical occupations; **III (N)**—Non-manual skilled occupations; **III (M)**—Manual skilled occupations; **IV**—Partly skilled occupations; **V**—Unskilled occupations.

3. The UK National Statistics Socio-Economic Classification (NS-SEC), introduced in 2001, still uses occupation and employment status to place people in one of eight analytic classes which reflect the employment market more accurately. Thus semi-skilled and unskilled workers are in

semi-routine and routine occupations respectively, and there are separate categories both for small employers and the self-employed ("own account workers"), and for those who have never worked and the long-term unemployed. For full details, see David Rose and David J. Pevalin, "The National Statistics Socio-Economic Classification: Unifying Official and Sociological Conceptualisation and Measurement of Social Class," ISER Working Papers, 2001–2004, Colchester, University of Essex.

4. The importance of these factors was finally acknowledged in the Great British Class Survey, conducted by the BBC, in 2011, which asked questions on social and cultural capital and produced over 160,000 internet responses. Researchers analyzing the results have come up with a new structure of seven classes: an "elite," whose wealth separates them from an established middle class, a class of technical experts and a class of "new affluent" workers. At the lower levels of the class structure, alongside an ageing traditional working class, there is a "precariat" characterized by very low levels of capital, and a group of emergent service workers. For full details, see Mike Savage et al., "A New Model of Social Class: Findings from the BBC's Great British Class Survey Experiment," online at http://soc.sagepub.com/content/early/2013/03/12/003803851348428, accessed 12 November 2014.

5. *The Frost Report* was a spinoff from *That Was the Week That Was*, a groundbreaking satirical show first broadcast in 1962 whose sketches vigorously, irreverently and systematically derided the political, religious and social Establishment. The two programs shared the same presenter, David Frost, later himself to become an Establishment figure.

6. "Episode = familiar status quo → ritual error made → ritual error corrected → ritual lesson learned → familiar status quo" David Marc, *Comic Visions: Television Comedy and American Culture*, Malden, MA: Blackwell, 1989, 190–91; "Sitcom episodes have a 'classical' narrative structuring in that the narrative process is inaugurated by some disruption of or threat to a stable situation, necessitating the movement towards the reassertion of stability. [...] The end of the episode represents a return to the initial stability." Steve Neale and Frank Krutnik, *Popular Film and Television Comedy*, London: Routledge, 1990, 17.

7. Simon Morgan-Russell, *Jimmy Perry and David Croft*, Manchester: Manchester University Press, 2004, 15.

8. Paul Cornell, Martin Day and Keith Topping, *The Guinness Book of Classic British TV*, Enfield: Guinness Publishing, 1996, 65.

9. Glen Creeber, *The Television Genre Book*, London: BFI, 2003, 61.

10. Mick Eaton, "Television Situation Comedy" in Tony Bennett et al. (eds.), *Popular Television and Film*, London: BFI/Open University Press, 1981, 26.

11. *The Design Dimension*, series 2, program 1, "Know Your Place," BBC Radio 4, 18 November 2014. Hanley was born and raised on Birmingham's Chelmsley Wood, at the time the largest council estate (social housing development) in Europe.

12. Another Reliant three-wheeler appears in episodes of *Mr. Bean* with the same comic effect.

13. Local accents are, of course, watered down and dialect features are eliminated to ensure a sufficient level of understanding by a general television-viewing audience.

14. The more carefully-spoken working-class Sid Abbott (*Bless This House*) and Stan Butler (*On the Buses*) limit their swearing respectively to "O' my Gord" and "Cor Blimey" and many other working-class Britcom characters of the same period pay similar attention to the demands of propriety.

15. E.g., "I didn't get where I am today by taking a gift horse to water after the stable door was opened"; "Bit of a cock up on the unemployment front ... hand caught in Labour Exchange door."

16. This Britcom holds the record for longevity: it was first broadcast in late 1973 and continued for 27 years through 295 episodes.

17. A nod to a contemporary event, the Church of England's decision in 1992 to ordain women priests.

18. The Grace Brothers' store appeared more and more antiquated over the 13 years and ten series of this Britcom.

19. Homosexuality was decriminalized in England in 1967.

20. The last national servicemen were called up in 1960. The series referred to here are, in chronological order of first broadcast: *The Army Game*, *Dad's Army*, *It Ain't Half Hot Mum* and *Get Some In*.

21. *Dad's Army* is an exception for it features a striking example of role reversal: in the Home Guard platoon on which the series centers, the officer is aggressive and lower-middle-class while the refined and smooth-talking sergeant is clearly of superior status. Set in 1940, it falls outside of the time frame of this article.

22. Arguably the most middle-class (and politically correct) Britcom of all and compulsory viewing in 10 Downing Street when Margaret Thatcher was prime minister.
23. Quaint though it may now seem, this was not an anachronism at the time.
24. The idea of faked suicide by drowning does have a contemporary echo. To escape corruption charges, MP and former minister John Stonehouse did just this in Miami in 1974. He was eventually found in Australia and imprisoned.
25. This comment applies not only to the deliberately short-lived *The Young Ones*, *Girls on Top* and *Bottom*, but also to *Men Behaving Badly* and *Absolutely Fabulous*, cult Britcoms of the 1990s.
26. The final episodes of *To the Manor Born* (1981) and *Only Fools and Horses* (1996) both attracted 24 million viewers.

Works Cited

Cornell, Paul, Day Martin, and Keith Topping. *The Guinness Book of Classic British TV*. Enfield: Guinness Publishing, 1996.
Creeber, Glen (ed.). *The Television Genre Book*. London: BFI, 2003.
Eaton, Mick. "Television Situation Comedy" in Tony Bennett, Susan Boyd-Bowman, Colin Mercer and Janet Wollacott (eds.), *Popular Television and Film*. London: BFI/Open University Press, 1981.
Halsey, A. H. *Change in British Society*. Oxford: Oxford University Press, 1995.
Marc, David. *Comic Visions: Television Comedy and American Culture*. Malden, MA: Blackwell, 1989.
Morgan-Russell, Simon. *Jimmy Perry and David Croft*. Manchester: Manchester University Press, 2004.
Neale, Steve, and Frank Krutnik. *Popular Film and Television Comedy*. London: Routledge, 1990.
Rose, David, and David J. Pevalin. "The National Statistics Socio-Economic Classification: Unifying Official and Sociological Conceptualisation and Measurement of Social Class." ISER Working Papers, 2001–2004, Colchester, University of Essex.
Savage, Mike, Fiona Devine, Niall Cunningham, Mark Taylor, Yaojun Li, Johs Hjellbreke, Brigitte Le Roux, Sam Friedman Sam, and Miles Andrew. "A New Model of Social Class: Findings from the BBC's Great British Class Survey Experiment." Online at http://soc.sagepub.com/content/early/2013/03/12/003803851348428.

Alphabetical List of Britcoms Cited

Title [No. of Series]	First Broadcast	Full-Length Specials
Absolutely Fabulous [3]	1992–95	1996
Are You Being Served? [10]	1972–85	1975, 1978, 1979, 1981
The Army Game [5]	1957–61	
Bless This House [6]	1971–76	
Bottom [3]	1991–95	1995
Bread [7]	1986–91	1988, 1990
Butterflies [4]	1978–83	1979
Citizen Smith [4]	1977–80	1977, 1980
Drop the Dead Donkey [5]	1990–96	
The Fall and Rise of Reginald Perrin [3]	1976–79	
Fawlty Towers [2]	1975–79	

Title [no. of series]	First Broadcast	Full-Length Specials
George and Mildred [5]	1976–79	
Get Some In [5]	1975–78	1975
Girls on Top [2]	1985–86	
The Good Life [4]	1975–77	1977, 1978
Hancock's Half Hour / Hancock [6]/[2]	1956–63	
It Ain't Half Hot, Mum [8]	1974–81	
Keeping Up Appearances [5]	1990–95	1991, 1995
The Last of the Summer Wine [18]	1973–97	1979, 1981, 1982, 1983, 1984, 1986, 1987, 1988, 1989, 1990, 1991, 1993, 1995, 1996, 1997
Likely Lads / Whatever Happened to the Likely Lads [3]/[2]	1964–66 / 1973–74	1974
Men Behaving Badly [5]	1992–97	1997
Mr Bean [separate episodes only]	1990–93	
The New Statesman [4]	1987–92	1994
The Office [2]	2001–02	2003
On the Buses [7]	1969–73	
One Foot in the Grave [5]	1990–95	1990, 1991, 1993, 1994, 1995, 1997
Only Fools and Horses [8]	1981–96	1982, 1983, 1985, 1986, 1987, 1988, 1989, 1990, 1991, 1992, 1993
The Rag Trade [3]	1961–63	
Rising Damp [4]	1974–78	1975
The Royle Family [3]	1998–2000	1999, 2000, 2006, 2008, 2009, 2010, 2012
Steptoe and Son [8]	1962–74	1973, 1974
Terry and June [9]	1979–87	1980, 1982, 1985
Till Death Us Do Part [7]	1966–75	1967, 1970, 1972
To the Manor Born [3]	1979–81	1979
The Vicar of Dibley [3]	1994–2000	2004, 2005, 2006, 2007
Yes Minister [3]	1980–82	1984
The Young Ones [2]	1982–84	

Authenticity and Performance of Class in British Factual TV Series

Jonathan Bignell

British "reality TV" is a hybrid of factual and fictional television genres, as signaled by the more accurate genre designation "structured reality" television. Its antecedents, notably documentary and soap opera, have their own traditions and conventions for representing social class. But from the 1990s onwards, in order to develop programs that are attractive to audiences and inexpensive to produce, program makers have focused on hybrids of dramatic and documentary modes. This essay argues that many recent reality TV programs privilege soap opera's emphasis on character, storyline and performance. This affects the ways that class authenticity is understood, undermining factual programs' usual claim to legitimacy based on reference to a reality that pre-exists them. Television "works through" reality, processing it and rendering it intelligible, across all of its genres.[1] This presupposes a kind of realism, and social value in the television medium's documentation, recording and reflection of the culture of which it is a part.[2] In Western Europe this is an aspect of public service broadcasting, a concept enshrined in the licensing and regulation of national television networks that requires them to inform, educate and entertain their audiences. The ways that this context impacts on hierarchies of power, and specifically class, in the case of reality TV are that reality TV adopts and transforms both highly-valued and low-valued types of program, and that many reality TV programs make class highly visible in particular ways.

The factual entertainment programs known as reality TV emerged from the daytime schedule into evening prime-time, and displaced program types like conventional documentary, popular drama and light entertainment that had previously dominated evening schedules. It often comprises the representation of ordinary people and ordinary events, transforming them both within the narratives of the programs and in the public discourses that accrete around them and around the programs in which they appear. In each of these senses, reality TV has a transformative effect on its material.

Unscripted participation programs began in the daytime genres of the talk show, the makeover show, and other programs in which ordinary people became the focus of attention.[3] They were guests, members of the audience invited to come in front of the camera, or contestants on game-shows with ordinary prizes. Some of these unscripted programs looked rather like documentary, but were distinct from the tradition of television and film documentary that is based on social observation and political intervention. Traditional documentary was evening programming, connected by proximity in the schedule, and often in terms of the personnel and institutions that made it, with news and current affairs. Daytime factual television, with its mix of programming aimed at female viewers, children and the economically inactive, was devalued and unregarded. But the remarkable success of some of these formats when transplanted into evening prime-time stimulated the invention of the forms and formats now known as reality TV. The ordinary people in them could be transformed into stars, or at least celebrities; they became performers.

Reality TV programs in the evening schedules cost much less than the investment needed to make scripted drama. They could be made in series forms with strong, repeatable narrative structures, distinguishing them from the single intervention with high prestige but high cost that characterized documentary. For example, in Britain, Channel 4's top ten rated programs in 2003 were headed by factual series.[4] *Big Brother* topped the list at 7.2 million viewers, followed by *Wife Swap* (5.9 million) and *How Clean Is Your House* (five million). The imported U.S. sitcom *Friends* was the fourth highest rated program for the channel at five million viewers, but the property-themed British factual programs *Property Ladder* and *Grand Designs* were eighth and ninth with 4.6 million viewers each. Channel 4 screened *Big Brother*, aimed at 16- to 34-year-old viewers, but diversified its factual television to address different audiences. *Operatunity*, in which members of the public competed to become opera singers, was aimed at more upmarket audiences, while the series about hairdressers *The Salon*, and *Wife Swap*, in which households swap partners, attempted to develop factual subjects in different ways for viewers seeking entertainment. Thus reality TV satisfied the different demands of the producing institutions and the audience. Channel 4 is a commercial network, funded by advertising, but like the other big commercial networks in the UK (ITV and Five), it is required to fulfill the requirements of public service broadcasting, informing, educating and entertaining its different constituencies of viewers with a broad mix of programs.

High profile game-docs and contests turned the daytime formats of the game show and the participation program into light entertainment. *Big Brother* and *Survivor* combined the social experiment documentary and the contest, and featured ordinary people in an extraordinary situation. Being in the *Big Brother* house or on the desert island of *Survivor* displaced them from their normal milieu, and put psychological and social pressure on them that tested their ability to create relationships with fellow participants (and the production team). The participants were required to perform, in the sense of crafting a *persona* that would suit their situation and endear them to the audience (in programs with public voting). They also had to undertake tasks that could be performed either well or badly.

The term "reality TV" was first applied to the combination of surveillance footage, crime reconstruction, voice-over narration and on-screen presentation in programs such as *Crimewatch UK* (1984–) and *America's Most Wanted* (1988–).[5] The term was extended to include "structured reality" programs such as *The Real World* (1992–) and *Castaway* (2000) where situations were devised for the purpose of shooting them, and docusoaps like *Airport* (1996) which impose on real events the conventions of soap opera, including editing techniques of parallel montage, character-focused narrative structure, and basis in a single geographical space and community. Reality TV increasingly diverged from documentary, changing its relationship with authenticity and explanation and emphasizing the performance of a classed identity.

The performance of identity and the testing of its authenticity and effectiveness have become ways of disciplining and stigmatizing class identities, often through processes of transformation or tests, or simply by showing participants coping (or failing to cope) with everyday challenges. As Gareth Palmer has argued, there is a class dimension to this since the people who feature in reality TV programs seem often to be trying to improve themselves according to expectations about appearance and behavior that shift them towards middle class norms.[6] Documentary has a history of representing and arguing for those in society who are the least privileged, the most vulnerable to exploitation, and the most marginalized. But reality TV can reinforce marginalization, by representing its subjects' performance of their own deviance from norms of taste and social behavior, and separating them and their actions from social and political contexts. It also invites the audience to recognize and stigmatize social divisions and position themselves within the norm from which deviance departs. From this perspective, reality TV has a deterrent effect, perpetuating hierarchies of class division and identifying marginalized, working-class culture as "the other." Bill Nichols argued that the emerging reality TV he saw on American television (like *Cops*, beginning in 1989), distanced the television audience from reality, rather than seeking to represent and interpret it, and narrativized and policed the real rather than observing and investigating it.[7] Palmer's work developed this argument in relation to class and other social divisions, portraying reality TV as an aspect of the governance of society.[8] Programs represent police dealing with offenders in *Cops*, nannies coping with unruly children and inadequate parents in *Supernanny*, or aspiring businesspeople trying to lead their teams in *The Apprentice*. Reality TV has increasingly comprised formats that set up situations where normative and deviant actions are explored and dramatized through unequal power relations, and audiences are invited to witness and evaluate the participants in relation to class as it is expressed through codes of taste and expression.

Class and the Documentary Tradition

Socially engaged documentary became significant in Britain in the period between World War I and World War II.[9] By the 1960s, the French tradition of *cinéma vérité* and the American direct cinema filmmakers[10] had refined the form into fly-on-the-wall and observational documentary. Television is by nature an intimate and immediate medium,[11] and the emergent British, American and French documentary traditions offered powerful forms of authenticity that would become significant in reality TV, without the paternalistic mode of address that characterized British documentary of the 1930s, for example. Structured reality programs retain and manipulate the residue of conventional documentary's social engagement when they place their subjects within a social context. As some examples of programs will demonstrate below, a personal experience might reveal something about an individual and a more broadly conceived public world involving work, institutions or communities.

Television took on the role of the primary broadcasting medium in the 1950s, and developments in technology enabled television documentary makers to record sound synchronized with the image, and drew on radio's practice of basing programs around interviews conducted on location and recording the ordinary speech of non-actors. While the shaping of documentary programs remained the province of directors and production teams distanced from their subject by their social class, expertise and professional status, the speech of ordinary people reflecting on their own experience and attitudes became an increasing feature of television factual programming. When lightweight 16-millimeter cameras became available to the makers of factual television in the 1960s, the possibilities for extended work on location following the activities of ordinary people became greater, and made innovations in documentary possible. Lightweight equipment gave more creative control to the program makers, and documentary could not only report the real, but intervene in it as it was being recorded and subsequently shape it through editing.

For example, the British program maker Paul Watson made the observational documentary series *The Family* in 1974, following the lives and relationships of the Wilkins family from the town of Reading in southern England. It was regarded as a landmark television program, because of the detail of ordinary speech and interaction traced by witnessing the conversations in the family home at a level of realistic observation previously absent in documentary. The "bad language" used by the Wilkins family attracted attention and controversy but added to the claim of the visual style to document interpersonal relationships realistically. *The Family* showed working-class people, followed verbal exchanges rather than physical action, and the family was headed by a strong matriarchal figure. In these respects *The Family* was similar to the social realist dramatic fictions on British television, centering on working-class communities, like the soap opera *Coronation Street* (broadcast since 1960). In the mid–1990s lightweight digital video cameras and high-speed digital editing suites became available. The first digital video cameras were introduced by Sony as a consumer format, but when equipped with professional standard microphones, these cameras could produce footage suitable for television, at much higher visual quality than analogue video. Digital editing arrived in the same period and television documentary producers were thus able to make their films relatively quickly, and have greater flexibility in manipulating sound and image. The recording of the everyday, using natural light and with synchronized sound, became much cheaper and the resulting footage could be manipulated quickly to produce complete programs.

By 1999, public and press confidence in the veracity of documentary was challenged by a series of controversies about "faked" footage and manipulation in factual programs.[12] Docusoap, an emergent television form deriving from both documentary conventions and soap opera drama, provided a ready way out of this crisis. Soap opera claims authenticity through its apparent reflection of a working-class social world. Storylines deal with apparently trivial interactions and events, but problems in relationships between individuals, families and communities (caused by divorce, birth, death, gossip, and antagonism between characters) generate new storylines. Dramatic conflicts are also a principal attraction of docusoap, which adopts them from the soap opera form, and they serve the function of illuminating character. Docusoaps have never aspired to the same respect for actuality as conventional documentary, and were less subject to criticism for that reason. The lessening ability of documentary makers to gain access to locations like workplaces, because once there they might cause trouble for the hotels, hospitals or other institutions they featured, meant that conventional documentary was becoming more difficult to make. If situations were constructed by the program maker, these problems of access were much less significant. Docusoaps tracked the day-to-day working lives of mainly working-class and lower-middle class participants, working in service industries where their interactions with the public provided a constant source of novelty.

The arrival of *Big Brother*, in which the artifice of the format is central to its structure and appeal, added another impetus for factual programming to rely on material under the control of the program maker, rather than subject to the constraints of found subjects or locations. At the end of the 1990s, *Big Brother* arrived first in Holland and subsequently in other countries. It was only possible because of the digital technologies of cameras, radio microphones and high-speed editing software with which live streams and evening highlights programs were made. The same kinds of radio microphones and digital cameras can also be used on location, and in *Airport*, *Wife Swap* or *How Clean Is Your House*, large amounts of tape footage and recorded sound could be easily gathered in locations with cramped conditions and low available light, then quickly edited and shaped into complete programs.

Once Britain's Channel 4 had ceased to broadcast *Big Brother* (which was acquired instead by Channel Five), the channel sought new opportunities. It returned to the documentary serial by remaking the seminal observational documentary *The Family* in 2008, with the significant technical innovation of mounting fixed cameras around the subjects' house. Fixed camera documentary was regarded by Hamish Mykura, the channel's head of documentary programming, as a way of delivering "intimate stories told in a new way."[13] The technique was also adopted for the successful series made by Dragonfly Productions for Channel 4, *One Born Every Minute* (2009–) which follows the experiences of staff and patients in a Leeds maternity ward. Authenticity was a key attraction for Channel 4's commissioners, and Mykura contrasted the conventional practice of camera operators shooting on location with the different aesthetic that fixed camera shooting appeared to generate: "If people are being followed by a camera all the time they behave in a certain way. With fixed cameras they are more unguarded and more interesting."[14] In *One Born Every Minute*, remotely controlled miniature cameras are installed in unobtrusive housings on the walls and ceiling of the hospital, with their lenses covered by apertures that conceal where the lens is pointing. The setting of the hospital, in which medical equipment and security systems are also mounted on the walls of corridors and delivery rooms, further serves to make the camera rig relatively unnoticed. Such ambitious fixed camera series require the installation of a large infrastructure of equipment, operator skill in remotely controlling changes from close to long shots in the moment of shooting, careful thought to provide sufficient camera positions to facilitate coherent cutting between points of view at the editing stage, and of course the shooting of very large amounts of footage. But their attraction for producers and audiences is that they create a powerful sense of intimacy, and access to action that appears relatively unmediated and authentic.

While episodes of *One Born Every Minute* do document the working routines of midwives, and provide some insight into the process of giving birth and its management by professional staff, the majority of screen time is occupied with the interactions of expectant mothers with staff and relatives. Like a docusoap, the program is about work in an institution, and the flow of patients through the maternity department gives opportunities to compare and contrast people of different social classes. The detail of human interaction, and how different people respond to the hopes and fears associated with parenthood, are much more prominent than questions of medical policy, institutional politics or public health information. Episodes have a dramatic structure in which sequences alternate between characters, the different mothers and relatives in the hours before birth, leading in chronological sequences towards the moment of delivery when the fixed cameras show the birth itself (with post-production masking of intimate body parts). While births are the dramatic climax of each episode, the audience is invited to get to know the mothers, staff and relatives in the time preceding the birth, and to evaluate the ways that people behave with each other. Referring to a sequence in which a prospective parent considered whether to eat a biscuit, Mykura commented, "It is these custard-cream moments that really work" as character drama, rather than the event of birth itself.[15] The intimate but apparently inconsequential detail of wondering whether to eat a snack becomes as authentic as the traumatic moment of birth.

The high cost of fixed camera documentary makes it suitable for the series form, in which costs are amortized over a long run of episodes. Reality TV has always been associated with long runs of episodes in either the serial form in which programs follow a consistent group of characters, or the series in which a stable format permits a repeating structure. The association of fixed camera series with reality TV rather than conventional documentary can be seen in the ways that established documentary producers criticize prime-time factual series. The BBC's commissioning editor for documentaries, Charlotte Moore, commented that Channel 4's character-centered factual series lacked analysis: "When you are trying to purely entertain it is very easy to get something that works and play it again and again through the same prism. It is my job at a public service broadcaster to do more than that. We are not just trying to reflect life, we are trying to peel back the layers."[16] Class is one of the issues at stake here; Moore's criticism is partly that Channel 4's structured reality programs do not analyze class.

The matter of class became controversial in relation to another Channel 4 series, *My Big Fat Gypsy Wedding* (2011), which centers on members of the Traveler and Roma Gypsy communities and especially their wedding celebrations. Many of the wedding events involve very elaborate "fairytale" costume and costly, large-scale social events. In preparation for the loud and theatrical weddings, and during them, highly patriarchal and uneven power-relationships between sexes and generations are prominent. The genesis of the series was a one-hour documentary in the channel's *Cutting Edge* strand that specializes in films about contemporary social issues. The premise was developed into a series of five films, and by the second episode its ratings of 8.7 million had made it Channel 4's eighth most watched program ever. The independent production company Firecracker Films made the series, and its executive producer Jes Wilkins argued for it to be seen in the tradition of investigative social documentary: "The best part of eight million viewers are watching a quite serious documentary about women, domestic abuse."[17] The aim to document a specific fraction of British society seems to fit squarely within the traditions of public service broadcasting. Aesthetically, the series adopts the combination of voiceover, interview, and single camera shooting that is familiar from previous documentary forms.

But the documentary imperatives to inform and educate the audience were undercut by extensive viewer criticism of the program's subjects, especially in online forums, but also from its producers' fellow television professionals. As the journalist Vicky Frost reported, viewer comments on Twitter, for example, referred to the participants by the derogatory terms "gypo" and "pikey," and referred to the stereotypical stigmatization of Roma Gypsies and Travelers as thieves or scroungers claiming welfare payments they are not entitled to.[18] The participants on the series were being seen as a feckless and deviant underclass. Representatives of Roma Gypsy organizations, and of charities working for their welfare, criticized the series for reinforcing prejudices and representing the different social groups as homogenous rather than distinctively different in ethnic makeup and cultural traditions.

Producers of documentary face a problem of exemplarity whenever they make a factual program, since the subjects of the program will be chosen for a range of reasons that include their representativeness of a specific group or issue, but also their exceptional characteristics that the audience might find interesting or entertaining. This is a familiar issue that reality TV programs have encountered, when choosing contestants from public auditions on the basis not only of their talent but also their potential appeal as character types (the tough guy, the joker, the ringleader, etc.). Choosing to shoot Traveler weddings that are designed as visual spectacles and in which conflicts between family members are more likely to occur than in everyday situations makes character typing and dramatic incident expected rather than exceptional. Commenting on *My Big Fat Gypsy Wedding*, the BBC commissioning editor for documentary Charlotte Moore regarded the program as "judgmental of its people in its tone," adding: "Had we made it I would have taken it deeper and deeper to ask bigger questions about how they live their life, what they believe and who they are. I would have wanted it more layered."[19] The boundaries between observational documentary with social purpose, versus factual entertainment based around character, have become blurred to the extent that the same program can be perceived in very different ways.

Narrative Structure

The majority of recent reality TV programs are distinct from observational documentary because of the highly structured nature of their narrative form. The most common of these forms are the contest, the swap in which a participant is displaced from their own milieu and placed in another, and the masquerade in which participants take on a disguise. According to Stephen Lambert, head of programs at the British production company RDF that made *Wife Swap*, the program is "just about character."[20] Reality TV as an entertainment form has been most successful when it promises to reveal character, even if its participants and settings are offered to the audience as authentic.

In the British context of public service broadcasting, with imperatives to bring into visibility the variety of the nation's people and to air differences that can then be understood and worked upon, reality TV has a strong class dimension. The reality that is offered to the audience is one that is evidently conditioned by the relative social power of the participants. The discourse of the programs therefore inhabits a tension between assuming a program of improvement and yet also making a spectacle of differences in social power and class.[21] Representing class diversity both grants visibility to under-represented groups (especially working-class people), but also opens up possibilities for judging a program's participants against middle-class social norms that they might fail to satisfy. For example, Channel 4 has commissioned programs like *Supernanny* in which "problem children" are observed and treated by professional intervention. The program draws on the heritage of expert social intervention that formerly characterized state institutions' ways of identifying and addressing social problems through social work, state medical care or infrastructure investment in housing or education. But in *Supernanny*, an individual (not an institution) intervenes into a single household (not a region or socio-economic group). Similarly, Channel 4's *Secret Millionaire* is a series in which wealthy benefactors disguise themselves as volunteer helpers at small local charities, businesses or support networks. At the end of the program, the wealthy individual makes a significant financial donation that can transform the situation for the better. Further examples of this interventionist individualism include *You Are What You Eat* (in which dietary expertise is given) and *What Not to Wear* (where participants' self-confidence is increased as a result of fashion advice).

These series do not identify problems that governments or state agencies might be able to fix through, for example, better housing, education or health care. Instead they are narratives of personal improvement and aspiration. Wishes are made to come true, or individuals are transformed into happier and more socially integrated members of society. In *Ladette to Lady*, for example (another Channel 4 series), the participants begin by being represented as socially abject, loud, impolite, improper, lacking in taste and self-control. By being trained in the social skills and bodily rituals of a higher social class, so that they can converse pleasantly, dress elegantly, and eat with good manners, they gain a different perspective on themselves and are set on a path to effective social integration. Lifestyle programming in the gardening and cookery genres is affected by these same narratives, whether by recommending no-fuss, quick recipes for the working single person, family dinners where all generations can eat sociably together, or comfort food that rewards the stressed modern professional with indulgent high-calorie treats.

Whereas traditional documentary might focus on a specific community or geographical region, the casting and dramatic structure of reality TV mean that the people featured in programs are not representative of where they live, but instead they are cast because they will constitute an ensemble of dramatically interesting characters. Recent British examples include *Geordie Shore* (MTV, about people living in the Newcastle area of northern England), *The Only Way Is Essex* (ITV2, about young people in southeastern England), and *Mersey Shore* and *Desperate Scousewives* (about the Liverpool area). *The Only Way Is Essex* won the British Academy of Film and Television Arts (BAFTA) audience award as a result of public voting in May 2011. Its participants are young, self-obsessed and vain, and all live in the outer London suburbs of Brentwood, Chigwell and Buckhurst Hill. The independent production company Lime Pictures cast the series from respondents to advertising on Facebook and local media.[22] The first to be selected was beautician and model Amy Childs, who had auditioned for *Big Brother*, *The X Factor* and other programs in the hope of becoming a celebrity. Some of her friends had done the same, and it was from this friendship group that Lime Pictures cast the remainder of the main participants. The series is based around the character relationships among the group, notably the on-off dating between Mark Wright and Lauren Goodger whose nine-year relationship repeatedly broke up and restarted during the program's first series. Storyline producers have the task of looking for dramatic arcs that will anchor the everyday interactions between the participants. These arcs are based on the giving and withholding of knowledge, gossip and intrigue that are the staple ingredients of soap opera, and it is no accident that Lime Pictures also makes the teen soap opera *Hollyoaks*.

The story producer for the first series of *The Only Way Is Essex* was Daran Little, who also worked on *Made in Chelsea* (made for the E4 channel), about wealthy and privileged young people in London. The romantic lives of the participants drove the narratives of both series. Little had experience in the U.S. as a writer for the soap *All My Children* and also in Britain as a writer for the two most popular soap operas *Coronation Street* and *EastEnders*. He explained when interviewed for a newspaper article on *The Only Way Is Essex*:

> If there's a boy and a girl in a scene, you'll pull them over individually and you'll say: "Right, in this scene I want you to ask her what she did last night." Because I know what she did last night, but he doesn't. Then we start the scene and they just talk it through and if it gets a bit dry, we'll stop and pull them to one side and we'll say: "How do you feel about him asking you that? Because I think you feel more emotional about it. I think you're pulling something back. Do you think it's fair that he's asking you this?"[23]

What is at stake, therefore, in the context of reality TV's interest in character and environment, is emotional realism. Emotional realism is a term that derives from analysis of U.S. soap opera, in Ien Ang's work on the 1980s prime-time soap *Dallas*.[24] The storylines in *Dallas* about rivalries among millionaire oil barons and their families were patently unrealistic, and the social world represented was very distant from the experience of the vast majority of the soap's audience. But Ang argued that the emotional lives of the characters were actually what appealed to many viewers, especially women viewers, and that the emotional connection audiences felt with the characters led to viewers experiencing *Dallas* as a realistic program. What Little was doing when talking to participants during the shooting of *The Only Way Is Essex* was trying to bring out their emotional reactions to events, since it would be those emotions and not the events themselves that would be appealing to viewers. As Faye Woods argues:

In shifting docusoap closer to fictional storytelling, tension is created between the glossy "drama" aesthetic and the British casts' inability to convincingly perform their everyday life. This tension creates a tone of cringing comedy familiar from British sitcoms, disrupting the emotional investment encouraged by the melodramatic content and offering the British youth television audience a detached viewing position that flatters their genre literacy—their awareness of reality TV's construction.[25]

Soap opera commonly adopts a melodrama style, and reality TV in some of its recent forms has also used this dramatic mode in order to connect with audiences on the level of emotional realism rather than documentary observation. *The Only Way Is Essex* focuses on expression of emotion and the performance of interpersonal dynamics. As Little said when asked about casting Ollie Locke and Gabriella Ellis for the parallel series *Made in Chelsea*:

> They had been together for a year. I talked to them together and their body language was completely different to what they were saying. And I thought, this is a relationship which is crumbling and she's not too aware of it. And he's hurting her. Oh my goodness, this will actually make very good television.[26]

Subsequently, Ollie ended his relationship with Gabriella in the third episode of the series and "came out" as bisexual. In advance of shooting, these structured reality series depend on relationships established between participants and the production team, so that storyliners are informed about what the participants may do and can discuss how and when to develop a storyline element. Ollie had informed the producers that he planned to break up with Gabriella, and the scene was scheduled for shooting in the ironically romantic location of a pleasure cruiser on London's river Thames.

While *American Idol* and *Supernanny* appear very different, they each represent character and environment in highly structured ways that invite viewers to assess the participants' performances and evaluate them. But what distinguishes the performance of reality TV participants from actors in television fiction is that reality TV participants lack an actor's training in creating character, and this has consequences for the production of programs. In constructed reality TV like *The Only Way Is Essex*, *The Hills* or *Made in Chelsea*, performances in scenes that have been planned with and by professional storyline producers are very likely to include moments of inauthenticity from at least some of the characters. As in melodrama, people are likely to look as if they are acting. Production teams avoid doing retakes of scenes in order to preserve the impression of authenticity, which requires them to cover scenes as fully as possible to generate a mass of footage that can be worked on at the editing stage. Tony

Wood, creative director of Lime Pictures, said in relation to *The Only Way Is Essex* that the question of authenticity was intended to be part of the pleasure for viewers in the series: "At the heart of this was always a desire to put in the audience's mind: 'Is it real? Are they acting? Is it scripted? Is it not?' and to leave that as an open question for them."[27]

Aesthetic devices from television fiction, especially melodrama, include the use of point of view to guide viewer identification with characters, music to underscore emotional tone, and dramatic structuring through editing. These are used both to invite the audience to engage with reality TV as if it were fiction, but at the same time to contrast with the uneven and sometimes inauthentic performance by non-actors that connotes realism. John Caughie notes that "the dramatic look creates its 'reality effect' by a process of mediation so conventionalized as to become invisible," referring to these systems of *mise en scène* and narrative adopted in the majority of television fiction.[28] However, on the other hand, "the documentary gaze depends on systems of mediation (hand-held camera, loss of focus, awkward framing) so visible as to become immediate, apparently unrehearsed, and hence authentic."[29] The program text becomes inherently dissonant, and thus potentially reflexive about the conventions that structure it. As Jon Dovey has argued: "documentary and factual television now exist in a space that is neither wholly fictional nor wholly factual, both yet neither."[30] An explicit invitation for viewers to experience this simultaneous adoption and disavowal of both fictional and documentary discourses occurred in *The Only Way Is Essex* when, in episode two, the participants were shot watching themselves on TV in the opening episode of the series. Production planning in which shooting and editing took place over only three days made this possible, in distinction to almost all other reality TV series.

Reality TV is not a genre, but a label that can usefully be given to programs that adopt a certain attitude to the functions of television, its audiences and its subjects (by which I mean its subject-matter and also the individuals who are represented on screen and who make the programs).[31] Television has been analyzed by exploring the tensions between its characteristics of immediacy and intimacy.[32] In news, or sports programs, for example, television claims to relay real events to its viewer, and the medium's history of live broadcasting is still important to its role today. Intimacy, on the other hand, describes how television programs set up emotional relationships between viewers and the factual or fictional worlds represented on screen. Television also exhibits tensions between being like a window and like a mirror.[33] News, current affairs and documentary are realist in their assumption that they offer viewers a window onto the real world. But like a mirror, television represents the domestic world, everyday life and ordinary people. Reality TV is a kind of television that has roots in documentary, and thus it often emphasizes immediacy and the role of the screen as a window onto a real world. However, many examples of reality TV programs emphasize intimacy, and invite viewers to assess how far the lives of its participants mirror their own. As Woods puts it: "the nonnatural situation of the structured reality process prompts a performance that creates tension with any remnants of documentary naturalism."[34] Like drama, the intimacy of many reality TV programs comes from their focus on character, social interaction and emotion. There is a wide spectrum in reality TV from programs that record a reality of social class whose authenticity pre-exists the production process, to programs that construct a scenario for the performance of class as authenticity.

Notes

1. See John Ellis, "Television as Working Through" in Jostein Gripsrud (ed.), *Television and Common Knowledge*, London: Routledge, 1999.
2. See Jonathan Bignell, "Realism and Reality Formats" in Laurie Ouellette (ed.), *A Companion to Reality Television*, New York: Wiley-Blackwell, 2013. For definitions of different concepts of realism, see Raymond Williams, *Keywords: A Vocabulary of Culture and Society*, London: Fontana, 1976, and Williams, "A Lecture on Realism," *Screen* vol. 18, no. 1, 1977.
3. See Rachel Mosely, "Makeover Takeover on British Television," *Screen* vol. 41, no. 3, 2000.
4. Maggie Brown, "Why I Can't Wait for Kevin," *The Guardian*, media section, 15 September 2003.
5. On the evolution of reality TV, see Jonathan Bignell, *Big Brother: Reality TV in the Twenty-First Century*, Basingstoke: Palgrave Macmillan, 2005.
6. Gareth Palmer, *Discipline and Liberty: Television and Governance*, Manchester: Manchester University Press, 2003.
7. Bill Nichols, *Blurred Boundaries: Questions of Meaning in Contemporary Culture*, Bloomington: Indiana University Press.
8. See Palmer, *Discipline and Liberty: Television and Governance*.
9. John Corner, *Television Form and Public Address*, London: Edward Arnold, 1995.
10. On the development of these different documentary forms, see Graham Barnfield, "From Direct Cinema to Car Wreck Video: Reality TV and the Crisis of Content" in Dolan Cummings (ed.), *Reality TV: How Real Is Real?* London: Hodder and Stoughton, 2002, 47–66; Sam Brenton and Reuben Cohen, *Shooting People: Adventures in Reality TV*, London: Verso, 2003; Jonathan Dovey, *Freakshow: First Person Media and Factual Television*, London: Pluto, 2000.
11. On intimacy and immediacy in television, see Jostein Gripsrud, "Television, Broadcasting, Flow: Key Metaphors in TV Theory" in David Lusted and Christine Geraghty (eds.), *The Television Studies Book*, London: Arnold, 1998, 17–32.
12. John Ellis, "Documentary and Truth on Television: The Crisis of 1999" in Alan Rosenthal and John Corner (eds.), *New Challenges for Documentary*, Manchester: Manchester University Press, 2005 [2nd ed.], 342–360.
13. Hamish Mykura quoted in Ben Dowell, "Channel 4 Corners Market for Fixed-Camera Observational Documentaries," *The Guardian*, media section, 10 January 2011, 2.
14. Ibid.
15. Ibid.
16. Charlotte Moore, quoted in Ben Dowell, "Moving on from Lagos," *The Guardian*, media section, 6 June 2011, 3.
17. Jes Wilkins quoted in Vicky Frost, "Channel 4's Big Fat Ratings Winner," *The Guardian*, media section, 7 February 2011, 3.

18. *Ibid.*
19. Charlotte Moore, quoted in Ben Dowell, "Moving on from Lagos," 3.
20. Stephen Lambert quoted in Matt Wells, "Top of the Heap," *The Guardian*, media section, 11 August 2003, 2.
21. See Helen Wood and Bev Skeggs (eds.), *Reality Television and Class*, Basingstoke: Palgrave Macmillan, 2011.
22. Julia Raeside, "Virtual Reality," *The Guardian*, media section, 1 June 2011.
23. Daran Little quoted in *Ibid.*, 7.
24. Ien Ang, *Watching Dallas: Soap Opera and the Melodramatic Imagination*, London: Routledge, 1989.
25. Faye Woods, "Classed Femininity, Performativity and Camp in British Structured Reality Programming," *Television and New Media*, vol. 20, no. 10, 2012, 5.
26. D. Little quoted in Julia Raeside, "Virtual Reality," 8.
27. Tony Wood quoted in *Ibid.*
28. John Caughie, *Television Drama: Realism, Modernism and British Culture*, Oxford: Oxford University Press, 2000, 111.
29. *Ibid.*
30. Dovey, *Freakshow: First Person Media and Factual Television*, 11.
31. Bignell, *Big Brother: Reality TV in the Twenty-First Century*.
32. Jostein Gripsrud, "Television, Broadcasting, Flow" in David Lusted and Christine Geraghty (eds.), *The Television Studies Book*.
33. *Ibid.*
34. Woods, "Classed Femininity, Performativity and Camp in British Structured Reality Programming," 11.

Works Cited

Ang, Ien. *Watching Dallas: Soap Opera and the Melodramatic Imagination*. London: Routledge, 1989.
Barnfield, Graham. "From Direct Cinema to Car Wreck Video: Reality TV and the Crisis of Content" in Dolan Cummings (ed.), *Reality TV: How Real is Real?* London: Hodder and Stoughton, 2002, 47–66.
Bignell, Jonathan. *Big Brother: Reality TV in the Twenty-First Century*. Basingstoke: Palgrave Macmillan, 2005.
Bignell, Jonathan. "Realism and Reality Formats" in Laurie Ouellette (ed.), *A Companion to Reality Television*. New York: Wiley-Blackwell, 2013, 97–115.
Brenton, Sam, and Reuben Cohen. *Shooting People: Adventures in Reality TV*. London: Verso, 2003.
Brown, Maggie. "Why I Can't Wait for Kevin." *The Guardian*, media section, 15 September 2003, 2–3.
Caughie, John. *Television Drama: Realism, Modernism and British Culture*. Oxford: Oxford University Press, 2000.
Corner, John. *Television Form and Public Address*. London: Edward Arnold, 1995.
Dovey, Jonathan. *Freakshow: First Person Media and Factual Television*. London: Pluto, 2000.
Dowell, Ben. "Channel 4 Corners Market for Fixed-Camera Observational Documentaries." *The Guardian*, media section, 10 January 2011, 2.
Dowell, Ben. "Moving on from Lagos." *The Guardian*, media section, 6 June 2011, 3.
Ellis, John. "Television as Working Through" in Jostein Gripsrud (ed.), *Television and Common Knowledge*. London: Routledge, 1999, 55–57.
Ellis, John. "Documentary and Truth on Television: The Crisis of 1999" in Alan Rosenthal and John Corner (eds.), *New Challenges for Documentary*. Manchester: Manchester University Press, 2005 [2nd ed.], 342–360.

Frost, Vicky. "Channel 4's Big Fat Ratings Winner." *The Guardian*, media section, 7 February 2011, 3.
Gripsrud, Jostein. "Television, Broadcasting, Flow: Key Metaphors in TV Theory" in David Lusted and Christine Geraghty (eds.), *The Television Studies Book*. London: Arnold, 1998, 17–32.
Mosely, Rachel. "Makeover Takeover on British Television." *Screen*, vol. 41, no. 3, 2000, 299–314.
Nichols, Bill. *Blurred Boundaries: Questions of Meaning in Contemporary Culture*. Bloomington: Indiana University Press, 1994.
Palmer, Gareth. *Discipline and Liberty: Television and Governance*. Manchester: Manchester University Press, 2003.
Raeside, Julia. "Virtual Reality." *The Guardian*, media section, 1 June 2011, 6–9.
Wells, Matt. "Top of the Heap." *The Guardian*, media section, 11 August 2003, 2.
Williams, Raymond. *Keywords: A Vocabulary of Culture and Society*. London: Fontana, 1976.
Williams, Raymond. "A Lecture on Realism." *Screen*, vol. 18, no. 1, 1977, 61–74.
Wood, Helen, and Bev Skeggs (eds.). *Reality Television and Class*. Basingstoke: Palgrave Macmillan, 2011.
Woods, Faye. "Classed Femininity, Performativity and Camp in British Structured Reality Programming." *Television and New Media*, vol. 20, no. 10, 2012, 1–18.

Part Two

Going Beyond Stereotypes?
Social Class in Documentaries
and Docudramas

"The only way is UP"
Social Mobility in Michael Apted's UP Documentary Series

SABINE HILLEN

When Margaret Thatcher entered Downing Street in 1979, she claimed that she wanted her fellow citizens to stop thinking in terms of class. According to her, this "Communist" concept implied that one group of people possessed power while others did not, that one group was "working" while others were not. The idea of exploitation and class struggle had to be overcome. During the 1980s, the very existence of social classes was even denied, to a certain extent, as Thatcher insisted that people should only be seen as individual men and women, and as families. Often portrayed as a grocer's daughter, the Conservative prime minister was actually more middle class than she was willing to admit. She grew up in Lincolnshire and her father taught her a form of hostility towards collective action but also a commitment to middle-class values such as self-improvement and enterprise.[1]

Regardless of Thatcher's views on the matter, some researchers in social science have come to reach similar conclusions, arguing that the notion of class needs to be revised. The wealth of the upper classes no longer relies on real estate and land property, but mainly on shares and holdings. Outsourcing and the development of technology, on the other hand, have contributed to downsizing the working-class population in Europe, while an increasing proportion of its members have gained access to higher education.[2] In around 1900, the working classes in Great Britain occupied 75 percent of all available jobs. Only one third of these workers had received education, while another third were half-schooled and the remaining group could neither read nor write.[3] The privilege of taking up a liberal profession belonged to the happy few who could afford it. From the 1950s onwards, however, the situation changed significantly. The working classes decreased because of automation and translocation to low-wage countries. The introduction of computers and technological tools made many jobs unnecessary. The middle classes were expanding slowly and the class system changed. Women took up part-time jobs. An increasing number of workers were able to buy television sets and radios, phones and computers. The economic gaps that existed within society progressively narrowed. All of a sudden, everyone belonged to the middle classes in a more horizontal society.

In his book *Chavs: The Demonization of the Working Class*, Owen Jones offers another hypothesis, which reveals a different, more vertical, approach to society. When it comes to defining the figure of the working-class hero, Jones refers to a Marxist definition of the working classes as having nothing but their labor to sell, yet lacking autonomy and control over their labor. This notion also comprises a sense of cultural identity, of history, and of place. Nonetheless, working-class heroes are seldom represented on television, and when they are, they are reduced to negative stereotypes, according to Jones. The author often refers to the sitcom *Little Britain* (BBC, 2003–06), which characterizes laborers and single mums as members of an uncivilized, uneducated underclass.[4]

To have some insight in this debate, I would like to investigate the *UP Series*—a collection of documentary films based on the life journey of fourteen children. The filmic experiment started in 1964 with the selection of these children from a group of twenty to represent a variety of socio-economic backgrounds. The filmmakers explicitly assumed that social class would predetermine the children's future. The series's director, Michael Apted, later conceded that he was asked to find children at the extremes of the social ladder.[5] Since the *UP Series* covers a very large period—from 1964 until 2012—it prompts us to question the constitution of classes that we have discussed earlier. This program may well confirm the recent social inquiry mentioned above, illustrating the rising middle classes and the prevailing focus on individual initiative. On the other hand, the documentary could also support Owen Jones's approach and show that disparity continues to exist, that solidarity has disappeared, especially among the working classes since Thatcher's premiership. The long-term experiment might also help us measure whether education has an influence over several generations.

Social studies have established that children born of highly educated parents have larger chances of reaching a higher level of education.[6] Young people acquire social status even before they enter the labor market. It should also be noted that the digital era, the emancipation of women and the translocation of industry have had a deep impact on the composition of social groups. Comparing the years from 1964 to 1979 with those that include and follow Margaret Thatcher's premiership (from 1979 to 2012) allows us to note the progress of individualist values and the emergence of a new social categorization identifying working-class youngsters as "Chavs" in the terminology of Owen Jones. According to the latter, the 1970s were organized around community life with the coalmine representing not only the beating heart of the industry, but also the entity around which everything revolved, including work, social life and recreation. The old and the young generations relied on each other: respect for the older miners was a matter of trust; no one would offend a co-worker who could save your life the next day. Miners and strikers were, to a certain degree, protected from mass redundancies by strong trade unions, whose power was such that they could bring the country to a standstill by cutting off its energy supplies. The election of Margaret Thatcher marked the beginning of a new era, as the notions of "rootedness" and solidarity began to weaken. As Jones concludes: "The new Briton created by Thatcherism was a property-owning, middle-class individual who looked after themselves, their family and no one else."[7]

The *UP Series* started on the premises that a child's future is predetermined by his social background, concluding each episode by the same sentence: "Give me a child until he is seven and I will give you the man."[8] As the series was prolonged into a unique filmic experiment that has so far spanned almost 50 years, was this initial statement proved right or not? How did it stand to the test of time?

The Filmic Experiment

Michael Apted established the project of the *UP Series* in the early 1960s for Granada, a broadcasting company with the reputation of being an "elitist" channel. However, the appointment of a new director for the current affairs programs changed the whole production approach. ITV's *World in Action*, which had already been set up, became a weekly current affairs program dealing with relevant and accessible social issues. After the release of its pilot episode, the *UP Series* became known as a drama-documentary, a format that "uses the sequence of events from a real historical occurrence or situation and the identities of the protagonists to underpin a film script intended to provoke debate."[9]

The first episodes revolved around access to private schools, which was believed to make some youngsters more successful than others: "The original idea was to reunite a gang of seven year olds, to shoot it in a square while asking: 'Who of you is going to be successful? Step forward!' The next step was to examine the ones that were not successful and to see if it was the class system

"The only way is UP" (HILLEN) 79

"The original idea was to reunite a gang of seven-year-olds": Jackie, Lynn and Susan (from the left at the top of the slide) in *7UP-1964* (Paul Almond/Michael Apted, 1964) (© Granada Television/Photofest).

that was responsible" (*42UP-1998*). But beside the issue of class determinism, most episodes rely on nuanced personal testimonies. Although the subjects are always aware that they are being filmed, the long-term relation between them and the documentary-maker guaranteed the natural development of the whole project.[10] During the first series, the *mise en scène* is not really innovative—a lot of talking heads reduce the impact of entertainment—and one could even say the producers have given priority to the scientific, educative value of their initial idea.[11]

Apted had three weeks to choose the children. In his comments, he mentions it was not obvious from the start that it would be interesting to follow the participants: "This idea came along after five years, when a colleague working for Granada suggested seeing what had become of all these youngsters" (*42UP-1998*). Even after moving to America, Apted continued to work on the program, because he saw the value of it. He decided to establish a more or less fixed production team to continue the interviews with the same participants after several years, reckoning the aging of the actors would increase the emotional impact on the audience.

As viewers, we are introduced to the children in a location that is removed from their everyday life. We meet them during a group visit to the London

Zoo, where the narrator announces how the experiment was set up: "We brought these children together for the first time." In the first episode, some of the seven-year-olds explain in a plain manner which schools they will attend, while others hardly know what a university is. Every seven years since then, Apted filmed those who were willing to join him, reporting the most important achievements in their lives. The latest episode to date, *56UP*, premiered on British television on May 14, 2012, interweaving recent interviews and archive footage from previous episodes. From the second episode onwards, scenes from the past are shown again to remind viewers how the subjects behaved as children, how they did as youngsters and then as young adults. These flashbacks increase the involvement of the audience whilst also creating an atmosphere of familiarity and sympathy.

Continuity was a rather difficult aspect to achieve over a period that spanned five decades. The techniques of documentary filmmaking changed thoroughly, by means of the addition of color and the release of new cutting software. The editing techniques used in the series underline the main hypothesis, namely the initial belief that there is a continuum between the life of the child and the human being that he or she becomes as an adult. This idea is implied by the use, in every new episode, of extracts from the previous ones. Given the gap of seven years between each installment, this repetition is necessary to stress the continuity in the life of each individual. We see that Tony was very active at the age of seven—climbing over fences, running in the courtyard, and fighting with his friends during recess; in the *42UP* series this image of childhood is linked to a more recent one where he plays football. We hear Neil as a child saying loud and clear: "When I grow up, I will never have children because they always do naughty things and they make the house untidy" (*7UP-1964*). At 35, bearing his difficult living conditions with courage, he repeats the same idea: "I always knew I would never have children, because children inherit something of their parents. Even if my wife was the most balanced and normal person on earth, there would still be a fair chance my child would not be happy" (*35UP-1991*). However, the continuity the editing creates can be misleading, especially when the viewer remembers that at the age of 21 Neil was dreaming of a stable family life and being married.

Although the notion of class is not often used explicitly, Michael Apted obviously highlighted the differences between his subjects: the settings, furniture and clothing do provide information on the participants, and so do their accents and their ability to speak in front of others. While it is possible for these signs to produce their own narrative, the meanings of these images are always directed by the omnipresent voice-over. The latter insists on the educational background of the children, the economic status of their parents, the schools they attend, etc. The documentary-maker's presence is pervasive in the first episodes.

Apted produced the project with fourteen children: seven of them represented the working classes or the lower middle classes in the pilot episode (Symon Basterfield, Paul Kligerman, Tony Walker, Nick Hitchon, Jackie Bassett, Lynn Johnson, Susan Davis), three of them the upper middle classes (Bruce Balden, Peter Davies, Neil Hughes), and four of them the upper classes (Suzanne Lusk, Andrew Brackfield, John Brisby, Charles Furneaux).

Some examples indicate how the path of a few subjects is smoothed for them, even before they are old enough to take decisions themselves. Attending a preparatory school in the rich neighborhood of Kensington, John Brisby and Andrew Brackfield could already name, at the age of seven, the colleges they intended to join. They would actually do so a few years later, although John also had to cope with the death of his father at a young age and insisted on the hard work he had to do in order to get where he intended. Suzanne Lusk, whose father owned a 4000-acre estate, married a solicitor and they had three children. Jackie and Susan enrolled in comprehensive schools in the East End, then married and divorced at a fairly young age, living in modest conditions. At first glance, 7UP shows us life as it is supposed to be. Social segregation in the British education system is a reality and the chances of mobility are fairly small.

As the youngsters grow older, Apted uses the same parameters to introduce his interviewees: firstly, the place they were brought up in (a city or the countryside); secondly, the school they went to (comprehensive school, state school, grammar school or preparatory school); thirdly, their professional activities and their relations with significant others, children, friends and so on. The participants themselves are aware of these parameters. They refer to other social groups to comment on their respective positions; they sometimes explain the changes in their lives as changes in their social backgrounds. Their self-representation seems honest and spontaneous up to a certain extent. The presence of the camera prompts them to keep up appearances or to keep up a façade, as Erving Goffman would say.[12] The awareness of being filmed not only obstructs the openness towards journalists and viewers, it also creates, every seven years, a strange kind of pressure and seems to reduce the possibility to experiment, take risks or even to fail. Furthermore, the serial form exerts some influence in itself. After each episode, the subjects can control their own image and evaluate the way in which they have been presented. Even if Michael Apted did not intend to work with actors, he unwillingly offered some youngsters the opportunity to become performers.

Being Upper Class

In the first episodes, we see how the education of English upper-class children is preplanned and paid for. For John, Andrew and Charles, a number of choices are clear from the start: from the primary school they will attend to the colleges that will follow, from Charterhouse to Trinity Hall, choices have already been made. The English they use to mimic their parents' is, even at an early age, well developed. Their awareness of social differences emerges already, for instance when Andrew states, "Rich children always make fun of poor children," while Charles adds, "Yes, they say 'Oh, look at that poor sissy over there!'" (*7UP-1964*). Their speech delivery contrasts with the accents and dialects of others. In the 1964 pilot episode, the three boys sit on a sofa and pretend to read the *Financial Times* or *The Observer*, avoiding to meet with members of other classes.

Still wearing their ties and suits at the age of 21, John and Andrew seem ready to carry out their responsibilities. According to Charles Furneaux, who, with the hindsight of experience, was able to view the situation differently, the process of segregation linked to higher education continues further on: "Oxbridge isolates you; you mix with the same sort of people" (*21UP-1977*). Wearing a comfortable green sweater with jeans and boots and sitting next to John and Andrew, he remarks that attending prestigious schools does not necessarily lead to better qualifications, and admits that fulfilling others' expectations may be more important than satisfying one's personal aspirations. On the other hand, these characters are well aware of their exposure to a broad audience. If projects are not turning out the way they should have, they prefer not to be open about them. Visual signs of wealth are exhibited with discretion. In the final year of their law degree, Andrew Brackfield appears briefly in a snowsuit while John Brisby stands in front of a small library that opens up to a kitchen. The selection of the filmed material and the remarks of the voice-over generate criticism among them. At 21, John mentions: "We went to the institutions we were supposed to go to, but it was presented as a kind of birthright. The poring over our books, the suffering and the sleepless nights weren't obvious to the viewer" (*21UP-1977*).

Charles Furneaux explains in one of his last appearances in front of the camera: "It seems as if all options are attainable for us ... as long as we reckon with our families' desires, our fatherland and the background we were born in" (*21UP-1977*). In other words, amazing privileges do not guarantee independence. During the most dramatic moments in the *UP Series*, the upper-class members act as subjects who experience a lack of freedom. Consumers, clients and even television viewers will entrust them with their duty to serve.[13] Their solidarity is not absent, but has an impersonal and abstract destination.

Being Middle Class

Although the voice-over suggests that life is unfair—some people get all the luck, while others have to suffer—the testimonies of middle-class subjects reveal another kind of reality: life can be easier when one is neither rich nor poor. When one walks in the middle of the road, one gains more leeway. Jackie, Lynn and Susan agree in that respect: "We all could have gone anywhere at the time, within our own capabilities. We all chose our own jobs. But we only had a limited choice anyway. We didn't have the choice of private education because we could not have afforded it anyway" (Susan, *21UP-1977*). The middle classes gather a large variety of people in terms of descents and education, but its members do experiment the most extraordinary cases of mobility. A few of the participants encounter setbacks and successes at specific moments in their lives. On these bumpy roads, they have to relate to all kinds of backgrounds, to the migrants and the unemployed.

If a rather abstract, impersonal solidarity can be observed among the upper class, the middle classes are characterized by the degree of political and social commitment of its members. Bruce Balden is an idealist who was, at a young age, concerned with poverty and racial discrimination. He wanted to become a missionary, and was educated in a prestigious boarding school whose teaching staff was not too narrow-minded: "They do not sort of enforce upper class things like that [...]. They suggest that you do not have long hair and they teach you to be reasonably well-mannered but not to sniff at the poorer people" (*14UP-1970*). At 21, he studied mathematics at Oxford University and, later on, used his education to teach children in the East End of London and in Sylhet, Northern Bangladesh.

Being Working Class

In 1978, the working-class participants were already working in the service industry. Even before Thatcher's revolutionary politics, they earned enough to defend their own interests. At first glance, judging by the representation of their everyday activity and their homes, they do well financially and the differences between them and the lower-middle classes are rather small. In this respect, Tony can be considered a convincing example of upward mobility. A few years after his career has moved from jockey to taxi driver, he is shown enjoying himself at the golf club or abroad, at holiday resorts and on beaches. As children, either orphaned or born of a single mother, Paul and Symon lacked financial support and were brought up in a children's home. At a fairly young age, Symon realizes that the poor are those who know they are missing something. They support each other. In the dorms of their boarding school, they make their beds and express their dislike of the greens of the bad-tasting meals. At 21, Symon was interviewed in a kitchen, explaining that he missed his father and worked in a freezer room in London where he carried boxes and drove a truck. He then got married and had five children. Paul moved to Melbourne, where he is shown playing with his wife on the beach and some moments later, laying bricks and building a house in a natural setting.

In 1964, the period in which Apted started filming, miners, dockworkers and car workers still made up more than a fifth of the labor market. However, the misery and the hard work in factories are not represented. We see the interviewed children without their parents, their games outside at the zoo or their dancing experiments at an informal party. Exterior shots of larger social environments are exceptional. Only Symon's mother appears occasionally, in a working-class neighborhood with an empty shopping bag, leaving the house and crossing the street; or the camera captures the area around Liverpool as Neil walks about in a warm coat. When most subjects reach the peak of their career, Apted rarely films the working area; most of the interviews take place in the private environment of the living room and the documentary seems to concentrate more and more on personal matters. Therefore, the initially relevant investigation of the public domain—are classes and the education system responsible for success?—seems to lose some of its importance along the way.

Even if an interesting mix of children was chosen to participate, political issues are only addressed in an indirect way. A vertically structured society appears in the first episodes with different categories being identified by significant signs (accent, clothes, leisure activities, housing, etc.). Concrete situations—having access to university, failing or passing an exam etc.—give indications about possible success in later life. But despite these elements, the sensitive interview style of Michael Apted only tackles these issues in order to avoid ideological statements in front of the camera. All in all, after the first episodes, the interviewees are no longer represented as members of a group. They slowly become individuals in front of the camera. The awareness of being filmed strongly compels the participants to try and produce a good impression. By the time they reached the age of 28, the subjects were more experienced as actors. They obviously wanted to show the best of themselves and be portrayed, if not as winners, at least as happy persons. In this respect the sociological evidence of the program is relative.

This trend is confirmed in the episodes starting from the beginning of the 1980s, where the signs separating the social groups become less traceable.

Narrative themes like love, children and dislocation gain more importance than education and work.

From Social Documentary to Docudrama

With this perspective in mind, the documentary unravels some familiar insights. It is not surprising that, in most cases, education does not take place in the countryside but in cities, that private schools are more likely to lead to a liberal profession and that a stable family life, with care and attention, provides a better environment to study. Besides this insight, *7UP* still displays a contrast between the rich and the poor, between those who are educated and those who are not, and between white- and blue-collar labor.

As said earlier, even the last episodes barely take into consideration new phenomena such as migration and minorities: among the fourteen interviewees, only four are women and only one is a (second-generation) immigrant. When a journalist asks Symon, who has become the head of a large family, "Do you want a better job?" he just replies: "I suppose I just like hard work [...]. I want an easy life" (*28UP-1984*). And when asked whether it is hard to be black in English society, he states: "It depends. If you just want to live in it: no, it is not hard. If you want to fight it, yes it is hard" (*28UP-1984*). It seems as if public opinion isolates the actors that express strong views on political matters. Obviously, criticism of Margaret Thatcher's government was not encouraged, especially not in a documentary wishing to attract a wide audience. Peter Davies, who went to the same suburban school in Liverpool as Neil, obtained a university degree. By the age of 28, he had become a schoolteacher, but already expressed dissatisfaction with his job. He left the series after *28UP*, following a tabloid campaign that portrayed him as an "angry young Red" for having criticized the Thatcher government's education policy in his interview.[14]

7UP shows no explicit long-term unemployment, no drug addicts or alcoholics, no badly paid part-time jobs or internships. Many interviewees divorced or separated from their partners, often the father or mother of their children (Jackie, Symon, Susan, Nick, Peter). And yet, they succeeded in finding new love. There is, at this stage, a focus on the emotional life of Susan, walking by the seaside with a new lover, on Jackie's health issues or on the turning points in the life of Nick whose love life dramatically changed. Save a few exceptions, the interviews avoid interactions and conflicts between the participants. Sometimes, however, the subjects experience internal turmoil—Neil wonders how to reach stability and use his talents —and disagreements between Apted and the interviewees are also hinted at in some of the episodes. When Apted asks

Jackie, "Do you think you had enough experience with men before getting married?" she sharply replies to him that the question is inappropriate.

The viewers of the most recent episodes probably find pleasure in this more emotional approach. Values like love, happiness and care for children are likely to be shared by an audience that strongly identifies with the characters. These matters arouse more identification than the original motif of the documentary. Whereas the original idea laid emphasis on a vertical approach of society and on the differences between grammar schools, comprehensive schools, etc., the continuation of the series shifts its focus on the theme of equality among the individuals. Susan Davies, Bruce Balden and Symon Basterfield, all had their share of professional difficulties. At key moments in their lives, Suzanne Lusk, Tony Walker and Jackie Bassett were united because they also went through difficult times on a personal level. The sequences unfold a horizontal image of society as if the producers had come to terms with their initial message: however bright, protective and sustaining an education may be, in the end, love, health and family will always win over all money-related issues. Characters appear, if not equal, at least similar in their humanity.

Even in a political context in which individualism was championed, solidarity was not a common good that had suddenly disappeared. It is among the members of the middle classes that *7UP* shows most examples of solidarity. By the age of 21, Neil Hughes had already dropped out of Aberdeen University and was living in a squat in London, living off casual work on building sites. By the age of 42, with the help of Bruce, he had gained some stability, and got involved in local council politics as a Liberal Democrat: "Neil stood in the 2010 general election as the Liberal Democrat candidate for Carlisle where he finished third, receiving 6,567 votes" (*42UP-1991*). The subjects do not automatically help their fellow workers in the same social groups. Solidarity exceeds the boundaries of one particular class to extend to others in need. However, it often remains limited in time. At 42, Bruce Balden was back in the East End, in a more traditional school, running the mathematics department. When Apted asks him why he changed schools, he stresses how difficult it is to reach those who have less opportunity in life: "I could not continue to do this until I was sixty. Therefore I had to change" (*49UP-1998*). According to Bruce, "there is a class society and [...] probably schools help its continuance." Consequently, the message is that we have to strive to keep the best places open to those who deserve it.

Michael Apted shows testimonials that foster sympathy and identification with the interviewees. After a rather ambitious pilot episode, the quality of the documentary lies, in my opinion, in its modest scientific aspirations and in the dignity it gives to all the subjects without taking sides. Jonathan Bignell explains this tension between science and convention in the following words:

> The documentary subject will almost always be aware that he or she is being recorded, witnessed or even pursued by the camera operator, and often also by a sound recordist. [...] While the finished programme may acknowledge the presence of the documentary-maker, it is often the case that documentaries imply that the subject is behaving "naturally" or at least representatively. So there is a tension between producing a documentary that is representative and "accurate," and providing the audience with a program that conforms to the conventions of argument or storytelling.[15]

Various cases of mobility (especially upward) refute the initial claim of the series. Real political issues are seldom discussed in the open, because the presence of the camera creates the need for a façade and participants have to submit, more than once, to the beliefs of public opinion. As a medium, television seems poorly suited to spontaneous confessions. Some of the interviewees lose the openness they had as children and prefer not to share their private lives. Their faces reveal a part of the truth they are living, a part of the discourse they have in mind. Maybe we could even state that the continuing pressure of the program was so strong that most participants felt obliged to reach their full potential, because, in the end, who wants to be a loser in front of the camera?

The verbal and visual signs, that initially separate the groups of interviewees, lose their impact after several episodes. After being portrayed as children and youngsters, Jackie, Suzanne and John transform into larger-than-life characters. This does not mean that they lose their credibility or become stereotypes. It simply makes us aware of the impact of the serial effect: the repetition of the images and the regularity of the episodes familiarize the viewer with the face, the love life, the qualities and the gestures of the interviewees. The latter can watch the episodes and control the presentation of their own selves in everyday life. *7UP* displays a double kind of dependency: the participants are vulnerable for they do not control all the aspects of the production. Nevertheless we could state that the vulnerability of Michael Apted is even more important. If he fails to represent his "actors" correctly, there will be no next episode. This dependency not only influences the content of the program. It also transforms the scientific set up in quite a difficult challenge.

Notes

1. Owen Jones, *Chavs: The Demonization of the Working Class*, London: Verso, 2011, 46.
2. "The Good News, Dave: We're ALL Middle-Class Now," *Daily Mail*, 6 December 2005. The

article's analysis about the extension of masses and the broader impact of individual taste can also be found in Bernard Lahire, *La Culture des individus*, Paris: La découverte, 2004.

3. Walter Weyns, *Inleiding tot de sociologie*, Universiteit Antwerpen: Acco, 2009, 155.
4. Jones, *Chavs: The Demonization of the Working Class*, 140–145.
5. Interview of Michael Apted, commentary of the *42UP* DVD. The first installment of the series (*7UP-1964*) was directed by Paul Almond to whom Michael Apsted was an assistant. Apsted has directed all the other episodes.
6. Mark Elchardus, *Sociologie, een inleiding*, Amsterdam: Pearson Benelux, 2007, 208.
7. Jones, *Chavs: The Demonization of the Working Class*, 71.
8. This is the motto of the Jesuit Order, usually attributed to the Order's co-founder, Francis Xavier.
9. For the notion of drama-documentary, see Derek Paget, *No Other Way to Tell It: Dramadoc/ Docudrama on Television*, Manchester: Manchester University Press, 2011 [1998], 82. Also mentioned by Jonathan Bignell, *An Introduction to Television Studies*, London: Routledge, 2013 [3rd ed.], 196.
10. See Bignell, *An Introduction to Television Studies*, 221–230.
11. See Frances Bonner, *Ordinary Television: Analyzing Popular TV*, London: Sage, 2003, 138.
12. Erving Goffman, *The Presentation of Self in Everyday Life*, London: Penguin, 1990 [1956].
13. John Brisby refers more than once to his parents in Bulgaria and to the recent legal adjustments that he does not approve of.
14. See Anita Singh, "56 Up: Whatever Happened to Peter Davies?" *The Daily Telegraph*, 14 May 2012: http://www.telegraph.co.uk/culture/tvandradio/9263321/56-Up-whatever-happened-to-Peter-Davies.html.
15. Bignell, *An Introduction to Television Studies*, 221.

Works Cited

Allen, Robert C., and Annette Hill. *The Television Studies Reader*. London: Routledge, 2004.
Bignell, Jonathan. *An Introduction to Television Studies*. London: Routledge, 2013.
Bonner, Frances. *Ordinary Television*. London: Sage, 2003.
Elchardus, Mark. *Sociologie, een inleiding*. Amsterdam: Pearson Benelux, 2007.
Jones, Owen. *Chavs: The Demonization of the Working Class*. London: Verso, 2011.
Lahire, Bernard. *La Culture des individus*. Paris: la découverte, 2004.
Paget, Derek. *No Other Way to Tell It: Dramadoc/Docudrama on Television*. Manchester: Manchester University Press, 2011 [1998].
Weyns, Walter. *Inleiding tot de sociologie*. Universiteit Antwerpen: Acco, 2009.

Race and Class in Luisa Dantas's Land of Opportunity

DELPHINE LETORT

Many documentaries were produced in the wake of Katrina, investigating the slow process of reconstruction in New Orleans. From Spike Lee's *When the Levees Broke: A Requiem in Four Acts* (2006), which relates stories of survival in the months that followed the hurricane, to Jason Hosein's *Independent America: Rising from Ruins* (2009), which points to the difficult reopenings of small businesses in a city that many people have abandoned, nonfiction films provide valuable insight into the social, economic and political struggles that underpin reconstruction.[1] The filmmakers view the situation through a different lens, spotlighting the hurdles which they consider impede progress. Luisa Dantas's *Land of Opportunity* spans a five-year period and emphasizes the race and class dynamics that underlie New Orleans project of urban renewal. Based on a series of interviews that construct a crisscross portrayal of the city, the documentary sheds light on the "silent salience of class" which shaped the debates. Sociologist Mary Pattillo argues that "Americans talk *around* class by using the vocabulary of status and lifestyles" instead of referring to socioeconomic power.[2] While striving to present a detailed picture of reconstruction processes, the film captures the implicit class distinctions that permeated the rationale for devising a series of priorities—affecting land use and home maintenance.

Land of Opportunity encompasses two interwoven projects: a web platform was developed to further the viewing experience of the documentary, inviting browsers to probe other internet sources that broaden their perspectives on the issues addressed by the filmed participants.[3] The platform provides additional footage that widens the scope of the documentary, drawing attention to recent developments that are broached through constant updating. It offers two types of entry ("video by issue" and "video by character"), reflecting the documentary's double structure around characters and issues. Ranging from affordable housing and disaster recovery to food security, immigration and urban planning, the characters portrayed in the film are affected by a common set of issues: Andres Duany (urban planner), Alfred Aubry (urban gardener and homeowner), Vanessa Gueringer (Lower Ninth neighborhood activist), Elza F. and Marcio P. (Latino immigrant workers), Tr'vel Lyons (teenager displaced to Los Angeles), Kawana and Sharon Jasper (public housing activists) embody a diversity of socioeconomic experiences and lifestyles.

The title of the whole project ironically suggests that New Orleans turned into a *Land of Opportunity* after Hurricane Katrina washed over the city, creating a sort of *tabula rasa* on which new projects could be experimented unhindered by the past. The documentary, however, points to the legacy of a geography of class as the camera captures the power relations that are ingrained in the landscape of a city divided along racial lines. Making herself invisible behind the camera, Luisa Dantas offers her footage as raw documents that provide evidence of an ongoing process of gentrification. Approaching the film as an expression of the filmmaker's "social engagement and distinctive vision,"[4] which film theorist Bill Nichols deems as documentary values, this article endeavors to question the legacies of race and class embedded in the documentary images.

Seeing Space through Race and Class

Luisa Dantas portrays New Orleans through a focus on its residents, whose personal stories of reconstruction illustrate socioeconomic differences between homeowners and public housing residents in neighborhoods that are segregated along racial and income lines. From the Lower Ninth Ward to Gentilly, the documentary depicts the dichotomies that determine how residents organize themselves and their interests. The juxtaposition of interviews emphasizes the distance between the priorities of the speakers, which reflect their social status: the film conveys a socioeconomic gap between homeowner residents, who do not face the same challenges depending on the location of their abode.

The extent of devastation caused by Katrina exposes the imprint of historic segregation, leaving some areas such as the Lower Ninth Ward without electric power or clean water for a longer period than other quarters. The film opens in the dead of night with a few residents driving to the Lower Ninth Ward to celebrate New Year's Eve 2006: the neighborhood is still plunged into darkness four months after the floods covered the area, thus unveiling the lack of progress in a quarter where very few people had settled back then. When Vanessa Gueringer visits the same area in plain daylight six months later, the landscape still lies in ruins and waste. Some people have moved in trailers, but there is yet no sign of rehabilitation; the camera captures the efforts of individuals who are left to cope on their own.

Rough editing points out the fragmentation of the social fabric across the city, where a pool of citizens are expected to pick urban planners to refurbish their neighborhood. Rather than promote a global plan for the city, reconstruction is devised according to geographical lines that acknowledge social class segregation. For example, the citizens of Gentilly address a distinct set of issues, which urban planner Andre Duany formulates when walking down the streets of the neighborhoods he was chosen to rejuvenate—Gentilly and the French Quarter. Holding a cigar in his hands, which marks his self-confident power, the urban planner views the land in commercial and aesthetic terms. He expresses his concern with the marketable value of Gentilly's retail center as he imagines the improvements that can be brought to rebuilding a square that might well become the best located "retail spot" in the city.

Editing underlines the fact that priorities differ from one neighborhood to another and from one social class to another: the focus on retail in Gentilly denotes the local residents' middle-class background, making the demolition of the Saint Bernard housing projects located in the same neighborhood a minority issue. While Duany articulates his architect's desire to preserve New Orleans's particular character, which according to him is gradually disappearing through suburbanization,[5] Lower Ninth residents are worried about saving their homes from demolition, for the government decided to have them bulldozed when damage was estimated at beyond 51 percent of their market value.[6]

Lower Ninth residents occupy their houses to prevent their demolition whereas Gentilly homeowners think about how to make their neighborhood more attractive for business and consumers. Filmmaker Luisa Dantas makes it clear that the project of New Orleans rejuvenation was geared to gentrification, leaving the underlying structures of inequality intact. The urban renewal plans called for the replacement of low-income housing developments with mixed-income housing, denying poor, often black, residents the possibility to return. When Duany advocates the HOPE VI program as an opportunity to revitalize Gentilly, he draws a rosy picture that betrays a neoconservative view associating poverty and crime:

> We're proposing to demolish the outside crust [of the 1940s' St Bernard housing projects] and to replace that with houses that feather down from the high-density existing but good-looking houses down to townhouses, shotguns, and single-family houses. [...] The good thing is that people like it and don't trash it, the bad thing is that you lose about 70% of your unit.

His speech illustrates an easy correlation between crime and place, arguing that the housing projects spawn bad behavior.[7] When Duany broaches the subject of demolition with an audience constituted of black and white residents, he is able to arouse identification with middle-class values and to erase race from the debate, gaining the support of the concerned citizens in opposition to the vociferous protests expressed by a housing projects heckler.[8] The scene demonstrates that the politics of neighborhood change in New Orleans occurs at the level of developers and among residents, favoring the building of communities across identical class values.

The filmmaker attended several public meetings that highlighted the struggles of power behind all post–Katrina urban choices. The trappings of power appear as body rigidity, opposing the stiffness of city council members to the disorderly movements of the people soon to be tasered to silence. The city's iconic Superdome epitomizes the economic priority local authorities set forth, endeavoring to restore the city's public image to host the Saints' games and attract more tourists. Although the film uses no voice-over to guide the viewer through the film, it resorts to a written narrative voice that articulates an ironic, critical view that complicates the interpretation of the unfolding events. Written comments appear over the image and underline the paradox of reconstruction, suggesting that concern for prestige comes first although the main facilities are still missing—including certified water in the Lower Ninth Ward. The following words turn the viewers into readers, inviting them to ponder the information that cannot be construed from the visuals only, thereby unveiling the limits of the camera to relate complete stories: "Neighborhoods have gathered to choose from a prestigious pool of architects and urban planners from all over the country." The narrator thereby frames the interpretation of the recorded footage, calling attention to the invisible politics of class.

Luisa Dantas offers a critical analysis of reconstruction by showing behind-the-scene insight, opening screen space for illegal Brazilian workers to testify about their life and work conditions in the shadows of the Superdome. The director addresses political issues through an individual focus that allows her to overcome stereotypes and racial categories. Elza F. and Marcio P. stand for the community of illegal immigrant workers who provided cheap manpower for the corporations employing them. Latino workers express archetypal beliefs in the American dream, yet they hardly make a living through a series of odd jobs. The five-year time span of the film enhances growing disillusion as the years go by and the land of opportunity turns into the land of disillusion for immigrant workers. In describing the predicament of Latino workers, Dantas uses her camera to bear witness to their exploitation and translates their powerlessness through the film's episodic structure which points to their social isolation.

The Politics vs the Individuals

The collected interviews are dispersed in the narrative and interweave several storylines together, presenting an overview of the problems that arose in post–Katrina New Orleans. The documentary thereby sheds light on structural divisions along the lines of race and class: there seems to be no homogeneous community in the filmed city. The documentarian draws attention to the specific cases of individuals whose efforts and interests conflict with each other, resulting in slow recovery throughout the city. The internet platform developed to further the viewing of the film does not shape a linear narrative either, symbolically echoing the fragmentation of society into diverse groups competing for power and resources. The videos appear in separate windows, resonating with the film's narrative structure which is composed of juxtaposed sequences that convey a sense of social division. Editing magnifies the filmed participants' social isolation, which the internet platform represents through a focus on people who are identified with labels denoting their social status: "cultural bearers," "developers," "homeless," "politicians," "public housing residents" and "immigrant workers." While these people shape the fabric of society in New Orleans, they belong to different social groups and their priorities in the context of post–Katrina diverge. The platform's methodological organization makes use of stereotypes so as to better show the social class division that undermines the sense of belonging to the city community.[9] It also endorses a multicultural perspective, which produces division rather than cohesion. Dantas, however, suggests that these boundaries can be overcome by accessing the same videos under several entries. New media scholar Lev Manovich underlines the specificity of browsing internet platforms when noting that: "Many new media objects do not tell stories; they don't have beginning or end [...]. Instead they are collections of individual items, where every item has the same significance as any other."[10] The web platform allows Dantas to erase the social hierarchy that pervades her filming the city.

In the film, the documentarian is able to circumvent these social signs by delving into the intimacy of the presented characters. She lingers on the demolition of the housing projects as diggers move in to tear them down; the camera focuses on a few lying objects, hinting at the symbolic destruction of a lifestyle.[11] Sharon Jaspers relates the stories of her everyday life in front of the barred housing projects, introducing an emotional dimension in the narrative of demolition and reconstruction. Missing from the architect Duany's vision is the emotional aspect that permeates local residents' comments on the homes they wish to rebuild. Try as he might to integrate the local social fabric by buying a house in Marigny, Duany fails to understand the citizens' attachment to rebuilding their communities and lifestyles.

The land does not bear the same meaning for the characters of the film: Duany sees the abandoned retail stores as commercial assets that can be developed, planning New Orleans's reconstruction according to its "zoning codes," which he relates to the imprint left by the French on its architecture, while the broken houses signify irretrievable loss among New Orleanians whose everyday life was transformed by Katrina. Although Tr'vel Lyons builds himself a new life in Los Angeles, integrating the local community through going to school there and eventually gaining a scholarship into UCLA, the film shows that he is gradually becoming aware of discrimination in his home city. The commemoration of the deaths five years after Katrina makes him realize that New Orleans has denied him the right to return. When he visits his own family home and finds a stranded domino in the grass, he recalls images of the past and restrains the tears that childhood memories trigger. The film turns the domino into a signifier for the loss and destruction of the past, which is encompassed in a few embedded sequences made of home videos.

The documentary includes three home movie sequences that represent the only archive footage of the film, delving into the participants' personal, subjective memories of New Orleans. Quite interestingly, although they were filmed in different parts of the city, these sequences point to childhood memories that could bring people closer to each other: all of them focus on children either playing on the lawn outside the St Bernard projects, cycling in front of an uptown family house in Gentilly, or rope skipping on the streets of the Lower Ninth Ward. The inclusion of home movie extracts is suggestive of an absence in the present of the film. The spotlight on children sheds light on past times of happiness and joy, which contrast with the silence of the present. The change of film grain underlines the rupture between the present and the past, making the archive footage an expression of irretrievable loss. They also represent an idealized vision of the past seen through the nostalgic lens of memory, focusing on images of happiness rather than discontent.

These embedded sequences also signify what has been destroyed since Katrina, for they are evocative of the home atmosphere the speakers mention, highlighting the sense of their uprootedness in the present. Urban scholar David Harvey explains that places are constructed through socio-spatial practices; home is not just identified to the place where one lives, it is endowed with cultural and social values as individuals weave their individual life stories into the local narrative:

> Places are constructed and experienced as material ecological artefacts and intricate networks of social relations. They are the focus of the imaginary, of beliefs, longing and desires (most particularly with respect to the psychological pull and push of the idea of "home"). They are an intense focus of discursive activity, filled with symbolic and representational meanings, and they are a distinctive product of institutionalized social and economic power.[12]

The home movie extracts convey that sense of place by capturing the intimacy of family life, constituting a metadiegetic level that further suggests the psychological impact of destruction. Most of the filmed interviewees behave like mourners expressing the pain of loss, but their grief is not considered in reconstruction projects.

The documentary heightens the opposition between the emotion pervading the residents' speech and the cold arguments of authoritarian bureaucrats. Dress codes highlight the distance between ordinary citizens like Vanessa Gueringer, who wears a red tee-shirt when demanding support for the Lower Ninth Ward, and the stern figures of men wearing dark suits that underline their patriarchal power and their upper-class background. The images of the city council public hearing organized on December 20, 2007, betray the gap between ordinary citizens and decision-makers whose language espouses a dominant, exclusive view. The treatment of the housing projects residents reflects the sense of otherness imposed on a neighborhood which is framed through negative clichés, associating poverty with cultural, social, moral and political mediocrity. The film fashions an intimate portrayal of the women who lived and grew up in the projects, highlighting the distorting prejudices that undergird the ideological framework of reconstruction.

The filmmaker calls attention to the ongoing human cost of reconstruction, depicting the psychological effects of a policy decision-making process that resonates with the segregationist practices of the past. Gentrification features battles over land use and makes visible social divisions, which sociologist Pierre Bourdieu associates with political power: "The power to impose and to inculcate a vision of divisions, that is, the power to make visible and explicit social divisions that are implicit, is political power par excellence."[13] Here resides the documentary value of the film, which gives us a glimpse into the social and power dynamics at work behind the gentrification of New Orleans. The filmmaker underlines the point that resources and wealth were channeled away from reconstruction in the poor quarter of the city, leaving homeowners and renters in the housing market to cope for themselves. Alfred Aubry expresses this isolated standpoint, having been waiting for more than two years that his flood-ravaged house be razed down.

Filming as a Tool of Social Activism

Luisa Dantas adopts the participatory mode of documentary filmmaking to portray post–Katrina New Orleans, the strengths of which lie in the observation of subjective, localized experience. Documentary theorist Bill Nichols emphasizes the physical engagement of the filmmakers who adopt that mode:

> Filmmakers who seek to represent their own direct encounter with their surrounding world and those who seek to represent broad social issues and historical perspectives through interviews and compilation footage constitute two large components of the participatory mode. As viewers we have the sense that we are witness to a form of dialogue between filmmaker and subject [...] that stresses situated engagement, negotiated interaction, and emotion-laden encounter.[14]

The documentary's focus on people who are determined to protect their lifestyle makes it a tool of social activism. Dantas sides with the people whom she gives a voice to through her filmmaking, drawing deeply sensitive portraits that counter stereotypical views. She expresses her commitment to social justice by retracing the untold stories of reconstruction, debunking the sense of "otherness" created by official speeches that criminalize the poor. As a Brazilian-American filmmaker who has been a resident in New Orleans for the past seven years, Luisa Dantas expresses her political commitment through the film. She denounces the neoliberal policies that were implemented in the wake of Katrina, using her documentary and the website platform to counterbalance the sense of powerlessness of those minorities, whose voices were not taken into account throughout the process of reconstruction.[15] Both the film and the platform restore their agency, allowing the viewer to follow their fight for decent housing beyond the time span of the film. Rather than shed light on their status as victims, the filmmaker reveals that their grassroots struggle comes from a larger world resistance: the collective protest reflects a political awareness that is grounded in race.

After homeowner Vanessa Gueringer has collected signatures to help organize Lower Ninth Ward residents in view of the meeting that will shape the Unified City Plan demanded by federal authorities prior to any funding, she marches with other women outside the City Hall to demand that certified water be turned on in her neighborhood; Endesha Juakali speaks up for the housing projects residents during a Housing Authority of New Orleans (HANO) meeting, leading the activists to occupy the projects slated for demolition; Sharon Jasper addresses the city council on the subject of demolition speaking for all the displaced. But on the whole, the film captures an imbalanced struggle for power with renters being deprived of a say during public meetings.

Although the film is based on the participatory documentary mode, exploring the encounters between Dantas and her environment, the director never appears on screen and her questions can rarely be overheard. Her commitment is expressed by her invisible presence alongside those she portrays in the five-year time-long making of the film. She does not intrude in the frame, leaving more visual and aural space to her filmed subjects. Their voices and their stance of resilience are put forward as she uses her camera to bear witness to their acts of unflinching courage. The camera is placed in the crowd during the council meeting, capturing the indifference of its members in opposition to the raw emotions of the citizens demanding housing. By giving voice to New Orleans African American poor whom she follows in the Lower Ninth Ward or in the barred St Bernard Projects, the filmmaker depicts people who refuse to be treated as victims, thus emphasizing their determination in the face of injustice. She strives to overturn the stereotypes which prevail in the speech of the Department of Housing and Urban Development president Alphonso Jackson: "I want only the best people in public housing.... I want people who will pay their rent, work every day. I don't want gangbangers and drug dealers in our housing developments." Because the housing projects in New Orleans were occupied by a majority of African Americans, his comments racialize and criminalize poverty—thus echoing the framing of Katrina by most conservative media.

Dantas, however, portrays working-class people whose efforts to make ends meet are compromised by low wages and high rental rates. The web platform refers to events that happened after the film was completed; it depicts housing activist Sharon Jasper demonstrate outside Columbia Park for more public housing, thereby suggesting that the fight continued beyond the film's time frame. The mixed-income development that replaces St Bernard projects offers too few apartments for former tenants to settle back in the city. The filmed participants may embody specific community dynamics and views in relation to reconstruction choices; however, Dantas is keen to point out the connections between local and nationwide issues through the documentary website. She is able to pinpoint that the situation in New Orleans reflects broader trends, noting for example that the emergence of tent cities in Seattle illustrates the persistent increase in homelessness due to the demolition of housing projects standing as national policy advocated by the Department of Housing and Urban Development (HUD). Under the label "get involved," the platform directs the website browsers to other social networks prompting them to commit themselves as concerned citizens. The web platform offers paths of action that counter the powerlessness of the filmmaker when confined to view the world through the viewfinder of the camera. Although the film has been shown all over the world—it was broadcast via Arte in Europe on the fifth anniversary of Katrina (2010) and had its festival premiere at the *It's All True Festival* in Brazil (2011)—it is nonetheless difficult to assess its impact on local politics.

Rather than promote a more equitable city, the reconstruction of New Orleans has further exposed race and class differences, which Luisa Dantas demonstrates by spotlighting the struggle of housing activists in favor of the rehabilitation of the housing projects. Her interviewees voice acute awareness of the institutional discrimination which pervades city planning. Some of the speakers have become local figures through endorsing an activist stance in other nonfiction films—Phyllis Montana-Leblanc has accrued her visibility and uses her celebrity status to speak out; Endesha Juakali has become a recurrent figure standing for the housing projects.

As an interactive documentary, *Land of Opportunity* remains an on-going production that can be modified according to news events—like Hurricane Sandy. Lev Manovich argues that new media are characterized by this "variability,"[16] a term encapsulating the idea that projects in new media are dynamic, open to constant modification by the filmmaker, the participants or the community built around the topic treated in the film.[17] Through filming New Orleans's reconstruction, Dantas revises the American myth of an open society, which allows for the working class to dream of economic justice. The film portrays a society which has relinquished equality and reveals conflicts between official representatives and ordinary citizens, whose opinions were discarded in the citywide plan of reconstruction presented to obtain federal aid. In December 2007, the city council unanimously voted in favor of demolition: four housing projects were concerned, which made it impossible for poor residents to return to New Orleans. Rents increased in the city due to the limited supply of undamaged rental housing, which was made worse by the fact that owners of rental property benefited from a very small percentage of the recovery grants allocated by the Department of Housing and Urban Development's Community Development Block Grant (CDBG).[18]

Notes

1. Among them, *When the Levees Broke: A Requiem in Four Acts* (Spike Lee, 2006), *Katrina's Children* (Laura Belsey, 2008), *Katrina Story* (Tenth Ward Buck, 2006), *Katrina: Man-Made Disaster* (Big Noise Film, 2008), *I Won't Drown on That Levee and You Aren't Gonna Break My Back* (Ashley

Hunt, 2006), *Independent America: Rising from Ruins* (Hason Hosein, 2009), *Faubourg Tremé* (Lolis Eric Elie and Dawn Logodon, 2008), *Cut Off* (Broderick Webb and Edward Holub, 2008), *By Invitation Only* (Rebecca Snedeker, 2006), *Neo Black Leaders and Politicians* (Ready Mills, 2007), *If God Is Willing and Da Creek Don't Rise* (Spike Lee, 2010).

2. Mary Pattillo, *Black on the Block: The Politics of Race and Class in the City*, Chicago: University of Chicago Press, 2007, 304.

3. http://www.landofopportunitymovie.com/. A new interactive website was launched after this essay was written, further testifying to the innovative tools developed to further the viewing of film. It includes three videos that evoke the landscape of a rebuilt New Orleans through the portrayals of three residents: http://landofopportunityinteractive.com, accessed on January 12, 2014.

4. Bill Nichols, *Introduction to Documentary*, Bloomington: Indiana University Press, 2010, 2.

5. "These demolitions happened without prior notice to the building owner (Nossiter, 2006) and even inadvertently included the demolition of houses undergoing renovation (Denhart, 2006). This left many homeowners, especially impoverished ones whose sum wealth resided in the broken structure, living in a state of anxiety wondering if their home might be next." Hazel Denhart, "Deconstructing Disaster: Psycho-social Impact of Deconstruction in Post-Katrina New Orleans," *Cities*, vol. 26, no. 4, August 2009, 195.

6. Duany declares: "I'd love to go to the heart of the problem which isn't just people are unhoused, this and that doesn't work. The problem is that this city is becoming more and more like other over time and that is a cultural tragedy. We could lose New Orleans. The world loses New Orleans. A city is a result of its codes. A code is like a zoning code, is what shapes a building, is what functions can happen in the building. New Orleans is a highly coded city. The French Quarter has that particular character because the French had rules. New Orleans has gone from a city with great character into a city that has gradually become suburban."

7. Pattillo, *Black on the Block*, 264.

8. Hazel Denhart states that low-income residents were strongly discouraged from going back to New Orleans by the loss of affordable housing: "Over 70% of New Orleans' housing was either destroyed or severely damaged by the hurricanes of 2005. By late 2007, about 70% of the population had returned but tens of thousands of homes remain damaged. Returning residents face high unemployment rates and a scarcity of construction materials for rebuilding, complicated by inflated prices for materials that were available. Since the majority of low-income housing was destroyed (and very little of it was back in place 2 years later), those returning to the city in the early years after the storm were those who had the money to return. Large numbers of low-income residents were threatened with being priced out of the rebuilding effort. [...] Before the Hurricane, the Housing Authority of New Orleans (HANO) operated 5100 low-income units in four sites. By late spring, 2008 only 880 families had been allowed to return to this low-income housing." Hazel Denhart, "Deconstructing Disaster: Psycho-Social Impact of Deconstruction in Post-Katrina New Orleans," 196.

9. The city of New Orleans appears to be geographically and socially divided: no social cohesion seems to emerge from Katrina, which reinforces divisions along income lines throughout the city. Depending on where they live in the city and on their social status as homeowners or housing projects residents, New Orleanians do not face the same issues and do not expect the same policies. More often than not, these divisions highlight the structural racial legacy of the past—although some African Americans have moved up the social ladder, which leads them to identify with middle class values. The film illustrates that point when recording the debates taking place with urban planner Duany in Gentilly.

10. Lev Manovich, *The Language of New Media*, Cambridge: MIT Press, 2001, 194.

11. Pattillo, *Black on the Block*, 13.

12. David Harvey, *Justice, Nature and the Geography of Difference*, Oxford: Blackwell, 1996, 316.

13. Pierre Bourdieu, "Social Space and Symbolic Power," *Sociological Theory*, vol. 7, no. 1, 1989, 23.

14. Nichols, *Introduction to Documentary*, 187.

15. Luisa Dantas collaborated with Robert Greenwald on the making of *Wal-Mart: The High Cost of Low Price* (2005), an activist film that critically explores the internal policies of the multinational company and its consequence on the national economic landscape.

16. Manovich, *The Language of New Media*, 36.

17. The latest innovation of the website includes the development of another experimental website, including several new videos that pursue Dantas's investigation into the transformation of

urban communities: http://beta.landofopportunityinteractive.com, accessed on December 14, 2013.

18. Matthew J. Scire, *Disaster Housing: FEMA Needs More Detailed Guidance and Performance Measures*, Report to Congressional Requesters, United States Government Accountability Office, 28 August 2009, 11–14. (The full report can be accessed on Google Books).

Works Cited

Bourdieu, Pierre. "Social Space and Symbolic Power." *Sociological Theory*, vol. 7, no. 1, 1989, 14–25.
Denhart, Hazel. "Deconstructing Disaster: Psycho-Social Impact of Deconstruction in Post-Katrina New Orleans." *Cities*, vol. 26, no. 4, August 2009, 195–201.
Harvey, David. *Justice, Nature and the Geography of Difference*. Oxford: Blackwell, 1996.
Manovich, Lev. *The Language of New Media*. Cambridge: MIT Press, 2001.
Pattillo, Mary. *Black on the Block: The Politics of Race and Class in the City*. Chicago: University of Chicago Press, 2007.
Nichols, Bill. *Introduction to Documentary*. Bloomington: Indiana University Press, 2010 [2nd ed.].
Scire, Matthew J. *Disaster Housing: FEMA Needs More Detailed Guidance and Performance Measures*. Report to Congressional Requesters, United States Government Accountability Office, 28 August 2009.

"Gizza job! I can do that!"
The Unmaking of the British Working Class in Alan Bleasdale's *Boys from the Blackstuff*

Carys Lewis

October 2013 marked the fiftieth anniversary of the publication of E.P. Thompson's *The Making of the English Working Class*, a book whose author had a precise purpose in mind when selecting the words of the title: "*Making*, because it is a study in an active process, which owes as much to agency as to conditioning. The working class did not rise like the sun at an appointed time. It was present at its own making."[1] Thompson goes on to define the other crucial terms of his study: he understands "class" to be "a historical phenomenon," which he does not see as "a 'structure,' not even as a 'category,' but as something which in fact happens (and can be shown to have happened) in human relationships."[2] The notion of human relationships is deemed by Thompson to be the bedrock of the notion of class; just as love cannot be embodied without the example of "real people in a real context," neither can class. It is therefore embedded in a historical context, and it is real people's awareness of their various human experiences that enables them to articulate class consciousness. Yet it is Thompson's insistence on the historical, on anchoring people in different times and places, that is particularly important in the representation of the working class. Staking out his territory and positioning his study in opposition to two schools of historians,[3] Thompson criticizes what he sees as the tendency "to obscure the agency of working people, the degree to which they contributed by conscious efforts, to the making of history."[4] His will be a different ambition as he sets out to remember the "blind alleys, the lost causes and the losers themselves,"[5] in an attempt to "rescue" the craftsmen and artisans of a dying tradition from becoming the "casualties" of history.

How apt therefore that Thompson's choice of words should echo questions of agency and active process when examining *Boys from the Blackstuff*, a television drama that many commentators have deemed to be a representation—a making present?—of the unmaking of the British working class.⁶ Questions of representation, however, need to be defined more precisely when dealing with a visual work of art and, more especially in the field of film or television, since the representational codes of the latter generate meaning for the audience through their particular cultural practices. To consider representation in film or television as a mere depiction of reality is to diminish the importance of these codes and the way in which a particular audience, through culture, will perceive and make sense of the reality encoded by a televisual or filmic representation. In the words of the critic John Fiske: "There may be an objective, empiricist reality out there, but there is no universal, objective way of perceiving and making sense of it. What passes for reality in any culture is the product of that culture's codes, so 'reality' is always already encoded, it is never 'raw.'"⁷

Determining the codes of a television drama—dress, environment, behavior, sound, camera work, lighting, music, editing—can also serve as a means of situating the specific point of view that a writer or a director has adopted in bringing a work to our screens. This is all the more helpful when a given drama is represented through a realist type of filming, as many works of British television have chosen to do when representing the working class. Realism, however, may be fraught with the double-edged encoding of ideology, in other words it may be used by dominant formations to lull audiences into viewing reality in a certain way. It is precisely here that the "unmaking" of representations of the working class can lead to more fertile, radical discourses that audiences can participate in at the moment of reception.

Once something is "unmade," there are of necessity two outcomes: there is either a general acknowledgement that the thing unmade is well and truly defunct, unfit for purpose, and a period of mourning and nostalgia sets in; or the unmade is deemed to have been merely transcended by a new process and through the pain of loss something is remade or reconfigured to serve in different conditions. Before we can safely say that *Boys from the Blackstuff* partakes of either of these processes, it is imperative to examine the representational ethos of the plays through the use of realism and non-realist filming techniques. However, it might be useful to give some of the important facts surrounding the plays, their impact and their historical context.

Boys from the Blackstuff: Origins, Impact and Historical Context

First transmitted on BBC2, which was at that time considered to be the more "arty" of the two BBC channels, *Boys from the Blackstuff* was shown as part of the BBC's *Play for Today* series, a flagship for "quality television" in which the BBC could justly claim to be adhering to its public service broadcasting obligation by producing programs "to educate, inform and entertain." The first play in the series went out on October 10, 1982. The fifth and final play in the series was transmitted on November 7, 1982. Such was the success that the plays were repeated on the more general public BBC1 channel the following January, thus giving *Boys from the Blackstuff* its status as "TV drama event of the eighties on the grounds of the exceptional intervention the program made in British culture in the autumn of 1982."[8]

The author of the plays, Alan Bleasdale, a former high school teacher, had turned to writing drama partly because he felt that nothing seemed to mirror the reality of Liverpool's working class whose children he taught every day. A Liverpudlian himself, Bleasdale first came to the fore as a playwright in Liverpool's Playhouse Theatre along with the likes of Willy Russell. He summed up his motivation in writing the script in these words: "I didn't write *Boys from the Blackstuff* for the bishops and knights and kings and queens and people who have got castles. I wrote it for and about pawns."[9] Bleasdale's past in the theater no doubt accounted for the exuberant and truculent dialogue that *Boys from the Blackstuff* would later be noted for and contributed to the credibility of the characters as representations of working class heroes.

Boys from the Blackstuff was four years in the making, from Bleasdale's initial proposal to its transmission. In fact, it came about as a sequel to a previous television play Bleasdale had written called simply *The Blackstuff* (1980).[10] In this first play, the viewers were introduced to the characters followed up in the later series of plays. The "blackstuff" in question was the slang word used by Liverpudlian building workers for tarmac. In the first play the five Liverpool building workers—Dixie, Chrissie, Loggo, George and Yosser—are sent up to Middleborough to lay tarmac on a construction site. In an attempt to outdo their crooked employer, they decide to go along with Yosser's ambitious plan to make a few bob on the side and "do a foreigner," i.e., they use their employer's building material and equipment to complete a contract they themselves have negotiated. But the boys' attempt at being early Thatcherite golden boys ends in failure and they are all fired.

Boys from the Blackstuff takes up their stories as they come face to face with chronic unemployment in their native Liverpool. The five plays in the series follow the destiny of each one:

- "Jobs for the Boys," an episode in which they are moonlighting on a building site whilst on the Dole and in which the almost

caricature socialist character of Snowy is killed whilst trying to flee the Department of Social Security inspectors.
- "Moonlighter," a play centered on Dixie, the most dour and authoritarian of the boys, forced to work as a security guard in the docks and to turn a blind eye to organized pilfering by union employees.
- "Shop Thy Neighbour," centered around Chrissie and Loggo as they evade DHSS inspectors and then on Chrissie and his wife Angie, where the latter taunts her husband with his apathy leading to Chrissie's snapping.
- "Yosser's Story," centered around the character of Yosser Hughes, whom we see steadily stripped of everything—work, wife, home, children, identity—only to end in defiant despair, head-butting all that try to hold him down.
- "George's Last Ride," in which George, ex-trade unionist, reminisces about his politically active past, but dies as he is wheeled around the derelict Liverpool docks by Chrissie. His funeral briefly causes the main characters to reunite.

The series was blessed in being directed by one of the UK's most experimental and innovative television directors of the day, Philip Saville.[11] Whilst the scripts were already carefully crafted to accommodate humor and pathos, Saville insisted on a certain amount of improvisation through slowing down the pace of the acting: "What I did was give the characters a sort of *distance* and space which no doubt the public became deeply involved with."[12]

The third pillar of the team was Michael Wearing, the producer. He had worked on previous television plays at the BBC and was well versed in finding practical and financial solutions to the innumerable problems that could arise with such productions. However, in *Boys from the Blackstuff* he also had great input into directorial and script decisions, such as suggesting that the surreal, carnivalesque scene in the pub be placed in the final play after trade unionist George's funeral: "I somehow had this notion that we needed an objectifying, almost alienating device which counterpoints the sheer sense of the life-force in George and what his life had stood for."[13] The trio of writer, director and producer were also admirably served by a formidable cast, most of whom had already worked with Bleasdale in theater.

The series was also innovative in that it was produced in the much freer atmosphere of BBC Pebble Mill in Birmingham, where the BBC's English Regions Drama Department was based. Working outside London and shooting on location in Liverpool was always going to leave a fresher, less "establishment" mark on the series. But added to that was the technological innovation that *Boys from the Blackstuff* made use of, namely the Light Mobile Control Room. Of the five plays, four were filmed using the cheaper Outside Broadcasting location video format. The play entitled "Yosser's Story" was the only one to be filmed in 16mm film. The lightweight video format, using Ikigami video cameras with a 200-foot shooting radius, enabled the director to give a more documentary-like feel to the plays since the hand-held cameras could follow the actors around and give a hands-on immediacy to the filming. The video format, using two to four cameras, also allowed Philip Saville to shoot wide-angles and close-ups at the same time. At the end of a day's filming, with the video technique Saville would spend time in the mobile control room with the video editing staff, rubberstamping all decisions. However, for "Yosser's Story," the film editor Greg Miller stated in an interview that he worked on his own since 16mm film meant that Saville had placed the camera where he wanted it and got the shot he felt was right for the sequence.[14]

If, as previously stated, "unmaking" representations of the working class allows audiences to participate in more radical narrative discourses at the moment of reception, this may seem to be confirmed when we consider the viewer ratings of *Boys from the Blackstuff*. Firstly, regional differences in the viewer ratings, with significantly higher ratings in the North West—for obvious reasons—but also in the Border, Central Scotland and the North East regions, compared to London and the South West,[15] would seem to suggest that *Boys from the Blackstuff* belongs most definitely to the Northern realist tradition of TV drama[16] and that its subject matter underlined a North-South divide in 1980s Britain. *Boys from the Blackstuff* would therefore appeal to a working-class audience from the North of England inasmuch as they could identify with the ordinary, everyday depiction of a way of life familiar to them. The sense of community could be channeled through television: "Media *mediate* between different individual audience members to create a sense of communal belonging in terms of national, city, regional, local or neighbourhood interests."[17]

Secondly, the unprecedented speed at which the series was repeated—a mere nine week interval between its first and second airings—shows that the series hit a nerve in those parts of the UK that were feeling the bite of high unemployment. Similarly, it might be said that the writerly qualities of the script transcended from screen to page, as the scripts were published in both play and novel form soon after the initial transmission, hinting at the exemplary critical value of the texts.

In Liverpool, the series was officially adopted by Liverpool City Council as epitomizing the problems faced by the inhabitants of the city in the 1980s. However, subsequent 1990s TV programs based in Liverpool distanced themselves from the "Blackstuff" legacy, as they no doubt felt that the constant portrayal of the city's inhabitants as scroungers or layabouts no longer resonated with audiences more intent in the late 1980s and early 1990s with viewing more societal storylines. Channel 4's *Brookside* (1982–2003) is a case in point, in which more controversial storylines, such as the first pre-watershed lesbian kiss on British television in 1994, were intended to appeal to a younger audience, with the new-build estate of Brookside Close an ideal setting for the middle-class Liverpool families who had climbed up the social ladder that had been so abruptly pulled from under the feet of the "Blackstuff" boys.

The character of Yosser Hughes became a folk hero, and not just in Liverpool. In an exceptional example of boundary-crossing from fiction to reality, Yosser's manic utterances became catchphrases in 1980s Britain, with strikers and dole claimants chanting his "Gizza Job" and even the Kop, the Liverpool football supporters, taking up Yosser's "I can do that" each time a player scored. There were Yosser look-alike competitions, Yosser posters, t-shirts, pop records and—more worryingly—a rash of Yosser head-butting in primary schools.[18] In today's age of the internet, video-on-demand, streaming and gifs, Yosser would provide much interaction for a devoted fan base.[19]

As far as the historical context of the series goes, it was somewhat of a turn of fate that it was finally broadcast as the unemployment figures hit the three million mark, ironically heightening the series' relevance. The Toxteth riots of July 1981, although officially put down to racial tension between the black community of this Liverpool inner-city area and the police, only served to reinforce the realism of the plays. Indeed, Snowy in "Jobs for the Boys" refers explicitly to the riots.

Boys from the Blackstuff was aired in 1982, three years into Margaret Thatcher's first term of office. However, the fact that Bleasdale had written the plays in 1978 has led to many questioning whatever political message, if any, the writer intended since 1978 saw a Labour government in power, plagued in its death throes by the "Winter of Discontent." Bleasdale has stated that his writing is not there to carry a political message. Indeed, the plays were almost expressly written in opposition to the militant Marxist realism of such TV dramas as Ken Loach–directed and Jim Allen–scripted *The Big Flame* (Ken Loach, 1969). Despite the softened politics some may detect in *Boys from the Blackstuff*, the series' wide-ranging audience and its capacity to appeal to a working-class audience in particular seem to bear out Bleasdale's ethos as stated here: "I think life's a farce—an absurd, mad, black farce—and that's how I write; but within that I try not to score any easy political points where there's no easy answer. I never give answers; I just ask a few questions on the way."[20]

I should now like to turn to two scenes from "Yosser's Story" in which I will examine questions of working-class masculinity and identity, before finally assessing the "complex seeing" the series gave *of* and *to* the working class.

A "knowable community"

The scene I will now focus on appears almost halfway into "Yosser's Story." Yosser has by now lost his job, his wife and soon he will lose his children as the social services swoop down. Filmed on the pier head above the Mersey, these images capture the rapidly disintegrating world of Yosser and his children.

Yosser's growing paranoia is apparent in his manic repetition—"I'm Yosser Hughes"—a phrase reinstating his fluctuating identity that is so reminiscent of "I'm not a vagrant" in Jeremy Sandford's 1971 television play *Edna the Inebriate Woman*. Here Yosser comes across as a figure of loss, one of lost identity, and more especially of lost male identity. Indeed, *Boys from the Blackstuff* supplied a redefinition of masculinity in 1980s Britain, as the figure of the male breadwinner collapsed under the altered state of unemployment. The series in fact provided few opportunities to view unemployment from a female standpoint, the one notable exception being Angie, Chrissie's wife, in the third play.

However, the character of Yosser provided viewers with an almost fetishistic identification with a violent male hero, his constant head butting symbolizing the only physicality that he has left. Work in a patriarchal capitalist society plays an important role in producing masculinity, but, in the words of John Fiske, "it is not without its contradictions."[21] Working men are thus subjected to the constraints of working conditions, which in turn renders them both dependent and powerless. Although the role of "breadwinner" may seem to all intents and purposes to bestow upon men a sense of power, it also confines men in a prison, thus depriving them of masculine independence and freedom. Yosser's behavior, mired in his growing frustration with the forces of society that are all leagued against him, captures the contradictions that Fiske highlights in the role of "breadwinner": "The concept 'breadwinner' contains within it the domains of work and of the family and the contradictions in both, for in it the masculine role is experienced as a constant vacillation between power and subjection, between freedom and restraint."[22]

Many of the empowering features of working-class masculinity have disappeared from the lives of the characters in *Boys from the Blackstuff*: the camaraderie of a "night out with the boys" depicted in an inverted, tragic-comic scene when Yosser Hughes comes across the Liverpool football player Graeme Souness in a pub; the pet ducks that Chrissie keeps in the backyard and that he savagely massacres with a shotgun; the masculine solidarity of the trade union, the demise of which is saluted in the death of George Malone. These constitute indeed a series of losses that contribute to masculine working-class "unmaking." However, the process of remaking, the transcendence previously mentioned as a reconfiguration of working-class life, is ultimately what *Boys from the Blackstuff* chooses to foreground: after George's funeral, Chrissie and Loggo enter a pub where the locals and the landlord are drinking heavily, leading to scenes of total mayhem and, as a "redundancy party" walk in, Chrissie and Loggo choose to leave. They are caught up by Yosser. Chrissie in despondent mood says everything George stood for has died with him. Yet, the scene is a testimony to some form of resistance as they turn their backs on the abject drinkers in the pub, most of whom are unemployed like themselves. There can be no going back to the male-dominated working-class culture of the past, but there are signs that something else may arise from the ashes.

The scene with the "wino" and the prostrate figures on the bench hints at the condition of Liverpool's working-class in the 1980s. The first male figure, flat-capped with newspaper in hand, reminds the viewer of that other male working-class hero, Andy Capp, the cartoon strip character created by Reg Smythe featured in the *Daily Mirror* newspaper since 1957. The figures are filmed in a low-angle tracking shot and the dialogue between Yosser and the "wino" is filmed from below, bottom-up and not top-down, reinforcing the viewer's identification with the unemployed. They sit on the pier head in front of the Royal Liver Building, an iconic Liverpool landmark, symbolizing the past industrial glory of the city.

As Yosser's existence crumbles, he indulges in nostalgia. Looking back to his childhood in the 1950s, he states in broken, hesitant speech how different things were then: "When I was little.... There was so much to look forward to." Yosser's insistence on "When I was little…" ominously suggests that "being"—"when I WAS"—is now not enough for existence, that identity is shaped through work, belonging, community, although in Yosser's case, his has always been a personalized individual identity rather than the collective identity of class. The "unmaking" of Yosser's working-class identity is synonymous with the darker side of loss: contemporary viewers of the plays in 1982 might well have felt some nostalgia for the strong sense of community that traditional working-class communities could provide. Yet, Yosser, whose individual initiative in *The Blackstuff*, the original play that introduced the boys, first brought about his fellow-workers' downfall (they are fired after doing a job on the side), can also be seen as an embodiment of the alienated working-class that Thatcherism was to prey on so steadfastly. His "unmaking" is partly on account of his own denial of community.

This scene captures what Raymond Williams would have termed the "structure of feeling" of 1980s Britain, a term Williams used to determine what was "realizable through experience of the work of art itself, as a whole,"[23] a term he once defined using the metaphor of a chemical process in which the everyday elements of life were distilled down into a precipitate until you end up with "a kind of recognition, a connection with something knowable but not yet known."[24] As Yosser's identity falls apart, he senses that the knowable community of working-class male camaraderie, with its male-female division of labor and the known domestic sphere of the home is slipping away. What will replace it is yet to be understood.

The scene also affords us with an inverted notion of the male knowable community. When Yosser insists in his megalomaniac diatribe that "I'm Yosser Hughes 'better looking by far.' Everybody knows me. Everybody notices me.... Everywhere I go I get noticed. That's me," his warped thinking is based on a super-inflated notion of self: in his eyes, he is better-looking by far than Graeme Souness, the Liverpool football player he meets in a pub early on in the play; everybody knows him, but for the wrong reasons—because of his head-butting and his desperate behavior. Similarly, the "wino" (played by James Ellis, PC Bert Lynch from the BBC's *Z-Cars* police TV drama) has his own warped notion of community: brandishing his bottle of whisky, he declares: "Yosser, they water this stuff down, you know. They do. In the factory. I know. I have contacts." This inverted logic only strengthens the undermining of the notion of community.

The bathos of the scene falls apart in Yosser's final words: "I built sandcastles. And.... I sometimes think that's all I've ever done." In the script version of *Boys from the Blackstuff*, "*I built sandcastles*" appears in italics, as if Yosser is already quoting himself, as if he is already caught up in some form of distancing from both himself and the community that has made him what he is. The nostalgic veneer of childhood is, however, disrupted in Yosser's final words—"I sometimes think that's all I've ever done"—as sentimentality turns into dark irony.

Complex Seeing and Brechtian Alienation

Prior to the scene with the "wino," "Yosser's Story" opens with a scene which many commentators have qualified as "surrealist" or "Brechtian."[25] As the opening sequence of the fourth play in the series, the tone is set with the dream-like, expressionist quality of the images. Indeed, for many commentators, the beginning of "Yosser's Story" is the most potent illustration of the innovative and experimental elements that led to *Boys from the Blackstuff* gaining a reputation as "art television" for a popular audience.[26] It was also through such scenes that realism in television drama could be reassessed with "Yosser's Story" setting the tone for audience appraisal of the entire series. As Richard Paterson put it: "Yosser's Story's emotional power, which quite transcended the conventional bounds of social realism, had an important determining effect on the shape and production of the whole series."[27]

The shot of Yosser and his children looking through a window is an obvious reminder of the wire grille through which the boys speak—or don't speak in Yosser's case—at the Social Security office. However, I would like to examine this particular image in light of a remark Raymond Williams makes on the relationship between television and the outside world in his 1974 study, *Television: Technology and Cultural Form*.[28] As television as a medium took off in an era when social communication was no longer centered in the home, there was a need for new kinds of contact with the outside world. Williams notes that there was already some trace of this in the theater of the 1880s and 1890s, citing both Ibsen and Chekhov, in whose plays characters are seen sitting beside windows, looking out, anxiously waiting for news from the outside which was bound to have repercussions on their private domestic lives. For Williams, the domestic television set served the same purpose. As Yosser looks out through the window, there is a need to make sense of what is happening in his fast-disintegrating life. In a mode of intense interaction, viewers of "Yosser's Story" find themselves looking at someone looking at them, a mirror image of their need to understand what the condition of the working class in 1980s Britain had come to. This yearning for meaning is also heightened by the interspersed images of the people in the park: some are pointing at Yosser in bewilderment; others cradle their children, fearing the worst might happen. The removal of the barrier between viewer and viewed in this opening scene is the clearest example in *Boys from the Blackstuff* of a Brecht-like estrangement or alienation effect. As in Brecht's theater, where the artist tore down the existence of the fourth wall beside the three walls of the stage, thus forcing the audience to understand that they were no longer an unseen entity, the disruptive nature of this first scene from "Yosser's Story" forces the viewers to take up a critical, analytical stance of their own passive acceptance of the images. Television is often taken to be a technology that offers unmediated access. What *Boys from the Blackstuff* succeeds in doing in scenes such as this is remind viewers of the mediating forces at work in television by distancing them from what essentially might be taken for reality.

Once again, Raymond Williams pinpointed the importance of recognizing the use of distance in television; more particularly when the discourse it produces is "controlled by the culture of distance" and reaches its "morbid last phase, in the culture of alienation."[29] Although Williams found this to be most apparent in television news, he intuitively felt that the same process was at work in the way mass unemployment had been distanced in 1980s Britain. Writing in June 1982 during the Falklands War, Williams draws attention to the central technical claim of television, that it can show distant events (*tele*, the Greek for "afar" drawing its roots from *telos*, an "end"). The distancing of war that Williams was witnessing every day on British television was, he argued, reason enough for people to be wary of what the dominant culture was arranging. Williams, however, felt that the distancing of mass unemployment was perhaps even more sinister: "But the larger argument that now needs to be stated [...] is about the culture of distance, the latent culture of alienation, within which men and women are reduced to models, figures and the quick cry in the throat."[30]

Yosser Hughes is reduced to "the quick cry in the throat" as he blurts out the names of his drowned children—"Dustin! Anne-Marie!" He is by now alienated from everything and everyone: George Malone floats past in a boat, but the stalwart of the Liverpool docks can do nothing to help; Chrissie and Loggo are pictured gliding past, dressed in Henley Regatta–type clothes, sipping champagne, as if they too are out of reach, in a different class, as seen through Yosser's paranoid eyes; finally, there is no help for Yosser from Maureen, his ex-wife.

But it was all a dream. Although Millington has already pointed out that the experimentation of dramatic new styles in television drama realism that *Boys from the Blackstuff* is noted for is in fact contained within a more traditional narrative, as here when Yosser wakes up from his dream, thus explaining the opening sequence in realist terms,[31] it might be more worthwhile to take a different approach and consider *Boys from the Blackstuff* as an example of popular television offering audiences the possibility of finding meaning in a variety of modes. Fiske states that "to be popular [...] television must be both polysemic and flexible."[32] Consequently, "this requires a flexible definition of the television text."[33] Among the definitions Fiske suggests is the "producerly text," which he insists must be attributed when considering television as a popular medium and he goes on to equate the producerly television text with many of the characteristics one might find in a more radical text, in particular in its capacity to produce a radical frame of mind in the spectator. He goes on to list some of the qualities of the producerly text:

> It draws attention to its own textuality, it does not produce a singular reading subject but one that is involved in the process of representation rather than a victim of it, it plays with the difference between the representation and the

real as a producerly equivalent of the writerly mixing of documentary and fictional modes, and it replaces the pleasures of identification and familiarity with the more cognitive pleasures of participation and production. But it does not do this in a so-called "radical" way: it does not emphasize differences between itself and more familiar modes of representation, it does not address itself to a minority, alienated group in society. Rather it treats its readers as members of a semiotic democracy, already equipped with the discursive competencies to make meanings and motivated by pleasure to want to participate in the process.[34]

The traditional realism gives way to more pleasurable, multiple meanings and renders the viewers active in the remaking of their own representation.

This paper began with a question: whether *Boys from the Blackstuff* could be said to have reconfigured the representation of the working class through the aesthetic discourse of television drama. As I close this essay I find the question has been answered in the popular reception given to the drama since the appeal the series had among a working-class audience would seem to validate its credentials as a work of art—a re-presentation—that has problematized the everyday working-class condition of the 1980s. Rather than cutting its audience loose in a sea of self-identification with its working-class characters as so many classic social realist television productions might have done, *Boys from the Blackstuff* has succeeded in instilling in its audience a desire to question the dominant cultural representations that the mere specularity of a realist drama might not have enabled them to achieve.

Notes

1. E.P. Thompson, *The Making of the English Working Class*, Harmondsworth: Penguin, 1963, 8.
2. *Ibid.*
3. *Ibid.* He particularly takes umbrage with what he terms the historians of the "Fabian orthodoxy," "in which the great majority of working people are seen as passive victims of *laissez faire*" (11) and, secondly, with "the empirical economic historians," in whose eyes "working people are seen as a labour force, as migrants, or as the data for statistical series" (11).
4. *Ibid.*, 12.
5. *Ibid.*
6. Critical applause for the series came from all sectors of society, from academic film and television critics: "a seminal drama series [...] a warm, humorous but ultimately tragic look at the way economics affect ordinary people [...]. TV's most complete dramatic response to the Thatcher era and as a lament to the end of a male, working class British culture" (Phil Wickham, *Boys from the Blackstuff: BFI Dossier 20*, London: BFI, 1984); or "the effectiveness and impact of *Boys from the Blackstuff*, [...] was in its readiness to deal with the lived experiences of a large number of people faced or dealing with the prospect of unemployment" (John Kirk, *Twentieth-Century Writing and the British Working Class*, Cardiff: University of Wales Press, 2003, 84) or from journalists looking back at the series: "a powerful depiction of the despair of unemployment in the early 1980s" (Paul Coslett, "*Boys from the Blackstuff*," BBC Liverpool, October 11, 2007) and from local Liverpool reporters again reassessing the writing of Alan Bleasdale: "Bleasdale started a debate and brought

drama into a new era. He made people laugh and cry and I think that this was his golden time—with *Blackstuff*, he was like a modern-day Dickens" (Paddy Shennan, *The Liverpool Echo*, August 20, 2011).

7. John Fiske, *Television Culture*, London: Routledge, 1987, 4–5.

8. Bob Millington, "*Boys from the Blackstuff*" in George W. Brandt (ed.), *British Television Drama in the 1980s*, Cambridge, Cambridge University Press, 1993, 119.

9. Alan Bleasdale quoted in Gordon Eaton, "*Boys from the Blackstuff*: Progressive Television" in *Boys from the Blackstuff: BFI Dossier 20*, 30.

10. This has therefore led many to believe that Alan Bleasdale had not set out on a mission to demolish the policies of Margaret Thatcher as she was first elected in May 1979. However, Bleasdale has stated that by the time the series was broadcast, the fate of the unemployed in Liverpool, as depicted in the plays, resonated with what many were then experiencing in the city. Liverpool in the 1970s and 1980s, Bleasdale recalls, was a city built on casual labor and it was precisely this workforce that was going to have to pay the heaviest price in the new economic era that was being ushered in. Bleasdale simply had enough nous to sense that, at the time of writing, a politician like Thatcher was the most likely outcome at the end of the 1970s: "That battering hadn't occurred while I was writing it [*Boys from the Blackstuff*], but you would have been a fool not to know it was on the way." Alan Bleasdale in interview with Paddy Shennan, *The Liverpool Echo*, August 20, 2011.

11. Philip Saville (born 1930 in London) began his career as an actor in the 1950s before turning to television drama direction. He was well-known for his innovative visual style, which first came to the forefront in the ITV series *Armchair Theatre*. The rapid, intricate camera work, which was his hallmark, was doubled by a keen interest in psychological states and subjective viewpoints, both of which feature in his direction of *Boys from the Blackstuff*. In the mid–1960s he began using video tape to film on location (his *Hamlet in Elsinore* was shot on location using this method in 1964). He pursued further experimental techniques, mixing video production with the techniques of film. Saville was a late-in-the-day choice for the direction of *Boys from the Blackstuff*, but the techniques he brought with him undoubtedly contributed to the series' huge success.

12. *Boys from the Blackstuff: BFI Dossier 20*, 18.

13. Ibid.

14. Greg Miller interview on http://www.pebblemill.org/blog/boys-from-the-blackstuff-video-of-film-editor-greg-miller/, accessed August 2013.

15. Richard Paterson, Introduction to *Boys from the Blackstuff: BFI Dossier 20*, 2.

16. Northern realism is defined by Bob Millington as "an influential generic trend in British fiction that extends across print and screen media. Northern realism fulfils a significant and socially progressive role in TV by providing a space for the exploration of working-class life. [...] The fictions characteristically focus on the day-to-day lives of individuals living in an industrial 'Northern' (or at least regional) setting and stress the resolution of social problems within narratives focused on personal events, such as the task of winning a suitable partner." He lists plays such as *Our Day Out* (script by Willy Russell, 1977), police series such as *Z Cars* (BBC, 1962–1978) and sitcoms such as *Liver Birds* (BBC, 1969–1978) and—the longest-running drama program on TV—*Coronation Street* (Granada, 1960–) as emblematic of Northern TV fiction. While *Boys from the Blackstuff* shares some of these conventions (unemployment, domestic space, self-betterment), it is noticeably devoid of any sexual or romantic intrigue. Millington, "*Boys from the Blackstuff*" in George W. Brandt (ed.), *British Television Drama in the 1980s*, 124.

17. Tony Thwaites, Lloyd Davis, Warwick Mules, *Introducing Cultural and Media Studies: A Semiotic Approach*, London: Palgrave, 1994, 145.

18. See Millington, "*Boys from the Blackstuff*" in George W. Brandt (ed.), *British Television Drama in the 1980s*, 119.

19. With the rise of websites such as *9GAG* (http://9gag.com/) or *Giphy* (http://giphy.com/), audiences have made a habit of transforming various "cultural resources" into different formats (animated images—or "gifs"—stills taken from films or series, etc.). There is now evidence that character cues in dialogue are also being used in this way. Today's technologically-astute audiences would have a field day with the catchphrases of Yosser Hughes.

20. *Boys from the Blackstuff: BFI Dossier 20*, 11.

21. Fiske, *Television Culture*, 205.

22. *Ibid.*, 206.

23. Raymond Williams, *Politics and Letters: Interviews with New Left Review*, London: New Left Review Books, 1979, 159.

24. Raymond Williams, "The Tenses of the Imagination" in *Writing in Society*, London: Verso, 1983, 264–263.

25. Gordon Eaton, "*Boys from the Blackstuff*: Progressive Television?" in *Boys from the Blackstuff: BFI Dossier 20*, 31.

26. Bob Millington does point out, however, that even the surrealist experimentation in the opening scene of "Yosser's Story" is contained within a logical, coherent framework, as the viewers are invited to understand the images as one of Yosser's dreams: "In this way, the viewer is able to accept the experimentation with dramatic style with some confidence and accept the surprises produced in the narrative as broadly representative of the vicissitudes of life." Millington, "*Boys from the Blackstuff*" in George W. Brandt (ed.), *British Television Drama in the 1980s*, 127–128.

27. Richard Paterson, "Introduction" to *Boys from the Blackstuff: BFI Dossier 20*, 12.

28. Raymond Williams, *Television: Technology and Cultural Form*, London: Fontana, 1974, 27.

29. Raymond Williams, "Distance," in *What I Came to Say*, London: Hutchinson Radius, 1989, 39. See also Alan O'Connor (ed.), *Raymond Williams on Television: Selected Writings*, London: Routledge, 1989, 16. Essay originally published in *The London Review of Books*, 17–30 June 1982, 19–20.

30. *Ibid.*, 43.

31. See note 28.

32. Fiske, *Television Culture*, 84.

33. *Ibid.*

34. *Ibid.*, 95.

Works Cited

Brandt, George W. *British Television Drama in the 1980s*. Cambridge: Cambridge University Press, 1993.

Coslett, Paul. "*Boys from the Blackstuff*." BBC Liverpool, October 11, 2007.

Eaton, Gordon. "*Boys from the Blackstuff*: Progressive Television" in *Boys from the Blackstuff: BFI Dossier 20*. London: BFI, 1984, 30–34.

Fiske, John. *Television Culture*. London: Routledge, 1987.

Kirk, John. *Twentieth-Century Writing and the British Working Class*. Cardiff: University of Wales Press, 2003.

Miller, Greg. Interview: http://www.pebblemill.org/blog/boys-from-the-blackstuff-video-of-film-editor-greg-miller/, accessed August 2013.

Millington, Bob. "*Boys from the Blackstuff*" in George W. Brandt (ed.), *British Television Drama in the 1980s*. Cambridge: Cambridge University Press, 1993, 119–139.

Paterson, Richard. "Introduction" in *Boys from the Blackstuff: BFI Dossier 20*. London: BFI, 1984, 1–3.

Shennan, Paddy. Preview to *Boys from the Blackstuff*, reunion program on Radio 4, *The Liverpool Echo*, August 20, 2011.

Thompson E. P. *The Making of the English Working Class*. Harmondsworth: Penguin, 1963.

Thwaites, Tony, Lloyd Davis, and Warwick Mules. *Introducing Cultural and Media Studies: A Semiotic Approach*. London: Palgrave, 1994.

Williams, Raymond. *Television: Technology and Cultural Form*, London: Fontana, 1974.

Williams, Raymond. *Politics and Letters: Interviews with New Left Review*. London: New Left Review Books, 1979.

Williams, Raymond. "The Tenses of the Imagination." *Writing in Society*. London: Verso, 1983, 259–268.

Williams, Raymond. *What I Came to Say*. London: Hutchinson Radius, 1989.

From Documentary to Docudrama
Post-War British Television and the Social Issues of the Lower Classes

GEORGES FOURNIER

Authored television programs helped make social classes more visible although, according to the wildest detractors of the new medium, television used social and political issues as an alibi designed to increase its legitimacy. Opponents of the new medium disparaged it even before it became popular and, from their point of view, television was intrinsically entertaining.[1] Fortunately, for television's supporters, this criticism did not rally a general consensus in Great Britain and from the mid–1950s onwards many, among the eminent documentary makers of the interwar period, decided to become involved in the new challenge.

After the failure of Group 3,[2] a filmmaking training structure which he chaired from 1951 to 1955, John Grierson, usually considered as the father of the British documentary movement, pioneered for television. From 1957 to 1967, he shared the adventure of STV, a private channel. He was in charge of *This Wonderful World*, an eclectic documentary series which he produced, edited and presented almost single-handedly. For both John Grierson and young filmmakers, it marked a transition from cinema to television and from documentary to intergeneric formats. The time had come for hybrid productions, designed to inform in an entertaining way, to flood British screens, both big and small. Such is the conclusion Stephen Frears reaches in his movie about British cinema: *Typically British* (1995). In this film, the director blames popular Hollywood productions for the fatal decline of post-war British cinema and the supremacy of fiction. Very early in the history of filmic representations, American cinema producers became aware of the interest fiction represented for the industry of entertainment; conversely British cinema openly favored a political usage of it.

Another reason for the decline of British cinema was the unrivalled attraction television held over talented British moviemakers. After World War II, most British directors were trained by television and, more precisely, by the BBC. The first productions for television, to which British viewers answered enthusiastically, promoted educational and political issues. The results of the British Film Institute investigation[3] carried out among viewers in 2000 and regarding the best twenty programs ever broadcast on British television screens prove it. The final results of this investigation listed a large number of docudramas among which was *Cathy Come Home* (1966), Ken Loach's early television film about the plight of the homeless, which held the second place, all categories included. These television undertakings aimed to arouse the political consciousness of the population, even though not all the British households were equipped with TV sets and those who were wealthy enough to have one were not necessarily sensitive to the representations of the issues of the downtrodden. As for the few not-so-wealthy who yet had one, it was more an element of socialization than education or information.[4] An examination of the representations of the underprivileged should provide key elements to understand how filmmakers used television, and in particular a hybrid genre like docudrama, to increase the visibility of political issues.

Documenting Social Classes

In the wake of the 1929 Great Depression, King Vidor shot *Our Daily Bread* (1934), which offered the audience a harmonious narrative that combined evidential information about the population's condition of rural exodus and a fictional story around the survival of a group of individuals. About *Our Daily Bread*, King Vidor declared:

> Today, when I run my film *Our Daily Bread* (1934) for new audiences I am always asked if the performers were real down-and-out people or they were cast through an actor's agency in Hollywood.[5]

The same realistic[6] touch pervades *The Grapes of Wrath* (1940) by John Ford adapted from John Steinbeck's book. Once again, fiction and reality overlapped and the director anchored his fictional narrative to the lives of migrants among whom he had lived. These movies are reminiscent of the realist tradition which King Vidor defined in the following terms:

> I began to feel I was developing a style that could integrate the seemingly disparate styles I had worked with before: the dramatic, entertaining story line with the realism and credibility of a Flaherty-type documentary.[7]

This statement was echoed years later by Tony Garnett[8] who declared:

Our own anger is reserved for the phoney objectivity, the tone of balance and fairness affected by so many programmes. We deal in fiction and tell the truth as we see it. So many self-styled "factual" programmes are full of unacknowledged bias. I suggest that you really are in danger from them and not us.[9]

Tony Garnett gave this explanation during the stormy debates which followed the distribution of *Days of Hope* (Ken Loach, 1975).[10] It encapsulated the choice of fiction to document reality, which he shared with Ken Loach. This way of reporting on reality through fiction did not undermine the documentary nature of the project in any way and the success of these productions largely inspired British representations of social issues.

By comparison with U.S. television, "British TV was small, dull, slow, poor, starved and amateurish"; this statement extracted from Waldman's 1953 Report[11] highlighted the serious and unappealing character of British fiction, as seen by foreigners. As a recommendation, the report advised the British film profession to imitate the American model: "The U.S. dominates the international export market, and its style, presentation and formats tend to vary markedly from UK models."[12] An explanation for this was the treatment, by British filmmakers, of social subjects through aesthetic practices which were reminiscent of the traditional documentary, defined by Bill Nichols as the "expository documentary."[13] The same conclusions had been reached by executives from the ITV in the 1960s who resorted to the talent of Sydney Newman, a Canadian producer, to give dynamism to British drama.[14] Realistic aesthetics was seen as the most convenient way to allow viewers to have access to projects that would consist in documenting the real. Dramatized documentaries, as works that purport to document reality by resorting to fiction, were particularly suited for it. Scriptwriters and filmmakers alike were encouraged to work along these lines and to strengthen the political ambition of the new medium by presenting films which were not only entertaining but which also had a testimonial discourse. This approach was so popular at the time that even journalists were encouraged to employ it:

> Granada Television's dramatised documentary department, led by Leslie Woodhead, dramatised sequences for such documentary strands as *World in Action* (ITV, 1963–98) and made dramatised documentaries which extended the social reach of current affairs investigations.[15]

Likewise, television filmmakers gradually became aware of the appeal the new medium had on a much wider segment of the population than cinema and of the possibility to use it as an instrument to unveil the nationwide phenomena of poverty and destitution. For John Grierson, the division between fiction and documentary was not made along purely aesthetic criteria and the subject, more than its aesthetics, determined the documentary approach. From his point of view, the documentary was ontologically linked to reality. This is what he spells out in *Principles of Documentary*:

> A succeeding documentary exponent is in no way obliged to chase off to the ends of the earth in search of old-time simplicity, and the ancient dignities of man against the sky. Indeed, if I may for the moment represent the opposition, I hope the Neo-Rousseauism implicit in Flaherty's work dies with his own exceptional self. Theory of naturals apart, it represents an escapism, a wan and distant eye, which tends in lesser hands to sentimentalism.[16]

According to John Grierson, the superiority of the documentary rested on its representation of social and political issues, in the fact that it dealt with reality, and that, above all, it was neither an alibi to make moving pictures nor a form of escapism. As a committed documentary maker, John Grierson felt compelled to show the hardship of the working classes and he was particularly successful with *Drifters* (1929), *Industrial Britain* (1933) and *Coal Face* (1935). For him, the choice of sensitive, and somehow controversial issues, defined the documentary which he did not think of as a form of artistic expression. He also defined himself as a sociologist and he saw in films a means to an end. In an interview granted to *Sight and Sound* in the winter of 1934, he declared:

> I have no interest in film as such [...]. For the absolute pleasure of form a man would more wisely look to painting and be done with it [...]. I look on cinema as a pulpit and use it as a propagandist.[17]

Television greatly benefited from John Grierson's work and thinking on film. According to him, television fiction required the realistic mode which, though likely to generate hybridity, was the mode most likely to make viewers aware of the corporeality of the world:

> Realist documentary, with its streets and cities and slums and markets and exchanges and factories, has given itself the job of making poetry where no poet has gone before it [...]. It requires not only taste but also inspiration, which is to say a very laborious, deep-seeing, deep-sympathizing creative effort indeed.[18]

From the beginning of the 1960s onwards, the creation of groups or think tanks[19] on television documentary forms, designed to explore the potentialities of new hybrid genres, clearly indicated the particular place occupied by creations devoted to social and political causes.[20] The collective approach to the filmic treatment of such issues on television was innovative. Documentary makers, scriptwriters and producers of fictionalized documentaries were dedicated to spreading politically committed statements that distinguished their productions from other filmic and fictional productions meant to entertain the population. In the 1960s, such was the case with Ken Loach and Peter Watkins, who both worked for television and for cinema, and who experimented with both the documentary and the fictionalized documentary genres. *The Wednesday Play* (BBC, 1964–1970) and *Play for Today* (BBC, 1970–1984) were programs that welcomed their filmic productions among which were *3 Clear Sundays*,[21] *Up the Junction* (1965), *Cathy Come Home* and *Edna, the Inebriate Woman* (1971). These productions were closer to journalistic programs, like *Panorama* (BBC, 1953–2008) and *Tonight* (BBC, 1957–1965), than to purely entertaining ones like *The Quatermass Experiment*, BBC's sci-fi series (1958–1959), and *Monitor*, BBC's art program (1958–1964).

Television spectatorship, which was shaped by the realistic mode made familiar by Hollywood, largely benefited from this combination through the hybrid form of the docudrama. The television directors of the 1960s offered British viewers docudramas that remained faithful to the social and political issues of the time, although they reassessed the fictional dimension of their representations, particularly in the way the filmic material was articulated.

Sources of Inspiration

Television was not very creative in its early years, yet it possessed the power to mix and to reprocess formulae already tested in other domains, be it literature, drama, cinema or radio. *Homeless Families*, the 1960 radio program made by Jeremy Sandford, gave birth a few years later to *Cathy Come Home* which borrowed extensively from the vocabulary and dialogues first heard in the radio broadcast.[22]

At its outset, and in many respects, television was heavily dependent on radio. Television appropriated the flagship programs tested on the radio and adapted them to its audience.[23] Very early on, radio was edged out by television in terms of audience records and it could but witness the dazzling rise of the new medium, at least quantitatively. As explained by Renée Dickason in her book on British radio and television, from the mid-1950s television outstripped its rival. One of the most popular ways the radio reported on the day-to-day realities of the population in a hybrid way was represented by *Radio Ballads*,[24] a program broadcast on BBC2 from 1958 onwards and that later became a genre.[25] Charles Parker, its creator, defined it in the following terms:

> A form of narrative documentary in which the story is told entirely in the words of the actual participants themselves as recorded in real life; in sound effects which are also recorded on the spot, and in songs which are based

upon these recordings, and which utilise traditional or "folk-song" modes of expression.[26]

Radio Ballads largely inspired television docudrama filmmakers. Its purpose was to inform listeners about the workers' lives by means of songs and music. A preliminary work of documentation was undertaken, during which testimonies were recorded. The result was then inserted into a narrative so that eventually it would be suitable for folk music adaptation. In many respects, this formula was reminiscent of the story documentary[27] since it was highly informative. Forerunner to the docudrama, the story documentary had much in common with the radio ballad. Both highlighted the everyday through the lives of ordinary individuals who were represented in emblematic situations. Both owed much to the documentary tradition to which British cinema was strongly anchored. Both used new techniques to report on reality, not a reality that was glamorous and fascinating, but the reality of the everyday life of the working class, in a way that was at once original and capable of eliciting belief and credence. Because lyricism largely pervaded these creations, their credibility rested on the fact that they rang true: emphasis was put on the right choice of lexicon and on regional accents which were suggestive of the social class that was described. The selected terminology endowed the songs with credit by referring to the everyday life of the people. The highly suggestive nature of this terminology contributed to the accuracy of the representation; it was designed to echo the collective images which were conveyed by the documentary nature of the work. Themes, which were very similar to those of the story documentary, would be the opportunity to investigate jobs in the steel industry and in the fishing industry with narratives which were reminiscent of the drama-documentary.[28] *The Ballad of John Axon*[29] is a good example of such a genre: through the life and the accidental death of the hero of this elegy, it tells the epic story of rail in Great Britain the way Basil Wright did in *Night Mail* (1936).[30]

Radio ballads abode by the rules laid down by the documentary: the search for information was followed by a search for the adequate narrative treatment to be applied and the final touch to the construction was brought by the capture of sound effects designed to evoke the atmosphere of the place and time. They did not refer to some distant past and *The Ballad of John Axon* was broadcast less than a year after the accident in which this railroad employee lost his life. As in the drama-documentary, the names of the people, the names of the places, the dates and the circumstances of the events referred to were scrupulously respected. More than the fatal accident John Axon was the victim of, this ballad evoked the conditions of the working class, the way Ken Loach showed them in *Up the Junction*. *Radio Ballads* were remembered as social testimonies about the difficulties people were going through and the subjects and titles of the sequels made by the BBC, at the beginning of the 21st century, testify to it: *The Song of Steel, Thirty Years of Conflict, The Ballad of the Big Ships, The Ballad of the Miners' Strike.*[31]

The hybrid nature of these creations lay in the association of testimonies, of fragments of information taken from the radio news reports, as well as from songs; the lyrics were then laced with evidential elements that served to flesh out the portrait of the people chosen to illustrate the issue. The porosity between information and entertainment stood at the origin of the controversy about the intentions of hybrid genres like the radio ballads and the docudramas: were they designed to be informative or propagandist in their treatment of social issues?

In search of aesthetic criteria that would be suitable to convey a strong political message, documentary fiction also turned to work done by political playwrights; it drew much of its inspiration from Berthold Brecht's political pieces. In Great Britain, the German playwright's work found echoes, during the interwar period, in the experiments carried out by Joan Littlewood. In a BBC1 program broadcast on April 19, 1994, and dedicated to her company, she explained how she experimented with the fictional treatment of topical events with committed drama, better known under the name of *Living Newspaper*. Famous at the time in the United States,[32] Russia and Germany, the formula consisted in the extraction of pieces of information from the press to which the theatre companies would bring a critical treatment. This constituted the foundation of the fiction. Joan Littlewood would compare this type of performance to journalistic "happening." She saw in her work of dramatized information a political manifesto designed to make the spectator more aware of her controversial standpoint.

Regarding the production teams of the 1960s, she was particularly influential among scriptwriters who proved highly sensitive to her progressive ideas. Jim Allen (*The Lumpfish*, 1967; *The Big Flame*, 1969), Jeremy Sandford (*Cathy Come Home*, 1966; *Edna, the Inebriate Woman*, 1971) and Nell Dunn (*Up the Junction*, 1965; *Poor Cow*, 1967) followed in her footsteps and opted for the treatment of politically committed subjects which would regularly hit the headlines. In the 1960s and 1970s, these topics were abortion (*Up the Junction*, 1965), the lack of healthy accommodation (*Cathy Come Home*, 1966), uncertainties regarding employment (*The Lumpfish*, 1967), labor disputes (*The Big Flame*, 1969), old age (*Edna, the Inebriate Woman*, 1971) and social determinism (*Poor Cow*, 1967). The working class origins of some of these scriptwriters, Jim Allen and David Mercer in particular, made them more liable to report on what they had been through. Their experience, which became invaluable first-hand material, gave a documentary dimension to all the fiction films they would take part in.

Politics and Fiction

After the years of rationing which followed the Second World War, the British mobilized around the social claims which had been silenced by the war efforts. The demand for more welfare measures had already been articulated long before the war: *Bread* (1934), a collective film from the Kino Production Group and *Housing Problems* (Edgar Anstey, 1935) were two major movies which dramatized the concerns of the poor. New filmmakers from the middle class, who found training at the BBC, resumed the cinematic project of the representation of the lower class.[33] The ambition these new recruits nurtured for the television of the 1960s was for it to be by the people and for the people.

At the time, scriptwriters and filmmakers would often opt for docudrama because its melodramatic dimension, which afforded an elegant compromise between comedy and tragedy, lent itself to an attractive presentation of important issues. Among the most prominent issues were poverty, alcoholism, abortion and the placement of children in foster homes. A subtle plot would allow for the complex development of issues instead of a sociological or philosophical treatment that might be deemed too austere for television viewers. While such programs fitted John Reith's vision of quality television as an educational medium, they also aimed to make up for the lack of secondary education of a large section of the population by providing them with contents that would not only entertain, but also inform them.[34]

Melodrama occupied an important role in the fiction films mentioned above: while Culture, with a capital "C," claims sovereignty over tragedy, a genre that speaks about those who hold power, melodrama is all about those who are subjected to it. While tragedy is esoteric and its hidden meaning must be revealed, melodrama is exoteric and its meaning is explicit and concrete, hence its use for a less literate audience. The adaptations of novels and plays from literature by the filmmakers of the 1960s were soon replaced by fiction films from scriptwriters who tapped into their experiences of the working class.[35] In this type of fiction film, heightened emotions are dramatized and the moral of the story must meet both ethics and popular justice. Cathy, in *Cathy Come Home*, induces empathy and the viewer follows her through the joys and carelessness of youth and through the distress and confusion of early motherhood when her children are put in foster families because she fails to provide decent accommodation for them. Cathy and her husband, Reg, are unprepared for urban modernity and are consequently easy prey: they have not mastered the codes of both urbanity and modernity and their improvidence makes them vulnerable to unsympathetic landlords and civil servants.

The documentary-fiction films of the 1960s on British public channels set up the matrix of what became a genre intended to educate the population. Originally, British public television was fashioned on a social-democratic pattern. Following the Fabian outlook on social issues,[36] it set the education of the masses as its main political objective. The filmmakers' works were eminently political. They confronted viewers with situations of distress, with disaster scenarios to make them aware of the dangers that threatened them so as to spur them to challenge politicians on social progress: from the day after its broadcasting *Cathy Come Home* shook British society and contributed to the publicity around the creation of Shelter two weeks later, on December 1, 1966,[37] and to the revision of the law on accommodation, namely the 1924 Housing Act.[38]

Similarly, the opposition of Harold Wilson's Labour government to the broadcasting of Peter Watkins's *The War Game* (1966) proved that the pioneers of television were right and that Peter Watkins's movie reached its goal in terms of public awareness of the dangers of nuclear power.[39] The originality of this docudrama consisted in adopting a different approach to the topic and turning a recurring issue into a topical one. The debate over the usage of nuclear power for military purposes and its impact on civilians had been going on for a long time, in particular ever since the Hiroshima and Nagasaki bombings. By turning this information into a topical issue, Peter Watkins changed its status and shed an unusual light on it. The same treatment was applied to the housing problem which suddenly, with Cathy and the difficulties she was going through, was no longer an abstract political issue, but a personal one that was treated in a human way. By giving a face to homelessness, Ken Loach extracted the housing problem from the invisibility into which it had fallen because of the repeated usage politicians and journalists had made of it, without ever solving it. With *Cathy Come Home*, it really became a top-priority for the British society and for its politicians. The strength of this movie lay in its capacity to be a documentary despite its trappings of fiction.

All the films mentioned in this paper revolved around a fluid narrative that rested on the principles of analogy, projection and identification, which are typical of fiction.[40] Yet, these features did not undermine the documentary intention of the filmmakers but, on the contrary, increased it by giving the films heightened credibility. Though Ken Loach had no intention of deceiving the viewer with regards to the fictional nature of Cathy and her family's (mis)adventures, he nevertheless stressed the testimonial value of his work. The precariousness of the livelihoods of a growing part of the population was then becoming a reality of modern England and the insertion of testimonies from experts in the film made this plain.

British Television as a Window onto Political Issues

Television works as an amplifier; it selects and revisits issues previously tackled by other media and offers them to a national audience. The BBC, because of its monopoly as unique British public channel, has often been accused of taking advantage of its privileged status to encourage socially and politically oriented works, as explained by James MacTaggart: "It [the BBC] could absorb, indeed it needed, a lot of controversial, energetic, imaginative, young people to push it on apace, even in front of 20 million people."[41] The broadcasting of a committed program like *Days of Hope* by Ken Loach, on BBC1 in 1975, stands as a perfect illustration of this. The series of four episodes was designed as a saga that spanned a period of over a decade—from the First World War to the General Strike of 1926—and dealt with the everyday difficulties of a working-class family. The purpose of the trio that initiated the saga—Jim Allen, Tony Garnett and Ken Loach—was to embolden the population, to urge them to think and act politically in a period which was conducive to it: the social movements of the 1970s in the British industry were reminiscent of those of the 1920s. *Days of Hope* started a spate of scathing articles in the British press from both the army and the political circles.[42]

Concerning the channels, the partition between the public and the private corresponds more to a myth than to a reality: though the BBC succeeded in avoiding deregulated policies for a few decades after the resumption of television, its executives very quickly gave in to pressures from politicians who encouraged "joint ventures between public service broadcasters and private companies."[43] The praiseworthy comments made to the BBC for its courage, its commitment and its righteousness can however, and in many respects, also apply to the private sector. While the BBC scheduled *Up the Junction* on November 3, 1965, ITV had broadcast nine months earlier, on February 4, 1965, a documentary on the subject: *Abortion—A Law for the Rich?* This program showed how the poor were more likely to be affected by unwanted pregnancy and how they would be less likely to obtain help from the social services.[44] Actually, it had almost gone without being noticed though it was relevant both in its approach and its treatment of abortion as a social and political issue; its title stood to prove it. Two years earlier, on October 3, 1963, the same team from *This Week*, the ITV weekly information magazine, had already raised the subject for the first time with a less catchy and more consensual title, *Birth Control*. Nevertheless, with *Up the Junction*, Ken Loach's movie about abortion, the BBC was breaking fresh ground: up until then the subject had never been treated through fiction. Ken Loach's choice of a publicly-owned channel proved wise: because it was broadcast on the BBC, his film reached a wide audience despite it being offensive to many.[45] Nevertheless, ITV, the private channel, had proved even bolder by running the risk of displeasing advertisers who would not necessarily appreciate connections with a program that promoted abortion.

The representation of social classes was facilitated by programs like *The Wednesday Play* (1964–1970) and *Play for Today* (1970–1984) intended to perpetuate the political vocation of television by offering hybrid fiction films meant to be disquieting without being antagonizing.[46] For many years after the resumption of television, the political dimension of the publicly-owned channels consisted in offering filmic productions of the classics of the world's literature in an effort to make up for the absence of secondary education among large sections of the population. For many years, *The Wednesday Play* fulfilled this assignment. Yet with the gradual disappearance of the older generation of television executives, *The Wednesday Play* changed from an "academic" program to a public agora. With new recruits, including educated people from the working class, *The Wednesday Play* started offering the British population the first filmic representations of the difficulties of those who, up until then, had only been represented tangentially on television. The stories in *Z-Cars* (ITV, 1962–1978) and *Dixon of Dock Green* (BBC, 1955–1976) would often take place among the destitute, yet it was the criminal aspects that were emphasized.

The evolution from *The Wednesday Play* to *Play for Today* further accentuated this trend and a gradual change from dramatic and literary classics to social realism took place. Fiction proved invaluable to this new generation of television filmmakers. *Edna, the Inebriate Woman*, broadcast on October 21, 1971, stands as emblematic of this new approach of television: Irene Shubik, the then producer of *Play for Today*, qualified it as a "blockbuster."[47] The huge success this movie met among viewers and in the profession alike is undoubtedly to the credit of Jeremy Sandford who was the screenwriter, and who, a few years earlier, had worked on *Cathy Come Home*. Because of its focus on Edna, a poor and homeless character, *Edna, the Inebriate Woman* allowed the public service corporation to renew with the British tradition of documenting the lives of the less fortunate in a realistic way. The images of poverty were without concessions to political correctness; both language and manners were coarse and Edna was both violent and uncompromising.

Authored Television and Collaborations

In the early years of television, executives were undecided about what the new medium should be aesthetically and thematically: was it doomed to offer filmed drama and promote classical culture *ad infinitum*? It is only in the early 1960s, when freed from the constraints of studios, that it acquired the fluidity and the flexibility for which it has since become so popular. In the wake of the newly acquired freedom from technological constraints came the freedom to opt for topics less likely to please the ruling classes, who had worked to promote it, but more likely to please its mainstream audience. Docudrama was strongly fashioned, in its early years, by scriptwriters, such as Jim Allen and David Mercer, who were acclaimed for instilling in their works the personal and professional experiences of men and women from the working class.

"For the young in the 1950s, there were more opportunities than ever before,"[48] and directors like Ken Loach and Stephen Frears belonged to the first generation of those who enjoyed the benefits of facilitated access to education. As a token of loyalty to their origins, these filmmakers took advantage of their place at the heart of the mainstream medium to grant visibility to those scrupulously neglected by an ethic of Reithian inspiration, which sought to mimic an upper-class model. Ken Loach and Jim Allen's works reflected Jim Allen's faith in a revolutionary socialism and testified to his past in the industry as a trade union member and grassroots activist.

Competing in the exploration of filmic hybridity, the channels set up structures composed of scriptwriters, directors and professionals which were designed to create popular though challenging television programs.[49] These professionals were assigned to explore the limits of the documentary model within the television medium. These structures would often hinge on tandems—scriptwriters and directors—which gave television its most famous political productions and gave visibility to different social classes. Their successes earned them the title of "school." The notion of "school" is traditionally used to mention the works produced for and by the BBC between the 1950s and the 1960s. This is the way the Loach–Garnett tandem was referred to: their main characteristic was the choice of social subjects to which the scriptwriter and the director would apply a realistic treatment. Their detractors would call this "naturalist." The Loach-Garnett School corresponded to the naturalistic-style docudrama, after the fashion of *Up the Junction*. "School" referred to a way of narrating and to the choice of subjects which represented major disruptions to what was then the rule on television and to what was expected by viewers.

The notion of "school" for the scriptwriter-director tandems meant shared views and opinions regarding the future of filmic practices on television. More prosaically, for reasons of budgetary constraints, television did not originally have directors and this responsibility would often be shared by the scriptwriter and the director, which meant teamwork, a feature specific to television.[50] As television programs sprang from collective work, they would then stand in sharp contrast with the personal and brilliant vision of the "movie director" of feature films which would reduce their authorship.

Attached to the notion of "school" is that of "author," around which is crystallized the contrast between art and industry, between cinema and television. Because it corresponds to a personal and committed claim, docudrama contributes to the bridging of this gap between the two media and confers on the channel which welcomes it the opportunity to offer viewers a moment of authored television. Retrospectively, docudrama stands as the standard by which the quality of programs on television can be assessed as proved by the 2000 British Film Institute investigation.[51] The popularity of this genre is accounted for by the fact that docudrama lends itself to the treatment of social and political issues and that it uses empathy as the means to achieve it.

The working classes have been the object and subject of very popular series to which prominent British directors and producers, like Ken Loach and Tony Garnett, contributed. Both started their career in the fiction department of the BBC in the early 1960s and took part in the very popular police series *Z-Cars* in which the hardship of the new urban working classes was staged. Ken Loach's collaboration with Tony Garnett,[52] a native of the Midlands too, proved crucial. In the innovative environment of public broadcasting of the 1960s, they both contributed to the implementation of fiction films which pioneered new filmic terrains both in the choice of subjects and aesthetics. As a producer, Tony Garnett was constantly in search of new scenarios that would be major breakthroughs and that would introduce changes from the staging of classic literature. For Ken Loach, public-service broadcasting represented an ideal structure for the adaptation of the then new technologies to his political ambitions as director. *The Wednesday Play*, the weekly formula that would accommodate unprecedented works of fiction, offered once-in-a-lifetime opportunities to these television reformers. The filmic adaptation of sensitive issues, something which had never been done up until then, was introduced to a very wide audience in prime-time slots. Retrospectively, *The Wednesday Play* afforded an insight into the evolution of the modern lifestyle. Although

Cathy Come Home—from the *Wednesday Play* series—is neither Ken Loach's first film nor his most shocking, it has remained in the memory of the British viewers because it prompted social mobilization and helped advance the cause of those in distress. This movie represented the prototype of the documentary drama as fashioned by the Loach–Garnett tandem. The "realistic" adjective attached to it corresponds to the choice of a theme anchored in the everyday lives of those who are threatened with unemployment, evictions, promiscuity, and harassment from cold-hearted civil servants. The avant-gardism of its aesthetics rests on the choice of light and handy filmic material, which allowed for effects of immediacy: the image is as close as possible to observed reality and to what both the documentary and the news report genres would offer. The choice of an asynchronous sound, of natural light, of scenarios on which amateur actors would improvise increased the feeling of closeness and credibility. Although the success of his creations made Ken Loach one of the most acclaimed British filmmakers, he has remained loyal to television, which he considers to be an unrivalled way to get political messages across.

While the British documentaries of the inter-war period had shown British workers at the workplace carrying out their professional activities, the television docudramas of the 1960s entered the households, dissected the human soul and considered the links between social problems and the difficulties which most of the disadvantaged classes encountered. It also succeeded in fulfilling the political vocation that John Reith had originally bestowed upon television film: namely to entertain, educate and inform. The reverberations of these programs on British society as a whole were numerous and politicians and parliamentary men would carefully follow the broadcasting of these programs, as they proved indicative of evolutions to come. Their impact was all the more effective as the documentary widely borrowed from fiction in an attempt to become more appealing to a popular audience. However, under pressure from the politicians who wished to abolish its monopoly, public television soon ceased to be openly political and the privately-owned channels took over the challenge by offering programs designed to "rock the boat and make mischief."[53] One-off docudramas and mini-series on both Channel 4 and ITV, by prominent docudrama filmmakers like Peter Kosminsky and Paul Greengrass, have recently helped raise the awareness of the British viewership on such issues as politics, both domestic and international, and integration. Yet, the social issues and the representation of the poor are no longer topics that inspire producers of docudramas and fiction films. Continuity has been maintained differently in this field with programs such *EastEnders* and *Coronation Street*, whose broadcasting, for decades,[54] has aimed at a greater understanding of the social issues of the lower class, though in a tangential way.

Notes

1. "Since television programmes and television regulations have been largely made by well-educated and socially powerful elite groups in society, the underlying ideology of television regulation has considered the less socially powerful and less well-educated mass audience of television as vulnerable and prone to bad influences in the same way that children might be. Theodor Adorno and the Frankfurt School considered that the mass media perpetuated what we now call 'dumbing down.'" Jonathan Bignell, *An Introduction to Television Studies*, London: Routledge, 2004, 242.
2. "Placed under the aegis of the National Film Finance Corporation, Group 3 had as function to supply young talents of the cinema, whether they were actors or directors, with the assistance of experienced professionals. Having failed, at the end of four years, to make a profit out of the investments granted by the State, the structure was dissolved." Guy Gauthier and Philippe Pilard, *Télévision passive, télévision active*, Paris: Téma Éditions, 1972, 100 (translation by the author of the present article).
3. BFI TV 100: http://en.wikipedia.org/wiki/BFI_TV_100, accessed 20 September 2014.
4. A TV set would often gather many households and different generations together.
5. King Wallis Vidor, *King Vidor on Filmmaking*, New York: David McKay, 1972, 186.
6. In the present paper, "realism," when applied to aesthetics, refers to what John Fiske and John Hartley in *Reading Television* define as "the mode in which the fictional story is presented [...] the natural representation of the way things are: a story may be fictional, but the way it is related tells it like it is." As for realism to refer to topics, it is to be understood as synonymous with "naturalism."
7. Vidor, *King Vidor on Film Making*.
8. "From the mid-1960s to the end of the 1970s Tony Garnett was one of British television's most controversial figures, responsible for producing some of the most politically radical drama ever to have been made in the UK, much of it in collaboration with director Ken Loach." http://www.screenonline.org.uk/people/id/467672/, accessed 12 December 2014.
9. http://www.screenonline.org.uk/tv/id/467647/, accessed 12 July 2014.
10. *Days of Hope* (1975) was a four-episode TV series produced by Tony Garnett, written by Jim Allen and directed by Ken Loach. It dealt with the lives of a working-class family from the First World War to the General Strike of 1926, but had a strong contemporary resonance in a context of industrial unrest. http://www.screenonline.org.uk/tv/id/467647/, accessed 7 September 2014.
11. Susan Sydney-Smith, *Beyond Dixon of Dock Green: Early British Police Series*, London: I.B. Tauris, 2002, 93.
12. Ibid.
13. "Expository films adopt either a voice-of-God commentary (the speaker is heard but never seen), such as we find in the *Why We Fight* series, *Victory at Sea* (1952–1953), *The City* (1939), *Blood of the Beasts* (1949), and *Dead Birds* (1963), or utilize a voice-of-authority commentary (the speaker is heard and also seen), such as we find in television newscasts." Bill Nichols, *An Introduction to Documentary*, Bloomington: Indiana University Press, 2001, 105.
14. Tony Currie, *A Concise History of British Television, 1930–2000*, Tiverton: Kelly Publications, 2004, 55.
15. http://www.screenonline.org.uk/tv/id/1103146/, accessed 12 December 2014.
16. John Grierson, *Grierson on Documentary*, London: Faber and Faber, 1946, 38.
17. Leila Wimmer, *Cross-Channel Perspective: The French Reception of British Cinema*, London: Peter Lang, 2009, 60.
18. Grierson, *Grierson on Documentary*, 41.
19. "Programmes calling themselves 'drama-documentaries,' or to which others have applied that (or a similar) label, have emerged in British television on many occasions, for example: at the BBC, between 1946 and 1960, the Dramatised Documentary Group made a number of documentary programmes which demanded dramatisation, due to the undeveloped state of recording technology." Andrew Goodwin and Paul Kerr, *Drama-documentary, Dossier 19*, London: BFI, 1984, 3.
20. "In 1946, the BBC's postwar resumption of television transmissions had been marked, among other things, by the formation of a new unit, the Dramatised Documentary Group. Developing out of the BBC's obligation to document the new postwar Britain, the group was an outgrowth of the Illustrated Talks Department and was soon responsible for a large number of what the Radio Times

described as 'story documentaries' with scripts, sets, and actors reconstructing (and thus 'documenting') an inaccessible world." Andrew Goodwin and Garry Whannel, *Understanding Television*, London: Routledge, 1992, 77.

21. Ken Loach's 1965 docudrama against death penalty.

22. Derek Paget, "Tales of Cultural Tourism" in Alan Rosenthal (ed.), *Why Docudrama? Fact-Fiction on Film and TV*, Carbondale: Southern Illinois University Press, 1999, 52.

23. "The formula organized by 'Radio Ballad', broadcast on BBC2 from 1958, represented an important source of inspiration for television." Official site of BBC2, http://www.bbc.co.uk/radio2/r2music/folksong//, accessed 10 November 2014.

24. "Radio Ballad" refers to the radio program and "radio ballad" to the genre it spawned.

25. Renée Dickason, *Radio et télévision britanniques*, Rennes: Presses universitaires de Rennes, 1999, 272.

26. BBC Press Office, *The 2006 Radio Ballads*: http://www.bbc.co.uk/pressoffice/pressreleases/stories/2006/02_february/05/ballads.shtml, accessed 12 June 2014.

27. "The Story Documentary was one of the forms used by the official documentarists of the Second World War." John Corner, *The Art of the Record: A Critical Introduction to Documentary*, Manchester: Manchester University Press, 1996, 34.

28. Georges Fournier, *British Docudrama*, InMeda, no. 3, 2013: http://inmedia.revues.org/591, accessed 20 September 2014.

29. Broadcast by BBC Radio 2, 2 July 1958.

30. Ballad available on BBC Radio 2 and accessed 15 November 2007: http://www.bbc.co.uk/radio2/radioballads/original/johnaxon.shtml.

31. "The following ballads were broadcast between 2006 and 2010: *The Song of Steel* on the decline of the Sheffield and Rotherham steel industry (27 February 2006); *The Enemy That Lives Within*, on HIV/AIDS (6 March 2006); *The Horn of the Hunter* on foxhunting (13 March 2006); *Swings and Roundabouts* on travelers who run fairgrounds (20 March 2006) *Thirty Years of Conflict* on the sectarian conflict in Northern Ireland (27 March 2006); *The Ballad of the Big Ships* on the shipyards of the Tyne and the Clyde (3 April 2006), and in 2010 the BBC broadcast *The Ballad of the Miners' Strike* to mark the 25th anniversary of the 1984–1985 Miners' Strike: http://www.bbc.co.uk/radio2/radioballads/2006/index.shtml, accessed 12 December 2014."

32. In the United States, *Newspaper Theatre* was part of the project set up by Franklin Delano Roosevelt to give work to people of the show, following the 1929 crisis. Often renewed, this initiative was definitively abandoned under McCarthyism because of the links artists of the time supposedly maintained with the European left.

33. "As a vital form, though, documentary was being lost to television in the 1960s and a new generation of filmmakers that included Ken Russell, Ken Loach, Roger Graef and Peter Watkins." Alan Burton and Steve Chibnall, *Historical Dictionary of British Cinema*, Lanham: Scarecrow Press, 2013, 142.

34. John Reith was the first general manager of the BBC (1922–1927) and its first director-general (1927–1938). His ambition was for television to be intellectually challenging and politically committed.

35. From the very beginning, British television has relied on literature and drama for a significant proportion of its output.

36. "Fabianism: British organization of socialist inspiration. Opposed to the Marxist ideology of class struggle, its members advocated equality for all by the collectivisation of property and the democratic control of national resources. Particularly active in the educational domain, they did not however establish a political party, but helped in the creation, in 1900, of the Labour Representation Committee, which gave birth, in 1906, to the Labour Party." Patrick de Laubier, *Histoire et sociologie du syndicalisme, XIXe–XXe siècle*, Paris: Masson, 1985, 78 (translated by the author of the present essay).

37. "Thanks to dynamic leadership and perfect timing of a drama documentary, *Cathy Come Home*, SHELTER raised £3 million in its first three years." Peter Williams, *Directions in Housing Policy: Towards Sustainable Housing Policies for the UK*, London: Sage, 1997, 106.

38. Revision of the 1924 Housing Act by the 1966 Housing Development (Control and Licensing) Act.

39. The people who appeared in his film were ordinary citizens who had been evacuated from London to the countryside because of the threat of a Soviet nuclear attack on the country.

40. Christian Metz, *The Imaginary Signifier: Psychoanalysis and the Cinema*, Bloomington: Indiana University Press, 1982, 42.
41. Bob Franklin, *Television Policy: The MacTaggart Lectures*, Edinburgh: Edinburgh University Press, 2005, 41–42.
42. "Letters to the *Radio Times* protested against the serial's portrayal of the Army in the First World War as 'disgusting,' 'lamentable tripe' and a 'jolly bad show.'" George W. Brandt, *British Television Drama*, Cambridge: Cambridge University Press, 1981, 28.
43. Michael Beesley, *Privatization, Regulation and Deregulation*, London: Routledge, 2013, 422.
44. "A woman who already has ten children is pregnant again, and wants an abortion. She describes how she was given pills by her GP to induce an abortion. These didn't work and she was referred to several doctors, none of whom would agree to perform the operation. She recounts how she was told that her husband's permission was necessary before she could have an abortion but she was still unable to find a doctor to perform the operation. No reasons were given; she assumed it was because it was against the law": http://www.screenonline.org.uk/tv/id/475063/synopsis.html, accessed 12 December 2014.
45. Mary Whitehouse and her National Viewers' and Listeners' Association, among others.
46. http://www.screenonline.org.uk/tv/id/454700/ and http://www.screenonline.org.uk/tv/id/454719/.
47. Chap. 10: "The 'Blockbuster': *Edna, the Inebriate Woman*" in Irene Shubik, *Play for Today: The Evolution of Television Drama*, Manchester: Manchester University Press, 2000, 105.
48. Pink Dandelion, Douglas Gwyn, Rachel Muers, Brian Phillips and Richard E. Sturm, *Towards Tragedy: Reclaiming Hope—Literature, Theology and Sociology in Conversation*, Aldershot: Ashgate, 2004, 84.
49. See note 20.
50. "Television is a team game in production." Derek Paget, "True and Truer Stories: Documentary and Drama," *Média: In Between Fiction and Reality*, Dijon: PRISM, 1994, 221.
51. http://en.wikipedia.org/wiki/BFI_TV_100, accessed 20 September 2014. These data are no longer available on the site of the British Film Institute.
52. Susan Sydney-Smith, *Beyond Dixon of Dock Green: Early British Police Series*, 264.
53. "Peter Kosminsky: Making Mischief? It's an Essential Part of the Job," *The Independent*, 16 June 2008.
54. Since 1960, for *Coronation Street*, and since 1985, for *EastEnders*.

Works Cited

Barr, Charles and Stephen Frears. *Typically British: Short History of the Cinema in Britain.* London: BFI, 1997.
Barrot, Olivier, Philippe Pilard, and Jean Queva. *L'Angleterre et son cinéma: le courant documentaire, 1927/1965.* Paris: Cinéma d'aujourd'hui, 1977.
Beesley, Michael. *Privatization, Regulation and Deregulation.* London: Routledge, 2013.
Bignell, Jonathan. *An Introduction to Television Studies.* London: Routledge, 2004.
Brandt, George W. *British Television Drama.* Cambridge: Cambridge University Press, 1981.
Burton, Alan, and Steve Chibnall. *Historical Dictionary of British Cinema.* Lanham: Scarecrow Press, 2013.
Corner, John. *The Art of the Record: A Critical Introduction to Documentary.* Manchester: Manchester University Press, 1996.
Currie, Tony. *A Concise History of British Television, 1930–2000.* Tiverton: Kelly Publications, 2004.
Dandelion, Pink, Douglas Gwyn, Rachel Muers, Brian Phillips and Richard E. Sturm. *Towards Tragedy: Reclaiming Hope—Literature, Theology and Sociology in Conversation.* Aldershot: Ashgate, 2004.
De Laubier, Patrick. *Histoire et sociologie du syndicalisme, XIXe–XXe siècle.* Paris: Masson, 1985.

Dickason, Renée. *Radio et télévision britanniques*. Rennes: Presses Universitaires de Rennes, 1999.
Freedman, Des. *Television Policies of the Labour Party: 1951–2001*. London: Frank Cass, 2003.
Franklin, Bob. *Television Policy: The MacTaggart Lectures*. Edinburgh: Edinburgh University Press, 2005.
Gauthier, Guy, and Philippe Pilard. *Télévision passive, télévision active*. Paris: Téma Éditions, 1972.
Goodwin, Andrew, and Paul Kerr. *Drama-documentary, Dossier 19*. London: BFI, 1984.
Goodwin, Andrew, and Garry Whannel. *Understanding Television*. London: Routledge, 1992.
Grierson, John. *Grierson on Documentary*. London and Boston: Faber and Faber, 1946.
Metz, Christian. *The Imaginary Signifier: Psychoanalysis and the Cinema*. Bloomington: Indiana University Press, 1982.
Nichols, Bill. *An Introduction to Documentary*. Bloomington: Indiana University Press, 2001.
Paget, Derek. "True and Truer Stories: Documentary and Drama." *Média: In Between Fiction and Reality*. Dijon: PRISM, 1994.
Paget, Derek. "Tales of Cultural Tourism" in Alan Rosenthal (ed.), *Why Docudrama? Fact-Fiction on Film and TV*. Carbondale: Southern Illinois University Press, 1999.
Paget, Derek. *No Other Way to Tell It: Docudrama on Film and Television*. Manchester: Manchester University Press, 2011.
Shubik, Irene. *Play For Today: The Evolution of Television Drama*. Manchester: Manchester University Press, 2000.
Sydney-Smith, Susan. *Beyond Dixon of Dock Green: Early British Police Series*. London: I. B. Tauris, 2002.
Vidor, King Wallis. *King Vidor on Filmmaking*. New York: David McKay, 1972.
Williams, Peter. *Directions in Housing Policy: Towards Sustainable Housing Policies for the UK*. London: Sage, 1997.
Wimmer, Leila. *Cross-Channel Perspective: The French Reception of British Cinema*. London: Peter Lang, 2009.

Part Three

Representing Class Divisions in Films

The Representation of Strike in British Cinema Since 1956
From Class to Gender and Ethnicity

ANNE-LISE MARIN-LAMELLET

Although British cinema has taken an interest in the working class for a long time, it has rarely represented labor disputes since only a dozen films have really tackled the issue of strike over the last fifty years. This somewhat limited corpus is nevertheless a good indicator of various contemporary conceptions and ideologies related to the representation of working-class strike actions. The films dealing with the subject, whether the strike is the mainspring of the narrative or just a sort of backdrop, can be divided into two main periods. The first period (1956–1979) from the rise of the affluent society in the late 1950s to the early signs of the late 1970s crisis is that of the post-war settlement, often referred to as the Keynesian consensus around the policies of the mixed economy and the welfare state. It includes *I'm All Right, Jack* (John Boulting, 1959), *The Angry Silence* (Guy Green, 1960), *Flame in the Streets* (Roy Ward Baker, 1961), *Carry On at Your Convenience* (Gerald Thomas, 1971), and *Love Thy Neighbour* (John Robbins, 1973). The second period (1979–2013), starting with Thatcherism, is that of the rise of neoliberalism and the establishment of a new consensus among the elites around the notions of free-market economy and reduction in government spending. It includes *Britannia Hospital* (Lindsay Anderson, 1982), *Business as Usual* (Lezli-Ann Barrett, 1987), *Brassed Off* (Mark Herman, 1997), *Face* (Antonia Bird, 1998), *Dockers* (Bill Anderson, 1999), and *Billy Elliot* (Stephen Daldry, 2000). *Ratcatcher* (Lynne Ramsay, 1999) and *Made in Dagenham* (Nigel Cole, 2011) have a special status in that they are re-enactments of strikes that took place in the first period. Adopting a contextual reading of the films mixing sociological, historical and cultural sources, the present essay will show that the evolution of the representation of strike in British cinema has shifted from a class to a post-class perspective, which can thus give the impression of fragmentation at a class level despite the potential rise in new forms of solidarity at a sub-class level.

1956–1979: Open Season on Strikers, Unions and the Media

The representation of strike is not always in favor of strikers and has evolved throughout the decades. Until the 1970s, strike films were satires used to portray a lost and confused society (*I'm All Right, Jack, The Angry Silence, Carry On at Your Convenience, Love Thy Neighbour*). The films pit excited workers against corrupt bosses who add fuel to the flames. Workers are derided and seen alternatively as idle, idiotic or clownish figures. The reasons behind stoppages are eccentric, strikes are repetitive and endless. The attempts to resolve disputes only lead to status quo or chaos.

"The shop stewards behind their leader": Peter Sellers (as Fred Kite) in light suit surrounded by (from left to right) Bruce Wightman, John Comer, Cardew Robinson, Sam Kydd (behind P. Sellers), Bill Rayment and Tony Comer in *I'm All Right, Jack* (John Boulting, 1959) (© 1959 Studiocanal Films Ltd.).

Satire is also aimed at trade unions which are sometimes perceived as Bolshevik henchmen. The Red Scare (*I'm All Right, Jack*), Trotskyist entryism, the domino theory (*The Angry Silence*), the possibility of an international labor movement (*Carry On at Your Convenience*), even though they are all dealt with in a comedic way, were recurrent themes in those days. The strikers are pictured like an army marching behind its leader (*I'm All Right, Jack*), an impression which is sometimes reinforced by the soundtrack playing a military tune (*Carry On at Your Convenience*). The shop stewards who are unsure about whether to officially support these spontaneous strikes are quickly overwhelmed by the rank-and-file (*The Angry Silence*). If it is not Bolshevism, it is the anarchism or the nihilism of the younger generation which is pointed out (*Flame in the Streets, The Angry Silence*).

In these films, the main character never directly takes part in the stoppage since he is either a mole—though his ingenuousness makes him harmless (*I'm All Right, Jack*)—or a strike-breaker exposed to what seems like an unbridled and raging mob (*The Angry Silence*). Strikers use all possible means to impose their rule against those they consider traitors to the cause. If coaxing fails, the "Coventry treatment,"[1] then threats and intimidation are used, such as breaking windows and flower pots, cutting clothes lines, burning cars, insults and molestation. *Love Thy Neighbour* and *Carry On at Your Convenience* show the same escalation in violence despite their overall lighter humorous tone.

As a rule however, trade unions rather tend to be represented as corrupt organizations defending their vested interests. Because most of them are in favor of co-management or mild reforms, they are considered to be part of the Establishment. Agreements between management and unions to the detriment of workers are criticized in *I'm All Right, Jack* and *The Angry Silence* in which talks take place behind closed doors, thereby excluding ordinary workers from all discussions. The shop stewards who rise to higher positions in their unions and therefore go up the social ladder are increasingly cut off from the grassroots in what looks like an inescapable process of embourgeoisement (*Flame in the Streets*). Those films do not focus on the political nature of the strikes, but show unions resorting to the war of nerves with management in order to obtain satisfaction on details. Unions, even when they are in a minority position, systematically block all negotiations and local representatives can only make a decision after consulting the union's highest authorities (*Carry On at Your Convenience*). In the films of the first period, the most recurrent criticism made about union officials is what French sociologist Henri Weber called "*le crétinisme du spécialiste*" (the idiocy of the expert).[2] The same archetypal figure is found in *I'm All Right, Jack, The Angry Silence, Carry On at Your Convenience* and *Love Thy Neighbour*. The union representative appears like a cultivated but conceited, eloquent but pompous, rigorous but tyrannical man who is familiar with the intricacies of the job but prone to quibbling, always protesting but cowardly, in a word, hypocritical. Only *Flame in the Streets* offers a more nuanced portrait of its shop steward.

British films also focus on how the fighting working class is presented in the media and show that the press and television are not very favorable. Their global lack of interest is only interspersed with sudden peaks of attention when a situation seems promising in terms of luridness. They then blow things out of all proportions and their ideological bias sometimes verges on propaganda in the way they present facts. The obsession of journalists with "the human angle in the story" does not hide the fact that they are first and foremost seeking sensationalism. For example, when they bring together the various members of a dispute in a television studio, it is with the hope that the stormy debate will shoot the ratings up (*I'm All Right, Jack, The Angry Silence*).

The representation of strike in the films of the first period is thus quite critical in a cinema that is rather known for its empathetic view of the working class.[3] Distrust of unions and more generally of all institutions can sometimes reflect the political opinion of directors. For example, Roy Boulting said he had made fun of the trade unions in *I'm All Right, Jack* because they were part of the Establishment and thus deserved a film that would complete his satirical filmography on the subject.[4] The "hatred of proletarian crowds" in *The Angry Silence* can, according to some film critics, be put down to the right-wing ideology developed by director Guy Green and scriptwriter Bryan Forbes in a film that was attacked as the British version of another controversial film: *On the Waterfront* (Elia Kazan, 1954).[5] Moreover, the choice of classical narrative conventions to film the working class can lead directors to focus primarily on one central character rather than on a group of workers and, subsequently, the individuality if not the individualism of the hero.[6] The resolution of the problem then seems to rely on a personal change and not a social one. The individualization process is particularly problematic when the point of view adopted is that of the strike-breaker. Because he is the only character endowed with psychological depth, he may look like the only free spirit opposed to a bunch of moronic fanatics (*The Angry Silence*).

However, the highly satirical and humiliating representation of some ringleaders and shop stewards is not only the mere product of a film industry anxious to make any strike action ridiculous. These films mirror the opinion of that time and echo Michael Shanks's *The Stagnant Society* (1961). This book which was a real best-seller is a scathing criticism of the weakness of the British economy of the time. The author blames this economic failure on both amateurish and incompetent managers and narrow-minded workers led by unions stuck on their archaic view of society.[7] These films can also be interpreted as a reaction to the numerous strikes that took place at the time, most of them being wildcat strikes. They were all produced during the Conservative Decade[8]—that is to say the thirteen years during which no fewer than four Conservative Prime Ministers succeeded one another between 1951 and 1964—or in the early 1970s, another period of great social unrest in the UK. As such, they reflect the exasperation felt by a part of the population, especially people who were directly concerned by the events as the comments heard in those films and the enthusiastic reaction of the audience of that time make it clear.[9] Lastly, these films are a reminder of the fact that the British working class is not a monolithic entity and that in its midst are staunch Conservative supporters who think the social order in place as natural.[10] This deference, not to say complex of inferiority, towards the upper class seen as the incarnation and defender of good taste and manners is felt on screen through the inseverable bond that seems to unite the top and the bottom of the social ladder, such as the one between Lady Dorothy and union representative Kite's wife in *I'm All Right, Jack* or the one struck up via the series of trans-class weddings redolent of a spirit of one-nation Toryism in *Carry On at Your Convenience*. The attraction of a part of the working class for Conservatism is sometimes reflected by the more or less comic debates organized between workers (*The Angry Silence, Carry On at Your Convenience, Love Thy Neighbour*). For example, the workers in *Carry On at Your Convenience* look passive and deeply bored with their shop steward's vehement speeches. Only his workmate and best friend supports him with some powerful slogans whereas the others only wake up when a lewd joke is made. They vote against the strike or rapidly turn against it because all they want is to work hard to save their firm from bankruptcy. The latter is incidentally bailed out by the foreman's horse race winning bets.

1979–2013: Sympathy for the Strikers

The onset of Thatcherism and more generally of the profound social and economic changes resulting from the adoption of neoliberalism seem to have been a watershed in the way strikes are represented. After being disparaged until the late 1970s, they are now defended on screen. If the films of the first period were inspired from the general mood of labor relations at the time, all the films produced since the 1980s have been inspired by real and specific strikes such as those of hospital workers (*Britannia Hospital*), miners (*Face, Billy Elliot, Brassed Off*) and dockworkers (*Dockers*). Each time, workers are presented as the victims of the Thatcher, Major and Blair governments. Stoppages and strikes aim at protesting against privatization or restructuring—an understatement for layoffs—but all the strikes in the name of saving jobs are bound to fail. With deindustrialization, strikes always seem to mark the end of an era, a last-ditch struggle of pointless resistance in a dying world, hence the sometimes very bleak tone of some films (*Business as Usual, Brassed Off*).[11]

Remarkably, the point of view has changed between the films of the first and the second period (1979–2013) since strikers are now always in the foreground. The vision given is much more nuanced. Films make a point of showing the reasons that lead some workers to go on strike and others to keep on working. Scabs are workers who are crucified between their financial needs and their loyalty towards their workmates (*Business as Usual, Brassed Off, Dockers*). Retaliation still exists and makes life difficult for them. The decision to go on strike or not tears families apart but sadness ultimately prevails over anger (*Business as Usual, Billy Elliot, Dockers*). Despair leads some strike-breakers to extreme acts such as suicide because nothing is worse than being a class traitor in times of hardship and struggle. If scabs are harshly treated, forgiveness is often granted in the end (*Brassed Off, Dockers*).

What is the most striking aspect compared with the comedic disputes of the first period is the violence of the head-on confrontation between the strikers and the state. The army and the police are indeed seen as the strong arm of the government, strike-breakers or repressive, inhuman and at times truncheon-happy agents (*Britannia Hospital, Business as Usual, Face, Dockers*).[12] That may be why, so as to downplay its impact, violence is sometimes choreographed, as in *Billy Elliot* in which the editing draws a parallel between Billy's boxing and dancing training sessions and the clash between the miners and the police in Durham.

The portrayal of union representatives is usually just as unflattering as in the films of the first period. Shop stewards are still criticized for their co-management tendency and their little concern about the fate of their union members (*Britannia Hospital, Dockers*), if they are not the victims of their own stupidity (*Business as Usual*).[13] What has changed though is the reason of the criticism. Unions used to be blamed for their exaggerated power. Now they are blamed for their increasing absence. In their defense, it must be said that times are changing and the well-known techniques used in an industrial world become ill-suited in a growing service economy. As explained by Mark and Babs (*Business as Usual*), it takes even more courage and motivation to picket a clothes shop than it does to picket a plant: a 1-hour strike on shift is impossible and a 9-to-5 picket is required to ensure the boycott, constantly inventing new ways of catching the media and people's attention. The balance of power now tilts in favor of the bosses in an era extolling the manager's right to manage.

If the employer tried to obtain peaceful industrial relations at all costs in the 1960s and 1970s (*I'm All Right, Jack, The Angry Silence, Flame in the Streets*), a new corporate culture was established in the early 1980s owing to anti-union legislation (through the 1980, 1982, 1988, 1990 Employment Acts and the 1984 Trade Union Act). The (in)famous closed shop policy—the obligation to join a particular union as a precondition to employment—an obligation referred to as "obsolete" in *Britannia Hospital* and said to be the cause of many strikes in the films of the first period (*I'm All Right, Jack, The Angry Silence, Love Thy Neighbour*), is now abolished.[14] Union representatives are implicitly led to understand they are now giants with feet of clay (*Business as Usual*).[15] The secret ballot reform (established by the 1984 Trade Union Act) shows its impact in *Brassed Off*. Despite public statements and polls, the result swings in favor of the non-strikers. The fear unions have of supporting spontaneous strikes partly explains the way the Transport and General Workers' Union (TGWU) lets the longshoremen down because the leaders do not want to pay any fines (*Dockers*). Employers' sense of omnipotence is evident. They threaten to call the police at the slightest claim from their employees. They gloatingly watch strikers getting beaten up by the police in front of their shops (*Business as Usual*). They get rid of their "problems," as they call union representatives, hence the gradual disappearance of such characters on screen. Because the dockworkers who make too much fuss over the non-respect of the rule book are not taken on again let alone reinstated (*Dockers*), because the leaders of the miners' strike are blacklisted (*Brassed Off*),[16] the workers who survive this streamlining, not to say purging, strategy are the most docile and/or those whose political culture is the weakest. The big difference between the films of the first and the second period is the loss of what some sociologists call trade-union consciousness.[17] Pushed to extremes—to the point of ridicule—in the late 1950s, it eroded and finally disappeared in the late 1990s.

If unions get blamed for their lack of responsiveness, so does the Labour Party. In the very few films that include politicians, these people are derided and mocked by the workers. Films usually show them as little concerned by the problems of their constituents who, consequently, lose all hope in any political alternative. New Labour, in which the obsession with image and communication has replaced the core principles of Old Labour as well as its historical alliances, is sharply criticized in *Dockers*. *Business as Usual* shows that, even in the mid–1980s, the only political parties sympathetic to the cause of threatened workers and employees were far left groups with Trotskyist leanings or groups soon to be expelled from the Labour Party, like Militant which was excluded by Neil Kinnock in 1986.[18] In keeping with Liverpool's reputation as the Red City because of the resistance it put up to the Conservative government during that decade—as evidenced by the numerous flags glimpsed—they seem to be the only ones to believe in a potential alternative.

The criticism of the media continues as well but the comic/satirical tone of the first period has turned into more tragic/ideological attacks. Journalists are either seen as inefficient people (*Business as Usual*) or accused of relaying the government's policy. Always on the lookout for sale-boosting scoops, the media only focus on degenerating demonstrations. They use connoted words and give an apocalyptic view of the country inspired by the Winter of Discontent (*Britannia Hospital*).[19] Conversely, they can remain purely factual when they present the human misery generated by premature pit closures (*Brassed Off, Billy Elliot*). The few activists seen show they know how to use television to their advantage to convey their message but the opportunities of hearing an alternative discourse are extremely rare (*Business as Usual*). Films denounce the repercussions of such media coverage which leads to a form of indoctrination of the population (*Billy Elliot*).[20] *Dockers*, written as a response by the real people involved in the strike that opposed the Liverpool dockers to their management for two years and a half from 1995,[21] is a good summary of the various attitudes the media usually display towards striking workers and emphasizes their share of responsibility in the political and ideological failure of the country. Initially, they are uninterested in the subject or just interview the management. Only support from local football player Robbie Fowler catches their attention for a short while, but the debate focuses on a footballer's right to have a political consciousness. The t-shirt he wore to show his support then briefly becomes the object of a new fad, which is used by the dockworkers for their own ends in the hope that it will help them publicize their cause before journalists' interest wanes again. In a world that has become the society of the spectacle,[22] the working class only gets bad press in the UK and British cinema offers itself as a medium of resistance to the hegemonic discourse of a given period of time.

Towards the Fragmentation and Depoliticization of the British Working Class

Whatever the genre[23] and the hero chosen to deal with the subject of strike—resulting in a change in tone and/or perspective—British cinema has remained very critical throughout the decades, even though its target varies according to the power struggle thought to be in place at the time of production. Strikers or strike-breakers, union officials, politicians, police forces, the media are all, to various degrees, deemed to be responsible for the fragmentation and the depoliticization of the British working class.

While strike action should stand as a moment of cohesion, it is rarely the case. Only the dockers' demonstration at the peak of their mobilization seems to be a festive and unifying moment over the fifty years covered by this essay. The general trend is rather towards distrust that destroys all potential bonds and feeling of solidarity. Some workers dissociate themselves from the picket when the strike is not official (*Dockers*). Others only think of the short term and prefer to take the redundancy money offered by employers who try to divide and rule, which undermines the credibility of those who remain mobilized (*Brassed Off*). When a strike ends up in failure, the group explodes (*Brassed Off*). Once they have lost, workers become estranged and lose sight of one another (*Business as Usual*).

The other phenomenon observed over fifty years is the gradual shift towards depoliticization. The transmission of working-class political culture from one generation to another weakens. As early as 1956, a generation gap emerged. Young workers who lack references and general knowledge invariably turn towards the older generation in order to know what to do, what to think, and what to vote during general meetings. To some, this is the illustration of how easy it is to manipulate workers because they look infantilized (*The Angry Silence*) and somewhat uninterested in politics unless it is part of the family culture (*Flame in the Streets, Business as Usual*). To others, on the contrary, it is the proof that working-class political culture is acquired through the experience of fighting (*Dockers*). The chronological evolution shows that the previous generation is always endowed with a sort of aura and respected for its fights (*The Angry Silence, Brassed Off, Dockers*). However, since the 1990s it seems it has been increasingly difficult to convince young workers to unite and defend their rights.[24] Although there are still debates among the workforce, young workers are unconvinced as to the real power of unions and seem incapable of planning any really organized political action (*Dockers*). In one generation, workers have gone from solidarity and collective fights for long term rights to an individualistic and erratic sense of rebellion. Pragmatism has won over ideology in a sort of vicious circle. The decline of unions' power and the drop in union membership—from 13 million in 1979 to 6.5 in 2013[25]—are both the cause and consequence of this general depoliticization.[26]

Over fifty years, films testify to the disappearance of a certain political or politicized view of this class, which may reflect the gradual dismantling of the historical strongholds of the working-class aristocracy known for its strong trade-union and political culture. It may also reflect a general feeling of disillusionment. Even if this nostalgia for an older, more united working class has something to do with the myth of the Golden Age and is noticed at all times, the fact remains that this class is getting away from politics, a trend that has gained momentum since the early 1980s.[27]

From Class to Gender and Ethnicity

The fragmentation process in the representation of the so-called traditional working class is nonetheless counterbalanced by other types of resistance, new moments of cohesion between different kinds of workers. Women, for example, awaken to political consciousness and often remain very politicized (*Business as Usual*, *Made in Dagenham*). From merely supporting their husbands, fathers and/or brothers, they start leading working-class movements on screen, these characters often being inspired by real women (*The Ploughman's Lunch*, *Business as Usual*, *Brassed Off*, *Face*, *Dockers*). They are those who make moving speeches—although they are fully aware of what is at stake—in front of activists from other unions who are more educated and therefore more impressive in order to convince them that unity is strength. Workers from ethnic minorities also embody a wind of change and keep the spirit of revolt alive. In recent films, it is highly significant that those who still appear to have a real political consciousness are foreigners, like Pakistani Hussein (*My Beautiful Laundrette*, Stephen Frears, 1985), Paraguayan Jorge (*Ladybird, Ladybird*, Ken Loach, 1994) and Nicaraguan Carla (*Carla's Song*, Ken Loach, 1996). So far, migrant workers who are swelling the ranks of the working class have not protested much in British films.[28] However, in a foreign context, *Bread and Roses* (Ken Loach, 2000) has shown the gradual politicization of this new proletariat in Los Angeles. Why not imagine a similar action in a British context in a not-too-distant future?[29] The idea is not as unrealistic as it may sound, all the more as many British films already show signs of solidarity and cohesion among these workers against their exploiters (*Dirty Pretty Things*, Stephen Frears, 2002; *Gregory's Two Girls*, Bill Forsyth, 1999).

If women and, to a lesser extent, ethnic minorities seem to be becoming the new channel by which the strike is represented on screen, the very nature of their fight is also changing. The stress put on the increase in feminist and ethnic claims in a world that had so far been essentially male and white reveals a change of times reinforced by a new conception of the defense of workers' rights. They do not see themselves or are not apprehended through the lens of social classes (a Marxist view) but through that of minorities (a post–Marxist view).[30]

The presence of ethnic minorities in the British working class disturbs the usual class perspective. *Flame in the Streets* and *Love Thy Neighbour* underline the fact that workers tend to give more importance to ethnic origins than socio-professional categories. In the first film, the shop steward only saves his union thanks to his eloquence. To counter some of the workers' racist attitude he explains that if white workers decide to apply the color bar, they will weaken their union. Either black workers will de-unionize or they will leave to create unions according to skin color, which is exactly what happens in the second film. In other words, the "us v. them" dichotomy has to remain a class struggle and should not become an ethicized conflict. However, this stance seems increasingly difficult to maintain in a context of heterogenization or, at any rate, redefinition of identities.

The class perspective is also undermined by the growing number of women on the labor market. Their difficult working conditions probably explain why they go on strike. However, their claims are not strictly speaking those of workers or employees. The diluted class perspective comes from the double if not triple yoke imposed on women in a professional context— boss/man/white versus worker or employee/woman/black (*Business as Usual, Made in Dagenham*). The growing ambiguity between class struggle and sex war applies at several levels. First, it is seen in the speeches made by all these female strikers. Contrary to Jean's speech (*Dockers*) whose class perspective is beyond doubt, Babs's (*Business as Usual*) and Rita's (*Made in Dagenham*) speeches are more blurred. The "we" they use to thrill the audience of activists can stand for the "us" of the "us v. them" dichotomy as well as the "us" of women in a sex war perspective. The ambiguity can also be felt in the private sphere. Babs's (*Business as Usual*) and Connie's (*Made in Dagenham*) emancipation as women and not as employee and worker—although the two aspects are linked—can be seen in the way their sudden decision to get involved in the public arena negatively impacts their couples.[31] Ambiguity pervades all levels of the world of work and society: rank-and-file workers, unions,[32] employers, government, the media (*Carry On at Your Convenience, Business as Usual, Made in Dagenham*). Faced with this sexism which is often the source of convenient and unholy alliances, women realize how isolated they are and how they must unite not to fail or yield[33] since class solidarity is an illusion, or in any case, a one-sided affair.

British cinema seems favorable to this evolution on the whole. Strikes, which are always criticized as a potential channel for the expression of class struggle, are celebrated when they are turned into the mouthpiece for the emancipation of minorities opposing a so-called traditional working class seen as phallocratic, racist, in a word, reactionary. Films can operate by inverting values.

Carry On at Your Convenience thus celebrates women who are objectively strike-breakers for their sensible and courageous reaction against their striking and sheep-like husbands. *Made in Dagenham* uses the Swinging London context with its booming soundtrack, sparkling colors and allusion to David Bailey in order to insist on the modernity of the female workers compared with the unions. They bring vividness, just like their colorful dresses, to a purely masculine world which is as grey and drab as the suits these men all wear. Films can moralize the cause of the strike to justify the fight and rally support. In *Business as Usual*, Babs's protest against her unfair dismissal is coupled with Josie and Paula's fight against sexual harassment to reinforce viewers' indignation.[34] The film plays on this deep feeling of injustice by combining industrial relations and the condition of women and minorities. *Made in Dagenham* uses the same device. A parallel is drawn between the fight for equal pay and the resistance to Nazism—through Connie and George's couple and Rita's final speech in front of the Trades Union Congress (TUC)—and the suffragette struggle in the ending credits. It is a just cause that is above any sort of divides, contrary to a mere labor dispute. The strike is here supported because it quickly goes beyond its initial goal, pay rise, a motive of many male strikes perceived to be mean.[35] Claiming to be the first women's strike in British history, it quickly becomes a model for the emancipation of women throughout the world. The fact that all these women are not activists paradoxically reinforces the purity of their cause. They simply wish to be recognized as citizens. The feminist perspective applied to female strikers is felt in the way these films often try to promote female over class solidarity. Depending on the ideology conveyed by the film, it is a failure (*Dockers*),[36] a partial success (*Business as Usual*) or a complete success (*Made in Dagenham*).

The shift in the representation of strike from illustrating working-class fights to depicting the struggle of women and minorities against the established white male order can be accounted for by several factors. This choice can of course be interpreted as the result of the ideology of the film industry which is also guided by economic interests pushing it to universalize the cause of the strike beyond strictly political divisions in order to widen the appeal of the film. It can also result from the individualization process. A strike film will only be made—read produced—if the class perspective is altered, taking for example the angle of women.[37] However, just as in the films of the first period, these films also go together with social change and integrate on the one hand the post-Marxist view used by many sociologists, politicians and media to represent society and on the other hand the influence of neoliberalism which has more or less eradicated the language of class from the public sphere for thirty years.[38] The elegiac view of strike as a potential occurrence of class struggle can be interpreted, depending on one's political opinion, as a reflection of reality or of the desire expressed by the current neoliberal consensus. Ironically, British social-realist cinema which, for some, is synonymous with working-class empathy would represent strikes in order to better bury them. And maybe strikes are defended in the films of the second period because they herald the welcome end of an era. *Made in Dagenham* released in 2011 takes place in the context of the films of the first period (1968) and combines this double perspective which confirms the change in point of view that occurred over the last fifty years. The vision of workers and unions blends the initial satirical imagery and the neoliberal critique whose early signs can actually be strongly felt in the discussion between the Ford representative and the Secretary of State for Employment and Productivity.[39] The power and the passivity of trade unions, now clearly associated with their eminently macho character, turn women into a vector for a new social and economic order.

Since 1956, the representation of strike in British cinema has shown a rather clear evolution from a class to a post-class perspective, which reflects a change of society and economic organization. That is probably why most films today waver between a feeling of mounting anger at an individual level and of dispirited listlessness at the collective level. Despite some embryonic experiences of new forms of solidarity, the individual fight for survival in a brutal world remains prevalent. In order to get by, the only hope left is being able to transcend one's social condition thanks to a given talent. The emblematic film of the period, *Billy Elliot*, set in 1984 that is to say the key date of the demise of the British working class after the failure of the miners' strike, shows a highly symbolical turning-point since the father disowns his past and his class by becoming a scab to pay for his son's departure to London. Beyond the reorientation from class to the limited and private scope of the family circle, the indispensable condition of success, Billy's enrolment in a prestigious ballet school means a clean break from his native milieu and the start of an uprooting process. His admission is known the day the strike ends. This patent failure of the political culture of the working class is counterbalanced for the father by the promise of a better future for his son. Billy will become a leading dancer and make his neighborhood proud. The moral of the film illustrates a well-known speech by Margaret Thatcher entitled *Let Our Children Grow Tall*, a metaphor used to promote individual success based on innate talent, work ethic and entrepreneurial spirit.[40] However, the film says nothing about the future of those who cannot "grow tall," the other children in Durham who stayed up north. British strike films therefore offer the vision of a heterogeneous working class which struggles as it can in an increasingly blurred world.

Corpus

Billy Elliot (Stephen Daldry, 2000)
Brassed Off (Mark Herman, 1997)
Britannia Hospital (Lindsay Anderson, 1982)
Business as Usual (Lezli-Ann Barrett, 1987)
Carry On at Your Convenience (Gerald Thomas, 1971)
Dockers (Bill Anderson, 1999)
Face (Antonia Bird, 1998)
Flame in the Streets (Roy Ward Baker, 1961)
I'm All Right, Jack (John Boulting, 1959)
Love Thy Neighbour (John Robins, 1973)
Made in Dagenham (Nigel Cole, 2011)
Ratcatcher (Lynne Ramsay, 1999)
The Angry Silence (Guy Green, 1960)

Notes

1. The (old) Coventry treatment, or sending someone to Coventry, is a British idiom used notably in *The Angry Silence* to refer to the way strikers refuse to speak to strike-breakers as a punishment.

2. Henri Weber, *Marxisme et conscience de classe*, Paris: Collection 10–18, no. 982, 1975, 274. He writes: "Far from producing its own antibodies, the process of bureaucratization keeps increasing as bureaucrats get more autonomous. Because full-time officials do not try to stop it. Quite the opposite. For multiple reasons, they become its conscious and active agents. Convinced of the incompetence and immaturity of the rank-and-file as well as of its own superiority, the proletariat officialdom is little inclined to conform to the democratic ritual. These full-time officials think they are the qualified representatives of the masses who know better what is in the latter's interest [...]. In certain highly specialized sectors such as trade unions, they soon fall victim to the '*idiocy of the expert*' syndrome [author's italics]" (translated by the author of the present essay).

3. Many British directors have been deemed empathetic towards their working-class characters such as Ken Loach (Alan Burton and Steve Chibnall, *Historical Dictionary of British Cinema*, Lanham: Scarecrow Press, 2013, 270; Geoff Mayer, *Guide to British Cinema*, Westport: Greenwood Press, 2003, 305), Mike Leigh (Ray Carney and Leonard Quart, *The Films of Mike Leigh: Embracing the World*, Cambridge: Cambridge University Press, 2000, 115, 160, 187, 226, 244) or Shane Meadows (Martin Fradley, Sarah Godfrey and Melanie Williams, eds., *Shane Meadows: Critical Essays*, Edinburgh: Edinburgh University Press, 2013, 13) for the best known. More generally, the former Cannes Film Festival President, Gilles Jacob, wrote in his essay on British film that "British cinema also shows empathy for a working class that, contrary to the title of the Italian Elio Petri's famous film, rarely goes to paradise." Gilles Jacob, "United Kingdom," 24 October 2013: http://www.festival-cannes.com/en/article/58044.html, accessed 24 August 2014.

4. Peter Stead, *Film and the Working Class: the Feature Film in British and American Society*, London: Routledge, 1991 [1989], 181–182.

5. Raymond Durgnat, *A Mirror for England: British Movies from Austerity to Affluence*, London: Praeger, 1971, 52, 72–74. Stead, *Film and the Working Class*, 183.

6. John Hill, *Sex, Class and Realism: British Cinema 1956–1963*, London: BFI, 1997 [1986], 55–57, 137–138, 143. This type of criticism is not new. Jeremy Hawthorn (ed.), *The British Working Class Novel in the 20th Century*, London: Edward Arnold, 1984, vii, made the same observation

about the working-class novel which is often presented as a clash between its bourgeois form and its working-class content. See also Guido Aristarco, *Marx, le cinéma et la critique de film*, Paris: Lettres Modernes Minard, 1972, 94–99, about the dead-end of naturalism in fiction which leads to individualism.

7. Michael Shanks, *The Stagnant Society*, London: Pelican Book, 1972 [1961], 63–69, 214–217. The shop stewards who are so much mocked on screen are also criticized by the author. He thinks they are not very representative of the other skilled workers, whom he finds apathetic, an impression which is also felt in the films of the period. The expression used for the title of the film, *I'm All Right, Jack*, is typical, he says, of modern British trade unions, a mix of conservatism and individualism.

8. The expression is used by British historian Stephen J. Lee in his book *Aspects of British Political History 1914–1995*, London: Routledge, 1996, 193–208.

9. Peter Stead, "A Paradoxical Turning Point: 1959 to 1960" in Sheila Rowbotham and Huw Beynon (eds.), *Looking at Class: Film, Television and the Working Class in Britain*, London: Rivers Oram Press, 2001, 46–51, gives details about the context of production and the undeniable success of these films. Robert Murphy, *Sixties British Cinema*, London: BFI, 1992, 45, explains 1960s critics were astonished to see that the most conservative films, like *The Angry Silence*, were the ones the workers liked the most. See also Durgnat, *A Mirror for England*, 71–74. Only the *Carry On at Your Convenience* DVD trivia notes (ITV DVD, Special Edition, 2003) explain that, before it became a classic just like all the other films in the series, this film had not been as successful as expected when first released because it made too much fun of its usual target audience.

10. This sometimes overlooked fact dates back, at least, as far as the late 19th century franchise reforms and it is confirmed by the significant titles of various contemporary sociological studies such as Robert T. Mackenzie, *Angels in Marble: Working Class Conservatives in Urban England*, London: Heinemann Educational, 1968; Eric A. Nordlinger, *Working-Class Tories: Authority, Defence and Stable Democracy*, London: MacGibbon & Kee, 1967; Frank Parkin, "Working-Class Conservatives: A Theory of Political Deviance," *British Journal of Sociology*, vol. 18, no. 3, 1967, 278–290. Incidentally, this trend might explain why the Labour Party failed to secure a majority in the general elections until 1945, although Ramsay MacDonald formed two minority governments in 1924 and 1929. It might also explain why Thatcher was initially quite popular among some members of the working class—35 percent of manual workers voted for her in 1979 compared to 24 percent for Heath in 1974. See Jacques Leruez, *Le Phénomène Thatcher*, Brussels: Editions Complexe, 1991, 145; and David Cannadine, *Class in Britain*, London: Penguin, 2000, 179.

11. Michel Etcheverry, "La fabrique de l'identité nationale" in Bertrand Lemonnier (ed.), *Médias et Culture de Masse en Grande-Bretagne depuis 1945*, Paris: Armand Colin, 1999, 159. He defines *Brassed Off* as follows: "At once elegiac and revolted, resigned and dynamic, *Brassed Off* is the film that best symbolizes the post Thatcher era." Jean-Michel Frodon, *La Projection nationale*, Paris: Odile Jacob, 1998, 143–144, explains: "*Brassed Off*, etc., are films that mourn the British working class and the loss of a certain age-old social relation that was destroyed by Margaret Thatcher, thus wiping the slate clean for Tony Blair to build 'something more modern'" (translated by the author of the present essay). *Made in Dagenham*, being a re-enactment of a 1968 strike, does not deal with striking under Thatcherism. Its lighter tone therefore does not undermine the general impression given by all the other films produced in the second period.

12. That was already felt in some films produced or set during the first period. The close-up on the stern faces watching a police van arrive in dead silence in front of the picket line (*The Angry Silence*) underlines the distrust and the hatred policemen inspire as their job is to protect the strike-breakers and get them safe and sound inside the factory premises. When the army is called out to collect the rubbish after three weeks of stoppage by the refuse collectors, it is thought to be breaking the strike by the locals (*Ratcatcher*).

13. In *Business as Usual*, Kieran, Babs's husband, is a former union representative whose constant will to negotiate with the management is seen as partly responsible for the closure of the sugar refinery where he used to work. His belief that the interests of the local management could converge with those of the workforce against European directives or the government's policy proved to be an illusion. His disappointment has evidently not shaken his convictions since he keeps encouraging his wife to negotiate with her employer rather than fighting against her unfair dismissal. He is another example of the embourgeoisement of union officials for which he is symbolically punished. As the journalist who follows him explains, he had become a full-time representative who worked

hand in hand with management. The betrayal of his native class made him lose a lot as he became estranged from his friends after moving out to a more residential area and he lost his job.

14. It was actually progressively reduced by the 1980s Employment Acts and finally abolished by the 1990 Employment Act.

15. In this film, unions are not necessarily considered as partners worth listening to. The end of the strike is required as a precondition for negotiations. A discussion between the London boss and the firm's lawyer alludes to the—then newly established (by the 1980 Employment Act)—ban on secondary picketing.

16. This type of retaliatory measures is mentioned by the real miners involved in the 1984 strike in the documentary by Philippe Moreau and Christophe Weber, *Working Class Heroes* (2001). Out of the 100,000 miners who were on strike, half of them never managed to find a new job. Some of them were declared disabled because of the serious injuries inflicted by police brutality. Others were put on police file and blacklisted, "a real banishment from British society" the commentator explains.

17. Henri Weber, *Marxisme et conscience de classe*, 104, defines it as follows: "the consciousness of the exploitation and the oppression of the working class, of the antagonism opposing it to employers and the State, thus of the necessity to organize and fight to obtain as many advantages as possible" (translated by the author of the present article).

18. John Hill, *British Cinema in the 1980s: Issues and Themes*, Oxford: Clarendon Press, 2005 [1999], 187, explains: "The Militant Tendency was a Trotskyist grouping operating within the Labour Party. Following the local elections of 1983, Militants controlled the Labour majority of the Liverpool City Council which it led into a confrontation with national government over 'rate-capping.' The then Labour leader, Neil Kinnock, famously denounced Militant at the 1985 Labour Party Conference and, following a report on Liverpool Militant to the Labour National Executive in 1986, a number of leading Liverpool Militants were expelled from the party."

19. *Ratcatcher*, a film set in the suburbs of Glasgow during the refuse collectors' strike, also alludes to this period. Television talks about the government's worries over public safety while decomposing rubbish attracts rats and vermin. But that makes children happy as they play football with the bin-liners.

20. The criticism of the biased press is a source of gags in *Love Thy Neighbour*. While Eddie laments because the postman has inverted the newspapers with the neighbor again, his wife retorts: "It's all the same news!" He exclaims: "How can it be the same news? It's a Tory newspaper. It's biased!" "Oh and your Labour paper isn't, I suppose?" she says ironically. "'Course it is but it's biased the right way!" he concludes.

21. For more details about the scriptwriting workshop behind the film, see the Channel 4 documentary "Dockers: Writing the Wrongs" (Solon Papadopoulos, 1999) available on the *Dockers* DVD (Prism Leisure, 2001).

22. After Guy Debord, *La Société du spectacle*, Paris: Folio, 1992 [1967].

23. *Britannia Hospital* is the only satirical film of the second period, opposing irresponsible strikers to zealous union leaders and stupid management. All the others are closer to chronicles.

24. Jean-Noël Evanno, "Les travaillistes et l'éducation" in Emmanuelle Avril and Richard Davis (eds.), *Comprendre la Grande-Bretagne de Tony Blair: Bilan d'une alternance politique*, Lille: Presses Universitaires du Septentrion, 2001, 46, writes: "recent studies have shown that 34% of young people, that is to say 7% more than in 1994, have no interest in politics whatsoever and, unsurprisingly, most of them are to be found amongst the least favored social classes" (translated by the author of the present essay).

25. According to official statistics released by the Department for Business, Innovation and Skills, "Trade Union Membership 2013: Statistical Bulletin, May 2014" available at https://www.gov.uk/government/uploads/system/uploads/attachment_data/file/313768/bis-14-p77-trade-union-membership-statistical-bulletin-2013.pdf, accessed 25 August 2014.

26. Stephen Edgell, *A Measure of Thatcherism: A Sociology of Britain*, London: HarperCollins Academic, 1991, 17, notes that after 1979, "rampant individualism replaced creeping collectivism." Leonard Quart, "The Religion of the Market: Thatcherite Politics and the British Film of the 1980s" in Lester Friedman (ed.), *Fires Were Started: British Cinema & Thatcherism*, Minneapolis: University of Minnesota Press, 1993, 33, adds: "Cultural and social structures that once reverberated morally and socially—and like left-wing politics, the unions, the church, and even the class system—no longer play the same social role."

27. For example, Ken Loach's filmography seems to show that the time of social struggles for a real political alternative occurred in the 1920s and 1930s when Stalinism had not yet stifled the hopes of an international labor movement (*The Wind That Shakes the Barley, Land and Freedom*). His feature films about contemporary British workers never really show any widespread political debates. If they do, politicized workers are an ultra-minority (in fact there is just one, like Larry in *Riff Raff*, or they are not British, as explained further down) and they get fired as mentioned above.

28. Off screen, some attempts to organize workers are led, for example, by office cleaners in Canary Wharf on the very premises where British dockworkers fought a century earlier as Paul Mason explains in his book. According to him, these workers belonging to a new global working class are those who could reinvent the labor movement and give birth to a new phase of class consciousness. Paul Mason, *Live Working or Die Fighting: How the Working Class Went Global*, London: Harvill Secker, 2007.

29. It is to be noticed that Ken Loach has so far never directed a feature film about a British strike, only a few documentaries and television dramas. He once said he thought the subject was too serious and urgent for fiction (see George McKnight, ed., *Agent of Challenge and Defiance: The Films of Ken Loach*, Westport: Praeger, 1997, 99, 125, 162–163) and that is why, for example, he shot *The Flickering Flame: A Story of Contemporary Morality* (1995) about the 1995 dockers' strike. *It's a Free World* (2007), although set in the world of migrant labor, focuses on a British employer running a recruitment agency and thus does not dwell on the political opinions of these people. The collective action put in place at the end of the film is as illegal as the status of the migrants Angie exploits.

30. According to *Encyclopaedia Britannica*, a minority is "a culturally, ethnically, or racially distinct group that coexists with but is subordinate to a more dominant group. As the term is used in the social sciences, this subordinancy is the chief defining characteristic of a minority group. As such, minority status does not necessarily correlate to population." Encyclopaedia Britannica, "Minority," 22 January 2014: http://global.britannica.com/EBchecked/topic/384500/minority, accessed 26 August 2014.

31. In *Business as Usual*, this is underlined by Kieran's refusal to attend the picket on the first day of the strike whereas his wife really wishes him to be there and by his fits of anger when Babs dares criticize his domestic inefficiency. His reaction during his wife's speech in front of activists also comes to mind: coming in late, he keeps grimacing at the back of the room before rushing out, jealous and ashamed of his loser's status in the undeclared war that opposes the couple.

32. Even the representation of the shop steward as a Pygmalion is ambivalent in that it turns these female workers or employees into puppets or parrots more or less used to promote a cause, of course a noble one, but whose impact is undermined by the fact that this progressive idea is initially a male one. The fact that the shop steward's admiration is often tinged with a loving or fatherly feeling can also be perceived as diminishing the strictly political nature of the cause (*Business as Usual*, *Made in Dagenham*).

33. The character of Sandra who wavers several times and nearly breaks the strike out of personal ambition is there as a reminder that many women revel in the worst phallocratic clichés. Although the codes of femininity are ultimately subverted to promote the cause—Equal Pay written in lipstick on Sandra's stomach as she is wearing a bikini—she appears to be a simple-minded, easily influenced girl.

34. Paula, a young black woman who undergoes a body search, is an irreproachable victim contrary to Josie who is depicted as a bit of a loose woman and can as such invite criticism.

35. This incidentally explains the media's support as they make the same observation. During the newsreel sequence, a bit of a sentence heard confirms the hypothesis: "what makes this strike different is that it's not about a specific."

36. The women's call to managers' wives in *Dockers* is inspired by a real action as Doreen McMally, one of the leaders of the Women of the Waterfront, explains in *The Flickering Flame*. Disappointment is bitter when she reads the answer sent by these women who explain they do not want to get "involved" in the dispute: "they're like gangsters' molls in films. They don't care about where the money comes from as long as it comes because they don't want to get 'involved.'"

37. For example, *Made in Dagenham* is as much a biopic or a bildungsroman—other than being a star vehicle for Sally Hawkins—as a strike film.

38. Thatcher's ambiguous use of class in her rhetoric is summarized by David Cannadine as follows: "The words, as usual, were carefully chosen: class war, yes; the language of class, no. All this

suggests that Thatcher's notion of Britain as a 'classless society' was one where she had won the class war, where they were no collective identities or class enemies left, and where she had driven class off the agenda of public perceptions and discussion. Yet to do this, she herself had to be obsessed with class, and that she seems to have been." Cannadine, *Class in Britain*, 178.

39. The American boss embodies a much more brutal form of capitalism than the one that was in place in the UK at the time and ushers in the rise of neoliberalism that was to become prominent at the end of the following decade. He does not hesitate to use the personnel files and records to threaten union representatives into fulfilling his wish—break the strike—and blackmails the unions and the Secretary of State with the threat of relocation.

40. Margaret Thatcher, "Speech to the Institute of Socio-Economic Studies ('Let Our Children Grow Tall')," delivered on 15/09/1975 at the St Regis Hotel in New York, posted on the Margaret Thatcher Foundation website: http://www.margaretthatcher.org/speeches/displaydocument. asp?docid=102769, accessed 3 July 2010.

Works Cited

Aristarco, Guido. *Marx, le cinéma et la critique de film*. Paris: Lettres Modernes Minard, 1972.
Avril, Emmanuelle, and Richard Davis (eds.). *Comprendre la Grande-Bretagne de Tony Blair: Bilan d'une alternance politique*. Lille: Presses Universitaires du Septentrion, 2001.
Cannadine, David. *Class in Britain*. London: Penguin, 2000.
Carney, Ray, and Leonard Quart. *The Films of Mike Leigh: Embracing the World*. Cambridge: Cambridge University Press, 2000.
Debord, Guy. *La Société du spectacle*. Paris: Folio, 1992 [1967].
Durgnat, Raymond. *A Mirror for England: British Movies from Austerity to Affluence*. London: Praeger, 1971.
Edgell, Stephen. *A Measure of Thatcherism: A Sociology of Britain*. London: HarperCollins Academic, 1991.
Fradley, Martin, Sarah Godfrey, and Melanie Williams (eds.). *Shane Meadows: Critical Essays*. Edinburgh: Edinburgh University Press, 2013.
Freidman, Lester (ed.). *Fires Were Started: British Cinema & Thatcherism*. Minneapolis: University of Minnesota Press, 1993.
Frodon, Jean-Michel. *La Projection nationale*. Paris: Odile Jacob, 1998.
Hill, John. *British Cinema in the 1980s: Issues and Themes*. Oxford: Clarendon Press, 2005 [1999].
Hill, John. *Sex, Class and Realism: British Cinema 1956–1963*. London: BFI, 1997 [1986].
Jacob, Gilles. "United Kingdom." 24 October 2013: http://www.festival-cannes.com/en/article/58044.html, accessed 24 August 2014.
Lee, Stephen J. *Aspects of British Political History 1914–1995*. London: Routledge, 1996.
Lemonnier, Bertrand (ed.). *Médias et Culture de Masse en Grande-Bretagne depuis 1945*. Paris: Armand Colin, 1999.
Leruez, Jacques. *Le Phénomène Thatcher*. Bussels: Editions Complexe, 1991.
Mason, Paul. *Live Working or Die Fighting: How the Working Class Went Global*. London: Harvill Secker, 2007.
McKnight, George (ed.). *Agent of Challenge and Defiance: The Films of Ken Loach*. Westport: Praeger, 1997.
Murphy, Robert. *Sixties British Cinema*. London: BFI, 1992.
Rowbotham, Sheila, and Huw Beynon (eds.). *Looking at Class: Film, Television and the Working Class in Britain*. London: Rivers Oram Press, 2001.
Shanks, Michael. *The Stagnant Society*. London: Pelican Book, 1972 [1961].

Stead, Peter. *Film and the Working Class: the Feature Film in British and American Society*. London: Routledge, 1991 [1989].
Thatcher, Margaret. "Speech to the Institute of Socio-Economic Studies ('Let Our Children Grow Tall')." Delivered on 15 September 1975 at the St Regis Hotel in New York, Margaret Thatcher Foundation website: http://www.margaretthatcher.org/speeches/displaydocument.asp?docid=102769, accessed 3 July 2010.
Weber, Henri. *Marxisme et conscience de classe*. Paris: Union Générale d'Editions, collection 10/18, 1975.

In Praise of the Working Poor
Archeology of Class Struggle through the Arts of Representation in *Comrades* and *The Fool*

NICOLE CLOAREC

In his essay *The English Ideology*, George Watson wrote: "All societies are unequal; [...] but they describe their inequalities variously."[1] While it is widely acknowledged that the British in particular have always been obsessed with class, the very definition of the concept of class has proved a much debated question. By now, though, most historians and sociologists consider that class is as much the result of economic factors, institutions and political discourse as a matter of culture and identity. In other words, class may be first and foremost a question of representation—through both self-representation and the others' look. This is the perspective that David Cannadine chose in his study on *Class in Britain*, where he analyzes the different ways British people have perceived themselves in class terms. Cannadine distinguishes three main models which, while being gross over-simplifications of the complexity of society, "have lain behind most popular perceptions and descriptions of social structure since the early 18th century,"[2] offering "different yet equally plausible accounts of the same contemporary social world."[3] One is the hierarchical model, in which society is perceived as a pyramid of layered ranks and orders, station and degree; another is a three-class system, a model favored by the middle-class that sees itself as the "virtuous social middle," holding society together,[4] and the last, a two-class system, which polarizes people according to one single divide between "us" and "them," high and low, the few and the many, the rich and the poor "between whom there is no intercourse and no sympathy; who are as ignorant of each other's habits, thoughts and feelings as if they were dwellers in different zones, or inhabitants of different planets; who are formed by different breeding, are fed by different food, and are not governed by the same laws" to quote Disraeli, who, in *Sybil* (1845), popularized this "two nations" image.

This vision of a deeply riven society is very much at the heart of the two films studied here—*Comrades* (Bill Douglas, 1987) and *The Fool* (Christine Edzard, 1990)—which both deal with the representation of social inequalities in 19th-century Britain. Both evoke key moments in the transformation of 19th-century British economy as *Comrades* records the changes in rural activity after the enclosures and the introduction of mechanization whereas *The Fool* testifies to the precarious living conditions in the streets of London, in a context of rural exodus, changes in manufacturing production and subsequent disruption of the labor market. What is more, both films dramatize instances that started to question the prevailing contemporary view of a social structure as the "natural" state of things, where inequality is providentially ordained and submission to this divinely ordained hierarchy the only possible response. In so doing, the two films eschew the disturbing grittiness of social realism as well as the more comfortable nostalgic outlook of the costume drama that prevailed in British film production in the late 1980s. Indeed, what is most remarkable is that while the two films are based on historical records and pay minute attention to the recreation of the past, they also develop sophisticated formal strategies to convey the questioning of any would-be "natural" class structure. And appropriately enough, this strategy involves the unusual foregrounding of arts of representation, a vast array of optical devices and entertainment in one, acting and the stage in the other. Through a highly self-reflexive *mise en scène*, the very artificiality of the arts of representation thus comments on and ultimately exposes the injustice and arbitrariness of the social class system.

Bill Douglas's *Comrades*[5] relates the story of the Tolpuddle Martyrs, six farm laborers in Dorset who were sentenced to seven years' transportation in 1834 after they protested against the repeated cuts to their pay by forming what they called a "Society of friends" or union.[6] Their case soon became well-known and protest was conducted through petitions, marches and meetings until they were granted full pardon in 1836.

The film faithfully follows the chronology of the main events, starting with a reference to the machine breaking and its subsequent retaliations that marked what was to be called the Swing rebellion that occurred in the early 1830s. In a few shots, Douglas sets out the sheer economy of his style and its tremendous evocative power which will characterize the whole film: no explanatory dialogue, no dramatic camera movements but some effective visual snapshots taken from the action and the use of metonymy—like a bloodstained hand raised against the sky—to evoke the violence of the repression and the crushing of hopes. Likewise, the whole film deliberately eschews all dramatic scenes: only one of the men's arrests is evoked and takes place off-screen behind a door, the trial itself is shot from the point of view of the families who are kept out of the court room and only attend the proceedings as a dumb shadow show seen through the frosted glass. The meetings of the union are first only suggested through the light of a window, the preparation of its banner, the creaking of floorboards and whisperings heard by the women knitting downstairs. Similarly, the setting up of the "London-Dorset Committee" in support of the Martyrs' cause is encapsulated by the image of its banner replacing the union's after the women have swept and dusted the attic where the men used to convene.[7]

Bill Douglas is a master of ellipsis, structuring his film through a pattern of scenes composed like organic *tableaux vivants* and simple striking images which encapsulate fundamental emotions and meanings. Moments are thus isolated, which, however trivial they may be, are endowed with meaningful depth. Through its *mise en scène*, the film privileges the small gestures, the imperceptible body language, all the simple events of ordinary life that was marked by the passing seasons and their corresponding activities. Dialogue is sparse, often reduced to some snippets of conversation whispered off screen, and the soundtrack, almost devoid of extradiegetic music, mainly foregrounds natural sounds.[8] The film is unsparing in its presentation of the harrowing conditions of life, the destitution and the dirt; but it also conveys a warm sense of community with gathering and singing around the fireplace and moments of great poetry through the evocation of popular entertainment, traditional festivals or the visit of itinerant street artists. This aesthetic approach of sober yet finely balanced compositions and a slow elliptical rhythm pays tribute to the lives of these ordinary people who are endowed with great nobility, conveying Douglas's sympathy for the dispossessed and the downtrodden.[9]

This sympathy is further conveyed by the film's casting strategy which relies on contrast and parallels the social relationships of the narrative. Douglas explained he wanted to cast virtually unknown actors to play the farmers and their family:

> I didn't want a Robert Redford standing in for George Loveless because I knew the audience would see Robert Redford and I wanted them to see instead the glory of this man. So I wanted actors who would be humble enough to want to share the same experience in presenting these men.[10]

Conversely, the upper class characters are played by famous actors, "the 'aristocrats' of their profession,"[11] from Robert Stephens as the Squire and Freddie Jones as the Vicar to Vanessa Redgrave and James Fox in the second part taking place in Australia.[12] Running counter to traditional casting strategies, Douglas uses the well-known actors to denounce the ruling class's hypocrisy, their performance stressing the gap between their smug patronizing speeches and their acts. The Squire and the Vicar in particular are shown telling blatant lies, as when Frampton promises to raise the men's wages only to cut their pay by one more shilling; they are shown cheating at cards and discussing the Martyrs' sentence in an outrageously callous and cynical manner[13] and one might object that the rather overblown performances of the two actors verges on Manichaean caricatures.

Surely enough, the film relies on a series of echoes[14] and contrasts to denounce the blatant injustice that the men incurred. Early in the film, George Loveless is heard saying grace while the camera isolates a chunk of bread: "Dear Lord we humbly beseech thee to accept our gratitude for this our daily bread. Give us the goodness of heart to share whatever we have. Amen." The next shot, although linked by the theme of communion, stands in sharp contrast with the displaying of the expensive and ornate decoration of the established Church. The contrast is further highlighted by the Vicar's sermon, quoting parts of Proverb 14:

> In all labour there is profit: but the talk of the lips tendeth only to penury. The poor is hated even of his own neighbour: but the rich hath many friends [...] In all labour there is profit and it behoves us to accept our lot in life and to work for our reward. [...] God the Father, in His infinite wisdom, created large men and small, white men and black, rich men and poor, wise men and fools. And we should not dare to presume to question His wisdom! [...] Hold fast to that which we know and have learned to value, the natural order of things, tried and tested down the ages of men.

Then in the next scene, the Vicar's sermon, advocating submission to the status quo, is again contrasted by the religious address delivered by Loveless in the Methodist chapel, preaching fraternity and equality:

> Give us the vision, Lord, to see past the narrow confines of the field the great and infinite glory of the world beyond. Help us to stretch ourselves to the full extent of our being that we might be one with all men. Neither master nor servant before thine eyes. Amen.

The introductory contrast between the Established and the Non-Conformist Church is used to encapsulate the ideological discourse underlying the social structure of the time. The Non-Conformist Church appears as a site of resistance and of solidarity, from which the "Society of Friends" or union is the logical development. The Martyrs' fate itself is treated as a parable: the six chairs which John Hammett has carved for the Squire function as metaphors for the six martyrs: like the men, the chairs are subjected to lowering price and contempt despite their elaborate craft and beauty, and it is no accident the men are asked to sit on them when they come as a delegation to plead for a decent wage.

Nonetheless, although the film is minutely documented and partly based on George Loveless's own writings,[15] which are quoted throughout the film and in the concluding speech, by no means is *Comrades* to be construed as a mere history lesson, or even a political plea. As the film's subtitle indicates—"Being A Lanternist's Account of the Tolpuddle Martyrs and What Became of Them"—the whole story is mediated by a key witness who first appears just after the opening scene of the machine breaking. The subtitle is further substantiated by the concluding speech made by Mr. Pitt, one of the members of the Dorset-London Committee that fought for the release of the men and celebrates their return in a theater: "Finally Ladies and Gentlemen, let us thank our friend the Lanternist, who through the power of optics and its magical transformations, has told the story here today. It was almost as though he had been present throughout himself. *Ars magna lucis et umbrae.*"[16]

Indeed, the character of the itinerant Lanternist is not only revealed as the main story teller but works as a chorus figure who appears throughout the film under a variety of guises, assuming no fewer than thirteen parts in all.[17] And more importantly still, each of his apparitions brings about some optical device or entertainment: from shadow play to thaumatrope, from peepshow to phantasmagoria, from *camera obscura* to photography—to name but a few—all indeed mastering the great art of light and shadow. Thus the film's opening shot of a white sun which is progressively eaten up by an eclipse, offering a superbly simple image that gives the men's fate a metaphysical dimension, recurs right at the end but this time the same image is revealed as the light circle of the magic lantern. Likewise, the subplot, retracing through numerous optical devices the history of pre-cinema, prompts the viewer to constantly reconsider what he/she has been watching. Now and again, people are transformed into characters of a shadow play, as with the Squire and his household or the Lanternist himself[18]; the journey to Australia is narrated through animated maps; the journey back through the slides of the Lanternist's triple lantern before it is shown on the stage and a similar series of slides serve as epilogue, relating what became of the Tolpuddle's Martyrs. In the same way, the integrity of the fictional world, along with its "willing suspension of disbelief," is disrupted on several occasions when the characters look straight at the camera in a direct address to the viewers. As James Hammett comes out of the shed on payday, he unexpectedly holds seven fingers to the camera, communicating the amount he has received just as he did in an earlier scene but to his Comrades.[19]

Ultimately the film's self-reflexive dimension sheds light on the laborers' increasing self-awareness of their condition and means of action, both depending on the notion of illumination and enlightenment, in a technical as well as philosophical sense.[20] Significantly, the first meetings of the "Society of Friends" are filmed exactly in the same way as the Lanternist's show, both depicted through a lit window from the outside. Not only is the Lanternist's lot closely linked to the Martyrs' but his avatars all conjure up a questioning of the "natural state of things" and its ordained social structure that can quickly appear literally upside down. In addition to the Vanity motif which runs through optical trickeries[21] and illustrates the union's motto ("Remember thine end") and its banner's design (a skeleton), optical devices are shown to provide subversive ironical comments on the powers-that-be or the ruling class. Sergeant Bell cheekily invites the Vicar to take a glimpse into his peepshow "to see the pictures from the Holy Book" which actually show "Eve—without her clothes on—in the garden." The French Silhouettist, after listening to Norfolk's sanctimonious speech describing himself as the agent of progress and order in the world,[22] commends him for his "liberal turn of mind," which reminds him of the French revolution and its *"raisons d'être."* He then proceeds to complete the silhouette and cuts off the head at the collar.[23]

Self-reflexivity culminates in the concluding scene when the film overtly displays its own status as fiction. The artificiality of the art of projecting images is then brought to the fore through the theatricality of the whole scene. As George Loveless delivers an impassioned plea for the working men to unite and shake off their slavish condition, protect their labor, preserve their wives and children from utter degradation and starvation and prevent "the interest of the millions [from being] sacrificed for the gain of a few,"[24] he is first filmed in a close up, face to camera, in a direct address to the audience; then as the camera slowly tracks out and tilts up, the stage progressively goes dark and isolates the speaker in a single spot light. By narrating the story of the Todpuddle's Martyrs through the mediation of pre-cinematic devices, through what can be called an archeology of cinema, *Comrades* presents the Martyrs' story as a founding narrative in the history of the trade union movement. Ultimately both seminal narratives reflect on each other, endowed with the same power to shed a critical light on the world.

Like *Comrades*, Christine Edzard's *The Fool* pays tribute to the working poor: set in the 1850s in London, the film is dedicated to "the anonymous men and women interviewed by Henry Mayhew in London between 1848 and 1861." Henry Mayhew, a journalist and writer,[25] started conducting a series of inquiries into the lives of thousands of street-traders and other street-folk, which were first published as news articles before being compiled into a book entitled *London Labour & the London Poor*. As Mayhew himself explains in the preface: "My earnest hope is that the book may serve to give the rich a more intimate knowledge of the sufferings, and the frequent heroism under those sufferings, of the poor." Although Mayhew shared with his contemporaries many preconceived notions about the poor, whom he classified into the deserving and the others, "those that will work, those that cannot work and those that will not work," to quote his very words, he also began to doubt "whether prevailing economic arrangements were either natural or necessary,"[26] questioning the vision of social structure as the natural order of things.[27] And what was most original is that Mayhew gave voice to the people themselves, attempting to give "a literal description of their labour, their earnings, their trials, and their sufferings, in their own 'unvarnished' language," to quote his preface again.[28] Director Christine Edzard and co-writer Olivier Stockman, who are best known for their internationally renowned company Sands Films,[29] which provides sets and costumes for period costume dramas, paid extreme attention to period details, evoking some of the now lost small trades that used to swarm the streets of London—the fly paper boys, the crossing sweepers, the grease remover sellers, the chickweed sellers, the pie sellers, the tricksters or the "pure finders" who gathered dog feces to sell to tanners—while recreating the tumult of the eager hawkers, the "cries of London" which so "astonished a Foreigner and frightened a Country Squire."[30]

In a fairly radical way, the film refuses any classical narrative development along a strong storyline and well-defined characters. What it offers instead is a series of tableaux which alternately depict life in the streets and in the salons of the High Society, busy with receptions, dinners and balls. If, on the one hand, the glaring contrast between the scenes emphasizes the "two-nations" image, the vision of a deeply fractured society, what is equally striking are the similarities between the scenes: both lower and upper classes are characterized by the constant vocal noise they make, the aptly named chattering classes being as loud and indistinct as the clamors of the streets. Significantly, many of the scenes are edited with sound bridges that follow the same conversation while places and characters have changed. Moreover, when snatches of conversation are overheard, they all address the same exclusive topic: money. Money appears as much an obsession for those who have as for those who have not, the wealthy are shown as worried about money matters as the destitute, and all are equally scheming, bargaining and using confidence tricks. What differs is the mere scale of it and it is no accident that the first scene amongst the genteel society opens on news of a fraudster, "the greatest rogue that ever was," who has just been found out after deceiving all the present members into investing into bogus financial schemes and who are left wondering: "and what would be left of the privileges of the privileged?"[31]

In between these two contrasted worlds are scenes set in a theater where again people are heard constantly chattering or declaiming more or less indistinctly; but, most importantly, the theater proves the central metaphor which articulates a critical representation of the social structure and it is only opposite that the film should open with Prospero's famous lines at the end of the masque,[32] highlighting the illusory nature of all representation, be it theatrical or social. On the one hand, the back lanes are filmed like the nooks and crannies of the backstage; on the other, the society salons echo the stage and balcony boxes surrounded with heavy drapes. Ultimately, as the recurring shots of backstage mechanisms indicate, what is laid bare are the springs, cogs and wheels, the complex mechanisms that underlie the social order.[33]

Accordingly, social status is exposed as a question of acting and dressing up.[34] The main protagonist, who first appears as a mere observer, remaining silent until the twenty-sixth minute, proves to be a social transvestite, leading a double life as Mr. Frederick, a humble, "non-descript" theatrical booking clerk, and Sir John, whose association every gentleman and gentlewoman seeks as he has acquired the reputation of being a financial wizard, making money virtually out of thin air. Both are introduced indirectly through name-dropping in other people's conversations, asking about either where or who he is. And significantly, whereas Mr. Frederick first appears on a descending platform stage amidst the workings of the backstage, Sir John's first apparition is filmed from his back into a mirror. Mr. Frederick–Sir John is indeed a master of impersonation, mimicking all types of voices and accents, recalling how appearance is everything.[35]

This Dr. Jekyll and Mr. Hyde personality actually leads to a climactic confrontation between the two sides of the character who confront their views on society. While Sir John asserts that plunder is the way of the world, that "this is a commercial country: everyone does it, a kind of dovetailing of shark practices. Everyone is at it, you know, not just the banks, so the shops but in your lanes, your courts and your houses and all your ten thousand people—all cheating for the value of a farthing here, a penny there, all the same," Mr. Frederick objects there is a fundamental difference between the social classes and their ethical relationship to need and money: "There's no common sense in that; no common justice." And although the scene ends with Mr. Frederick's existential crisis, asking, "Who is me? I'm so adaptable, you see," he eventually reveals his "true" identity to the genteel society he has just been manipulating into a vast financial speculation. His long tirade, exposing the financial skullduggery and stock market ebullience of the 1850s which engendered a world undermined by self-interest, fraud and corruption, sounds only too true nowadays after the series of recent financial scandals:

> Who knows to what pitch the science of manipulating investment funds will advance? Who knows what rules of oriental subtlety will be invented to cre-

ate the illusion of a separation between conflicting business interests? Who knows what contorted lines financial ingenuity will learn to draw between optimistic promotion and misrepresentation of fact, between craftiness and deceit, cunning and fraud? [...] I know, I know, I have fooled you and this very nearly fooled me. In the back street, in the yards, the lanes and courts where I come from, I see men, mere men, weak, deceitful sometimes, shabby, gullible, struggling to exist. Here I can see men, mere men, weak, deceitful sometimes, shabby, gullible, arguing about their bits of return on money for which they've done nothing.[36]

By subverting the Victorian class order, Mr. Frederick's class-crossing exposes both the vanity and arbitrariness of social status and the monstrous absurdity of financial speculation. The "insubstantial pageant" of the stage is thus both the reflection of the social world and the means by which it is exposed. If both Sir John and Mr. Frederick call the other a fool, the fool of the film's title indisputably refers to the King's jester and all his stage companions.[37] While the actors are rehearsing midway through the film, some lines can be heard from backstage, appropriately quoting Jaques in *As You Like It* (act 2, scene 7): "O noble fool! / A worthy fool! Motley's the only wear."

While both films are based on historical records that give voice to the dispossessed and downtrodden, Bill Douglas's *Comrades* and Christine Edzard's *The Fool* articulate a powerful denunciation of the social inequalities and injustice in 19th-century Britain with a self-reflexive *mise en scène* that foregrounds the arts of representation as a critical tool of social investigation. It may come as a sad paradox, though, that both films, while celebrating the poor and popular entertainment, have proved uncompromising art-house productions and failed to reach any mainstream audience.[38] Indeed, while set in 19th-century Britain, the films also provide an ironical comment on their own production time at the end of the 1980s, when unions' power and ethos were systematically undermined and attacked, when financial deregulation reigned supreme. Both are damning indictments of the Thatcher years, offering instead a powerful outcry against poverty and injustice along with a celebration of the magic and poetry of art.

Notes

1. George Watson, *The English Ideology: Studies in the language of Victorian Politics*, London: Allen Lane, 1973, 174.
2. David Cannadine, *Class in Britain*, London: Penguin, 2000, 20.
3. *Ibid.*, 19.
4. *Ibid.*, 29.
5. *Comrades* is Bill Douglas's fourth and last film. The other three films, *My Childhood* (1972),

My Ain Folk (1973) and *My Way Home* (1978), also known as *The Bill Douglas Trilogy*, relate the filmmaker's own destitute childhood in Scotland using a bleak, uncompromising black and white aesthetics. Douglas started working on the script of *Comrades* as soon as 1979 but it took him eight years to find the necessary funding and have the film made. He died in 1991 of cancer, leaving a number of projects he was unable to complete, testifying to his uncompromising attitude towards the film industry and his adamant refusal to give up full artistic control. For a detailed account of the difficulties Douglas encountered to shoot *Comrades*, see Duncan Petrie, "The Lanternist Revisited: The Making of *Comrades*" in Eddie Dick, Andrew Noble and Duncan Petrie (eds.), *Bill Douglas: A Lanternist's Account*, London: BFI, 1993, 173–204.

6. It should be noted that unions had been lawful since the Combination Acts were repealed in 1824. The men were charged with an obscure law prohibiting people from taking oaths in assemblies. The whole trial was an outrageous mockery of justice since the jury was composed of the Squire himself, his son, his step-brother and magistrates who had signed the arrest warrant.

7. Other examples include the agreement between the Hammett brothers whereby James took the place of his brother John, which is evoked as James discreetly outlines the gesture to keep one's mouth shut; all the spurious arguments and unfair proceedings of the trial are summed up in a single discussion between Mr. Pitt and Squire Frampton; the verdict is only indirectly announced by one of the women who answers a little girl asking what "transportation" means; the harrowing pain of departure is conveyed by three silent short takes, first of a road with the chain of the Todpuddle men walking along in the snow (there are five of them since George Loveless was ill at the time), a cut to one of the Todpuddle girls who is hearing the clanking of the chains while lying in bed, then the same road seen from the girl's point of view but empty; the same device is used for George Loveless's departure depicted in three simple shots: one of the ship near the Dorset cliffs, the next of Betsy Loveless, George's wife, walking away from the village, then the first shot again with Betsy looking away at an empty sea.

8. Duncan Petrie explains that composer Hans Werner Henze was ready to leave long sections entirely silent. See Duncan Petrie, "The Lanternist Revisited: The Making of *Comrades*" in Eddie Dick, Andrew Noble and Duncan Petrie (eds.), *Bill Douglas: A Lanternist's Account*, 192.

9. Bill Douglas referred to the type of effect he wanted to achieve as "emotional narrative" which focused on characters and their relationships rather than plot as such. See *Ibid.*, 189.

10. Quoted in *Ibid.*, 82.

11. Conversion with Bill Douglas: Q&A session at Bridport Film Society after a screening of *Comrades* on 31 October 1987, transcribed and originally published as a supplement to *Film, the Journal of the British Federation of Film Societies* in January 1988, 14.

12. The list includes Murray Melvin as the clerk, Michael Hordern as Mr. Pitt, or even Barbara Windsor as Mrs. Whetham, whose performance is very much in keeping with her best-known roles in the *Carry On* films. Ironically, Douglas first wanted to cast non-professional actors in the lead roles but was barred by Equity, the British actors' trade union. It is also worth noting that some of the little known actors like Phil Davis (young John Stanfield), Imelda Staunton (Betsy Loveless), Alex Norton (the Lanternist) or Keith Allen (James Hammett) have by now become quite famous.

13. One of the Gentlemen Farmers playing cards at Frampton's exclaims: "I think them jolly lucky. How I would love to visit Botany Bay! Have you read Cook?" Later on, another says disapprovingly: "Next thing we know the wives will be asking for Parish Relief!"

14. Pay day occurs three times, highlighting the repeated lowering of salary from eight shillings to six.

15. The film includes the poem that George Loveless wrote in prison, a letter to his wife and an excerpt from his pamphlet *The Martyrs' Account: The Victims of Whiggery*. The latter, which relates his and his companions' ordeal and transportation, is a plea for workers to organize themselves to overcome destitution and injustice and was often quoted at Chartist meetings. It was first published under the direction of the Central Dorchester Committee in 1837, reprinted by the TUC Tolpuddle Martyrs' Memorial Trust in 2005. Loveless also wrote *The Church Shown Up*, first published by the Dorchester Committee in 1838, reprinted by the TUC Tolpuddle Martyrs' Memorial Trust in 2005, which castigated the hypocrisy and indifference of the Church.

16. The phrase refers to the title of the work of 17th-century German Jesuit scholar Anathasius Kircher who has often been credited with the invention of the magic lantern whose principles he studied in the aforementioned book.

17. In addition to the Lanternist who entertains the children with shadow plays and his "galanty

show," the actor Alex Norton plays Sergeant Bell, a peg-legged old soldier who invites the Vicar to see into his "Royal Raree Show" or peepshow; the Diorama showman harboring a John Bull waistcoat who invites Loveless to his diorama of the battle of Waterloo; the "Laughing Cavalier" who appears in the three-dimensional picture at the Squire's manor, the usher who keeps the martyrs' family out the court room which then appears to them as a dumb shadow show seen through the frosted glass; Wollaston, one of the Squire's snobbish friends cheating at cards who uncovers a marked pack of cards foreshadowing the flicker book; the Ranger bringing relief money by stagecoach who gives the children a thaumatrope (showing appropriately the images of a bird and a cage); the tramp who picks up Loveless's message and is fairly puzzled by the optical effect known as Roget's wheel whereby the spokes of a wheel look curved when passing through vertical railings; the Captain of the convict ship who sells a toy panorama to the Foppish gentleman; the sadistic guard who isolates himself in a wood cabin where the principles of *camera obscura* operate; the French silhouettist who makes the portrait of Norfolk; the Witch who introduces the phantasmagoria and Gaviotti, the eccentric photographer who desperately tries to record the wonders of the Australian outback with his "patent steam heliotype." For a personal account provided by Bill Douglas himself, see "Bill Douglas: A Lanternist and his Comrades," originally printed in *The New Magic Lantern Journal*, vol. 5, no. 2, August 1987: http://www.exeter.ac.uk/bdc/lanternist.shtml, accessed 25 July 2013.

18. Even key dramatic scenes such as the reunion of five of the Martyrs after their ordeals in Australia is shot like silhouettes, thus echoing the Lanternist against the backcloth of the full moon. A very long shot eschews any easy emotion and provides a discreet reminder of the nature of the spectacle: as powerfully moving an image it may be, it is part of a representation.

19. Other instances include the mocking look of the "Laughing Cavalier," the sceptic look of the silhouettist, the knowing look of the Lanternist on the stage at the end.

20. George Loveless also uses some simple visual demonstrations to make his point as when appropriately he meets Squire Frampton in the print shop. After Frampton very patronizingly asserts that "folk are blind to their own interest," Loveless calmly replies: "folk are not blind, Sir, but it is those that master us that cannot see"; he proceeds with showing him an engraving of the Virgin Mary with her child and then places a coin on the head of Christ before asking "What prevents you from seeing it?"—"The silver of course!" answers the squire; "That's just it," Loveless concludes.

21. Also "The Blossom and Decay," the *trompe l'oeil* picture in the print shop's window that shows from a distance two young children who seem to play and proves to be a skull when seen closely.

22. "Now I regard the subjects of this province as my family. I'm a martyr to duty, public service, diplomacy. I think it's generally acknowledged I have promoted a measure of stability where before there was none."

23. There is further irony in the scene as the Silhouettist's speech expounding the tenets of the French revolution—"*liberté, égalité, fraternité*"—is immediately contradicted by his acts when he berates and abuses the poor blackfaced servant that brings some drinks to them. Deceitful appearances as well as the arbitrariness of "colors" are illustrated by the simple optical trick whereby the figure paper, although black, first appears light on a black backdrop before turning back to black.

24. The full speech goes: "Comrades. I believe that God works by means and man. Under such an impression I call upon every working man in England to shake off that supineness and indifference to their interests which leave them in the situation of slaves. (track out starts) Has not the working man as much right to preserve and protect his labour as the rich man has his capital? Such a measure, I'm well aware, will be dreaded, reviled, reprobated by the moneyed part of the nation; they would devise all those schemes, stratagems and policies that the art and cunning of man can invent to thwart and retard it. But let the working classes of Britain, seeing the necessity of acting upon such a principle, remembering that union is power, listen to nothing that might be presented before them to draw their attention from the subject, alike despising and conquering party, disputes, personal bickering and they will accomplish their own salvation and that of the world. Let every working man come forward from north to south, from east to west. Unite firmly but peaceably together as the heart of one man and then no longer would the interest of the millions be sacrificed for the gain of a few but the blessing resulting from such a change would be felt by us and our posterity, even to generations yet unborn."

25. Henry Mayhew (1812–1887) was one of the 17 children of a successful London solicitor. Like all his brothers, he opted for journalism and literature, falling into a middle-class bohemia. He

was the co-founder of *Punch* (with Gilbert Beckett) in 1841. In 1849 Mayhew was invited by the editors of the *Morning Chronicle* to act as metropolitan correspondent. He made three series of inquiries conducted over five years. About a third of the material published in the *Chronicle* was incorporated in his book *London Labour & the London Poor* published in three volumes in 1851 (an extra volume was published in 1861). In 1851 he also attempted a critique of political economy called *Low Wages* and in 1862 he started a survey of the prison population (*The Criminal Prisons of London*) that was only partially completed.

26. Henry Mayhew, *London Labour & the London Poor*, Ware: Wordsworth Classics, 2008, introduction by Rosemary O'Day and David Englander. They refer in particular to his "Answers to correspondents," letter no. 50, 22 November 1851. Another example is provided by the conclusion of Mayhew's preface: "My earnest hope is that the book may serve to give the rich a more intimate knowledge of the sufferings, and the frequent heroism under those sufferings, of the poor—that it may teach those who are beyond the temptation to look with charity on the frailties of their less fortunate brethren—and cause those who are in 'high places,' and those of whom much is expected, to bestir themselves to improve the condition of a class of people whose misery, ignorance, and vice, amidst all the immense wealth and great knowledge of 'the first city in the world,' is, to say the very least, a national disgrace to us." Henry Mayhew, *London Labour & the London Poor*, li.

27. *Ibid.*, xxvii.

28. The whole quotation goes: "It may surely be considered curious as being the first attempts to publish the history of a people, from the lips of the people themselves—giving a literal description of their labour, their earnings, their trials, and their sufferings, in their own 'unvarnished' language; and to portray the condition of their homes and their families by personal observation of the places, and direct communion with the individuals." *Ibid.*, xlix.

29. Christine Edzard was born in Paris in 1945, of German parents. She began a career in the theater, designed several productions for operas and theaters. In 1971, with her husband producer Richard Goodwin, she founded Sands Films, which was first conceived as a film production company but has become internationally famous for the making of 19th-century period costumes, providing wardrobes for numerous stage, opera, television and film productions, among which prestigious productions such as Mike Leigh's *Topsy Turvy* (1999), Mira Nair's *Vanity Fair* (2004), Joe Wright's *Pride and Prejudice* (2005), Sofia Coppola's *Marie Antoinette* (2006), Jane Campion's *Bright Star* (2009), Steven Spielberg's *Lincoln* (2012), Tom Hooper's *Les Misérables* (2012), Mike Newell's *Great Expectations* (2012), BBC1's *North and South* (2004), BBC1's *Lark Rise to Candleford* (2008–), HBO's *John Adams* (2008), BBC1's *Great Expectations* (2011). Edzard herself directed a much acclaimed adaptation of *Little Dorrit* (1987), an adaptation of Shakespeare's *As You Like It* (1991) and *The Chidren's Midsummer Night's Dream* (2011). Olivier Stockman was born in Paris in 1960 and moved to London aged 19 to pursue a career in film-making. He joined Sands Films in 1980 and is now its manager. He is the editor of *Little Dorrit* (1987) and *The Fool* which he also co-wrote with director Christine Edzard.

30. "There is nothing which more astonishes a Foreigner and frights a Country Squire, than the *Cries of London*. My good Friend, Sir Roger, often declares that he cannot get them out of his Head, or go to sleep for them the first Week that he is in Town. On the contrary, Will. Honeycomb calls them the *Ramage de la Ville*, and prefers them to the Sounds of Larks and Nightingales, with all the Musick of the Fields and Woods." Joseph Addison, *The Spectator*, no. 251, December 18, 1711.

31. One of the characters, Dowager Duchess, humorously recalls the South Sea Bubble of her youth.

32. "Yea, all which it inherit, shall dissolve,
And, like this insubstantial pageant faded,
Leave not a rack behind. We are such stuff
As dreams are made on; and our little life
Is rounded with a sleep."
—William Shakespeare, *The Tempest*, 1611, Act 4, scene 1, lines 148–158.

33. The metaphor is also made explicit by Mr. Frederick when he is confronted with the woman who has found out he was leading a double life. She thinks he might forget plain dealing and plain speaking, that he might be contaminated by the upper class's callous immorality and "their slippery eel-like courses." He then explains: "I'm studying them. There's a mechanism that wants looking at

and I mean to look at it. [...] I need to know how its springs, how its cogs, how its wheels, all fit together. I need to know its workings, all its workings."

34. Snatches of rehearsals are heard from *As You Like It* and *Hamlet* both stressing the analogy:
"O noble fool!
A worthy fool! Motley's the only wear.
[...] A worthy fool: One that hath been a courtier,
[...] O that I were a fool!
I am ambitious for a motley coat."
—William Shakespeare, *As You Like It*, c1600, Act 2 scene 7, lines 33–34, 36, 42–43.
"O, what a rogue and peasant slave am I!
Is it not monstrous that this player here,
But in a fiction, in a dream of passion,
Could force his soul so to his own conceit
That from her working all his visage wanned,
Tears in his eyes, distraction in's aspect,
A broken voice, and his whole function suiting
With forms to his conceit? and all for nothing!"
—William Shakespeare, *Hamlet*, c1601, Act 2, scene 2, lines 502–509.

35. As Mr. Frederick explains to the girl how his ambition to climb socially was thwarted by the shabbiness of his clothes, he recalls what he was told when he was a bank clerk: "The appearance, Mr. Frederick, the appearance leaves to be desired."

36. The speech goes on: "In the yards, in the courts, I see men, mere men struggling to exist [...]. Here I see men no better no wiser. It may be that so many years of balancing pounds, shillings and pence have given me a peculiar turn of mind. I've become sensible to the smallest irregularity, the merest discrepancy. But a million pounds in the hands of a man with the exact knowledge of ten thousand others, eking an existence out of five or six shillings a week, is a discrepancy unendurable." The speech recalls the woman's remarks about the radical difference between working and upper classes: "Those people they care for nobody. Nobody cares for them. They don't put themselves, only their money, into what they do. A man who has no money has to put himself into what he does."

37. After his near mental collapse, Mr. Frederick has apparently become part of the stage in the last scene, as he only speaks in rhyming couplets, addressing his cat Potiphar:
"Once upon a time, and it wasn't such a very good time,
But it is my time and your time and everyone else's time,
Some men I know, their blood is blue—
Swells, fops, bucks, a motley crew,
Toffs, gentlemen, a Lord or two,
Lawyers, brokers and bankers too,
Their deals are merely speak and act,
With friends and foes, and laws and facts,
In such a sweeping way.
Some men I know their house is poor,
Their shoe is worn, their trade obscure,
Whatever will some food procure,
Because tomorrow is never sure.
These men they know the price of bread
The landlord they've learned to dread
Yet they haven't spoken—yet."

38. *Comrades* was originally 3 hours and 25 minutes long and producer Simon Relph points out that even after the cuts Douglas consented to make, the film was still too long: "I think the reason we never really found precisely the right film is because Bill didn't understand the necessity of trying to get it down a bit to something that could be screened more widely." Quoted in Duncan Petrie, "The Lanternist Revisited: The Making of *Comrades*" in Eddie Dick, Andrew Noble and Duncan Petrie (eds.), *Bill Douglas: A Lanternist's Account*, 187. Although the film received very good reviews when finally released in August 1987, it played for only six weeks in one cinema house in London. *The Fool* had only a limited release and was hardly reviewed even when it was shown during the Toronto Film Festival in 1991.

Works Cited

Addison, Joseph. *The Spectator*, no. 251, December 18, 1711: https://www.gutenberg.org/files/12030/12030-h/12030-h/SV2/Spectator2.html#section251, accessed 15 January 2015.

Cannadine, David. *Class in Britain*. London: Penguin, 2000 [first published by Yale University Press, 1998].

Douglas, Bill. "Conversion with Bill Douglas: Q&A session at Bridport Film Society after a screening of *Comrades* on 31 October 1987." Supplement to *Film, the Journal of the British Federation of Film Societies*, January 1988.

Douglas, Bill. "Bill Douglas: A Lanternist and his Comrades." *The New Magic Lantern Journal*, vol. 5, no. 2, August 1987: http://www.exeter.ac.uk/bdc/lanternist.shtml, accessed 25 July 2013.

Loveless, George. *The Martyrs' Account: The Victims of Whiggery*. TUC, Tolpuddle Martyrs' Museum and Memorial Cottages, Tolpuddle Dorchester Dorset, 2005 [1837].

Mayhew, Henry. *London Labour & the London Poor*. Ware: Wordsworth Classics, 2008 [1851].

Petrie, Duncan. "The Lanternist Revisited: The Making of *Comrades*" in Eddie Dick, Andrew Noble and Duncan Petrie (eds.), *Bill Douglas: A Lanternist's Account*. London: BFI, 1993, 173–204.

Shakespeare, William, *As You Like It* [c1600] in Stanley W. Wells et al. (eds.), *The Complete Works*. Oxford: Oxford University Press, 1986.

Shakespeare, William, *Hamlet* [c1601] in Stanley W. Wells et al. (eds.), *The Complete Works*. Oxford: Oxford University Press, 1986.

Shakespeare, William. *The Tempest* [1611] in Stanley W. Wells et al. (eds.), *The Complete Works*. Oxford: Oxford University Press, 1986.

Watson, George. *The English Ideology: Studies in the language of Victorian Politics*. London: Allen Lane, 1973.

Ken Loach and the Geographies of Class

WENDY EVERETT

Just as it is impossible to think about British society without reference to class divisions, so too it is impossible to consider contemporary British cinema without reference to the films of Ken Loach, all of which are concerned with giving a voice to those who have traditionally been ignored, demeaned, or exploited: predominantly, of course, the working class (or its post–Thatcher incarnation as "underclass" or "post-working class").[1]

Ken Loach has been making radical, frequently controversial films, for both television and cinema, since the 1960s, and is internationally recognized as one of the most important (and prolific) of contemporary filmmakers.[2] He is equally happy working in fiction and documentary genres, and his films typically occupy the overlapping space between the two, an aspect which assumes a particular significance in discussions of their "realism." He is frequently seen as a thorn in the flesh of the British Establishment, is regularly reviled by the British popular press, and a number of his works have been censored, or pulled from television schedules at the last moment (particularly under Thatcher), in a move described by Newsinger as "the most dramatic and blatant epic of political censorship [...] since the Second World War."[3] In his unflinching commitment to the working-class experience, and his consistent refusal to patronize or compromise, Loach is one of a handful of filmmakers whose work can be demonstrated to have had direct social and political impact. He is, therefore, "in a uniquely important position in British cinema."[4]

Loach's films are generally situated within the British realist/social-realist tradition, and critical approaches to them tend to be historical and chronological, whether in highlighting the slight ideological shifts in perspective across his remarkably consistent concern with the lot of the working class, or in relation to the characters and narratives he creates. Typically, his films are positioned, as it were, along a vertical timeline which posits a direct correlation between historical event (as *cause*) and filmic production (as *effect*). Similarly, the history of Loach's collaborations with different writers, at different moments, is used to account for the changes in location, plot, and ideological content his films reveal.[5] While this linear approach has the merit of clarity, providing a stable framework in the restless world of film analysis, and accepting that the historical context of any film, particularly those with political intent, cannot be ignored, nevertheless, in combination with an unquestioning adoption of the realist label, the risk is a dangerously simplistic version of art as unmediated reflection of an external "reality" (see the passionate and on-going debates about the nature of realism). Moreover, because this approach so dominates critical studies of Loach's films, there is a risk that much of their extraordinary originality is ignored, making them tamer, somehow, and more predictable. (For example, frequent moments of comedy or the surreal are often left out of the discussion, simply because they do not fit comfortably into a realist account.)

My intention in this article is to see whether, by privileging not time and history but space and place, by adopting, as it were, a geographical perspective, a "horizontal" approach to the films, new insights might be gained, fresh lateral connections revealed. I hope that breaking away from the safe cause-and-effect narrative will enable me to open up new readings of Loach's films. What are their spatial subtexts, for example, and what might they show us about the significance of spatiality to social experience? How might a geographical reading of class enrich our understanding of the films' texts and contexts? And what is the real significance of location to this reading? I am concerned here less with providing clear-cut answers—Loach's films have already attracted too many—than with identifying questions and suggesting new routes into his work and, beyond that, into practices of film reading in general. Such a quest, within the parameters of a short article, inevitably imposes a number of short cuts, of course. The shifting and unstable concepts of realism have already received enough of an airing, and while I shall indicate something of the development of post-modern geography and its impact on film studies, this will be brief. Nor do I intend to engage in detail with the rather strange hostility that marks the space-place debate. Furthermore, given the immense corpus of Loach's work, while referring to it in general, addressing my comments primarily to his fictional cinema, I shall concentrate on two films in particular: *Raining Stones* (1993) will provide my main example, while I shall refer more briefly to his most recent documentary, *The Spirit of '45* (2013), by way of a conclusion. However, before beginning my argument, I shall provide a brief introduction to the fundamental aims and concerns of Loach, for those who may not be familiar with his work.

Ken Loach's Method

Loach is known for his obsessive search for authenticity. Using a mix of professionals and non-professionals, the latter often in the main roles, he insists on choosing people from the region in which the film is set, so that they have authentic accents and rhythms of speech. Because of this, a number of his films have been released with English subtitles, and when *Sweet Sixteen* was shown at Cannes, for instance, it ran with simultaneous French and English subtitles. Such practices are, of course, common in realist filmmaking, but Loach goes further in finding actors not only from the same region and social class as the characters they play, but also, if possible, with experiences in common. And while it may be predictable that he always films on location, and that he favors a distant, observational camera, his notion of "sympathetic" camera, and "democratic" lighting, are more original. For instance, by electing to light not the actors but the space that is being filmed,[6] Loach deliberately undermines any hierarchical content,[7] and grants the actors freedom of movement, while highlighting the *context* of that movement: the location of the shot.[8] He is, of course, famous for shooting chronologically: the actors often being unaware of what will happen to them next in the film (thus reacting "naturally"), and while the script is more-or-less adhered to, there is always room for improvisation and the unexpected. Loach works in close collaboration with his writers, and refuses to acknowledge film as anything other than a team experience. As has often been noted, it is, therefore, ironic that, whilst he passionately rejects the label of *auteur*, this is precisely the status he is accorded.

Of all these practices, the question of Loach's use of location has received by far the least attention, as if it were almost incidental; merely the result of practical or financial considerations. Attacking this view is my starting point. But before doing so, I need to touch upon the geographical concepts of space and place.

Space and Place

Modernist concerns were dominated by temporality, and it was not until the 1960s, inspired by a new breed of geographers, that the spatial was reintroduced into the critical landscape. However, in the process, a rift was created between the dual geographical elements of space and place. Space was linked with modernity and fluidity,[9] while place, if it figured at all (Lefebvre, for example, makes no mention of it in his seminal 1991 work, *The Production of Space*), was seen as static, traditional, and backward looking.[10] More recently, however, the concept of place too has made an important return to the agenda of postmodern geography,[11] and, more widely, to a whole range of theoretical disciplines—including film studies.[12] Moreover, the view of place as essentially static has given way to an awareness of its inherent mobility,[13] and its mediating role in social relations.[14]

Indeed, there is increasing recognition that space and place are inextricably linked, that you cannot have one without the other. For Tuan, who points out that architects will talk about the "spatial qualities of place," but may, just as easily, discuss "locational qualities of space," they are distinguished only by familiarity: what begins as undifferentiated space takes on the identity as place only as we become familiar with it.[15] If place is constructed through familiarity and social practices, its boundaries are both permeable and internally diverse, so that its interaction with individuals and communities is essentially fluid.[16] Given that our experience of the moving image is intimately connected to our experience of place,[17] it is clear that, in cinematic terms, place and space, reality and fiction, all meet in location, still one of the most underrated aspects of film studies. Despite its frequent role as generic marker (which does imply a recognition of fictionality), all too often, location is seen as little more than a backdrop: the place in which the film *happens* to have been made. Moreover, while the essentially fictitious nature of the characters and events is acknowledged, the place in which the action occurs is still frequently perceived as "real," situated—as it were—outside the filmic, beyond the diegesis.

If this somewhat dismissive treatment of location is true of the majority of feature films, how much more is this the case when dealing with "realist" films which actively encourage the illusion of camera as passive observer of "real" events and places. For example, it is assumed that British realist films will be set in gritty northern landscapes or grim urban topographies, as proof of authenticity, to such an extent that the function and significance of these settings within a particular film are scarcely discussed. A big mistake, I think.

Of course, despite its photographic relationship with reality, film is recognized as a constructed discourse. We need to remember that locations are a part of this discourse, not merely photographic reflections of "real" places, but also a "highly complex set of aural and visual signs."[18] Given that place and space are themselves constructs, it follows that film locations are doubly constructed; the resulting tensions may serve to open up the wider implications of a film narrative. In this essay, I shall argue that this is certainly true of the cinema of Ken Loach.[19] I shall therefore use locations—both their politically and socially motivated selection and their diegetic double construction—as a way of opening up a spatial perspective on his films.

Geographical Locations in the Films of Ken Loach

A broad view of the most widely known of Loach's films and documentaries reveals clear geographical clusters.

Scotland
    Riff Raff (1991)—Glasgow and London
    Carla's Song (1996)—Glasgow Strathclyde, and Nicaragua
    My Name is Joe (1998)—Glasgow
    Sweet Sixteen (2002)—Greenock/Clyde Estuary
    Ae Fond Kiss (2004)—Glasgow
    The Angel's Share (2012)—Glasgow

North of England
  Manchester:
    Questions of Leadership (Channel 4, 1983)
    Raining Stones (1993)
    Ladybird, Ladybird (1994)
    Looking for Eric (2009)
    Route Irish (2010)—Manchester, Liverpool and Jordan (doubling for Iraq)
  Yorkshire:
    Kes (1969)—Barnsley, South Yorkshire
    The Price of Coal (BBC1, 1977)—South Yorkshire
    Black Jack (1979)—North Yorkshire
    Looks and Smiles (1981)—Sheffield
    The Navigators (2001)—Sheffield
  Liverpool and Lancashire:
    The Golden Vision (BBC1, 1968)
    The Big Flame (BBC1, 1969)
    The Rank and File (BBC1, 1971)
    Land and Freedom (1995)—Liverpool and Spain
    Route Irish (2010)—Liverpool, Manchester and Jordan (doubling for Iraq)

London
    Up the Junction (BBC1, 1965)
    Cathy Come Home (BBC1, 1966)
    In Two Minds (BBC1, 1967)
    Poor Cow (1967)
    Family Life (1971)
    Riff Raff (1991)—London and Glasgow

11'09'01 (2002)
It's a Free World (2007)—East End of London, Katowice (Poland), and Kiev (Ukraine)

Ireland & Northern Ireland
Hidden Agenda (1990)
The Wind that Shakes the Barley (2006)
Jimmy's Hall (2014)

Outside the UK
In Black and White (aka *Save the Children Fund Film*) (1971)— Kenya and Essex (UK)
Carla's Song (1996)—Nicaragua and Glasgow Strathclyde
Bread and Roses (2000)—USA and Mexico
Tickets (2005)—Italy
Route Irish (2010)—Liverpool, Manchester and Jordan (doubling for Iraq)

While factors such as Loach's collaboration with different writers and his need to obtain financial support from different regions or countries are, of course, significant, nevertheless, there may be more fundamental political and ideological reasons for his choices of location and, in particular, the clusters we have noted. Given the primacy of location within each film, that is to say that the choice of actors, situation, language, and humor are tightly dependent upon location, and bearing in mind the close relationship Loach establishes between place and identity, it is useful to consider these clusters in slightly greater detail.

Three main sites can thus be identified: Glasgow and Clyde in Scotland, Manchester, Liverpool, Sheffield/Yorkshire in the north of England, and (the East End of) London. These places are linked in multiple ways. First, they all flourished and expanded in the 19th century, becoming major centers of manufacturing which attracted vast numbers of workers from across the world, and all played a key role in establishing Britain as a leading global power. Manchester, then center of the textile industry, is now recognized as having been the world's first industrial city.[20] At the same time, Sheffield dominated the world steel production, and Glasgow and Liverpool were major seaports.[21] They, along with the shipbuilding industry at Clydebank, Glasgow, played a vital role during both World Wars. Through its long and complex history of attracting immigrants to its overcrowded streets, London's East End developed countless industries (not least, textiles), and became a center for constructing and repairing ships. All of these cities and regions were once thriving, dynamic, and forward looking, at the forefront in developing new transport systems: for example, railways (the world's first intercity link was constructed between Liverpool and Manchester in 1830), shipping, and canals (for instance, the Manchester Ship Canal, 1894). All relied upon Britain's natural resources, not least iron and steel and—of course—coal, and upon an exploited and underrewarded workforce. Not surprisingly, all became vibrant centers of working-class culture, playing a key role in the development of trade unions, and the politicization of the workforce.

These same cities and regions continue to be highlighted in contemporary maps of the UK, but, unfortunately, for very different reasons. Glasgow, Manchester, Liverpool, Sheffield, and the East End of London are, today, areas of exceptionally high unemployment, with the worst national poverty rates, and the highest crime rates (particularly gang-related, organized crime).[22] It is in this bleak, post-industrial world that Loach's protagonists struggle to survive.

However, not concerned merely to show individual struggles, Loach wants us to engage with the causes of poverty, and this, of course, is a notoriously difficult project. "The mechanics of capitalism or the distribution of wealth are not 'Things' which can be seen, except in their effects," states Hill.[23] Gledhill too believes that since cinematic realism depends upon the proposition that reality equates with what we can see, it follows that the underlying forces shaping that reality cannot be portrayed.[24] Loach recognizes the problems. In discussing *Cathy Come Home*, for instance (his early television drama about the plight of the homeless, credited with leading to the development of the charity "Shelter," thus, actually contributing to social change),[25] Loach criticizes the film's failure to engage with the underlying structural causes of homelessness:

> Who owns the land? Who owns the building industry? How does housing relate to employment? How do we decide what we produce and where we produce it, under what conditions? [...] You can't abstract housing from the economic pattern. So it is a political issue; the film just didn't examine it at that level.[26]

However, I would argue that Loach's work *does* succeed in making us aware of the wider structural problems that underlie the personal struggles of his protagonists. And I suggest that the primary strategy for achieving this involves his use of location (*doubly* constructed). The clues are present in the above comments: who or what shapes the geographies of our world?

Clearly, the changing patterns of employment and mass-unemployment, poverty and wealth illustrated by Loach's preferred locations are not natural phenomena but the result of strategically motivated political and economic policies. The catalyst for the mass unemployment that marked the last decades of the 20th century in Britain and beyond (even if we now situate the problem within a wider, global context) was, of course, the coming to power of Margaret Thatcher's Conservative government in 1979. Thatcher's policies, which heralded a dramatic intensification of the class struggle (today reflected in the extreme disparity between the rich and the poor in the UK),[27] were characterized by aggressive anti-trade union legislation, the deliberate creation of record levels of unemployment (and, of course, the systematic provocation of industrial conflicts, as shown in Loach's *Questions of Leadership* (Channel 4, 1983). In her desire to "extend market forces to all areas of society,"[28] Thatcher was also responsible for weakening the notion of communal action, with consequences that are made clear in Loach's work.

Thatcher's policies, of course, are just one element within what Soja refers to as capitalism's "changing mosaics of uneven regional development."[29] In *Postmodern Geographies*, he argues that unequal regional (and national) development is fundamental to capitalism because (among other reasons) "it is the existence of underdeveloped regions, with high unemployment, that creates the reserves of labor able to respond to its spasmodic and contradictory flows."[30] Mass unemployment is thus a deliberate strategy, and uneven allocations of capital investment and social infrastructure are "deliberately maintained."[31] Thus, the poverty, frustration, hopelessness experienced by Loach's individual characters is grounded in the geography of power, and it is impossible to consider his films from a horizontal, spatial (geographic) perspective without becoming aware of this wider pattern, and extrapolating from it something of the deliberate policies that have already been noted.

Film locations import images of "real" (constructed) places into the filmic diegesis, where, flouting the conventional borders *between* truth and fiction, they are simultaneously literal and metaphorical. It is this complex space between documentary and narrative that opens up particular experience to the wider political structures of which the characters themselves have little or no understanding. Loach does also provide more obvious, less complicated clues: slogans, posters, and speeches constitute clear diegetic signposts, often full of irony as well as anger. But such elements play only a supporting role in the films' spatial geographies.

Raining Stones (1993) centers upon an unemployed worker, Bob Williams, and follows his attempts to support his family through a series of casual jobs and scams. A devout Catholic, Bob is determined to buy a *new* dress for his daughter's first communion, despite the fact that both his wife and the priest argue that a second-hand dress would be fine.[32] (The dress, of course, symbolizes Bob's attempt to retain some self-respect.) When his van is stolen (in a passing reference to Vittorio De Sica's *Bicycle Thieves*, 1948), finding work becomes even harder, and Bob is soon in serious debt, his family at risk from an unscrupulous loan shark. In desperation, Bob attacks the man, an act which leads to (but does not directly cause) the latter's death. In an unexpected twist, Bob's priest advises him not to tell anyone, and colludes in burning the list of debtors' names. Criticism of the film's apparently sympathetic treatment of the church, and its happy, even comic, ending misses the point: individual acts of frustration by a betrayed class cannot replace communal action, and it is the priest's understanding of this that enables his parishioners to survive.

This, apparently simple, tale has a powerful episodic structure in which Loach juxtaposes scenes of violence and hardship with comic episodes that remind us of the traditional importance of humor to working-class culture, as a way of forgetting problems or taking revenge. *Raining Stones* is also a film in which open, political messages are far less apparent than the more coded and complex subtexts, making it multi-layered and engaging in all sorts of ways. It was filmed over a period of six weeks, on the real-life Langley Estate, in Middleton (a suburb of Greater Manchester, just under nine kilometers north-east of the city center), constructed in the 1950s by Manchester City Council as part of their post-war slum clearance scheme.[33] This location, as "spatial imaginary rooted in the real,"[34] is thus rich with encoded cultural and political messages that root it in the wider context of capitalist exploitation. But, as filmic construct, it simultaneously situates its characters in that context, and enables

"Living off casual jobs and scams": Bruce Jones (as Bob) in *Raining Stones* (Ken Loach, 1993) (© Northern Arts Entertainment/Photofest).

us to understand and identify with them on an emotional basis. It is this aspect which will now be considered.

Positioned on the margins of the city, the estate is isolated and claustrophobic. Tight geometric framings confine and restrict Bob, his family and friends, showing us that they cannot escape, that their choices are severely limited. The grim, graffiti-covered high-rise blocks, and neglected, decaying spaces of the estate seem to stretch for ever. At one moment, as they watch a drug-fuelled fight by some young people (Loach frequently refers to this "wasted generation"), a character comments to Bob: "It's mapped out ... it's all cut and dried ... no work and no hope ... it's all despair."

Place, as we have seen, is actively constructed by "the ways in which [it] is [...] used, inhabited."[35] This is clearly shown in the film, as characters map their routes between the individual spaces of home, and the public spaces of the labor exchange, where the unemployed must "sign on," the tenants' association—private ownership having replaced council ownership—where they try to find help with their housing, and the post office, where they go to collect their social benefits. It might, just as tellingly, be mapped by what is not there. There are no banks, no department stores, no youth clubs, cinemas, or restaurants. Pubs, the traditional locus of working-class culture, do feature, and provide companionship and friendly banter; however, even they are increasingly contaminated and threatened by loan sharks and drug pushers. Conversations, whether amicable or threatening, generally take place on street corners, next to derelict buildings.

There are a few indications of the world outside the estate. The opening credit sequences are set in the countryside, as Bob and his friend Tommy attempt to catch a sheep (in a harebrained scheme to make money by selling the carcass to a butcher), but rather than providing a sense of freedom, the hills are filled with ditches and other pitfalls, and as the narrative starts, we are immediately transported to the confined spaces of the estate. On one occasion, Bob finds a job as a security guard in a nightclub in the city, but he is sacked that same night when he flies into a rage on discovering that his friend's daughter is selling drugs in the club. (Loach repeatedly highlights the irony of the fact that the drugs industry is almost the only one left flourishing today, as, for example, in *Sweet Sixteen*.) In another attempt to find work, Bob sets off to clean drains in a middle-class suburb close to where he lives. It might as well be a different universe, and the unfriendly response of the people on whose doors he knocks clearly reveals both the selfish philosophy fostered by Thatcher, and the "fractal geographies" of poverty and wealth.[36] Our only glimpse of this other universe occurs when a job he and Tommy are offered turns out to involve stealing turf from the impeccable bowling-club green of the local Conservative club.

However, if the film draws us emotionally into Bob's life, it simultaneously requires our intellectual involvement in what Loach presents as a corrupt social and political system. It never allows us to indulge in the current re-labeling of the poor as lazy, dishonest and undeserving, and while Loach neither sentimentalizes nor idealizes his characters, he does make us aware of the wider structures that have deliberately brought about their situation. The film also demonstrates that only collective action can change the system; that, alone, an individual is powerless.

By way of a brief conclusion to this geographical perspective on Loach's cinema, I shall briefly refer to elements of Loach's recent film *The Spirit of '45*, which revisit or underline the issues that have been explored in relation to *Raining Stones*. As a documentary, *The Spirit of '45* can present its message directly, rather than through the codes of fiction (although, with Loach, it is never quite that simple). Thus, while the apparent theme of the documentary is the historical construction of the welfare state in the 1940s, its real subject, I would argue is, in fact, its progressive dismantling, begun under Thatcher in the 1980s, continued under successive governments, and today at crisis point. The film combines original footage with the voices, past and present, of the participants in that footage, and provides a powerful, often passionate account of the ideals of those who were determined that Britain would never again know the poverty, exploitation, inequality, and mass-unemployment that had characterized pre-war existence. That henceforth, everyone would have the right to high-quality medical treatment, social support, and education, all without cost; that the state would be a community, owned by all its citizens, and run for their good. However, the film's structure reveals a less optimistic reading:

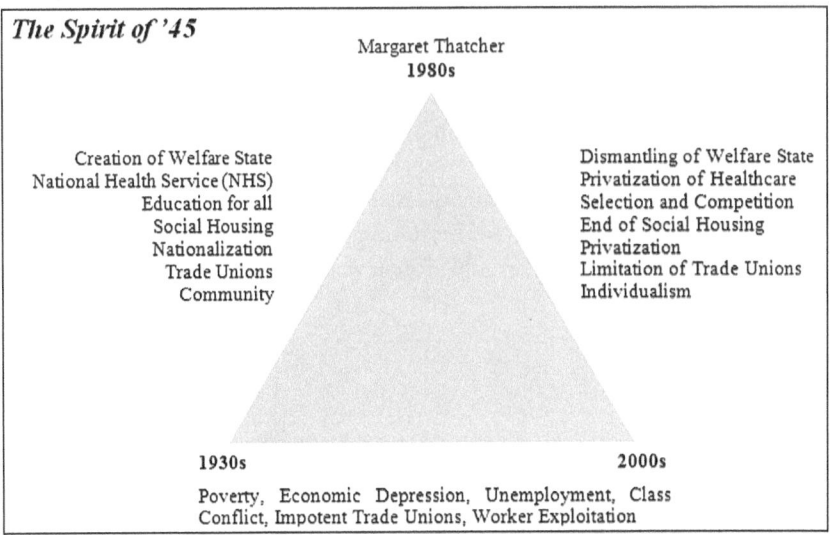

I have chosen to illustrate the film's triangular structure in diagrammatic form because this spatial analysis clarifies and highlights elements which might otherwise remain obfuscated. The triangle reveals quite strikingly, for example, the clear balance, at least in Loach's vision, of the creative reforms, seen on the left-hand side, and their systematic destruction, on the right. That Thatcher is positioned at the apex of the triangle clearly reveals the anger with which she continues to inspire Loach. But even more significant is the fact that the base line of the triangle, with its painful liturgy of poverty and suffering, refers, at the same time, to the bad old days of the 1930s, and the bad new days of the 21st century.

So what new light does this short documentary cast upon the fictional world of *Raining Stones*? It is important to note that the multiple messages of *The Spirit of '45*, both open and more coded, are most vividly expressed through images of particular places and spaces. Supporting my earlier argument, these directly reflect the geographical locations in which the majority of Loach's fiction films have been set: Glasgow, Manchester, Liverpool, and Sheffield. Place, with all its historical baggage, thus remains the dominant signifier. Moreover, as we watch real footage in which workers reminisce about the grim conditions of life in the 1930s, in Liverpool or Manchester for example, their historical accounts depressingly reflect the experiences and lives of the characters in the much more recent narrative of *Raining Stones* (or of almost any of Loach's fiction films). The warning sounded in *The Spirit of '45* is clear: the "bad old days" are here again, and the people who suffered most in the 1930s, those inhabiting Britain's bleak post-industrial landscapes, are again the most vulnerable.

Location, far from being merely incidental, is thus *precisely* targeted in Loach's work, and, as I have argued, he uses its complex dualities, its simultaneous realist and metaphorical identities as a way of situating the individual experiences of his characters within a wider, political, historical, and social context. By drawing the spectator into an open and ongoing debate involving the structural, social, and political causes of poverty and sufferings, Loach successfully overcomes the perceived limitations of cinematic narrative: he makes us aware of the underlying, invisible forces that shape all our realities.

Notes

1. The terms "underclass" and "post-working class" were originally used with pejorative implications, portraying a class which was dependent and work-shy, rather than merely unemployed. However, this is no longer the case. See, for example, Charles Murray, *The Emerging British Underclass*, London: Institute of Economic Affairs, 1990; and Claire Monk, "Underbelly UK: The 1990s

Underclass Film, Masculinity and the Ideologies of 'New' Britain" in Justine Ashby and Andrew Higson (eds.), *British Cinema, Past and Present*, London: Routledge, 2000, 274–287.

2. He has made some 25 feature films, and more than 40 television films and documentaries and, as Jerry Whyte, for example, has pointed out, Loach's work receives greater appreciation abroad than at home, perhaps because of his capacity to raise uncomfortable local issues while highlighting themes of internal concern. See Jerry Whyte, "Report on the Programmes Arranged by the British Film Institute to Celebrate the Work of Ken Loach: The Politics of Documentary, from Hidden Agenda to the Free World and Beyond, and the Political Films of Ken Loach," *Cineoutsider*, 2011: www.cineoutsider.com/articles/stories/k/ken_loach_politics_and_cinema.html, accessed 15 September 2013.

3. John Newsinger, "Scenes from the Class War: Ken Loach and Socialist Cinema," *International Socialism Journal*, vol. 2, no. 83, Summer 1999: www.marxists.org/history/etol/writers/newsinger/1999/xx/kenloach.htm, accessed 20 July 2013. As an example of extreme censorship, *In Black and White*, an hour-long documentary made in 1971 for the Save the Children Fund, was not cleared for screening until September 2011.

4. John Hill, "Finding a Form: Politics and Aesthetics in *Fatherland, Hidden Agenda*, and *Riff-Raff*" in George McKnight (ed.), *Agent of Challenge and Defiance: The Films of Ken Loach*, Trowbridge: Flicks Books, 1997, 125–143, 139.

5. See, for example, Jacob Leigh, *The Cinema of Ken Loach: Art in the Service of the People*, London: Wallflower Press, 2002; John Hill, *Ken Loach: The Politics of Film and Television*, London: Palgrave Macmillan/BFI, 2011.

6. See Loach in Graham Fuller (ed.), *Loach on Loach*, London: Faber and Faber, 1998, 4.

7. In classical Hollywood, of course, lighting was designed, quite literally, to highlight the star.

8. John Caughie neatly refers to this as "the rhetoric of the unplanned shot," in Leigh, *The Cinema of Ken Loach: Art in the Service of the People*, 17.

9. See, for instance, David Harvey, *Social Justice and the City*, Baltimore: Johns Hopkins University Press, 1973; Michel de Certeau, *The Practice of Everyday Life*, Berkeley: University of California Press, 1984.

10. For a detailed and coherent account of the conflict between space and place, see John Agnew and David Livingston (eds.), *Handbook of Geographical Knowledge*, London: Sage, 2011.

11. "Despite the seduction of endless space [...] place is beginning to escape from its entombment in the cultural and philosophical underworld of the modern West," in Edward Casey, *The Fate of Place: A Philosophical History*, Berkeley: University of California Press, 1997, 339.

12. See, for example, Catherine Fowler and Gillian Helfield (eds.), *Representing the Rural: Space, Place and Identity in Films about the Land*, Detroit: Wayne State University Press, 2006; Henri Lefebvre, *The Production of Space*, Oxford: Blackwell, 2006; John D. Rhodes and Elena Gorfinkel (eds.), *Taking Place: Location and the Moving Image*, Minneapolis: University of Minnesota Press, 2011.

13. Tim Cresswell, *Place: A Short Introduction*, Oxford: Blackwell, 2004.

14. See Allan Pred, "Place as Historically Contingent Process: Structuration and the Time-Geography of Becoming Places," *Annals of the Association of American Geographers*, vol. 74, no. 2, June 1984, 279–297; Doreen Massey, *Spatial Divisions of Labour*, Basingstoke: Macmillan, 1984.

15. Yi-Fu Tuan, *Space and Place: The Perspective of Experience*, Minneapolis: University of Minnesota Press, 1977, 6.

16. Robert David Sack, *Homo Geographicus*, Baltimore: Johns Hopkins University Press, 1997.

17. John David Rhodes and Elena Gorfinkel (eds.), *Taking Place: Location and the Moving Image*, Minneapolis: University of Minnesota Press, 2011.

18. Jeff Hopkins, "A Mapping of Cinematic Places: Icons, Ideology, and the Power of Misrepresentation" in Stuart C. Aitken and Leo Zonn (eds.), *Place, Power, Situation and Spectacle: A Geography of Film*, Lanham: Rowman & Littlefield, 1994, 47–65, 51.

19. Loach is famous for, in the 1960s, taking the television series, *Z Cars*, out of the studio and into the streets, in order to situate the narratives in their "real" contexts.

20. Alan Kidd, *Manchester: A History*, Lancaster: Carnegie, 2006.

21. By the early twentieth century, 40 percent of the world's trade passed through Liverpool.

22. See, for example, Alan R. H. Baker and Mark Billinge (eds.), *Geographies of England: The North-South Divide, Material and Imagined*, Cambridge: Cambridge University Press, 2004.

23. John Hill, *Sex, Class and Realism: British Cinema 1956–1963*, London: British Film Institute, 1986, 60.

24. Christine Gledhill, "Recent Developments in Feminist Criticism," *Quarterly Review of Film Studies*, vol. 3, no. 4, 457–493, 464.

25. Widespread public reaction to the film led the government to request a special screening attended by the Labor Minister for Housing, and to discussions in Parliament about how to solve the problem of the homeless.

26. Loach in Fuller (ed.), *Loach on Loach*, 24.

27. "Levels of income inequality [...] have now returned to their Victorian highs despite the increase in overall material wealth," Danny Dorling and John Pritchard, "The Geography of Poverty, Inequality and Wealth in the UK and Abroad: Because Enough Is Never Enough," *Applied Spatial Analysis*, vol. 3, 2010, 81–106, 94.

28. Hill, *Ken Loach: The Politics of Film and Television*, 157.

29. Edward W. Soja, *Postmodern Geographies: The Reassertion of Space in Critical Social Theory*, London: Verso, 1989, 3.

30. *Ibid.*, 105.

31. *Ibid.*, 109.

32. Since the influx of Irish migrants into Liverpool at the start of the 19th century, the city continues to hold more Catholics than any other British city. Thus, the Catholic element of the story serves as a further marker of place.

33. During the Industrial Revolution, Middleton—a town in its own right—was an important center for textile manufacturing, and first silk, then cotton production flourished there from the mid-nineteenth to mid-twentieth centuries. However, by the 1990s, factories were closed, unemployment was widespread, and soaring debt was feeding drug-related and other crimes, as well as fostering the sense of hopelessness the film explores.

34. John Orr, *The Art and Politics of Film*, Edinburgh: Edinburgh University Press, 2000, 138.

35. *Ibid.*, 137.

36. Dorling and Pritchard, "The Geography of Poverty, Inequality and Wealth in the UK and Abroad: Because Enough is Never Enough," 90.

Works Cited

Agnew, John, and David Livingston (eds.). *Handbook of Geographical Knowledge*. London: Sage, 2011.

Aitken, Stuart, and Leo Zonn (eds.). *Place, Power, Situation and Spectacle: A Geography of Film*. Lanham: Rowman & Littlefield, 1994.

Baker, Alan R.H., and Mark Billinge (eds.). *Geographies of England: The North-South Divide, Material and Imagined*. Cambridge: Cambridge University Press, 2004.

Casey, Edward S. *The Fate of Place: A Philosophical History*. Berkeley: University of California Press, 1997.

Chell, David. *Moviemakers at Work: Interviews*. Redmond: Microsoft Press, 1987.

Cresswell, Tim. *Place: A Short Introduction*. Oxford: Blackwell, 2004.

de Certeau, Michel. *The Practice of Everyday Life*. Berkeley: University of California Press, 1984.

Dorling, Danny, and John Pritchard. "The Geography of Poverty, Inequality and Wealth in the UK and Abroad: Because Enough is Never Enough." *Applied Spatial Analysis*, vol. 3, 2010, 81–106.

Fowler, Catherine, and Gillian Helfield (eds.). *Representing the Rural: Space, Place and Identity in Films about the Land*. Detroit: Wayne State University Press, 2006.

Fuller, Graham (ed.). *Loach on Loach*. London: Faber and Faber, 1998.

Gledhill, Christine. "Recent Developments in Feminist Criticism." *Quarterly Review of Film Studies*, vol. 3, no. 4, 1978, 457–493.

Harvey, David. *Social Justice and the City*. Baltimore: Johns Hopkins University Press, 1973.

Hill, John. *Ken Loach. The Politics of Film and Television*. London: Palgrave Macmillan/BFI, 2011.

Hill, John. *British Cinema in the 1980s*. Oxford: Oxford University Press, 1999.
Hill, John. "Finding a Form: Politics and Aesthetics in *Fatherland, Hidden Agenda*, and *Riff-Raff*" in George McKnight (ed.), *Agent of Challenge and Defiance: The Films of Ken Loach*. Trowbridge: Flicks Books, 1997, 125–143.
Hill, John. *Sex, Class and Realism: British Cinema 1956–1963*. London: BFI, 1986.
Kidd, Alan. *Manchester: A History*. Lancaster: Carnegie, 2006.
Lefebvre, Henri. *The Production of Space*. Oxford: Blackwell, 1991.
Lefebvre, Martin (ed.). *Landscape and Film*. New York: Routledge, 2006.
Leigh, Jacob. *The Cinema of Ken Loach: Art in the Service of the People*. London: Wallflower Press, 2002.
Massey, Doreen. *Spatial Divisions of Labour*. Basingstoke: Macmillan, 1984.
Monk, Claire. "Underbelly UK: The 1990s Underclass Film, Masculinity and the Ideologies of 'New' Britain" in Justine Ashby and Andrew Higson (Eds.), *British Cinema, Past and Present*. London: Routledge, 2000, 274–287.
Murray, Charles. *The Emerging British Underclass*. London: Institute of Economic Affairs, 1990.
Newsinger, John. "Scenes from the Class War: Ken Loach and Socialist Cinema." *International Socialism Journal*, vol. 2, no. 83, Summer 1999: www.marxists.org/history/etol/writers/newsinger/1999/xx/kenloach.htm, accessed 20 July 2013.
Orr, John. *The Art and Politics of Film*. Edinburgh: Edinburgh University Press, 2000.
Pred, Allan. "Place as Historically Contingent Process: Structuration and the Time-Geography of Becoming Places." *Annals of the Association of American Geographers*, vol. 74, no. 2, June 1984, 279–297.
Rhodes, John D., and Elena Gorfinkel (eds.). *Taking Place: Location and the Moving Image*. Minneapolis: University of Minnesota Press, 2011.
Sack, Robert David. *Homo Geographicus*. Baltimore: Johns Hopkins University Press, 1997.
Soja, Edward W. *Postmodern Geographies: The Reassertion of Space in Critical Social Theory*. London: Verso, 1989.
Tuan, Yi-Fu. *Space and Place: The Perspective of Experience*. Minneapolis: University of Minnesota Press, 1977.
Whyte, Jerry. "Report on the Programmes Arranged by the British Film Institute to Celebrate the Work of Ken Loach: The Politics of Documentary, from Hidden Agenda to the Free World and Beyond, and the Political Films of Ken Loach." *Cineoutsider*, 2011: www.cineoutsider.com/articles/stories/k/ken_loach_politics_and_cinema.html, accessed 15 September 2013.

Part Four

Social Class through a Gender Perspective

Vanishing Act
The Sexualization of the Workplace and Disappearance of Class in American Television Dramas (1990s–2010s)

Ava Baron

This essay explores the dramatic changes in how women workers have been represented on American television, focusing on hour-long television dramas from the 1990s to the present. Women workers' visibility in television drama in recent decades reflects the reality of their changed presence in the U.S. labor force. The multiplicity of women workers in television drama has served as daily reminders of the progress women workers have made in achieving equality. However, those same representations have distorted the nature of this progress, masking the gendered power relations of the actual workplace.[1]

Early research on women in television programs in the 1970s had pointed to the "symbolic annihilation of women," noting that in television shows, there were limited numbers of female characters, fewer of women at work, and even fewer in leadership positions.[2] When women did appear on television, they were stereotyped as temptresses, victims, or damsels in distress.[3]

However, in the 1980s new television dramas, such as *Cagney & Lacey* (1981), *Designing Women* (1986), *L.A. Law* (1986), and *Murphy Brown* (1988), featured women professionals as central characters, but these were still exceptional. In the early 1990s new television series with women as lead characters appeared, such as *N.Y.P.D. Blue* (1993), *Chicago Hope* (1994), *Dr. Quinn, Medicine Woman* (1993), and *E.R.* (1994). By the end of the 1990s, women workers appeared with regularity in television dramas, as lawyers, doctors and police detectives in such hit series as *Ally McBeal* (1997), *Family Law* (1999), *Judging Amy* (1999), and *Law & Order: SVU* (1999).

We might laud these trends as a sign that television programming policies have shifted towards presenting positive images of women in work settings.[4] This shift in programming follows changes in women's labor force participation rates during the past fifty years.[5] American women workers benefited from the expansion of civil rights legislation which prohibited sex discrimination in employment, and eventually from interpretation of these laws to prohibit sexual harassment at the workplace. American law considers sexual harassment at the workplace to be a "form of discrimination based on one's sex" not only when employers or supervisors coerce employees to engage in sexual relations as a condition of employment, but also when employers, supervisors or co-workers engage in "unwelcome sexual advances, requests for sexual favors, and other verbal or physical conduct of a sexual nature" that create "an intimidating, hostile, or offensive working environment," if its purpose or effect was "unreasonably interfering with an individual's work performance."[6]

The prevalence of women professionals, as lawyers, doctors, and police detectives in television dramas during the past decade highlights the progress women workers have made in achieving equality in the labor force. In most of these shows employment discrimination against women workers has largely vanished; indeed, in some of them there has been a gender reversal of power: women are represented as having moved into positions of authority at work and men have become the subordinates. In *Law & Order*, for example, the longest running drama series on prime-time television (1990–2010), in some seasons, a white woman is the head prosecutor and a black woman is chief of detectives; in addition, women of various ethnic groups appear as police detectives and assistant prosecutors. Similarly in a more recent program, *Body of Proof* (2011–2013), another white woman plays the lead character as medical examiner, and a black woman plays the role of police chief. The days of women workers on television only as "tokens" have passed; in the new television image of the workplace, women not only dominate in numbers, but also in power and authority.

While the placement of women workers at the center of numerous primetime television series appears to represent a sea change in the portrayal of women workers, this gendered transformation of television programming actually operates as a set of magic tricks which mask the reality of ongoing gender inequality at the workplace. One magic trick is the way television's foregrounding of women workers as professionals misrepresents the actual gender division and hierarchy of the American workplace. Since television dramas focus on lawyers, doctors and detectives, placing women as main characters wrongly suggests that most women workers have careers and lead upper-middle-class lifestyles. Even when women characters have working-class backgrounds, television shows typically focus on the skill and professional nature of the work, or the character's upward mobility. Poor and working-class women remain invisible, even as they appear in the background, performing typical women's work as hotel maids, nannies, waitresses and sales clerks, factory workers and welfare mothers.[7]

Another magic trick includes how television programs make the class and gender hierarchies of the workplace vanish by representing the workplace as a space in which sex discrimination is no longer a problem. A third is their erasure and distortion of current social and legal realities regarding discrimination at the workplace. The headlines of two newspaper articles in 2013 provide examples and stark reminders about the difficulties women workers in the U.S. continue to confront. In one article, the *New York Times* reported on the status of women at Harvard's Business School and the ways male students harassed them, and an array of other forms of discrimination women experienced at school, the wage differentials that followed them through their careers. The second article, from a local New Jersey paper, reported on a lawsuit brought by seven police officers for sex discrimination and harassment by the police chief.[8]

These articles foreground what the representations of women workers in television dramas now obscure—that the American labor force still is significantly segregated by sex, and that discrimination towards women workers continues.[9] Although women have made some strides in the types of occupations highlighted on television drama—lawyers, doctors and detectives—in reality they tend to be clustered in the lower rungs of these occupations with significantly lower wages.[10] Despite the dramatic increase of women in the U.S. paid labor force since the 1970s, gender inequities in salaries prevail, and numbers of complaints of sex discrimination made by women workers remain high.[11]

Although the representation of women workers does not neatly mesh with reality, a case can be made that these television dramas have contributed a positive image of women workers to the broader cultural discourse about gender relations and work in modern society. The repetition of images of women at work may make it easier for young women today, who expect that they will need to work for most of their adult lives, to imagine that they can feel "at home" at the workplace. My purpose is not to vilify television for its misrepresentations of reality, but to address the ways women workers' increased visibility on television simultaneously contributes to a cultural discourse that masks issues of conflict and power at work. Sex, and women's sexuality in particular, constitute the core of this discourse.

Two seemingly contradictory themes have characterized the increased representation of women workers in television dramas since the 1990s: the desexualization of the workplace on the one hand, and its sexualization on the other. The ways sexual relations at the workplace are fictionalized in television programs points to how social class issues operate as a silent subtext in TV fictions.

Desexualization: Banning Sex from the Workplace

When women workers began to appear with some regularity in television dramas by 1990, issues relating to women's sexuality at the workplace were downplayed. Primarily this was accomplished by minimizing representations of sexual difference between men and women, and by presenting women workers as being, and looking, like men. Clothing styles deemed fashionable, such as padded shoulders for women, exemplified this trend.

The modern workplace has long been culturally defined as "sexless," driven only by impersonal market forces and the efficient pursuit of profit, or in government and non-profits, the operation of bureaucratic rationality. From the vantage point of Western industrial capitalism, which dichotomized mind and body, work and home, men workers were deemed to be sexless beings whose rationality was jeopardized when women infected the workforce with their sexuality and its attendant emotion and irrationality.[12] A mixed sex workplace was believed to "naturally" result in sexual tensions and attractions which were disruptive to productivity and to managerial control of workers.

Early rulings about sexual harassment in American courts in the 1970s echoed these concerns about the consequence of women's presence at the workplace. Sexual harassment was considered "natural" and "inevitable" in sexually mixed workplaces. The only way to avoid that, as one federal judge put it, was to "have employees who were asexual."[13]

Throughout most of the nineteenth and twentieth centuries, legal, managerial, and cultural discourses attempted to maintain the workplace as "sexless" by restricting women's entry into the labor force, and by minimizing the acceptance of those women who entered. But by the 1970s, with women entering the workforce in ever larger numbers, an exclusionary strategy was no longer a viable option.

As if to build on the judges' advice quoted above, a broad range of cultural discourses began to proliferate, providing advice to would-be successful women about appropriate dress, comportment, communication and interaction style. Women workers remained defined by their sexuality, but they were advised that they could succeed if they masked or overcame it through a particular type of gender "performance." Countless books and articles provided advice to women workers about dress, behavior, and comportment that would enable them to act and look more like men. In the 1970s, for example, women workers were advised to get assertiveness training and adopt a particular "dress for success" style. By the 1980s, fashionable dress for women included mannish styled suits and heavily padded shoulders that imitated male physique in an extreme form. Shoulder pads in women's fashion increased in size throughout the 1980s, seeming to mimic football players. Television dramas such as *L.A. Law* picked up on this advice and costumed successful women in this form of "power dressing" that attempted to mask their feminine sexuality.[14]

During the 1990s, as padded shoulders waned in popularity, proper dress-for-success attire for women workers on television still built on the notion that women who wanted to be taken seriously should downplay their femininity and sexuality by donning supposedly genderless and asexual style uniforms or emulating the dress of middle-class professional men whose monochrome wardrobes of dark colored tailored suits conveyed the impression of competence and authority.

In reality as well as in television drama, the burden of becoming asexual was placed on women workers themselves. The message for women was that they had to lose their sexuality and become "asexual." But this created a problematic tightrope for women to walk: The path to becoming asexual was to adopt the manner and style of the opposite sex without adopting male sexuality. If women became too much like men, they would be labeled lesbian.[15] Women and men had to figure out how to identify the tipping point. In some instances, this eliding of asexuality and lesbianism is explicit.

Television drama series in the 1990s created a vision of the workplace that was sanitized of sexuality. In such settings, work relations follow the seemingly normal bureaucratic hierarchical chain of command with power difference represented as natural and reasonable. Organizational decisions, including employment decisions of hiring, firing and promotion, are not presented as based on irrational factors, such as gender, race, sexual orientation, or class background. Thus when the hardworking, smart and experienced Serena Southerlyn, a female assistant prosecutor in 85 episodes of *Law & Order*, is fired, she simply accepts her boss's explanation: She has not been fired for the irrational reason of her deviant lesbian sexuality, but because she is deemed *not masculine enough*; he believes she is "too emotional" to do the highly combative and masculine work of criminal prosecution. The gendered characterization of the work is presented as natural and necessary.[16]

Although at actual workplaces, sex discrimination and harassment remain real problems, rarely have these been visible in television dramas of the "asexual" workplace. Television's silence about these issues suggested that these problems no longer existed. The occasional inappropriate and irrational forms of discriminatory remarks were presented as a matter of individual deviance, separated from the hierarchical nature of work organization, and deemed remediable by internal organizational mechanisms or, if necessary, by legal action. By depicting such situations as the consequence of discrete instances of individual misbehavior, the structural and cultural foundations for this problem remained invisible.[17]

Sexualization of the Workplace

By contrast to the sanitized television workplace of the 1990s, shows featuring women at work in the past decade have been saturated with sex. To underscore the emphasis on sexuality, television dramas often open with sex scenes with a focus on women's bodies.[18] The "asexual" women workers who had pervaded television series have been largely displaced by those who flaunt their sexualized bodies and distinctly traditional style feminine sexuality. For women workers on television in such shows as *House* (2004–2012) and *Boston Legal* (2004–2008), "dress for success" meant revealing one's body, not covering it up.

Given the highly charged sexual environment depicted in these television shows, we might expect that sexual harassment would be a common theme. Quite the contrary. Like the "asexual" television shows, rarely are sexual encounters depicted as sexual harassment. We have countless episodes of men and women engaging in sexual flirtations, banter, innuendos and acts. Sexual relationships between co-workers are common, as are those between supervisors and employees. Yet none of this is defined as sexual harassment, because all of it is represented as "welcome" and consensual by both the women and men.

Television dramas in the past decade have been displacing the notion that sex should be banned from the workplace, with a vision of work as a sphere in which sexual relations, rather than class relations, predominate. For example, in *Private Practice* (2007 to date), a long-running medical drama series, doctors in the practice engage in sexual affairs with each other, changing partners and achieving almost every conceivable combination. Neither the race nor class of participants is treated as having power dimensions. Because the sexual relationships are between those in the same profession, issues of power appear irrelevant. The race of the participants is rarely addressed as problematic, despite the multiple instances of interracial affairs during the series, which is remarkable, given the ongoing salience of race in American society. Similarly, admission into the medical profession is represented as having erased the relevance of the class background of the show's characters.

Increasingly, since the turn of the 21st century, similar scenarios about sexual relationships at professional workplaces play out in television dramas. Sexual coercion is rarely depicted as a problem for women at the workplace. Even in instances involving organizational inequality, when a hierarchical supervisory relationship is involved, representing the relationship as consensual makes it appear that power is irrelevant. This pattern of depicting sexual relationships at the workplace as wholly consensual, regardless of status or power differences, is commonplace in television dramas in the past decade. These representations, which appear, for example, in *Bones* (2005 to date), *Body of Proof* (2011–2013) and *Conviction* (2006), even leave the impression that men no longer are sexually dominant, and that women are more eager than men to have sex.

Accompanying this sexualization of the workplace is the overrepresentation of women who are "in charge" of their own sexuality. In many shows, such as *Conviction, Grey's Anatomy* (2005 to date), and *Longmire* (2012–2013), women workers are depicted as sexually aggressive and as initiators of sexual relationships, even with their bosses. Numerous episodes depict women workers openly flaunting their sexuality at work with a "take charge" attitude. These women are shown ready and willing to use their sexuality to their own advantage.

Instead of women's bodies constructed as objects of the male gaze, contemporary television dramas present a portrait of female agency and female sexuality that is empowering. While sexuality might pervade the workplace, women are portrayed as capable of resisting unwanted sexual overtures. The portrayals of women workers as victims have been replaced by those which show women as strong, independent, and not in need of legal protection.

Such visions of women workers have the potential to disrupt demeaning images of women as passive and powerless. However, placed in broader social and cultural context, the same images that serve to disrupt hegemonic masculinity can also operate to reinforce it. Images of a sexualized workplace dominated by women workers dovetail with claims of a "litigation explosion" in which women workers have won outlandish sums for discrimination claims. With the news media giving attention to some high profile cases in the 1990s, a narrative of the law having gone "too far" began to proliferate. In this narrative, sex discrimination laws are faulted for giving women power over men at the workplace, resulting in an inversion of the natural order; at the same time, sexual harassment regulations are faulted for causing stilted social interaction and destabilizing the workplace. Sitcoms and dramadies, such as *Boston Legal*, and *Ally McBeal* (1997–2002), regularly mock the litigiousness of American women workers who sue because they are overly moralistic, because they cannot take a joke, because the women were provocative by their dress or manner, or simply because they want to cause "trouble."

Erasing Class and Power from the Sexualized Workplace

Television drama representations of the last decade increasingly have depicted the contemporary workplace as one in which sexuality is pervasive, normal, and unproblematic.[19] Television's focus on professional, non-bureaucratic occupations has facilitated this representation. Professional work emphasizes

"Flaunting their sexualized bodies": Jane Krakowski (as Elaine Vassal) in *Ally McBeal* (season 1, episode 10 "Silver Bells," 1997) (© Fox Broadcasting Co./Photofest).

work organization that is primarily collegial rather than hierarchical; unlike most work settings which utilize formal bureaucratic rules seeking to limit workers' discretion, professional settings tend to be more informal and allow workers much autonomy. Television dramas transform this professional collegiality into a depiction of work which appears to be non-hierarchical. In this setting, class distinctions disappear despite status and power differences between working-class and professional workers, and between supervisors and those they supervise, emphasizing instead that they both share the same profession or are part of the same "team." Instead television shows such as *The Newsroom* (2012 to date), *Private Practice*, and *Grey's Anatomy*, direct our attention to the relationships between characters as peers, and often as friends. The sexually coercive characteristic of hierarchical work settings vanishes.

Television's sexualization of work and representation of women workers contribute to cultural discourses that mask the ways class issues are implicated in gender inequality at the workplace, and the ways gender continues to be used to naturalize hierarchical work relations. Remarkably there has been little scholarly attention to these issues. By not treating these issues as problematic, this silence has further contributed to a discourse about sex at work in which class issues appear not to matter.

The sexualized workplace is devoid of the class power relations between employer and employee, supervisor and worker. Supervisory power is weak, and rules often unenforced. Its treatment of sexuality at work also erases the relevance of race as an axis of power. As I have shown earlier, men and women workers in television shows regularly have sexual relations with supervisors and/or co-workers of varying rank, race, ethnicity and class. In so doing, these images ignore scholarly literature that documents the ways "bodies" are viewed, not only in terms of sex, but also in terms of class and race, and that particular cultural notions of unequal sexual attractiveness, desirability, availability and vulnerability, are inscribed on bodies of different class and race. But in the television fiction of a workplace in which sex is rampant but sexual harassment does not exist, neither class background nor race are salient to how women workers are viewed and treated. Sexual attractions and attentions (wanted or not) are portrayed as uniformly applicable to women, be they black, Asian or white, or upper-class, middle-class or working-class.

Rarely visible on television workplace dramas are situations involving sexual harassment by a supervisor and coerced quid pro quo of job benefits for sex; nor are there many depictions of unwelcome sexual attentions by either supervisors or co-workers, or work environments that are intimidating or hostile to women generally, or to minority women, minority men, or to individuals based on their sexual orientation. In instances when male characters in high level supervisory positions have sexual relationships with women, there is imputed no harm to women; rather, often women are the ones who are portrayed as having power and control over these men, even their bosses. For example, in an episode of *Grey's Anatomy*, a black man, who is the attending supervisory physician at the hospital, confesses to an Asian female medical intern with whom he is having a sexual affair, that he has suddenly become aware of why this relationship is a problem. He concludes, quite ironically, that the problem is that she has power to unduly influence his professional decisions by exercising her feminine wiles, not that he has the power to control her future career opportunities.[20]

Sexual Harassment, Law and the Television Workplace

Contrary to mythologies about law circulating in popular discourses (in news, film, television) which depict the slightest innuendo as grounds for a lawsuit, a sexual harassment legal claim in the U.S. must demonstrate "sufficiently severe and pervasive" conditions that "unreasonably" interfere with a worker's performance and create an intimidating work environment. A plaintiff must prove that the sexually harassing conduct constituted discrimination *because of sex*, not that such conduct was "merely tinged with offensive sexual connotations." American courts have declared that there are "genuine but innocuous differences in the ways men and women routinely interact," that not all workplace harassment constitutes sex discrimination, and that the purpose of sexual harassment regulations is not to create a "general civility code" for the American workplace.[21]

Since the meaning of sexual harassment is a contested and problematic concept legally and culturally, the perception that a highly sexualized work environment is normal makes it harder to demonstrate the "reasonableness" of a woman worker's perceptions. The normalization of sexuality at the televised workplace makes it more difficult for women workers to demonstrate the existence of the harm of sexual harassment, for if sex at the workplace is "normal" then how can it be "harmful?" Media depictions of a sexualized workplace become part of the "broad social context" that judges and jurors have explicitly relied upon to interpret whether the behavior was normal or "unwelcome," sexual harassment or not.

Television drama representations of the sexualization of work fall into four broad themes: (1) mutual sexual tensions between male and female workers that are an integral component of the plot[22]; (2) men and women working together in an atmosphere in which there is no sexual relationship or attraction, or in which no negative or sexually inappropriate remarks or behavior occur[23]; (3) women using their sexual attractiveness as a "tool" to help them at the workplace; and (4) hostile work environment sexual harassment explicitly referenced, but in ways that trivialize (e.g., as comic or "innocent" or insignificant words or deeds) and/or demonize it (e.g., law suits which will yield horrific, unjust consequences, such as shutting down a company).[24]

These four themes, taken together, depict sexual relations between men and women workers based on the seemingly natural attraction between sexes, and therefore unavoidable. From this perspective, the sexualization of the workplace has nothing to do with relations of power: gender hierarchy is inverted, race is visible but irrelevant, and hierarchical work relations in a capitalist society are non-existent.

The logical conclusion drawn from these depictions of sexual harassment is that it can be, indeed it has been, sufficiently regulated, if not entirely eradicated. One of the few television drama series that seriously addressed sexual harassment was *Mad Men* (2007 to date). However, since the show concerns the early 1960s, an era prior to the naming of sexual harassment by the women's movement and its legal recognition by the U.S. Supreme Court in 1986, the series actually underscores progress by contrasting the "bad old days" when women workers were powerless underlings and sexual objects, to the contemporary era, not only allegedly free of all this, but in which women often hold power and act as sexual aggressors towards men.

To be sure, the legal recognition of both quid pro quo as well as hostile work environment forms of sexual harassment has been a major victory for women workers, and has provided women workers with increased legal rights and remedies. However, at the same time, sexual harassment law has also created new ways for the workplace to operate as a site to control of women's sexuality.[25] Sexual harassment regulations have created a regime for controlling sexuality in the workplace, and for redirecting workplace conflict in ways that make class conflict less evident. Sexual harassment law also defines some forms of sexuality at the workplace as legitimate and normal, and induces a struggle over how and where to mark that boundary in incremental terms. Sexual harassment codes of behavior legitimate the policing of worker behavior while also reinforcing traditional gender and racial stereotypes.[26] Further, sexual harassment law, like other issues of legal "rights" of workers, define the problem as an individual, not collective one.

The importance of class to sexual harassment is evident in multiple ways. It is apparent in the high rates of sexual harassment of women who work at the lower rungs of the occupation ladder[27]; it is implicated in the unequal distribution of power that derives from organizational work hierarchies; it derives from and reproduces gender discourses that have been shown to be embedded in work relations, labor processes, and occupational structures[28]; and it operates as a "technology of class" by creating additional workplace rules that enhance control and oversight of workers' behavior on a micro-level, co-opting control of workers' sexuality as a form of class resistance in an alienating work environment.[29] Laws forbidding sexual harassment at the workplace operate as a new regime of managerial regulations that have been set into place to observe, control, and punish.

Finally, sexual harassment law creates a modern Panopticon, encouraging workers to engage in continual self-surveillance, training them to watch and regulate their own behavior, dress, language, comportment and social interaction using the internalizing codes and rules that reproduce class hierarchies and identities. Yet the role of class remains a hidden dimension of work in legal and cultural discourses and an under-theorized component of sexual harassment.[30]

The reality constructed in television dramas entails a fantasy workplace in which organizations are hierarchical, but employers and workers relate as equals; bureaucratic rules proliferate, but their violation results in little consequences; and the rare dispute resembles the quickly settled family quarrels on *Leave it to Beaver* (1957–1963). In this Oz-like land, gender differences have been eradicated, and the female gaze now complements and balances the male gaze. Men, regardless of occupational rank, appear simultaneously as caring and sensitive but still bearers of hegemonic masculinity, while women are presented as able to retain their femininity despite attaining career success and the dominance and power that might otherwise mean. Although men are shown subject to women's voyeuristic gaze, women in various stages of "undress" are more typically subject to the male gaze. Indeed it is the normality of the male gaze that gives the reverse of the female gaze its carnivalesque and comic character.[31] This make-believe equality rooted in gender contradictions operates to mask not only the realities of gender at the workplace, but the ways gender and class hierarchies intertwine and reinforce each other.[32]

In the struggles over sexuality at work, class relations have remained a silent, but significant, force. From the vantage point of television dramas structurally based struggles over the nature of work do not exist. In the reality they have constructed, the workplace is not a site of conflict over the sexualization of the workplace but merely a normal and "natural" component of gender relations that are independent of class.

Class as a form of social relations rooted in hierarchical work processes and economic inequality vanishes in television shows by making them seem like they are not about the workplace at all. Instead, the workplace is characterized as a space in which power is irrelevant; hierarchical relations are portrayed as natural and reasonable, and conflicts at the workplace are depicted as based solely on individual disagreements. Class as the foundation for conflict, the ways intersecting discourses about gender, race and sexuality have operated to naturalize class relations and how work is organized are not part of television reality—they have magically disappeared.[33]

Appendix I: Workplace Television Dramas Sample[34]

Show Name	Years	Episodes	Network/Producer
Ally McBeal Legal dramedy	1997–2002	5 seasons 112 episodes	FOX/David E. Kelley
Body of Proof Crime drama/forensic examiner	2011–2013	3 seasons 42 episodes	ABC/Christopher Murphy
Bones Forensic examiner	2005–	8 seasons 166 episodes	FOX/Hart Hanson
Boston Legal Legal dramedy	2004–2008	5 seasons 101 episodes	ABC/David E. Kelley
City of Angels Medical drama	2000	1 season 22 episodes	CBS—Paris Barclay
The Closer Crime drama	2005–2012	7 seasons 110 episodes	TNT/Kyra Sedgwick
Conviction Crime drama	2006	1 season 13 episodes	NBC/Dick Wolf
Crossing Jordan Crime drama/forensic examiner	2001–2007	6 seasons 117 episodes	NBC/Tim Kring
Damages Legal drama	2007–2012	5 seasons 59 episodes	FX/Glenn Kessler, Todd Kessler, Daniel Zelman
The Defenders Legal drama	2010–2011	1 season 18 episodes	CBS/Niels Mueller
The Division	2001–2004	82 episodes	CBS/Deborah Joy LeVine
Emily Owens MD Medical drama	2012–2013	1 season 13 episodes	CW/Jennie Snyder
ER Medical drama	1994–2009	15 seasons 331 episodes	NBC/Michael Crichton
Family Law Legal drama	1999–2002	3 seasons 68 episodes	CBS/Paul Haggis

Golden Boy Police drama	2013	1 season 13 episodes	CBS/Nicholas Wootton
Good Wife Legal drama	2009–	4 seasons 91 episodes	CBS/Michelle King (I), Robert King (III)
Grey's Anatomy Medical drama	2005–	9 seasons 196 episodes	ABC/Shonda Rhimes
The Guardian Legal/court drama	2001–2004	3 seasons 67 episodes	CBS/David Hollander
Homicide: Life on the Streets Police drama	1993–1999	7 seasons 177 episodes	NBC/Barry Levinson
House Medical drama	2004–2012	8 seasons 176 episodes	FOX/David Shore
In Plain Sight Crime drama	2008–2012	4 seasons 61 episodes	USA/David Maples
JAG Military crime drama	1995–2005	10 seasons 227 episodes	CBS, NBC/David Bellisario
Judging Amy Court/legal	1999–2005	6 seasons 138 episodes	CBS/Amy Brenneman
Justice	2006–2007	13 episodes	FOX/David McNally
L.A. Law Legal drama	1986–1994	8 seasons 173 episodes	NBC/Steven Bochco
Law & Order Crime drama	1990–2010	20 seasons 457 episodes	NBC/Dick Wolf
Law & Order: CI Crime drama	2001–2011	20 seasons 457 episodes	NBC/Dick Wolf
Law & Order: SVU Crime drama	1999–	14 seasons 318 episodes	NBC/Dick Wolf
Longmire Crime drama	2012–2013	2 seasons 23 episodes	A&E/Christopher Chulack
Mad Men Historical drama, 1960s advertising agency	2007–	6 seasons 78 episodes	AMC/Matthew Weiner
The Newsroom	2012–	3 seasons 29 episodes	HBO/Aaron Sorokin
NYPD Blue Crime drama	1993–2005	12 seasons 263 episodes	ABC/Steven Bochco, Mark Tinker, David Milch
Political Animals	2012	1 season 6 episodes	USA/Greg Berlanti

Private Practice Medical drama	2007–	6 seasons 110 episodes	ABC/Shonda Rhimes, Mark Tinker
Rizzoli & Isles Forensics/crime drama	2010–present	4 seasons 52 episodes	TNT/Michael Katleman
The Shield Police/ Crime drama	2002–2008	7 seasons 88 episodes	FX-cable—Shawn Ryan
Strong Medicine	2000–2006	6 seasons 132 episodes	LIFETIME/James Stanley, John Perrin Flynn, Jeremy R. Littman
Third Watch	1999–2005	6 seasons 131 episodes	NBC/John Wells, Edward Allen Bernero
The Wire	2002–2008	5 seasons 60 episodes	HBO/David Simon
Without a Trace Crime drama	2002–2009	7 seasons 160 episodes	CBS/Hank Steinberg

Notes

1. Approximately 30 television dramas that aired between 1990 and 2013 were examined. See appendix for details.
2. Report of the U.S. Commission on Civil Rights, *Window Dressing on the Set: Women and Minorities in Television*, Washington, D.C.: GPO, 1997; Gaye Tuchman, Arlene Kaplan Daniels and James Benit (eds.), *Hearth and Home: Images of Women in the Mass Media*, New York: Oxford University Press, 1978; on symbolic annihilation in the media, see George Gerbner and Larry Gross, "Living with Television: The Violence Profile," *Journal of Communication*, vol. 26, no. 2, Spring 1976, 172–199.
3. Bonnie J. Dow, *Prime-Time Feminism: Television, Media Culture, and the Women's Movement Since 1970*, Philadelphia: University of Pennsylvania Press, 1996, xviii.
4. Amanda D. Lotz, "Introduction: Female-Centered Dramas after the Network Era," 1–36; and "Of Female Cops and Docs: The Reformulation of Workplace Dramas and Other Trends in Mixed-Sex Ensembles," 144–164, in Amanda D. Lotz (ed.), *Redesigning Women: Television after the Network Era*, Urbana: University of Illinois Press, 2006.
5. According to the U.S. Department of Labor, in 2010, 58.6 percent of American women were labor force participants (working or looking for work); the median weekly earnings of full-time women workers compared to men's was 81 percent, and women have entered a range of traditionally male professions, such as medicine and law. U.S. Department of Labor, Women's Bureau, "Women in the Labor Force in 2010," http://www.dol.gov/wb/factsheets/Qf-laborforce-10.htm; 54 percent of American women with children three years of age and under are in the labor force; 63 percent with children ages three to five, and 67 percent of women with children under 15. Data from the Organization for Economic Cooperation and Development cited by Pamela Druckerman, "Catching Up with France on Day Care," *New York Times*, 1 September 2013, Sunday Review, 12.
6. Title VII of the Civil Rights Act of 1964 (amended 1972); U.S. Equal Employment Opportunity Commission, http://www.eeoc.gov/laws/types/sexual_harassment.cfm, accessed 30 January 2014; *Meritor Savings Bank v Vinson*, 477 U.S. 57, 1986. On the differences between the legal and cultural status of sexual harassment in France and the U.S., see Abigail C. Saguy, *What Is Sexual Harassment? From Capitol Hill to the Sorbonne*, Berkeley: University of California Press, 2003.

7. Only a limited number of working-class women have appeared in television series, and most of these have been in comedic rather than dramatic shows. See Amanda D. Lotz, "Introduction: Female-Centered Dramas after the Network Era" in Amanda D. Lotz (ed.), *Redesigning Women: Television after the Network Era*, 1–36; and "Of Female Cops and Docs: The Reformulation of Workplace Dramas and Other Trends in Mixed-Sex Ensembles," Ibid., 144–164.

8. Jodi Kanter, "Harvard Business School Case Study: Gender Equity," *New York Times*, Education: http://www.nytimes.com/2013/09/08/education/harvard-case-study-gender-equity.html?ref=education, accessed 7 September 2013; and "7 Princeton Officers File Suit Against Town, Former Chief," *Trenton Times*, 7 September 2013, A1.

9. "7 Princeton Officers File Suit Against Town, Former Chief," *Trenton Times*, 7 September 2013, A1.

10. About four in ten women and men work in jobs that are at least 75 percent either female or male. In 1980s, American women constituted five percent of police detectives, 14 percent of lawyers and judges, and 14 percent of physicians. By 2010, those numbers only increased to 17 percent, 36 percent and 36, percent, respectively. Lisa Wade, "Job Segregation by Sex, 1972–2008," *Sociological Images*, 2 May 2010: http://thesocietypages.org/socimages/2010/05/02/job-segregation-by-sex-1972-2008/, accessed 30 January 2014; "Jobs Where Gender Segregation Persists," *New York Times*, 30 September 2012: http://www.nytimes.com/imagepages/2012/09/30/opinion/30coontz-gr1.html?ref=sunday, accessed 30 January 2014.

11. According to the U.S. Equal Employment Opportunity Commission, over 30,000 complaints of sex discrimination were made by women workers in 2012, an increase of 5,000 over the previous year. See EEOC charge data for sex based discrimination: http://www.eeoc.gov/eeoc/statistics/enforcement/sex.cfm. A wage gap still exists in almost every occupation. See the chart published by the *New York Times* (March 1, 2009, BU4) and online at: http://www.nytimes.com/interactive/2009/03/01/business/20090301_WageGap.html.

12. Vicki Schultz, "The Sanitized Workplace," *Yale Law Journal*, vol. 112, 2003, 2061–2192; See also Ava Baron and Eileen Boris, "'The Body' as a Useful Category for Working-Class History," *Labor: Studies in Working-Class History of the Americas*, vol. 4, no. 2, Summer 2007, 23–44.

13. *Corne and DeVane v. Bausch & Lomb*, 390 F. Supp. 161, 163–164, D. Arizona, 1975. See also judicial opinions in *Miller v Bank of America*, 418 F. Supp. 233, 236, N.D. CA, 1976. "The attraction of males to females and females to males is a natural sex phenomenon and it is probable that this attraction plays at least a subtle part in most personnel decisions." Quoted in Reva B. Siegel, "Introduction: A Short History of Sexual Harassment," in Catherine A. MacKinnon and Reva B. Siegel (eds.), *Directions in Sexual Harassment Law*, Yale University Press, 2004, 34, note 58. See also Catherine A. MacKinnon, *Sexual Harassment of Working Women*, New Haven: Yale University Press, 1979.

14. See Valerie Steele, *Fifty Years of Fashion: New Look to Now*, New Haven: Yale University Press, 1997; see also Duncan Kennedy, "Sexual Abuse, Sexy Dressing and the Eroticization of Domination," *New England Law Review*, vol. 26, Summer 1992, 1309–1393.

15. Ann Russo, "Lesbians, Prostitutes, and Murder: Media Constructs Violence Constructs Power" in Martha A. Fineman and Martha T. McCluskey (eds.), *Feminism, Media, and the Law*, Oxford: Oxford University Press, 1997, 259.

16. Serena Southerlyn was played by Elisabeth Röhm, NBC drama series *Law & Order*. The episode "Ain't No Love" (15th season) was her last appearance. According to the television character, District Attorney Branch, Serena is fired because she is "too sympathetic to defendants," and "lets her emotions get in the way" of her prosecutorial work.

17. On the tendency of other television formats, such as sitcoms to favor treatment of social issues as result of personal difficulties rather than structural and cultural problems, see Bonnie J. Dow, *Prime-Time Feminism: Television, Media Culture, and the Women's Movement Since 1970*, xxi, and Chap I.

18. Often opening shots are of women workers engaging in sex with a co-worker or supervisor.

19. Some feminists have argued that the sexualization of workplace culture operates to promote male solidarity rather than to destabilize it. According to Cynthia Cockburn, sexualized discourses at work are "a necessary part of the cementing activities with which senior men seek to bond men beneath them firmly into the fraternity, healing the contradictions of patriarchal and class structures that threaten to divide them." Cynthia Cockburn, *In the Way of Women: Men's Resistance to Sex Equality in Organizations*, Ithaca: Cornell ILR Press, 1991, 157–158.

20. *Grey's Anatomy*, season 2, episode 15: "Break on Through."

21. On Title VII as not intended as a general civility code, see, for example, the Supreme Court's ruling in *Oncale v. Sundowner Offshore Services*, et al., U.S. Supreme Court No. 96–568, 1998; Nor have the courts established the goal of law to eradicate sexual harassment at the workplace. Supreme Court rulings on employer liability have been widely criticized for determining liability in terms of how well employers comply with judicial rules (e.g., anti-harassment policies and grievance procedures) regardless of how well those rules address the underlying problem or whether they redress the injury when such harassment does occur.

22. See television drama series, such as *Cold Case, Bones, Burn Notice, Private Practice, House*, and a recent, though short-lived, cable series, *Emily Owens, M.D.*

23. See *Law & Order* and its various spin offs.

24. See *Suits*; these depictions are more frequently portrayed in television workplace dramadies such as *Boston Legal, Ally McBeal* (*Desperate Housewives*, which ordinarily focuses on the home, also has a few episodes which focus on the workplace and depict sexual harassment as somewhat comical).

25. See, for example, Katherine M. Franke, "What's Wrong with Sexual Harassment?" 49 *Stanford Law Review*, 1997, 691–772.

26. A significant body of research has explored the racially disproportionate rate of sexual harassment charges brought by women of racial minorities, with an eye to understanding the role that racialized sexuality plays in this disciplinary practice. See, for example, Catherine MacKinnon, *Sexual Harassment of Working Women*, New Haven: Yale University Press, 1979; Tanya Kateri Hernandez, "Sexual Harassment and Racial Disparity: The Mutual Construction of Gender and Race," *The Journal of Gender, Race & Justice*, vol. 4, Spring 2001, 183–224; Tanya Kateri Hernandez, "The Racism of Sexual Harassment" in Catherine A. MacKinnon and Reva B. Siegel (eds.), *Directions in Sexual Harassment Law*, New Haven: Yale University Press, 2004, 479–495; Sumi K. Cho, "Converging Stereotypes in Racialized Sexual Harassment: Where the Model Minority Meets Suzie Wong," *Journal of Gender, Race & Justice*, vol. 1, 1997, 177–211; Maria L. Ontiveros, "Three Perspectives on Workplace Harassment of Women of Color," *Golden Gate University Law Review*, vol. 23, no. 3, 1993, 817–893.

27. Historically, women workers with the least amount of economic and social resources—women in low skilled and blue collar jobs experienced the most severe forms of sexual harassment. See, for example, James E. Gruber and Lars Bjom, "Blue-Collar Blues: The Sexual Harassment of Women Autoworkers," *Work and Occupations*, vol. 9, no. 3, August 1982, 271–298; and Elvia R. Arriola, "'What's the Big Deal?' Women in the New York City Construction Industry and Sexual Harassment Law, 1970–1985," 22 *Columbia Human Rights Law Review* 21, 1990, 21–57.

28. On gender, race and class in work organizations, see, Joan Acker, "Theorizing Gender, Race and Class in Organizations" in Emma Jeannes, David Knights and Patricia Yancey Martin (eds.), *Handbook of Gender, Work and Organization*, Chichester: Wiley, 2012, 65–80.

29. Jeff Hearn, for example, argues that work is a central site for the reproduction of sexual identity, "Men's Sexuality at Work" in Andy Metcalf and Martin Humphries (ed.), *The Sexuality of Men*, London: Pluto Press, 1985, 110.

30. Kathleen M. Rospenda et al., "Doing Power: The Confluence of Gender, Race, and Class in Contrapower Sexual Harassment," *Gender & Society*, vol. 12, no. 1, February 1998, 40–60, examines gender, race and class as varied sources of power and suggest that study of sexual harassment can therefore help us understand the multiple ways that power operates in the workplace.

31. The concept of the "male gaze" highlights the importance of seeing/being seen as a crucial component of the production and reproduction of "masculinity" and "femininity." See Laura Mulvey's important essay in feminist film theory in which she dissects how Hollywood cinema incorporates the assumption of a male viewer and a female object of his gaze: "Visual Pleasure and Narrative Cinema" in Constance Penlye (ed.), *Feminism and Film Theory*, New York: Routledge, 1988, 57–68. On the cultural significance of carnival and ritual inversions of everyday hierarchies, see Peter Stallybrass and Allon White, *The Politics and Poetics of Transgression*, Ithaca: Cornell University Press, 1986.

32. On the ways print media has misrepresented sex and race discrimination, see Laura Beth Nielsen and Aaron Beim, "Media Misrepresentation: Title VII, Print Media, and Public Perceptions of Discrimination Litigation," *Stanford Law & Policy Review*, vol. 15, 2004, 237–265.

33. On how gender is implicated in class relations and organizations, see, for example, Ava Baron, "Happy Ending for Women Workers, or Tragedy for the Workplace? Cultural and Legal Narratives

of Sexual Harassment in the United States" in S. Dimakopoulou, C. Dokou and E. Mitsi (eds.), *The Letter of the Law: Literature, Justice and the Other*, New York: Peter Lang, 2013, 93–114; Ava Baron, "Masculinity, the Embodied Male Worker, and the Historian's Gaze," *International Labor and Working Class History*, no. 69, 2006, 143–160; Ava Baron and Eileen Boris, "'The Body' as a Useful Category for Working-Class History," *Labor: Studies in Working-Class History of the Americas*, vol. 4, no. 2, Summer 2007, 23–43; Ava Baron, "Gender and Labor History: Learning from the Past, Looking to the Future" in Ava Baron (ed.), *Work Engendered: Toward a New History of American Labor*, Ithaca: Cornell University Press, 1991, 1–46.
34. Sources: epguide.com; TVGuide.com; IMDb.com.

Works Cited

Acker, Joan. "Theorizing Gender, Race and Class in Organizations" in Emma Jeannes, David Knights and Patricia Yancey Martin (eds.), *Handbook of Gender, Work and Organization*. Chichester: Wiley, 2012, 65–80.

Arriola, Elvia R. "'What's the Big Deal?' Women in the New York City Construction Industry and Sexual Harassment Law, 1970-1985." 22 *Columbia Human Rights Law Review* 21, 1990, 21–57.

Baron, Ava. "Happy Ending for Women Workers, or Tragedy for the Workplace? Cultural and Legal Narratives of Sexual Harassment in the United States" in S. Dimakopoulou, C. Dokou and E. Mitsi (eds.), *The Letter of the Law: Literature, Justice and the Other*. New York: Peter Lang, 2013.

Baron, Ava. "Masculinity, the Embodied Male Worker, and the Historian's Gaze." *International Labor and Working Class History*, no. 69, 2006, 143–160.

Baron, Ava. "Gender and Labor History: Learning from the Past, Looking to the Future" in Ava Baron (ed.), *Work Engendered: Toward a New History of American Labor*. Ithaca: Cornell University Press, 1991, 1–46.

Baron, Ava and Eileen Boris. "'The Body' as a Useful Category for Working-Class History." *Labor: Studies in Working-Class History of the Americas*, vol. 4, no. 2, Summer 2007, 23–44.

Cho, Sumi K. "Converging Stereotypes in Racialized Sexual Harassment: Where the Model Minority Meets Suzie Wong." *Journal of Gender, Race & Justice*, no. 1, 1997, 177–211.

Cockburn, Cynthia. *In the Way of Women: Men's Resistance to Sex Equality in Organizations*. Ithaca: Cornell ILR Press, 1991.

Corne and DeVane v. Bausch & Lomb, 390 F. Supp. 161, 163–164, D. Arizona, 1975.

Dow, Bonnie J. *Prime-Time Feminism: Television, Media Culture, and the Women's Movement Since 1970*. Philadelphia: University of Pennsylvania Press, 1996.

Druckerman, Pamela. "Catching Up with France on Day Care." *New York Times*, 1 September 2013, Sunday Review, 12.

Franke, Katherine M. "What's Wrong with Sexual Harassment?" 49 *Stanford Law Review*, 1997, 691–772.

Gerbner, George, and Larry Gross. "Living with Television: The Violence Profile." *Journal of Communication*, vol. 26, no. 2, Spring 1976, 172–199.

Gruber, James E., and Lars Bjom. "Blue-Collar Blues: The Sexual Harassment of Women Autoworkers." *Work and Occupations*, vol. 9, no. 3, August 1982, 271–298.

Hearn, Jeff. "Men's Sexuality at Work" in Andy Metcalf and Martin Humphries (eds.), *The Sexuality of Men*. London: Pluto Press, 1985, 110–128.

Hernandez, Tanya Kateri. "The Racism of Sexual Harassment" in Catherine A. MacKinnon and Reva B. Siegel (eds.), *Directions in Sexual Harassment Law*. New Haven: Yale University Press, 2004, 479–495.

Hernandez, Tanya Kateri. "Sexual Harassment and Racial Disparity: The Mutual Construction of Gender and Race." *The Journal of Gender, Race & Justice*, no. 4, Spring 2001, 183–224.

Internet Movie Database: IMDb.com.
Kanter, Jodi. "Harvard Business School Case Study: Gender Equity." *New York Times*, Education. http://www.nytimes.com/2013/09/08/education/harvard-case-study-gender-equity.html?ref=education, accessed 7 September 2013.
Kennedy, Duncan. "7 Princeton Officers File Suit Against Town, Former Chief." *Trenton Times*, 7 September 2013, A1.
Kennedy, Duncan. "Sexual Abuse, Sexy Dressing and the Eroticization of Domination." *New England Law Review*, vol. 26, Summer 1992, 1309–1393.
Lotz, Amanda D. "Introduction: Female-Centered Dramas after the Network Era" in Amanda D. Lotz (ed.), *Redesigning Women: Television after the Network Era*. Urbana: University of Illinois Press, 2006, 1–36.
Lotz, Amanda D. "Of Female Cops and Docs: The Reformulation of Workplace Dramas and Other Trends in Mixed-Sex Ensembles" in Amanda D. Lotz (ed.), *Redesigning Women: Television after the Network Era*. Urbana: University of Illinois Press, 2006, 144–164.
Mackinnon, Catherine A. *Sexual Harassment of Working Women*. New Haven: Yale University Press, 1979.
Meritor Savings Bank v Vinson, 477 U.S. 57, 1986.
Miller v Bank of America, 418 F. Supp. 233, 236, N.D. CA, 1976.
Oncale v. Sundowner Offshore Services, et al., U.S. Supreme Court No. 96-568, 1998.
Ontiveros, Maria L. "Three Perspectives on Workplace Harassment of Women of Color." *Golden Gate University Law Review*, vol. 23, no. 3, 1993, 817–828.
Mulvey, Laura. "Visual Pleasure and Narrative Cinema" in Constance Penlye (ed.), *Feminism and Film Theory*. New York: Routledge, 1988, 57–68.
Nielsen, Laura Beth, and Aaron Beim. "Media Misrepresentation: Title VII, Print Media, and Public Perceptions of Discrimination Litigation" *Stanford Law & Policy Review*, vol. 15, 2004, 237–265.
"Report of the U.S. Commission on Civil Rights." *Window Dressing on the Set: Women and Minorities in Television*. Washington, D.C.: GPO, 1997.
Rospenda, Kathleen M. et al. "Doing Power: The Confluence of Gender, Race, and Class in Contrapower Sexual Harassment." *Gender & Society*, vol. 12, no. 1, February 1998, 40–60.
Russo, Ann. "Lesbians, Prostitutes, and Murder: Media Constructs Violence Constructs Power" in Martha A. Fineman and Martha T. McCluskey (eds.), *Feminism, Media, and the Law*. Oxford: Oxford University Press, 259–266.
Saguy, Abigail C. *What Is Sexual Harassment? From Capitol Hill to the Sorbonne*. Berkeley: University of California Press, 2003.
Schultz, Vicki. "The Sanitized Workplace." *Yale Law Journal*, vol. 112, 2003, 2061–2192.
Siegel, Reva B. "Introduction: A Short History of Sexual Harassment" in Catherine A. MacKinnon and Reva B. Siegel (eds.), *Directions in Sexual Harassment Law*. New Haven: Yale University Press, 2004, 1–39.
Stallybrass, Peter, and Allon White. *The Politics and Poetics of Transgression*. Ithaca: Cornell University Press, 1986.
Steele, Valerie. *Fifty Years of Fashion: New Look to Now*. New Haven: Yale University Press, 1997.
Title VII of the Civil Rights Act of 1964 42 U.S.C.A. § 2000e-4; Amended by the Equal Employment Opportunity Act of 1972, Pub. L. No. 92–261, March 24, 1972, 86 Stat. 103.
Tuchman, Gaye, Arlene Kaplan Daniels, and James Benit (eds.). *Hearth and Home: Images of Women in the Mass Media*. New York: Oxford University Press, 1978.
TV Guide Magazine: TVGuide.com.
U.S. Department of Labor, Women's Bureau. "Women in the Labor Force in 2010." http://www.dol.gov/wb/factsheets/Qf-laborforce-10.htm, accessed 30 January 2014.
U.S. Equal Employment Opportunity Commission: http://www.eeoc.gov/laws/types/sexual_harassment.cfm, accessed 30 January 2014.

U.S. Equal Employment Opportunity Commission: http://www.eeoc.gov/eeoc/statistics/enforcement/sex.cfm, accessed 30 January 2014.

Wade, Lisa. "Job Segregation by Sex, 1972–2008." *Sociological Images*, 2 May 2010: http://thesocietypages.org/socimages/2010/05/02/job-segregation-by-sex-1972-2008/, accessed 30 January 2014.

Wade, Lisa. "Jobs Where Gender Segregation Persists." *New York Times*, 30 September 2012: http://www.nytimes.com/imagepages/2012/09/30/opinion/30coontz-gr1.html?ref=sunday, accessed 30 January 2014.

The Gender and Class Politics of Social Realism in The Wire

T. ANN KENNEDY

HBO's *The Wire* (2002–2008) is one of those television series that has an iconic status—one of a handful of game changing shows that helped create the "brand" for an entire cable network.[1] Low rated as a series, like most legends, it gained in stature after its demise and much of the interpretation of its innovation is dependent on the creators' framing of the series as an innovative novel for television in the style of the great social realist novels of the nineteenth and twentieth centuries. For its creator David Simon, *The Wire* is a serious work of social critique, a story of class struggle that carries on the traditions of the serial novels of Dickens and the documentary journalism of Walker Evans and James Agee.

Simon has been an insistent interpreter of his own show and in a 2012 blog post entitled "I meant this, not that. But yeah, I meant it," he attempts to explain remarks he made in an interview that were critical of *Wire* fans for their "hacking [*The Wire*] into pop-culture nuggets" and ignoring the seriousness of the show's systemic social critique.[2] Instead of apologizing to fans for implying they didn't understand the show, Simon offers a fuller explanation of the context in which he believes the series should find its meaning, comparing it to James Agee and Walker Evans's *Let Us Now Praise Famous Men*: "Agee's classic is one of the most intimate studies of American poverty ever attempted, and at the point of publication, the author was somewhat aghast at the delicacy of the lives in the balance, the possible affront to the essential dignity of the broken, desperate world that he and Walker Evans had captured in prose and photograph."[3] Simon then quotes Agee:

> If I could do it, [...] I'd do no writing at all here. It would be photographs; the rest would be fragments of cloth, bits of cotton, lumps of earth, records of speech, pieces of wood and iron, phials of odors, plates of food and of excrement. Booksellers would consider it quite a novelty; critics would mur-

mur, yes, but is it art; and I could trust a majority of you to use it as you would as a parlor game....[4]

Simon shares Agee's frustration with the American public's ability to transform social critique into a pleasurable commodity and, like Agee, throws up his hands and ends his post by stating: "Is [*The Wire*] a parlor game? Exactly so. With Omar as the big winner."

As Frank Kelleter points out in "*The Wire* and its Readers," Simon's background as a Baltimore journalist and co-creator Ed Burns' years as a Baltimore homicide detective lend *The Wire* an authenticity that many network shows can only hope to aspire to through "the ripped from the headlines" sensationalism that marries the "man bites dog" news story to the fictional ideological neutrality of the criminal system. Kelleter demonstrates how lines from the publicity materials and interview commentary produced by Simon and HBO are taken up and repeated by television critics and bloggers across the media, becoming institutionalized ways of reading the series itself. He argues that Simon has "a reporter's confidence in the transparency of social reality; the aspiration is to capture unfamiliar life by sheer force of local knowledge."[5] But, according to Kelleter, Simon's faith in the transparency of reality and his journalistic motives are treated with equal transparency by sociologists as representative of contemporary life in urban America:

> Such sociological interest in the show's realism conflicts with the show's identity as a television series in at least two ways: Stringer Bell and Omar are hardly "ordinary" nor are they "people." To be able to treat them like people, that is, to use television series as "new fictional sources," sociologists and ethnographers have to explain the text's practice of storytelling as insignificant for their research interests.[6]

The Wire's success is based on this idea of authenticity so that the frame of representation itself disappears. Simon's concern is that the series will lose this authenticity if it becomes part of middle-class viewers' online entertainment-consumption practices. And when Simon imagines a challenge to *The Wire*'s authenticity, he borrows the metaphor of the bourgeois and feminized space of the parlor to express his disdain.

For Simon, and for many producers and critics working in cable television who draw on social realism for their structures of representation, authenticity has become linked with masculinity and industrial labor. Critics Kennedy and Shapiro argue that *The Wire* creates nostalgia for an imagined time when capitalism was once held in check by a social contract that protected male homosocial networks of labor. These homosocial networks are depicted as surviving in the mostly boys club of the urban institutions that make up *The Wire*'s focus, even when in reality those institutions such as the schools are made up primarily of women.[7] *The Wire*'s obsession with cultures of industrial masculinity means that it has little space for the representation of women's labor struggles, and this is particularly true of the struggles of working poor black women.

This is surprising since Simon's other insistent framing of *The Wire* is that the series is about class and not about race. In a lecture at USC in 2008, he goes so far as to argue that "*Homicide* [the series he created at NBC] already covered race. *The Wire* is about class."[8] However, by appropriating the social realism of industrial capitalism the series achieves its realist affect through the traditional linking of class struggle with masculine labor. In this, the show is not innovative but repeats the popular and historical construction of social class in the United States using the iconography of the white male worker.[9] Instead of challenging this picture of industrial capitalism, Simon contributes to the mythologizing of its primary symbol: the industrial white male. It's the familiarity of this icon that lends *The Wire* its emotional realism—the struggle of the white working class male against illegitimate claims of foreign capital and local perversions of domestic order.

This essay focuses mostly on season 2 because it most directly engages with the plight of the working class in late capitalism and with the global politics of America's local economies. In a 2005 interview, Simon describes the season as "a meditation on the death of work and the betrayal of the American working class."[10] When, in season 2, the creators use the masculine space of the docks to represent deindustrialization and globalization, they are making a choice to avoid telling the story of U.S. working-class women's displacement. In this way, the gendered and raced segregation of the labor force is marginalized as a social construction and reflected back in the series as a natural organization of labor.[11] While the male characters of *The Wire* are often differentiated through class, ethnicity/race, and sexual orientation, the characters share common cultural codes that effectively naturalize blue-collar industrial masculinity as an originary foundation for American masculinity itself.

The affective realism of *The Wire* comes from its depiction of white masculinity as representative of the struggles of the working class against capital, especially foreign capital, to earn a family wage. Drawing on popular images of white male injury and rescue, this works against the recognition of white women and people of color as members of the working class who have always struggled for decent work. Because of the narrative complexity and visual nature of the serial drama, which appears more real because of its detailed multiple storylines, it may appear to give voice to multiple versions of history, but instead the transparent metaphor of surveillance leaves little room for interpretive claims of historical difference.

This naturalism places women outside the class struggles of history and offers as a solution to working class struggles the reestablishing of patriarchal responsibility and "decent work" for men. A realist vision that marginalizes women and subsumes racial politics within a historical trajectory devoted to the death of meaningful work for white men helps support the structures it seeks to critique. Thus, *The Wire* subtly reiterates some of the most pernicious stereotypes of black women in U.S. family and work policy.

Trafficking in Jane Does

Despite Simon's insistence on *The Wire*'s difference from other crime procedurals, season 2's exploitation of the woman as sex-victim is typical of the genre. The season's incorporation of sex trafficking means that it takes part in a larger political discourse in the media that has its origins in early 20th-century white slavery narratives and is revived as a symbol of globalization during the Bush administration. According to Jamie L. Small, at least fifty-five U.S. films from 1996 to 2008 were on the subject of sexual trafficking.[12] Sex trafficking became a central tenet of the Bush administration's incorporation of feminist rhetoric into its faith-based internationalism. As Bush had taken up feminist rhetoric in his "war against terror" so too had the administration used feminist rhetoric to help wage a war on undocumented immigration and to help establish the Trafficking Victims Protection Act in 2000. In its approach to international law enforcement, the administration used the language of "sexual slavery" to help advance its agenda, focusing primarily on the humanitarian-framed issue of sexual trafficking of women and children, and downplaying women's increased economic migration.[13] Simon's use of this discourse to help tell his own story of white male working-class decline shows his reliance on traditional gendered rhetorics of labor and nationalism. In this way, gendered economic exploitation and violence become a vehicle for the real business of the story: the struggle to salvage American working-class masculinity in the era of global capitalism.

Union leader Frank Sobotka's control of both the physical space of the docks and the representation of that space is established early in the first episode by the use of his office as a location of both paternal and workplace authority. At the moment that the dead women are being discovered on the docks by Officer Beadie Russell, Sobotka is in his union office telling a rape joke: "what's the first thing a guy from local 47 does after he gets laid? Wipes the pepper spray from his eyes." This rape joke is not directed at the victim but at the members of local 47; however, it tells us very well how we should understand the scene as sirens interrupt Frank's laughter in the closing moments of the first episode. These sirens bring an end to the masculine world of the docks as the women's dead bodies are pictured spilling out of the container, surrounded by suddenly speechless men.

The traffickers smuggling the girls haven't bothered to tell Frank that he's smuggling humans in the containers for them. And when Frank confronts them, his indignation is met with scorn. The trafficker Vondas tells him: "Now, you want to know what's in the cans? Before, you wanted to know nothing, now, you ask. Guns, okay? Drugs, whores.... Vodka, BMWs, Beluga caviar ... or bombs, maybe, hmm? Bad terrorists with big nuclear bombs. Boom. I am kidding you, Frank, it's a joke. But you don't ask.... Because you don't want to know." Frank has lost control of the docks and is now the butt of the joke, his ignorance signaling his loss of legitimacy as an authority figure. Vondas reminds Frank that he has chosen ignorance so that he may retain an illusion of his own moral innocence. Throughout the season Frank is represented as being different in morals and motives from the traffickers because he sees himself as motivated by a working-class consciousness. Frank is portrayed as having a measure of plausible deniability about the realities of global economics and women's place in it, but in suppressing Frank's knowingness, the show draws a moral line between the national borders of that collective consciousness and the foreign elements (girls in cans, immigrant store owners, global traffickers, and robots) that are represented as "taking over" Frank's place in this nationalized class structure.

The stories that the dockworkers, the police, and the traffickers tell about the "girls in the can" tell us little about the victims, but establish an affective frame for how viewers should feel about those telling and hearing the story. At the moment of the discovery of their bodies the men on the docks identify the women migrants as "girls." Frank is told what the audience has already glimpsed: "It's fuckin' girls, man, young ones." Nick says: "There's like a dozen of them." Frank asks: "Dead? They're dead?" This emphasis on their youth and gender encourages viewers to see the women as children; as "girls" they have more currency in the global morality market and can be imagined as innocents. Frank's own words about the "dead girls in the can" are paternalistic. When the cops begin to question the dockworkers, he becomes enraged:

> The [detective] thinks we'd leave [those girls] there on the dock, in a box, dyin' there in the dark [...]. What reason would we have to want girls to die like that? [...] I got a wife. And three sisters. And they got daughters. And I got too much respect for women not to be pissed off at what's in your heads right now.

By comparing the dead girls to women in his own family Frank puts forth a common moral reasoning that he implies is universally understood. Morality requires that viewers imagine the girls in familial ways, similarly situated as American wives, sisters, and daughters. But, he is also making an argument for his own goodness and the goodness of the dockworkers generally. Frank's protective incorporation of the victims into his own domestic order helps viewers see him as a paternal figure in contrast to the traffickers who refer to the girls as whores, concerned only with their lost profit. Moreover, by focusing on their emotional appeal as dead girls, viewers can avoid seeing them as similar to the immigrant sex workers that are portrayed much differently later in the season but who remain silent, minor characters.

As Wendy Hesford notes, the technologies of capital that make possible migration for work and the trafficking in women are the same technologies that regulate and police the borders of citizenship, work, and sexuality.[14] Thus, while one group of undocumented migrants are autopsied and tagged for removal to the anatomy board, others throughout the United States are identified by governmental surveillance and moved to detention centers. The series depicts this flow of migration, surveillance, and detention early in the season when McNulty visits a federal detention center because he wants to give a "name" to one of the Jane Does. This visit shows viewers the incorporation of the Immigration and Naturalization Service into the Department of Homeland Security, marking the ideological fusion of security and immigration. At Homeland Security, McNulty sees a surveillance program that allows federal agents to pull up a GPS map of facilities where groups of Eastern European women are being detained for deportation. This mapping of containment facilities suggests the parallel techniques of criminality and governance in the management of migrant identities.

McNulty and the agent discuss what can be offered to the detainees in return for their cooperation in helping identify the Jane Doe. The agent tells McNulty: "You could marry one of 'em, make her an American housewife. Short of that, they're goin' back the fuck where they came from." The agent suggests that McNulty can give one of the detainees a "name" by marrying her and making her an American citizen in the Cold War era sense when political ideologies of gender represented the American housewife with her access to consumer goods as the chief beneficiary of capitalism. These national scenes at the containment facilities of Homeland Security incorporate the global politics of gendered statehood into the series so that we are able to understand these "girls" not only as "girls," but also as nascent capitalist gendered subjects capable of entering into the U.S. class system, in Frank's terms, as a daughter, a wife, a sister.

The agent's talk echoes the "kitchen debate" between Nixon and Khrushchev where the space of domesticity is the sign of America's capitalist triumph, representing the best that America has to offer to women.[15] As Nixon said then: "In America, we like to make life easier for women." Khrushchev rejected this as a "capitalistic attitude" but Nixon argued: "I think that this attitude towards women is universal. What we want to do, is make life more easy for our housewives." This easier life was represented by the modern kitchen and its domestic technologies designed to make women's labor more efficient. This is something that Americans—presumably men—want to do: "make life more easy for *our* housewives" (my italics).

McNulty's conversation with the agent implies that there are two temporal representations at work in *The Wire*, the one a representation of global capitalism when people and goods move across borders and another that struggles to keep the representation of women contained in capitalist domesticity. These temporal stages are gendered as the INS agent offers a Cold War solution to the problems confronted by female breadwinners in post–Communist nations, women who already live in capitalist societies. The women in post–Communist Eastern Europe can be incorporated into women's universal subject position in the class structure of capitalist patriarchy. This scene in *The Wire* is similar to dominant representations of Eastern European women in Western media that play into the idea that immigrant women could be moved into the surveillance of the American home by American men, offering a hope that the triumph of capitalism could actually be shared with the American working-class male through a globalized marriage market. Ursula Biemann's documentary *Writing Desire* (2000) examines the global marriage market and notes that one way matchmaking sites in Russia advertise women looking for a mate in the United States is to align them with ideas of Cold War American domesticity. Biemann argues in the video that the Russian woman is represented "[as] beautiful and feminine / she is loving and traditional / [...] she believes in a lasting marriage / and a happy home / she is a copy of the First World's past."[16]

As Nixon's idea of Americans making easier the lives of "our women" implies, women are identified as an essentialized universal class; part of this gender ideology is that "this attitude" toward making their lives "more easy" *should* be universal as well. Similarly, Frank assumes that his "respect for women" is universal, something that all men by virtue of their familial relations with women should understand. This American paternalism helps legitimate Frank in contrast to the foreign men who commit these acts, stages a contrast between those who tell rape jokes and those who rape, those who ignorantly allow women to suffocate and those who knowingly commit mass murder. The disrespect that would knowingly allow "girls" to die in a can demonstrates a capitalist disorder, but it is a foreign disorder.

Nixon's linking of capitalism, domesticity, and national identity echoes through *The Wire* as white male characters struggle to realign American labor and white masculinity with a proper capitalist domesticity. The global criminal ring of men from the Ukraine, Russia, Turkey, Israel, and Greece not only destroy girls but also take them away from American men who might give them a "name" and in the process claim part of the triumph of capitalism for themselves. If in the labor history of industrial capitalism *The Wire* uses the icon of the white blue-collar worker to indict global capital, then it incorporates dominant narratives of Eastern European women and cultures to emphasize the perversions of contemporary global capitalism.

Julietta Hua argues that most media stories of sex trafficking focus on its cultural as well as economic causes. In these narratives found in both media and in government publications, post–Communist Eastern Europe is represented as illegitimate and undeveloped in its approach to capitalism; the people are depicted as psychologically unable to adapt and, thus, focused on the acquisition of wealth without work. Throughout U.S. media, Russian men and women are represented as part of global criminal networks in storylines that imagine the "sexualized glamor" of capitalism leading to a culture of greedy exploitation. The U.S. state department, in a 2003 report, cited "images of wealth and prosperity beamed in through television or radio and lavish displays of wealth [that] send powerful messages to impoverished citizens about the benefits of material acquisition" as one of the causes of trafficking.[17] Similarly, a report Donna M. Hughes prepared for the International Organization for Migration argues that sex trafficking in Russia is not caused only by economic decline but also "psychological and attitudinal changes of people, especially women" that comes as a result of "images of glamour and wealth from the West by the media."[18] This report states that one of the causes of sexual trafficking is that "few [Eastern European women are] able to differentiate between liberalization and exploitation,"[19] and that how wealth is acquired does not matter; the American work ethic doesn't exist among these newly capitalist nations. The trafficker known as The Greek—who is not Greek—represents this unfettered capitalism corrupting the U.S. political and labor systems. In opposition to Frank, who turns to crime out of a sense of class consciousness and a desire to save his "way of life," The Greek rejects ideologies of work ethic and class and urges Frank to join the new world of consumerism: "It's a new world, Frank. You should go out and spend some of the money on something you can touch: a new car, a new coat. It's why we get up in the morning, right?"

The detainees refuse to cooperate with McNulty and since they can't be transformed into subjects of capitalist domesticity, legally they are as dead as the girls in the can. Instead of learning the individual story of a single sex worker as we did in season 1 with the African-American stripper Shardene, viewers learn about sex trafficking through the eyes of the detectives as they search for the connection between the Jane Does and the drug traffickers. In the process, we learn of the constant stream of foreign women coming through Baltimore; as one group is deported or dies, so another group of women arrives. These women are indistinguishable from the "girls in the can" but instead of being imagined as wives, sisters, and daughters, they are increasingly referred to as whores. Alive these women represent a threat to capitalist domesticity, a perversion of the material rewards and "easier" life Nixon promised women in capitalism. They are now defined—like many female characters of *The Wire*— by their aggressive sexuality and materialism and become part of the "joke" of the season. Frank is no longer in control of this joke, but McNulty emerges at the end of the season to take control of the telling.

When the detectives finally get a warrant to raid the condominiums where a different set of women perform sex work, McNulty is sent in as a customer to get the sex for money exchange on tape; the women are lined up in front of him and he jokingly asks for two women who then aggressively strip him, preventing him from saying the code word for the raid and resulting in his completing the sexual act that he must then write into his report. In this scene, the women are represented as sexually voracious aggressors who rape McNulty without any acknowledgement of the performative labor of sex work. As in the story with Frank, the women are used to convey men's lack of control of their surroundings; just as the Greeks are now in control of the docks, the women control McNulty's body. But it is McNulty who controls this story and writes it up so that his partner Bunk tells him: "You're famous behind this." Instead of giving a "name" to the Jane Doe, McNulty uses the women to legitimate his own identity in the social hierarchy of masculinity.

Similarly, the fate of the women is marginalized in order to mythologize Frank as the embodiment of masculine industrial labor. When he is finally arrested for his role in the trafficking, Frank gives an impassioned speech to the officers when one of them suggests that with a little cooperation the DA's office can help him: "Twenty-five years we been dyin' slow down there. Drydocks rustin', piers standin' empty. My friends and their kids. Like we got the cancer. No lifeline got throwed, all that time. Nuthin' from nobody…. And now you wanna help us. Help me. Where the fuck were you?" This scene secures Frank's own superiority over those—like us the viewers—who would allow a workingman and his family to drown as opposed to the dockworkers who would *not knowingly* allow girls to suffocate in cans. It secures *The Wire*'s social realist underpinnings as a drama about class by putting forth Frank as the tragic figure of the season. His body, like that of the Jane Doe who fought back against her rapists on the ship, washes ashore, but, while she remains anonymous and forgotten, Frank emerges as a working-class hero, his body coming to rest at the feet of the stevedores. His reelection posters, once a symbol of his refusal to give up his authority in the union to the black candidate Nat, now become a symbol of the solidarity and resistance of working-class masculinity.

Black Mothers and Capitalist Domesticity

In these scenes, the culture of poverty rhetoric is marginalized to use the women to tell a story about Jimmy's maverick behavior and Frank's tragic end.[20] But the culture of poverty rhetoric that influences the broader representation of sex trafficking is a rhetoric that influences *The Wire*'s social realist representation of gender more generally. As Hua notes, this culture of poverty rhetoric clearly parallels the culture of poverty thesis developed in 1960s America to explain welfare dependency and criminality in blacks.[21] Thus, the connection between social class, white masculinity, and women in *The Wire* is that women are often represented as having a disordered relationship to capitalism. While the "girls" in the can are victims and the sex workers in the hotel are transformed by greed into "whores," black women are also portrayed as having a disordered relation to wealth and domesticity.

The story of former stripper Shardene demonstrates the connection between this characterization of sex trafficking and the perversion of capitalist domesticity represented by black women. When the detectives visit the stripper friend of Shardene, she speculates that Shardene "must have found her a rich one to be out so long." Her friend assumes that wealth motivates Shardene's decision to give up dancing, but viewers know that Shardene lives with Lester Freamon, a lower-ranked older police officer who spends his evenings making doll furniture. From this, viewers can see that Shardene's friend misunderstands domesticity while Shardene has been appropriately redeemed into the capitalist home by the educational labor of paternal figure Lester. Once she is redeemed by Lester, Shardene never appears outside the home. She is put away as "saved" and her friend's question implies that Shardene does not hang onto old friends in her new life as a nursing student—a job that will allow her to legitimately perform the nurturing labor expected of women of color in neoliberal capitalism, although we never see her at school or work.

The most stereotypical and one-dimensional representations of women in *The Wire* are depictions of poor black women who are mothers. In U.S. popular and political discourse, black single motherhood has always been represented as a perversion of capitalist domesticity. Historically, mainstream white feminists have represented liberation from domesticity as central to feminist progress, but women of color have been much more likely to work and, therefore, on the one hand marginalized from the story of feminism but also incorporated into this false universalism of women's status. While Nixon brags about America's "housewives" in 1959, in 1965 the Moynihan report points to black matriarchs as a perversion of this familial ideal, citing black familial structures as a cause of poverty. Poor black mothers have been portrayed as "wolves" and "reckless breeders" who raise "disruptive" young men, and as "welfare queens" who cheat the system. These women aspire to material wealth but reject the American work ethic and domesticity, using their children as a means of getting what they want from others.[22] *The Wire* uncritically incorporates these images of black mothers while continuing to represent male characters of authority as redemptive figures.

The model for all other black mothers in *The Wire* is Brianna Barksdale, along with her boss/brother Avon, a leader in the Barksdale drug organization. Brianna appears in only twelve episodes of the series for less than an hour total screen time over the course of five seasons. She aligns the success of her family so closely with the success of the drug trade that she destroys her son D'Angelo ("D") by forcing him to serve time in prison instead of cooperating with the police. Brianna speaks the language of family loyalty to her son, but an earlier conversation with her brother shows that greed is a motivating factor in her urging D to reject a plea agreement. Avon warns her: "You like the car you driving there, right? You like this crib? I put you in this crib. You like it? Yeah, I mean, we all got a lot to protect here." Instead of arguing for her son's welfare, Brianna assures him of D's loyalty, "You ain't gotta worry about my child. I raised that boy, and I raised him right."

In fact, key repetitions in *The Wire*'s representation of black mothers are scenes in which black mothers force their sons to sacrifice their own desires for someone else's or reject or dismiss those sons out of apathy or greed. In season 1, Wallace's mother shows only anger at the disappearance of the basically good and nurturing Wallace, arguing with police detectives who are more concerned than she is that he's gone missing. Even a minor character like Donette who is the mother of D's child neglects to take her son to see his father in prison and seems most concerned with not losing the lifestyle to which she has become accustomed.

Two key developments in the series show the producers' construction of black mothers as representing deviance from capitalist domesticity. McNulty's final scene with Brianna in season 3 exemplifies *The Wire*'s disdain for black motherhood. Brianna learns that McNulty has been investigating D's prison suicide as a homicide and goes to confront him about his suspicions. When

Brianna asks him why he didn't come to her with his information, he tells her: "Honestly, I thought I'd tell someone who actually cared about the kid." While McNulty's sense of moral superiority is often undermined in scenes with more noble characters such as Greggs and Freamon, his words characterizing the relationship between Brianna and D'Angelo are allowed to stand as the final interpretation of her as a mother. Although Brianna's primary role in the series is as matriarch, we never see D's death from her perspective. Her grief is never depicted outside of the storyline of Stringer Bell's desire to avoid detection for D's murder.

In season 4, De'Londa, Namond's mother, is introduced as a "dragon lady" who is obsessed with material goods and having her son become a player in the drug trade like his father Wee-Bey. In Brianna's last scene in the series, she meets with De'Londa and Namond to tell them that they will receive no more financial help from the Barksdales. This meeting of the two mothers is an example of *The Wire*'s pattern of paralleling the stories of two characters. These parallels are representationally satisfying, but they also set up individual circumstances such as redemption by a father figure as primary factors in a character's fate. As Namond grows into manhood his story is paralleled with D's. Both young men are raised to deal drugs by mothers who are dependent on the game for their livelihood and whose materialism defines them. D'Angelo ends up murdered in prison. Namond avoids D's fate because of the intervention of the father-cop figure Colvin who tells Wee-Bey that Namond can be whatever he wants to be but not if he stays in West Baltimore with his mother. Wee-Bey then commands De'Londa to let Namond go. De'Londa's last words though are not about her son, but about herself: "you cutting me off too?" Wee-Bey tells her no, but that she is "going to let go of that boy."

As Roxana Galusca notes, the depiction of gender in relation to capitalist domesticity is racialized and nationalized. While "young girls" from Eastern Europe and Asia might possibly be assimilated into capitalist domesticity through marriage into citizenship and appropriate education in capitalist values, this can only happen with the help of legitimate paternal figures willing to give them a "name." The connecting narratives of foreign control and black women's misuse of matriarchal power aligns women with global consumer desires rather than with global labor no matter their class. As Galusca points out, the emphasis on sex trafficking marginalizes women's global status as workers, breadwinners, and citizens, ignoring "the flipside of neoliberal capitalism, the multinationals' global exploitation of cheap gendered and racialized labor."[23] In the end, *The Wire* uses poor women to realign the working class with masculinity and to align white American morality with patrolling the borders of a "good" nationalist capitalist domesticity. Women are aligned with a disordered global capitalism where social class is detached from the industriousness of "decent work" and with cultures of poverty represented by native black mothers, while foreign girls threaten American working-class structures of paternal authority.

Notes

1. On *The Wire*'s role in establishing HBO's reputation as part of the cable revolution in television programming, see Gary Edgarton and Jeffrey P. Jones, *The Essential HBO Reader*, Lexington: University Press of Kentucky, 2009; and Brett Martin, *Difficult Men: Behind the Scenes of a Creative Revolution from The Sopranos and The Wire to Mad Men*, New York: Penguin Press HC, 2013.
2. http://davidsimon.com/i-meant-this/, accessed 7 May 2013.
3. *Ibid.*
4. *Ibid.*
5. Frank Kelleter, "*The Wire* and its Readers" in Liam Kennedy and Stephen Shapiro (eds.), *The Wire: Race, Class, and Genre*. Ann Arbor: University of Michigan Press, 2012, 37.
6. *Ibid.*, 42.
7. Liam Kennedy and Stephen Shapiro, "Tales of the Neoliberal City" in Liam Kennedy and Stephen Shapiro (eds.), *The Wire: Race, Class, and Genre*, 158.
8. Quoted in Marsha Kinder, "Rewiring Baltimore: The Emotive Power of Systemics, Serality, and the City" in Liam Kennedy and Stephen Shapiro (eds.), *The Wire: Race, Class, and Genre*, 75.
9. On the representation of the working class as white and male, see for example Julie Bettie's "Class Dismissed? *Roseanne* and the Changing Face of Working-Class Iconography," *Social Text*, vol. 45, Winter 1995, 125–149. In the book I'm writing, I extend this argument to discuss the racial politics of class and masculinity and the feminist politics of *The Wire*'s representation of middle-class professional women.
10. "Totally Wired," Interview by Richard Vine, Blog post, *The Guardian*, 13 January 2005.
11. Hamilton Carroll in his essay, "Policing the Borders of White Masculinity: Labor, Whiteness, and the Neoliberal City in *The Wire*" argues that "Season 2 of *The Wire*, then, constitutes an example of the discourse of white male injury that has become a pervasive feature of contemporary U.S. culture" (265). Carroll's essay appears in Kennedy and Shapiro (eds.), *The Wire: Race, Class, and Genre*.
12. Jamie L. Small, "Trafficking in Truth: Media, Sexuality, and Human Rights Evidence," *Feminist Studies*, vol. 38, no. 2, Summer 2012, 417.
13. Julietta Hua, *Trafficking Women's Human Rights*, Minneapolis: University of Minnesota Press, 2011, 101–105.
14. Wendy Hesford, *Spectacular Rhetorics: Human Rights Visions, Recognitions, Feminisms*, Durham: Duke University Press, 2011.
15. http://teachingamericanhistory.org/library/document/the-kitchen-debate/, accessed 7 May 2013.
16. The Biemann quotations are taken from Wendy Hesford's *Spectacular Rhetorics*, 148.
17. "Trafficking in Persons Report" (June 2003), quoted in Julietta Hua, *Trafficking Women's Human Rights*, 60. See also Ralph Lindgren et al. (eds.), *The Law of Sex Discrimination*, Boston: Wadsworth, 2011, 435.
18. Donna M. Hughes, *Trafficking for Sexual Exploitation: The Case of the Russian Federation*, Geneva: International Organization for Migration, 2002, 7, quoted in Julietta Hua, *Trafficking Women's Human Rights*, 61.
19. Donna M. Hughes, *Trafficking for Sexual Exploitation*, 13, quoted in *Ibid.*, 91.
20. Jill Steans makes a similar argument about this scene in "Gendered Bodies, Gendered Spaces, Gendered Places: A Critical Reading of HBO's *The Wire*," *International Journal of Feminist Politics*, vol. 13, no. 1, 2011, 100–118. She also argues that "the fairly stark neglect of female characters who drive the drama, their stories and specific experiences, points to an unreflective attitude to women, girls and femininities that effectively naturalizes what is actually a fundamental dimension of social relations marked by inequality and power" (103).
21. Hua, *Trafficking Women's Human Rights*, 61.

22. On the historical specificity of black motherhood in U.S. history, see Patricia Hill Collins, *Black Feminist Thought: Knowledge, Consciousness, and the Politics of Empowerment*, New York: Routledge, 2000. On the Moynihan report and the representation of low-income black mothers, see, for example, Ange-Marie Hancock, *The Politics of Disgust: The Public Identity of the Welfare Queen*, New York: New York University Press, 2004, 57–59 and Jill Quadagno, *The Color of Welfare: How Racism Undermined the War on Poverty*, New York: Oxford University Press, 1994.

23. Roxana Galusca, *Projects of Humanitarianism: Sex Trafficking and Migration in the Twenty-First Century United States*, Diss. University of Michigan, 2011, 108, fn. 22.

Works Cited

Collins, Patricia Hill. *Black Feminist Thought: Knowledge, Consciousness, and the Politics of Empowerment*. New York: Routledge, 2000.

Galusca, Roxana. *Projects of Humanitarianism: Sex Trafficking and Migration in the Twenty-First Century United States*. Diss. University of Michigan, 2011.

Hancock, Ange-Marie. *The Politics of Disgust: The Public Identity of the Welfare Queen*, New York: New York University Press, 2004.

Hesford, Wendy, *Spectacular Rhetorics: Human Rights Visions, Recognitions, Feminisms*, Durham: Duke University Press, 2011.

Hua, Julietta. *Trafficking Women's Human Rights*. Minneapolis: University of Minnesota Press, 2011.

Kelleter, Frank. "*The Wire* and its Readers" in Liam Kennedy and Stephen Shapiro (eds.), *The Wire: Race, Class, and Genre*. Ann Arbor: University of Michigan Press, 2012, 33–70.

Kennedy, Liam, and Stephen Shapiro. "Tales of the Neoliberal City" in Liam Kennedy and Stephen Shapiro (eds.), *The Wire: Race, Class, and Genre*. Ann Arbor: University of Michigan Press, 2012, 147–169.

Kennedy, Liam, and Stephen Shapiro (eds.). *The Wire: Race, Class, and Genre*. Ann Arbor: University of Michigan Press, 2012.

Kinder, Marsha. "Rewiring Baltimore: The Emotive Power of Systemics, Serality, and the City" in Liam Kennedy and Stephen Shapiro (eds.), *The Wire: Race, Class, and Genre*. Ann Arbor: University of Michigan Press, 2012, 71–83.

Quadagno, Jill. *The Color of Welfare: How Racism Undermined the War on Poverty*. New York: Oxford Univesity Press, 1994.

Simon, David. "I meant this, not that. But yeah, I meant it." *The Audacity of Despair*, April 16, 2012: http://davidsimon.com/i-meant-this/, accessed 7 May 2013.

Small, Jamie L. "Trafficking in Truth: Media, Sexuality, and Human Rights Evidence." *Feminist Studies*, vol. 38, no. 2, Summer 2012, 415–434.

Steans, Jill. "Gendered Bodies, Gendered Spaces, Gendered Places: A Critical Reading of HBO's *The Wire*." *International Journal of Feminist Politics*, vol. 13, no. 1, 2011, 100–118.

The Wire. Home Box Office, HBO, 2002–2008.

Striking Women
Salt of the Earth, Norma Rae and Bread and Roses

PENNY STARFIELD

In *Behind the Mask of Innocence*, Kevin Brownlow describes the documentary *The Passaic Textile Strike* (Sam Russak, 1926; screenplay and titles by Margaret Larkin), a forgotten film of the silent era that resurfaced in the early 1980s. The strike took place in six textile mills in Passaic, N.J., starting in January 1926 and ending in February the following year.[1] Along with *Labor's Reward*, produced by the American Federation of Labor (AFL) (Rothaker Films, 1925), *The Passaic Textile Strike* provides an example of the poor treatment meted out to women workers, while describing their combat to improve working conditions through industrial action. Besides its intrinsic worth, the film provides documentary input and contributes to piecing together film history. Brownlow introduces a now generally accepted fact that the 1910s and 1920s were not just a time of entertainment and melodrama, but that the "social conscious" film as it is sometimes termed was very much present. In particular, Steven Ross emphasizes that, contrary to common thought, the working class exists in the United States, and a large body of "working-class" films appeared during the first decades of film.[2]

From another point of view, the anti-working class bias can be seen as part of an esthetic hierarchy that considers such subject matter to be esthetically unworthy. The class struggle belongs to categories of realism and naturalism, two esthetic styles that, as Frank Curot points out, have been criticized as non-artistic since their emergence in the 19th century.[3] Photography and film developed concurrently and, with their supposed capacity to reproduce their subject matter exactly, fueled the anti-realists and their objections to what they considered a non-esthetic focus on the more sordid side of life. In this context, the esthetic value of the social conscious film is minimized through its frequently close relation to real events. The three "strike films" studied here—*Salt of the Earth* (Herbert J. Biberman, 1954), *Norma Rae* (Martin Ritt, 1979) and *Bread and Roses* (Ken Loach, 2000)—depict actual strikes. Moreover, *Salt of the Earth* and *Bread and Roses* feature people who were involved in the strikes described, along with professional actors. Although set in Alabama, *Norma Rae* is based on a North Carolina strike in a textile factory in the mid–1970s, and the protagonist draws from Crystal Lee Sutton, the woman who led the movement to organize workers and improve conditions through joining the Amalgamated Textile Workers' Union. That the main focus of these conflicts involves women, minorities and immigrants, further downgrades the subject matter.

Yet, either as an intrinsic property of filmic discourse, or to counter the effects of this esthetic hierarchy—voluntarily or involuntarily in both cases—the supposed "slice of life" is frequently deviated cinematically. From an early stage, films that are the most closely linked to reality, such as news reels and documentary, learnt to incorporate fictional cinematic techniques, through the restaging of events, editing and narrative devices, for example.[4] Even fictional films that rely on naturalistic techniques, like some of D. W. Griffith's Biograph films that are linked to the Reform Movement or his *Broken Blossoms* (1919), or New Wave 1960s–1970s films, tend to esthetize their subjects by these very techniques. The "proletarian film," as Charles Eckert terms it, is frequently disguised by narrative or generic constraints. Class conflict may not necessarily occur in a specifically working-class environment, but is found, for instance, in the gangster genre via the relationship between the gangsters and the call-girls who work for them, revealing "existential rather than political or economic" conflict, governed by a "sense of disparity between being poor and being rich."[5]

Although relying largely on documentary, the early strike films incorporate the strategic use of fictional cinematic narrative. *The Passaic Textile Strike* contains narrative elements that reoccur in later strike films, suggesting that the limited narrative typology may be to blame for the limited appeal of such films. It depicts a mainly immigrant or minority community, their path to awareness and organization, the basically collective struggle, police brutality and repressive tactics, ending on their final achievements. However, a long fictional prologue allows for worker identification through the difficulties encountered by a Polish family of factory workers: long hours, harsh conditions, arbitrary pay cuts and firing, sexual harassment. In particular, the mother's arrival in America, the land of hope and promise, is symbolized ironically by a reverse shot of the Statue of Liberty, a common trope in films on immigration, used a few years earlier in Charlie Chaplin's *The Immigrant* (1917).[6] Although very much AFL propaganda, promoting union shops and an all-white anti-immigrant union, *Labor's Reward* also includes fictional elements as a means to transmitting its message, using flashback to describe to a sick woman how her fellow workers have gone on strike to protest against their poor working conditions.

Salt of the Earth, *Norma Rae* and *Bread and Roses* have in common their female protagonists, but their realistic "styles" are very different. *Salt of the Earth* draws from the American documentary schools of Flaherty and Strand, and Soviet idealization of the worker; *Norma Rae* is very much a Hollywood product, constructed around the eponymous central figure (played by Sally Field), whereas *Bread and Roses* belongs to the "docudrama" genre created by Loach. While films like *Blue Collar* (Paul Schrader, 1978) also depict strikes, the foregrounding of women's role in industrial conflict highlights not just issues of class, but also gender, ethnicity and minority origin. In general, the status of working-class women is further minoritized, as illustrated in *Salt of the Earth*, in which the miners, of Mexican origin, tend to dominate their wives. Although Norma Rae is from the white working class, a substantial number of the factory workers are African American. The focus in *Bread and Roses* on janitors reveals the exploitation of both African American women and a more recent immigrant population, mainly female, from Mexico and Eastern Europe. Whereas in *Bread and Roses* the janitors are visible minorities, Norma Rae can be considered a minority through her condition as a female worker in a southern state. By definition, being a minority is a question of quality and not quantity and involves those who are excluded from dominant society, workers, poor people, and women according to their background or the historical period. From the point of view of film narrative, certain characters may be minoritized according to the way they are presented within the narrative. For film history, this has been the case of the South, and in particular southern women. However, there is a difference between the romanticized "southern belle" in the plantation film, or her deviant side as depicted by Tennessee Williams, and the working-class white southern woman who, from the late 1960s with Arthur Penn's *Bonnie and Clyde* (1967) became the focus of attention.

Obviously, the particular period in American history is noteworthy, and the 1920s to the 1950s may have been more "strike-friendly," as were the 1970s, which also produced Barbara Kopple's documentary *Harlan County, U.S.A.* (1976), describing a 13-month miners' strike that owed much of its force to the staunch support of the miners' wives. *Harlan County, U.S.A.* was Kopple's first film and won the 1977 Academy Award for best documentary. The strike was sparked by the refusal of the owners of East Mining to sign the working agreement allowing the miners to organize via the UMW (Union for Mine Workers). The refusal led to demonstrations, strikes, problems with strike breakers, court orders against strikers, arrests, imprisonment, and even murder.[7] The year 1976 also saw the release of *Union Maids* (Julia

Reichart and James Klein), a historical documentary about women's role in labor movements since the 1930s. In her critique of *Union Maids*, Linda Gordon points out that women were not encouraged by the Congress of Industrial Organisations (CIO) to enter industry or to organize. Moreover, until 1940, 20 percent of women workers were domestic servants. Traditionally, women find themselves in the textile industry, as in *Norma Rae*, or in services as in *Bread and Roses*.[8]

Salt of the Earth: "Solidarity forever"[9]

Salt of the Earth adopts a semi-documentary style to describe a miners' strike in a zinc mine in New Mexico. The Mexican Americans are demanding wages and working conditions on a par with the Anglo-Americans. When the men are threatened with losing their jobs, the women take over the strike, proving even more tenacious. One of the aspects of strike films is to emphasize the collective nature of the struggle. As seen in *The Passaic Textile Strike* and the later films, the microcosm for this is a particular family or a few individuals in order to illustrate how exploitation of workers affects their lives and how they are prepared to sacrifice individual benefits for the community. This is particularly evident in *Salt of the Earth*, filmed with mostly blacklisted workers, notably the director, Biberman, who was one of the Hollywood Ten, and actor Will Geer, who plays the sheriff. The screenplay was by Michael Wilson, and the film was produced by Paul Jarrico, who also participated in the directing. Mexican actress Rosaura Revueltas plays the female protagonist, Esperanza Quintera, who is also the narrative voice, what Linda Dittmar terms the "narrative consciousness" of the film.[10] Her image and voice open and close the film, she is frequently seen in close-up and her voice-over comments on the events, often paraphrasing the Spanish dialogue. The film opens interestingly on a close-up of Esperanza's feet, not on her face. During the opening credit sequence, she is seen as an anonymous woman, with the camera cutting to various shots of her chopping wood and preparing a fire to boil water for washing clothes, each time showing her from the back or in profile. All of this is watched by her daughter, who vaguely helps by stirring the fire.

All three films focus on class differences by insisting on the humble habitat of the workers, their dress and their difficult living conditions. Linguistic differences are often revealed, through accent, speech patterns, more hesitant speech, or foreign languages as in *Salt of the Earth* and *Bread and Roses*. Here, Esperanza's voice-over introduces the miners' village, ending on the shack where she lives with her husband Ramon (Juan Chacon) and her two children.

Women are located at the bottom of the scale, as illustrated by Esperanza in the following sequences when she is pictured doing the chores. Her bowed head and downcast eyes as she hangs up the washing, irons or hands her husband a towel, reveal her total submission to her state. Later, she is visited by a delegation of "ladies," as she terms them, who want her to join them in their demands for better sanitation. Indeed, to call them "housewives"—a word that was fast developing during the 1950s with the return of women to the home— would suggest a place on the socioeconomic scale. She introduces herself as a "miner's wife." Whereas the men go on strike for equality with the Anglo workers, the women want to make the everyday problem they are confronted with— the lack of running water, let alone hot water—a demand as well. It would certainly enhance *their* daily life.

The gender difference is emphasized by the placards the women and men brandish. In front of Esperanza's house, the ladies' delegation reveals a sign saying, "We want sanitation not discrimination," while, later, the picketing men, carry signs reading, "Less talk more money" and "The union is our leader." Here, the siren from the mine, announcing an accident, interrupts the women's conversation and all rush anxiously to the scene. The men decide to strike and Ramon tells the mechanic to shut off the machinery. In the ensuing silence, the men raise their eyes to the hill where the women are grouped together, while the women's placard demanding sanitation is raised, by an anonymous hand. A reverse shot presents the men below, looking at them in admiration, followed by a low-angled long shot of the women on the hill, announcing the strike through the grouping around the placard, and serving as a prolepsis for their future picketing.

The first union meeting during which the strike is voted is also attended by four women, one of whom is Esperanza. While the main body of men sits in the middle of the room, they sit on the side and one has a baby in her arms. Finally, Consuela Ruiz (Angela Sanchez) asks for the floor, but is so intimidated that she can hardly speak. She goes to the platform on the men's request, and expresses the women's demands for sanitation and their wish to join the strike, as a "ladies auxiliary." This is scorned and rejected by the men. The strike begins the following day. Watched by the women sitting in a group on the hill, the male strikers below begin picketing, walking around in a circle as is customary in the United States. Throughout the film, the men's and women's participation and demands are shown in parallel. This comes to its height when a sequence of Ramon being beaten up by scabs is intercut with Esperanza's cries as she "goes into labor" for their third child in a makeshift hut near the picket line.

During the long months of the strike, the women gradually become involved, sometimes joining in the picketing, and generally supporting the miners by providing them with coffee and other types of support, until a court injunction forbids the men to strike. This leads to a second meeting in the same hall to discuss the situation. The next few sequences counterbalance those described above and are indeed symmetrically opposed both to the first meeting and the picketing. The second meeting differs by the strong presence of the women who now take up a larger space, sitting at the back of the hall, as well as along the sides. They propose to strike in lieu of their husbands, a suggestion that is first rejected, but accepted after a long discussion. The following sequence depicts the beginnings of the women's picketing. Now, the situation is reversed and the women are in the center, walking in a circle, while the men are on the outskirts watching, above on the hill or around them, some in pick-up trucks. The sequence is accompanied by Esperanza's voice-over as intradiegetic narrator, recounting the arrival of the women and the harassment they experience in the form of sexist comments. Like the men, the women are evenly-spaced and walk at an even pace, as in the union-made film, *Labor's Reward*.[11] Some women, like Esperanza, have been forbidden by their husbands to participate in the picketing. As she comments, she is standing on the hill next to Ramon, holding her newborn baby in her arms, but she steps out of her role as narrator when the sheriff's men attack the women physically. Passing the baby to her husband she becomes an active character, running to the defense of a friend whose assailant she stuns with her shoe. This triumphant moment is her first move to agency and empowerment. It is also the moment when her gaze ceases to look downward or to seek heaven-sent solutions. Esperanza can now look directly ahead.

Although the women are instrumental in bringing the strikers' demands to a more or less happy conclusion, their struggle is wrought with suffering on all sides. The women are frequently attacked by the company or its henchmen, both physically and verbally, and even arrested. Their husbands and other men experience their participation as a blow to their virility, which it is partially. However, the men do not understand that their virility is first undermined by the refusal of the company to take their demands seriously, forcing them to work in perilous conditions for low pay. The women are also affected by the fact that they may be neglecting their families, until their combat becomes more important and goes beyond self-criticism. Full empowerment is achieved when they are no longer surrogate strikers, but acting for themselves, as shown above with Esperanza. The men's and women's demands converge on one question, that of equality. For the men, this lies in equal pay and working conditions to those of the Anglo workers. For the women, it means equality for men and women, which is the final outcome of the film.

Norma Rae: "Child of a working man"[12]

Norma Rae and *Bread and Roses* adopt more mainstream fictional modes, describing how women workers are gradually led into the struggle to defend their rights. *Norma Rae* was a Hollywood product for Twentieth Century Fox. Although actresses like Mary Pickford or Nazimova had produced their own films during the silents, women like the female duo behind *Norma Rae*, Tamara Asseyev and Alex Rose, were a rarity in the 1970s. They particularly sought to stress the female, if not feminist side, to the story,[13] partially scripted by Harriet Frank, Jr., who worked alongside screenwriter Irving Ravetch. The film complies to a large extent with Hollywood narrative demands, although its director, Martin Ritt, had made several social conscious films, starting with his first feature, *Edge of the City* (1957), in which an African American foreman in a New York dock warehouse, played by Sidney Poitier, is attacked and killed by a racist white foreman. Closer in time and subject matter to *Norma Rae* is Ritt's *The Molly Maguires* (1970), set in Pennsylvania in the mid–1870s among Irish coalminers who fight against the mining company's exploitation. Ritt also directed *The Front* (1976), in which Woody Allen, playing a screenwriter during the McCarthy witch hunt, is asked to lend his name to a victim of McCarthyism, played by Zero Mostel, one of the many former blacklisted workers who participated in the making of the film and who, contrary to *Salt of the Earth*, could do so openly. In these earlier films, Ritt seems more concerned with masculinity, so *Norma Rae* could be seen as a shift to female characters, or a partial shift, judging by this statement regarding Sutton, the model for Norma Rae: "I've known a lot of women in my life, most of them much more educated and sophisticated, who would not have had the balls that she had."[14] As Corinne Oster underlines, Norma Rae is presented in masculine terms as noisy, drinking, muscular, going against the usual stereotypes of femininity.[15] Indeed, female activism is judged in terms of masculinity, exposing the difficulties of being a *woman* in American film.

Thirty-two-year-old Norma Rae is a single mother, with one young child from her first husband who died in a brawl, and a second child from one of the many men she has had relationships with since then. Norma Rae's parents, Vernon (Pat Hingle) and Leona (Barbara Baxley), work in the same factory, but both are worn out by their years of work. Leona never speaks and she is seen at the beginning temporarily deafened by the constant noise of the machinery. Norma Rae and Vernon have a close relationship, but he dies on the job. It would seem that there is not much work available for unskilled or semi-skilled workers, except in service industries. Early on in the film, she meets Sonny (Beau Bridges) and they get married. These personal moments of death and marriage are not treated emotionally or melodramatically, which is part of Ritt's "stylistic realism." Vernon's funeral is presented in a general shot, with the family seen from afar on the other side of the grave. The smallness of the party at the funeral, their smallness of scale within the shot, the rapidity with which a father's death is dispatched, all suggest suppressed emotion which the working class does not have the time to indulge in. Similarly, Norma Rae and Sonny's wedding, although presented at medium-close range within the interior of the pastor's home, has only two witnesses: Norma Rae's friend, Bonnie Mae (Gail Strickland), and the pastor's wife.

The film dwells in greater length on the relationship that develops between Norma Rae and Reuben (Ron Liebman), the union organizer who has come specifically to the small Alabama town to organize the workers in the textile factory. The Jewish trade unionist organizer is a recurrent filmic character, found also in *Bread and Roses* in the character of Sam Shapiro (Adrien Brody). Reuben meets with hostility until Norma Rae joins him in the struggle to unionize workers. Jewish organizers may be based on actual figures, like Albert Weisbord, the left-winger organizer in the Passaic textile strike.[16] Jews often serve symbolically in film—especially in the biblical epics of the 1950s, which coincide with the Civil Rights Movement—as representatives of freedom, following on Moses leading the Israelites out of bondage. Although the Mexican Maya (Pilar Padilla) does not see Sam as other than a man, a trade unionist who might help her personal cause and an American intellectual more than a Jewish American, for Norma Rae, Reuben is the epitome of otherness: a New Yorker, an intellectual, a union organizer—and a Jew. She has never met a Jewish person before, but only ponders on his ethnic origins toward the end of the film. She relates to him essentially as a co-worker. The fact that she does not relate to him as a woman, shows that she has moved away from her previous physical and emotional need for men. When she first meets Reuben, she has just broken off a purely sexual relationship with a man whom she has been seeing in the motel where he is staying. In a rage at being discarded, her lover beats her violently and Reuben gives her some ice to subdue the pain. From then, the motel ceases to be a locus for brief sexual encounters as frequently shown in American film, and the room where Reuben is staying becomes the center of union activities for discussion, printing tracts, etc. Norma Rae often works there with him.

Norma Rae's character should not be seen as one and unique throughout the film. It evolves from the beginning when, during the lunch-break, she tells Bonnie Mae, that she is on diet. She is at that stage still dependent on male approval of what is considered a perfect female body. This evolution takes place within the bounds of her working-class upbringing and against the social background of women's liberation and changing mores. These two yardsticks allow her to rebel against conditions that her parents' generation or other more settled contemporaries like Bonnie Mae accept. Confrontation with the physical toll that factory work takes on her parents, the sexist attitudes of her lover and later her husband, Sonny, the bosses' cynical manipulation, all combine in a practical experience of *consciousness raising*, one of the primary tools of the contemporaneous women's movement. Norma Rae has a rough veneer that enables her to speak out uncompromisingly, but she has a love of life that makes her enjoy simple things like picnics or swimming with people she loves, or just likes.

The height of her awareness comes when she goes against the company's ban on unionizing and is fired. She walks into the middle of the factory, climbs onto a table brandishing the sign of her own making with the single word "Union" written on it. Her fellow workers stare at her, and then one by one, they switch off their machines. It is interesting to note that the first to do so are the women, starting with her mother, followed by Bonnie Mae and other women, then African American workers. Finally, close-ups of anonymous hands, barely identifiable by gender or ethnic group, drop the switch of their machines until utter silence occurs. The scene is similar to the beginning of the strike in *Salt of the Earth*, except that here it marks the climax of the film. In both cases, the strike is marked by the absolute silence of the machines, and the female character(s) positioned above the others. This silence is all the more

"Coming to awareness": Sally Field (as Norma Rae) in *Norma Rae* (Martin Ritt, 1979) (© 20th Century Fox/Photofest).

powerful in that it is instigated by women who are usually associated either with innocuous chatter, hysteria, or docile silence.[17] Just as the hieratic pose of the women on the hill in *Salt of the Earth* reinforced the men's initiative, here Norma Rae's silent immobility causes a shut down in solidarity. Unlike the former film, it is a short-lived moment for Norma Rae, who is arrested and humiliated by being sent to prison. A shift from the individual to the general now occurs, as shown in the scene depicting the tabulation of the ballots for or against unionizing. To emphasize the historic moment, the fictional element gives way to naturalistic depiction, varying between general shots of the mass of people outside the factory, to close-ups of characters or anonymous characters, to the people counting the ballots, or their hands and the ballot papers. The sequence showing the tabulation before the results are announced lasts a full two minutes and is not accompanied by music or noise. The silence and the slowness add to the tension, as one anxious face after another is shown. The film ends on the personal element as Norma Rae and Reuben say goodbye. She has lost her job, but has the satisfaction of seeing the factory unionized. He leaves, having accomplished his mission and Norma Rae is left to carry on with her life. It would seem however that her experience has put her "above" factory work.

S. Ross remarks on the cross-cultural romance as a recurrent feature of 1920s class struggle films,[18] which could be attributed to the ambient melodramatic mode. This is absent from the three films discussed here, although there is a possibility of an affair between Norma Rae and Reuben,[19] and a short flirtation occurs in *Bread and Roses* between Maya and Sam. *Norma Rae* concludes rather on a cross-cultural *exchange* between her and Reuben: she has learnt about unionizing and Dylan Thomas, and he has been inspired by her personality and gumption.

Bread and Roses: "No nos moveran"[20]

Like *Norma Rae*, *Bread and Roses* concerns the right of workers to unionize—in this case, janitors in a high-rise building in Los Angeles. It centers on Maya, an illegal Mexican immigrant, who is first seen crossing the border. She joins her sister Rosa (Elpidia Carillo), who has been living in the United States for years and, like her, finds work as a janitor. The double irony of Loach's single film in the United States is that it is set not only on the outskirts of Hollywood, but also in what may be considered the underside of the film industry.[21] The building is owned by a group of lawyers, whose main clients are Hollywood stars. This is highlighted in a central scene when janitors stage a demonstration during a party organized by the owners of the office block. Many of the guests are actual Hollywood stars, like Ron Perlman and Tim Roth. While they are sipping their champagne, Sam leads in the janitors, who begin to vacuum in between the guests. Generally, janitors are invisible, doing the cleaning after hours. Here, the order of things is reversed and they become conspicuous in their red union t-shirts, knocking into stars, producers and lawyers, and drowning out the conversations by their hoovering, the type of incessant noise that is the worker's lot, as seen in *Salt of the Earth* and *Norma Rae*.

Maya discovers a world of corruption and exploitation. Perez (George Lopez), the janitor foreman, lays down the rules for hiring and firing workers, which may include sexual harassment. A typical ploy of bosses is to wield power over workers by promotion or salary raises. Norma Rae had been delighted to become forewoman because of the extra pay, but resigns when her former friends and colleagues shun her. This could be seen as a milder form of worker harassment, but it is a typical "divide-and-rule" tactic found in strike films. In *The Passaic Textile Strike*, Richard Deak is offered a job as foreman, which he refuses. In *Salt of the Earth*, Ramon is singled out by the bosses as the strike leader. When called over to their car, the superintendent cynically tells him that before the strike, they had intended to make him foreman. Ramon is not duped by this intimidation. In *Bread and Roses*, Berta (Maria Orellana) is less fortunate than Norma Rae. Perez offers her a job as forewoman in exchange for the names of those who attended a union meeting. When she refuses, she is fired. Rosa accepts the job to pay for her husband's medical fees, causing a rift between her and Maya and the other workers. Rosa has few illusions about work and the exploitation of women, having worked as a prostitute in Mexico in order to provide for her siblings. Maya learns the truth during an argument between the two and discovers that she owes her job to the fact that Rosa had slept with Perez in exchange for hiring her.

Ethnic groups may be played off against each other, like the Anglos and Mexicans in *Salt of the Earth*, or whites and African Americans in *Norma Rae*. Significantly, those just above the janitors in *Bread and Roses*, like the security guards and chief of police, are mainly minorities—second-generation Hispanics like Perez or African Americans. The janitors tend only to deal with them and not with the owners of the building. Direct contact with the bosses seldom occurs, two instances being when the janitors invade their cocktail party and when they invest the lobby of the building during the final demonstration. Now the white-collar workers are seen clustered together behind a glass partition on an upper floor, looking down on the strikers. This direct contact would seem to lead ultimately to the success of the movement with salary raises and improved working conditions.

Jean-François Baillon notes that in *Bread and Roses*, as in other Loach films featuring women, the female characters do not specifically defend a women's cause.[22] This is to a certain extent true of this film, as in *Norma Rae*, in which men are the guiding force. In *Bread and Roses*, the trade unionist Sam informs the workers of their rights and initiates them into the struggle. He is also the one with the intellectual know-how, who establishes the historical link between this movement and past industrial action during the final demonstration when he points to the banner with the slogan "bread and roses," explaining to the strikers the reference to the Lawrence textile workers strike of 1912, a movement that also involved immigrants. The explanation is simultaneously addressed to the audience, giving added meaning to the title, suggesting that, while Sam is a trade unionist, he is also an intradiegetic narrator and outsider— he faulted by leaving tracts in the building that later incriminate the workers, something that Reuben would not have done. In his capacity as both narrator and outsider, he represents the authors of the film, Loach and screenwriter Paul Laverty. Maya is an outsider too, as a new arrival to the United States, the job of janitoring, and unionizing. Much of the action is shown through her experiences and literally through her eyes. In the final demonstration, an over-the-shoulder shot allows us to see the approaching police force from her perspective, while reaction shots on her reveal the strength of Sam's words to the crowd.

Another force is present, represented by the Hispanic-American woman Teresa—an actual union leader—who accompanies Sam at each union meeting and who is seen during the demonstrations, talking to the lawyers or, as here, arguing with security guards and policemen. Teresa is never presented as a "character": not much is known about her, unlike Maya, Rosa, or some of the other women. She is a committed unionist and leads the chanting of slogans. From this it can be seen that Loach and Laverty constructed a narrative based on two parallel voices: that of the actors playing the parts of workers, recounting the greater story and the historical account, represented by Sam and Maya, and that of the actual janitors, led with quiet determination by Teresa and backed up by the other grass-roots janitors—many of whom are women—who reenact their own life and struggle.[23] They come together in this moment of industrial action, crossing the bridge that leads to downtown Los Angeles, storming the building and singing "we shall not be moved" in Spanish.

To conclude, each film presents the different paths to empowerment of the women characters as a personal struggle, but also one that is closely linked to a collective movement. While the films idealize workers to a certain extent, the interweaving of fictional and non-fictional narrative and cinematic techniques allows the working class to emerge as worthy of narrative focus. In this,

Loach takes a particular stand, intentionally estheticizing his working class in their daily life as in their struggles.[24] He has reiterated on several occasions his belief that the poor and socially disadvantaged need not be filmed in drab surroundings and are as entitled to romance, emotions and pretty clothes as, let us say, a Jane Austen heroine.

The statement for women's rights is more clearly marked in *Salt of the Earth*, as the women are seeking equality *along with* their men folk. When Esperanza returns home after being imprisoned for a few days with a large group of women strikers, she is buoyed up with determination and hope. Like Sonny in *Norma Rae*, her husband feels belittled at having to look after the children and do the washing and a violent argument breaks out between them. Her demand for full equality is achieved at the end when the couple is on the point of being evicted from their house. Husband and wife stand together in front of their house, surrounded by miners and their families from the village, by Mexican Americans and Anglos alike. Against such numbers, the sheriff gives up and the company bosses are forced to capitulate too. Esperanza has proved the strength of her conviction, of the slogan "Solidarity forever," and the film ends on her in close-up and her concluding words.

By portraying the workers' struggle essentially from the women's perspective, these three films underline not a dent in masculinity, but an enhancement of the workers' movement and its message. As Linda Gordon indicates, in the union hierarchy, women belong to the rank-and-file and their presence allows the union's base to be broadened.[25] Although May 1st is celebrated as Labor Day in many countries in the world, after strikes that occurred in Chicago in the mid–1880s,[26] organizing is depicted in American films as not appertaining to the working world and something that still has to be fought for. As shown in the films, there is a slow, difficult process to political awareness and where women workers are concerned, the workplace is gendered differently. Women suffer from sexist remarks levied at those who protest against their condition or who defend certain rights. What will be the aftermath in these women's lives? The women in *Salt of the Earth* will return to being housewives without pay. Although the workers gain the right to organize, Norma Rae will not be reinstated. The janitors' demands are met in *Bread and Roses*, but Maya is deported for stealing. These open-ended conclusions illustrate that the "struggle continues."

Filmography

The Accused (Jonathan Kaplan, 1988)
Bonnie and Clyde (Arthur Penn, 1967)
Bread and Roses (Ken Loach, 2000)

Broken Blossoms (David Wark Griffith, 1919)
The Devil Wears Prada (David Frankel, 2006)
The Front (Martin Ritt, 1976)
Harlan County, U.S.A. (Barbara Kopple, 1976)
Harlan County War (Peter Silverman, 2000)
Labor's Reward (Rothaker Films, American Federation of Labor, 1925)
The Molly Maguires (Martin Ritt, 1970)
9 to 5 (Colin Higgins, 1980)
Norma Rae (Martin Ritt, 1979)
The Passaic Textile Strike (Sam Russak, 1926)
Salt of the Earth (Herbert J. Biberman, 1954)
Union Maids (Julia Reichart and James Klein, 1976)
Working Girl (Mike Nichols, 1988)

Notes

1. Kevin Brownlow, *Behind the Mask Innocence, Sex, Violence, Prejudice, Crime: Films of Social Conscience in the Silent Era*, New York: Knopf, 1990; Alan Gevinson (ed.), *American Film Institute Catalog, Within Our Gates: Ethnicity in American Feature Films, 1911–1960*, Berkeley: University of California Press, 1997, 764–765; M. Keith Booker, *Film and the American Left: A Research Guide*, Westport: Greenwood Press, 1999, 19; Steven Higgins, *Still Moving: The Film and Media Collections of the Museum of Modern Art*, New York: The Museum of Modern Art, 2006, 117.

2. Steven J. Ross, *Working-Class Hollywood, Silent Film and the Shaping of Class in America*, Princeton: Princeton University Press, 1999. For the counter point of view, see Corinne Oster's short review of the literature in "'Mouth!': Voix et lieu de pouvoir dans *Norma Rae* de Martin Ritt" in Elizabeth de Cacqueray and Zachary Baqué (eds.), "Women, Conflict and Power," *Anglophonia / Caliban*, vol. 27, Université de Toulouse 2-Le Mirail, 2010, 75–77.

3. Frank Curot, *Styles filmiques: 2. Les réalismes—Cassavetes, Forman, Kiarostami, Loach, Pialat*, Paris-Caen: Lettres modernes Minard, "Etudes cinématographiques," vol. 69, 2004, 3–7.

4. *Ibid.*, 12–17.

5. Charles W. Eckert, "The Anatomy of a Proletarian Film: Warner's 'Marked Woman,'" *Film Quarterly*, vol. 27, no. 2, 1973–1974, 11.

6. A similar use of Lady Liberty is found in later films, like Elia Kazan's *America, America* (1963) or more recently in James Gray's *The Immigrant* (2013).

7. The fictional television film *Harlan County War* (Peter Silverman, 2000) starred Holly Hunter as a miner's wife.

8. See Linda Gordon, "*Union Maids*: Working-Class Heroines" in Peter Steven (ed.), *Jump Cut: Hollywood, Politics and Counter Cinema*, Toronto: Between the Lines, 1985, 153–154.

9. Lyrics by Ralph Chaplin (1915) for the IWW (Industrial Workers of the World), sung to the tune of *John Brown's Body*, which is also that of *The Battle Hymn of the Republic*. Songs were an important feature of the labor movement, and were often inspired by popular or folk music, see Dave Van Ronk and Elijah Wald, *The Mayor of MacDougal Street: A Memoir*, Cambridge: Da Capo Press, 2005, 30–1.

10. Laura Dittmar, "The Articulating Self: Difference as Resistance in *Black Girl, Ramparts of Clay*, and *Salt of the Earth*" in Diane Carson et al., *Multiple Voices in Feminist Film Criticism*, Minneapolis: University of Minnesota Press, 1998 [1994], 398.

11. This was a way of showing the workers' struggle to be dignified and orderly, and not composed of a mass of wild "Bolsheviks." See S. J. Ross, *Working-Class Hollywood, Silent Film and the Shaping of Class in America*, 163.

12. "Bless the child of a working man" is the opening line to the film's song, *It Goes Like It Goes*, sung by Jennifer Warnes, lyrics by Noman Gimbel, music by David Shire.

13. Oster, "'Mouth!': Voix et lieu de pouvoir dans *Norma Rae* de Martin Ritt," 78.

14. Martin Ritt, garnered from imdb trivia, under *Norma Rae*: www.imdb.com, accessed 7 October 2013.

15. Oster, "'Mouth!' Voix et lieu de pouvoir dans *Norma Rae* de Martin Ritt," 79–80.
16. Albert Weisbord, author of *The Conquest of Power: Liberalism, Anarchism, Syndicalism, Socialism, Fascism, and Communism*, New York: M. Secker & Warburg, 1937.
17. Corinne Oster, "'Mouth!': Voix et lieu de pouvoir dans *Norma Rae* de Martin Ritt," 81.
18. Ross, *Working-Class Hollywood, Silent Film and the Shaping of Class in America*, 157.
19. As a woman, Norma Rae is not taken seriously by the company. The bosses do not fail to spread rumors about a possible relationship between her and Reuben, using her previous encounters to suggest that she has loose morals. As in *The Accused* (Jonathan Kaplan, 1988), women—especially those of the "lower" classes—need a pristine record to be credible.
20. The demonstrators sing in Spanish "We shall not be moved," a union song that was also sung during the Civil Rights and 1960s protest movements.
21. For divergent reception of the film as regards right-wing and left-wing critics, and Mexican and European audiences, see Armida de la Garza, *Mexico on Film: National Identity and International Relations*, Bury St. Edmunds: Arena Books, 2006, 110–116.
22. Jean-François Baillon, "Pendre part ou prendre parti? La cause des femmes dans le cinéma de Ken Loach" in Penny Starfield (ed.), *Femmes et pouvoir*, Condé-sur-Noireau: éditions Corlet, coll. "CinémAction," 2008, 120–125.
23. The documentary, *Ken and Rosa* (2000), provides off-screen insight into the participation of these janitors.
24. Frank Curot, *Styles filmiques: 2. Les réalismes—Cassavetes, Forman, Kiarostami, Loach, Pialat*, 40.
25. Linda Gordon, "*Union Maids*: Working-Class Heroines."
26. May 1, 1886, was intended to mark the introduction of the eight-hour day across the board, but the movement was halted by police repression and the Haymarket Square riots on May 4, which led to the arrest of eight participants, four of whom were executed.

Works Cited

Baillon, Jean-François. "Prendre part ou prendre parti? La cause des femmes dans le cinéma de Ken Loach" in Penny Starfield (ed.), *Femmes et pouvoir*. Condé-sur-Noireau: éditions Corlet, coll. "CinémAction," 2008, 120–125.
Booker, M. Keith. *Film and the American Left: A Research Guide*. Westport: Greenwood Press, 1999.
Brownlow, Kevin. *Behind the Mask Innocence, Sex, Violence, Prejudice, Crime: Films of Social Conscience in the Silent Era*. New York: Kopf, 1990.
Curot, Frank. *Styles filmiques: 2. Les réalismes—Cassavetes, Forman, Kiarostami, Loach, Pialat*, Paris-Caen: Lettres modernes Minard, "Etudes cinématographiques," vol. 69, 2004.
Dittmar, Laura. "The Articulating Self: Difference as Resistance in *Black Girl, Ramparts of Clay*, and *Salt of the Earth*" in Diane Carson, Linda Dittmar and Janice R. Welsch (eds.), *Multiple Voices in Feminist Film Criticism*. Minneapolis: University of Minnesota Press, 1998 [1994], 391–405.
Eckert, Charles W. "The Anatomy of a Proletarian Film: Warner's 'Marked Woman.'" *Film Quarterly*, vol. 27, no. 2, 1973–1974, 10–24.
De la Garza, Armida. *Mexico on Film: National Identity and International Relations*. Bury St. Edmunds: Arena Books, 2006.
Gevinson, Alan (ed.). *American Film Institute Catalog, Within Our Gates: Ethnicity in American Feature Films, 1911–1960*. Berkeley: University of California Press, 1997.
Gordon, Linda. "*Union Maids*: Working-Class Heroines." *Jump Cut*, vol. 14, 1977, also in Peter Steven (ed.), *Jump Cut: Hollywood, Politics and Counter Cinema*. Toronto: Between the Lines, 1985, 151–157.
Higgins, Steven. *Still Moving: The Film and Media Collections of the Museum of Modern Art*. New York: The Museum of Modern Art, 2006.

Oster, Corinne. "'Mouth!': Voix et lieu de pouvoir dans *Norma Rae* de Martin Ritt" in Elizabeth de Cacqueray and Zachary Baqué (eds.), "Women, Conflict and Power." *Anglophonia / Caliban*, vol. 27, Université de Toulouse 2-Le Mirail, 2010, 75–82.

Ross, Steven J. *Working-Class Hollywood, Silent Film and the Shaping of Class in America*. Princeton: Princeton University Press, 1999.

Van Ronk, Davewith, and Elijah Wald. *The Mayor of MacDougal Street: A Memoir*. Cambridge: Da Capo Press, 2005.

Art and the Reversal of Hierarchies
Representing Women in Domestic Service in *Upstairs, Downstairs*

Delphine Lemonnier-Texier

For many viewers, the spatial dichotomy apparently contained in the title of the 1970s TV series *Upstairs, Downstairs*[1] mirrors the hierarchy of class in British society so aptly that the title has become a catchphrase for the representation of masters and servants in TV period drama along the lines of an aesthetics in which verticality defines class-identity. For instance on "Good Morning America" on October 12, 2013, the ABC host welcomed Julian Fellowes and the cast of *Downton Abbey* by defining the show as "our favorite upstairs-downstairs drama."[2] Overlooking the fact that both in real life and in corresponding TV series, servants occupied the downstairs *and* the attic parts of stately homes (as Sarah says about herself and Rose in "The Mistress and the Maids": "We've Got This Lovely Room up Top Together"),[3] the title of the show has thus been made into a synonym for a spatial class-divide that mirrors in its vertical paradigm the simple line between the upper and the lower classes.

However, what is in a title—or its history—reveals an eloquent and somewhat richer perspective upon a project that was radically new in terms of content at the time and which remains largely under-explored in critical writings, as Helen Wheatley notes.[4] The list of prospective titles for the series in the early 1970s speaks volumes about a decision to shift the representational focus of TV drama from the figures of the masters to those of the servants and more particularly those of female servants, an aspect that is prominent as early as the second episode of season 1 ("The Mistress and the Maids"). In the episode, the thematization of the artistic representation of the maids by a fashionable painter offers a perspective upon the very same aspect in the TV series itself, and invites the viewers to measure the amount of artistic and representational audacity contained in the fictional artefacts (the two paintings, the officially commissioned portrait of the mistress, and the one of the maids he paints in secret after having one of the maids pose for him in his studio in her time off) as well as in the episode itself, and invites a similar questioning regarding the series itself.

Rather than complying with a generally accepted view of the series as rather conservative, the episode questions and challenges representational and class-hierarchies by denying the class-divide from an artistic and aesthetic point of view, since both paintings are shown next to one another at the Royal Academy, much to the dismay of the Bellamys when they find out. The episode thus asserts the representational value of its own (and the series') core subject and elaborately scripts the differential filmic treatment of both paintings to set in relief the one representing the maids. The result does not only effect a leveling of class difference but also establishes—albeit temporarily—a new hierarchy in which a genre painting representing servants supplants the official portrait of their mistress.

Documenting the Existence of People in Service: "Two little maids in town"

Richard Marson's book on the original 1971 series[5] highlights the difficulty he faced when tracing the origins of the series because most of the available material on the subject was in the form of interviews with the media at the time when the series was hugely successful. Besides, Jean Marsh herself had admitted to having slightly simplified and altered facts for the sake of clarity in those interviews: "I started to compress the facts a bit. Nothing was a lie but it got re-edited."[6] The idea for the 1970s series originally stemmed from a simple enough canvas based on the creative agency of Jean Marsh and Eileen Atkins and their response to existing TV period drama—in which hardly any figures of servants were ever featured. In the light of their own family backgrounds, both having at least one parent who had been in domestic service, they identified a gaping hole in TV fiction which they thought should be remedied. As Marsh says: "We come from poor families and poor parts of London, and we both have a parent who was in service, and it just evolved gradually from that."

The project took shape around two female figures of domestic servants, who were to be played by both actresses, and a potential title for the series was *Two Little Maids in Town*. The original idea was therefore not so much to portray class division as to focus upon the figures of the two maids. As a result, the script for the other characters (servants and masters alike) was largely written around them, so that the first series' concern was primarily to document a historical dimension largely left aside in existing TV shows.

At the root of their idea lies a document whose nature was to have implications concerning the TV series: it is a photograph of Eileen Marsh's mother when she was in service. Jean Marsh explains:

> Eileen's father was an under-butler, and her mother a needlewoman and my mother was a housemaid for a time. The seed of the series really came from looking at some photographs of Eileen's family. If there was a moment, a key to the idea—that stack of photographs was it.[7]

The photograph in question, reproduced in Richard Marson's book, depicts a large group of servants on their day off, dressed in their Sunday best and photographed in a row. Looking at it was a trigger for both actresses:

> We thought about starting each programme with this photograph and zooming in on one of the servants, whose story we could tell in that episode but, at this stage, we were just talking about it, taking notes.[8]

Although the idea was not retained, it speaks volumes about the original idea for the series and the seminal nature of this photograph, which seems to have somehow reverberated onto the episode under scrutiny.

Such a radical change in perspective meant that at the level of production, script writing, acting and filming, a number of equally radical changes were necessary. At the time, the parts of servants in TV fiction were akin to those of "mobile props" as John Hawkesworth puts it: "To look at downstairs as carefully as upstairs for the first time was the pearl in the oyster, because really forever servants had been kind of mobile props."[9] The radically new angle in the project was not so much a thematic shift as a structural transformation: what really made *Upstairs, Downstairs* stand out was that the series developed for the first time servant figures into full-fledged characters (and no longer merely types or stock characters), a characteristic which mirrors the place of female servant figures in so-called "kitchen literature," a type of sensation literature that became popular in the 1860s,[10] featuring female servants as central figures, originally meant to be read by cooks and maids but which ended up with a far wider readership.

As Marsh and Atkins's project took shape, they submitted it to a number of producers and a number of prospective titles came up. Richard Marson lists them: two titles were proposed by Marsh and Atkins, *Below Stairs* and *Behind the Green Baize Door*. The first one could not be used because a book of memoirs had just been published under the very same title, and the second put too much emphasis on the downstairs part of the household. Freddy Shaughnessy then produced another three suggestions: *The Servants' Hall* (rejected for the same reason as the previous one), *Two Little Maids in Town* (perceived as too specific), and *75 Eaton Square* which was the address of a family house which he could use; it was subsequently changed for *165 Eaton Place*.¹¹ Finally, it was a line from a nursery rhyme which provided the inspiration for the title, and not a location-based or class-divide angle:

> Goosey goosey gander,
> Whither shall I wander?
> Upstairs and downstairs
> And in my lady's chamber.

Although Shaughnessy's second proposal (*Two Little Maids in Town*) was rejected, it is probably the one that best encompasses the core of Atkins and Marsh's initial idea, an idea which resurfaces explicitly as early as season 1, episode 2, "The Mistress and the Maids," where the issue of artistic merit concerning the representation of servants is developed through the artefact of portrait painting and where another one of the possible titles for the show is mentioned by the painter, Guthrie Scone (Anton Rodgers), when he denigrates the Bellamys' belief that he needed to go to Rose and Sarah's bedroom to be able to paint them in bed: "The bourgeois mentality! So they think I've been creeping through the little green baize door up to the attic, do they?" Scone's decision to paint in secret a picture of the two maids of the Bellamy house unbeknownst to their employers (as well as the official portrait of Lady Marjorie for which he was commissioned) is made all the more significant as the episode highlights in its theme, structure and choices of camera angles and shots the crucial issue of the servants' position as subjects. The paintings are thus used to highlight the TV series' deliberate choice of promoting the maids to the same level of artistic merit as their mistress.

Decentering the Mistress and Replacing Her with the Maid(s)

Originally intended to air under the title "The Model," the second episode of the series springs from a simple narrative canvas quoted by Richard Marson:

> Portrait painter comes re: Lady M. picture. Orpen, Sargent. Sarah helps with clothes for sitting. Gets a note. Strange assignation. By hansom cab to where? Painter's studio. Sits for erotic sideline picture. Academy or portrait society. Who is "The Girl in a Shawl"? Lady M.'s under-housemaid. Slight scandal. Painter/Bellamy rift. Rose appears disapproving of Sarah/artist but really it's sexual jealousy.¹²

The changes brought to the initial script highlight the change of perspective subsequently adopted in order to focus on the figure of the two maids. The title of the episode "The Mistress and the Maids" refers to its central characters (it features Lady Marjorie, Rose and Sarah) as well as to the two paintings being made in the episode, one for which the painter has been commissioned, and the other which he paints in secret. Both are revealed at the Royal Academy in an explicit artistic leveling of class division which makes quite a sensation in the episode.

The episode starts with Bellamy commissioning a portrait painting of Lady Marjorie. The artist is fictional and known as "Guthrie Scone, one of the most fashionable avant-garde painters." Sarah is soon involved in the practicalities of the process, delivering Lady Marjorie's favorite dresses to the painter's studio so he can pick one for the portrait. The viewers are given a red herring in the suggestion of an affair between Sarah and Scone that Rose thinks she can detect, a further indication of which seems to be the use of a double bed as a central prop upon which the camera lingers emphatically in the studio scenes. However the juxtaposition of the studio scenes with views of Sarah and Rose's bedroom featuring a very similar double bed subtly prepares the viewers at the same time for the revelation about the true nature of Scone's scheme: while he is officially painting a portrait of Lady Marjorie, he is also secretly painting an intimate picture not just of Sarah but of both maids as they go to bed at night in their attic bedroom, using Sarah as a model posing in her underwear, and imagining Rose and the room from what Sarah tells him about both.

The focus shifts quite rapidly from an opening centered on Lady Marjorie to Sarah, who is for Guthrie an object of curiosity and fascination. This thematic shift is the first and most obvious manifestation of the way in which the episode gradually dislodges Lady Marjorie from her apparently central position in the painter's creative process. Although the episode opens on her and her portrait being commissioned, in terms of shooting she is not central but largely peripheral: there are lingering medium shots and close-ups on the sketches made by Scone (see figure 1, 1'02), as well as upon his hand and Bellamy's; a striking cut-in shot insists on the three characters' hands (Scone's and Bellamy's in the foreground, and Lady Marjorie's in the background). The sketches symbolically replace the flesh-and-blood face of Lady Marjorie (1'12–1'15), a first indication perhaps that the painter's inspiration is not spontaneous but imposed by the transactional nature of the commissioned portrait, as the dialogue seems to point out: "SCONE: Husbands are a great trial to artists. They look at their wives as possessions and the portrait as a kind of display case."

These shooting choices effectively prevent the viewer from seeing Lady Marjorie as she poses for the painter, or when she is seen she is slightly out of

Figure 1: The artist's hand and sketch are central and in focus, not Lady Marjorie who is slightly blurry (1'02): Rachel Gurney (as Lady Marjorie Bellamy) and Anton Rodgers (as Guthrie Scone) in *Upstairs, Downstairs* (season 1, episode 2 "The Mistress and the Maids," 1971) (© ITV/Rex Features).

focus (figure 1), giving a first indication that despite appearances, her place in the episode might not be as central as could be expected.

A radically different filmic treatment is given to Sarah in the painter's studio when she brings a selection of her mistress's dresses for the painter to choose from. There are immediately a number of close-ups on her face and they are framed like portraits using the light to emphasize her features, just as the painter announces that he wants to paint her (14'31–14'50).[13] The focus on Sarah's face creates a filmic *tableau vivant*, highlighting the complex status of pictures in an episode that intertwines artefacts in the narrative (sketches and paintings) with the presence of structural *tableaux* created with filmic tools.

When a long shot is used, the camera plays with Sarah's reflection in the mirror (see figure 2, 8'30–8'34). The framed image thus created is an inserted *tableau*, a feature that makes sure not only that contrary to Lady Marjorie the viewer can admire Sarah's face whatever the angle of the shot, but also shows that mock portraits are created with the camera before the actual artefact is created by Scone in the narrative. Whereas Lady Marjorie's face was repeatedly

Figure 2: Scone and Sarah (in her mistress's gown); the camera angle plays with the reflection in the mirror as a framed picture (8'30): Anton Rodgers (as Guthrie Scone) and Pauline Collins (as Sarah Moffat) in *Upstairs, Downstairs* (season 1, episode 2 "The Mistress and the Maids," 1971) (© ITV/Rex Features).

cut out, it seems Sarah's face is omnipresent and the marked contrast in the filmic treatment of both characters is further emphasized when Sarah poses for Scone for the first time. The painter stands with his back to the camera, as he was when sketching out Lady Marjorie (figure 1) but whereas he was in focus and the Lady was blurry, this time he is blurry and it is Sarah the camera focuses upon (15'44).

While the shots highlight the central position of Sarah and her value as a model for the painter, the dialogue insists on the way Scone's artistic tastes are at odds with his social class. He tells Sarah that he has just come back from Paris, and he mentions Degas and one Renoir which he would have liked to buy for his aunt but "the dowager said she wouldn't have a servant hanging in her drawing-room," a remark which will prove somewhat proleptic. By relegating the mistress to the margins and placing the maid in the center, the episode establishes a filmic hierarchy and a chronology which reverse the social order, just as the filmic *tableau vivant* of Sarah in her close-up shot (14'31–14'50) and her full-length portrait in the mirror in her mistress's gown (figure 2) precede rather than follow the similar shots of Lady Marjorie wearing it (19'45–19'56) in the opening scene of part 2 in the episode.

The Maids Hanging Side by Side with *The Mistress*

Whereas the sketches of Lady Marjorie's portrait were central in the opening scene, the viewer is not shown much of the picture representing Sarah. No sketches are shown, and whenever the canvas itself is filmed as a work in progress, only a small part of it is visible (figure 3, 26'53). From what is shown, it is obvious Scone mixes what he can see as he observes Sarah posing for him with elements that he imagines from Sarah's description of her and Rose's little room in the attic, such as the candlestick clearly visible in the bottom left corner of the canvas—the same item was present in the scene taking place in the maids' attic bedroom but on the other side of the bed (15'53). Together with the similar metal bedstead in his studio and in the maids' room, this is a first hint given to the viewer about what his second painting represents, the revelation of which is delayed until quite late on in the episode.

Just as with the sketches, the treatment of the actual paintings representing Lady Marjorie on the one hand, and Sarah on the other hand, could not be more contrasted. Unlike the painting representing Sarah, which remains largely unseen, Lady Marjorie's portrait is shown in its entirety as Scone brings it already framed to the Bellamys. The painting is a copy of the filmic *tableau vivant* of Lady Marjorie (19'45–19'56; 28'41).

As in the opening scene with the sketches of Lady Marjorie, the painting is shot from an unexpected angle, revealing a man's foot on the left side of the screen (Scone's) and literally situating the portrait of Lady Marjorie as an object lying at the two men's feet (28'48). The shadow of Bellamy's head hinders the full viewing of the picture. As he shows the Bellamys the picture, Scone reveals his unexpected plan: "I would like to submit it to the hanging committee of the Royal Academy" (29'48–29'53).

As far as the second painting is concerned, the camera denies the viewer a full sight of the painting representing the maid. Sarah is shown the picture by Scone in his studio, in a scene of unveiling which recalls that of Lady Marjorie's portrait, except this time the canvas is on a stand, not on the floor and all the viewer can see is the back of the frame (30'05). Whereas the mistress's portrait was shown, here the viewer has to rely upon the dialogue to *imagine* what the picture represents, in a step-by-step process which moves from one revelation to the next, using the visual memory of the viewer: the location is the maids' attic bedroom (1), there is not one but two people in the picture,

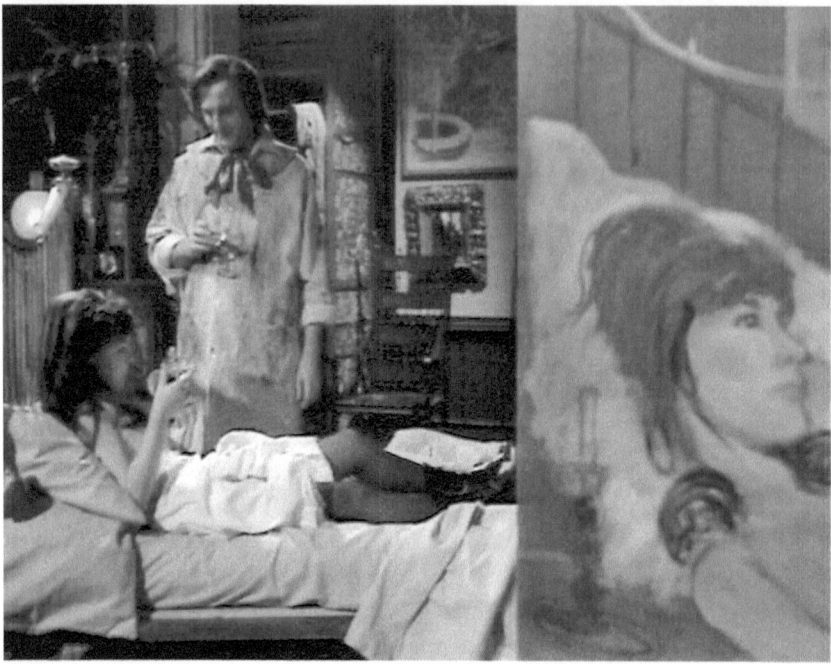

Figure 3: Part of the canvas is shown, a candlestick is sketched in its bottom left corner (26'53): Pauline Collins (as Sarah Moffat) and Anton Rodgers (as Guthrie Scone) in *Upstairs, Downstairs* (season 1, episode 2 "The Mistress and the Maids," 1971) (© ITV/Rex Features).

Sarah and Rose, who has been painted from a description (2), Sarah tells Scone he should add the plaque with the motto "To work is to pray" (seen earlier on in the same episode, 9'50) and the title of the piece is "The Maids" (4), a revelation which echoes and explains the episode title:

> **Sarah:** That's our room all right, but how do you know, you've never been there?
> **Scone:** I didn't need to.
> **Sarah:** Who's that behind me?
> **Scone:** Rose.
> **Sarah:** You've never seen Rose.
> **Scone:** I have. Through your eyes.
> **Sarah:** You won't mind me mentioning it, but here should be a little plaque with "To work is to pray" written on it. What are you going to call it?
> **Scone:** The Maids [30'58].

Not only is the painting left out and its contents scripted into a series of revelations relying on the viewers' imagination to form a mental picture based on the elements that the dialogue reveals, but it is also the center of the next scene in 165 Eaton Place, with the discovery Hudson makes in the next day's newspaper. Scripted with a certain amount of suspense, the scene centers on a mysterious article discovered in the day's paper by Hudson. Only after he has read it aloud are the contents of the paper revealed both to Sarah and to the viewers, as the title of the episode takes on a new dimension associated with a sensational display at the Royal Academy.

A process of step-by-step revelation similar to the unveiling of the painting to Sarah in Scone's studio is used here, as the viewers do not get to see the article or the photograph of the painting, and have to rely upon the dialogue: Hudson exclaims upon reading the day's paper and what he sees is so shocking that he tears the page apart (1); he lies to Bellamy about the delivery of the paper (2); upon returning to the kitchen he shows Sarah the article (3); Sarah identifies the picture as her painting (4); Hudson reads aloud the article which underlines eloquently the "fascinating counterpoint" formed by both paintings (5) as their titles are given: "The Mistress" and "The Maids." The event of the newspaper article is sensationalized in the episode in a process which mirrors the sensation at the Royal Academy described in the article:

> Sensation of this year's Academy are undoubtedly two striking pictures by Guthrie Scone artist nephew of the Countess of Abercraven, hung side by side in fascinating counterpoint the Mistress and the Maids, as this pair of canvases have already been called are both scenes from the house of Mr. Richard Bellamy MP and set a new fashion for home portraits. Asked to name the model for the scantily clad maid servant, in his canvas aptly entitled The Maids, Mr. Guthrie Scone referred our reporter to the servants' quarters at 165 Eaton Place [35'24–36'03].

The focus on the servants rather than on the masters and the revelation of the scandal before the Bellamys are shown arriving there place the masters in a situation of dramatic irony as the viewers expect to see them publicly humiliated, which is precisely what the next scene deals with. It obviously takes place in a gallery and the conversations that are overheard are about Bellamy. Again, the viewing of the painting is delayed and the figures of the master and mistress and decentered: as the Bellamys discover both paintings, their eyes glaze over (37'09), but the camera angle abruptly shifts to their backs now seen in the foreground with the paintings in the background and Lady Marjorie's portrait is clearly visible (37'12).

The same abrupt angle shift is used again: the look of shock on the master's and mistress's faces is plain for everyone to see (37'16), and again the camera shifts to their backs to reveal gradually more of the mysterious painting. The left side of the canvas featuring Sarah's face is shown, as well as the naked back of the seated figure of another woman in the background (37'17). The angle of the camera has shifted so that the portrait of the Lady is now completely obscured by Bellamy's hat while the two maids are clearly visible.

As the faces of the Bellamys are shown again, they look at one another and leave the room, after which the painting of the maids is shown again but this time in its entirety (figure 4, 37'35). The close-up of the framed canvas blends in the screen frame with the picture frame, an effect of proximity or analogy between both representational modes which is further conveyed by the superimposition of the canvas with the caption card announcing the end of part 2 (37'37).

The portrait of Lady Marjorie, a small part of which was visible for a moment at the beginning of the scene has simply been excluded from the screen, while the painting of the maids is gradually made narratively and structurally central in all possible ways including the superimposition of frames with the caption card. The moment when the viewers finally discover it is scripted as a sophisticated pitch at the heart of which the partial nudity of both

Figure 4: The framed picture gradually becomes central in the frame revealing Sarah's naked breasts (37'35): Scone's portrait of Sarah and Rose in *Upstairs, Downstairs* (season 1, episode 2 "The Mistress and the Maids," 1971) (© ITV/Rex Features).

female figures comes as a surprise, as this aspect was completely left out of the preceding dialogue referring to the picture (for instance when Sarah commented, "Good old Sarah, got your face in the papers, fancy," 36'38). After decentering the mistress, the episode excludes her completely to focus solely on the painting representing the servants.

As early as the second episode of the series, the issue of the artistic status of the representation of female servants is both central and seminal. Through the artefacts of the paintings, the core issues at work in the global project of the series surface: just as existing TV period drama tended to focus solely on the figures of the masters/mistresses and the series aimed at establishing a more balanced representation of the reality of those rich households, the episode features the commissioned conventional portrait of the mistress and the painter's initiative not only to paint the maids, but to have both paintings shown at the Academy. By hanging side by side a classical portrait and a genre painting including partial nudity, the artist deliberately subverts the hierarchy of genres as much as the hierarchy of class, just as the episode scripts the making of Lady Marjorie's portrait as an anti-climax whereas the picture of Sarah is turned into a suspenseful series of revelations which culminate in the revelation of the picture at the Academy, displacing the filmic and narrative focus of the episode onto the maid(s).

In a 2010 article, Steven Fielding wrote:

> Actors Eileen Atkins and Jean Marsh came up with the idea for the show, hoping it would give serious weight to lower-class as well as female characters. Unlike the BBC's iconic *The Forsyte Saga*, where servants were seen but not heard, they wanted *Upstairs, Downstairs* (the clue is in the title) to *give them parity with their supposed betters*.[14]

As Helen Wheatley notes in her feminist reading of the series, *Upstairs, Downstairs* is characterized by its recuperative endings which show women having to accept their restricted place in the world,[15] which does not necessarily dim out completely the subversive potential of the issues raised in each episode:

> In line with Newcomb and Hirsh's notion of cultural forum and the idea that "the raising of questions is as important as the answering of them in the television text," this reading would suggest that the constantly recuperative endings of *Upstairs Downstairs'* serial narrative are less significant than the issues raised through each episode.[16]

By decentering the figure of the mistress and replacing her with the maid(s) in the narrative as well as in the filmic structure, "The Mistress and the Maids" goes beyond the parity mentioned by Fielding and exposes a number of representational and artistic ambitions. Indeed the final scene (figure 5, 48'24),

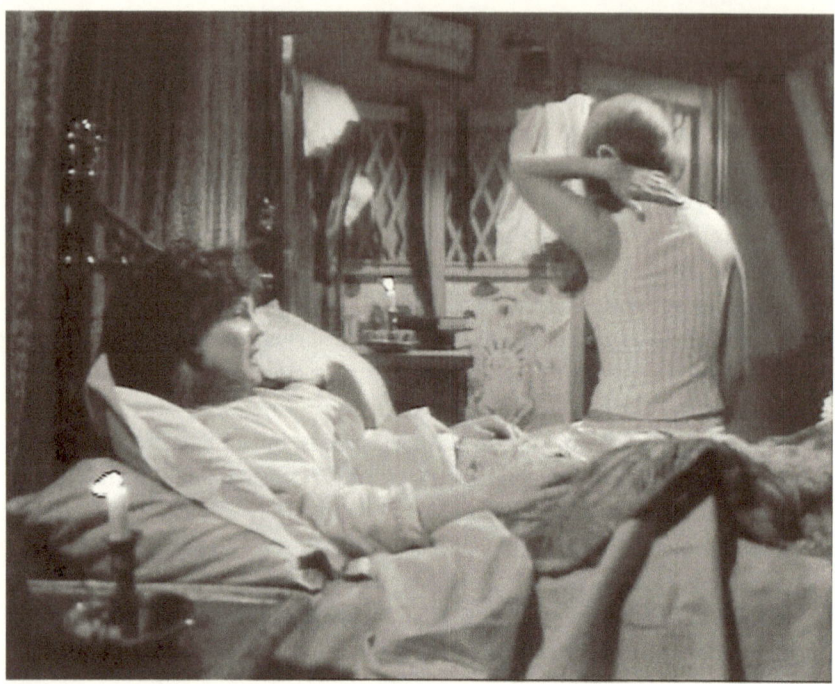

Figure 5: The two maids in their attic bedroom, in the same postures as in Scone's painting: Pauline Collins (as Sarah Moffat) and Jean Marsh (as Rose Buck) in *Upstairs, Downstairs* (season 1, episode 2 "The Mistress and the Maids," 1971) (© ITV/Rex Features).

which takes place in the maids' bedroom, replicates the postures of the two maids in the painting, nudity excepted. As in Scone's painting, there is a candlestick on Sarah's bedside table and Rose's posture with the palm of her left hand gently resting on the nape of her neck is the same as that in the painting.

> **Sarah:** Oh I wish you'd seen our picture, Rose, just once. We could still go you know, it's open to the public.
> **Rose:** We'd be recognized! No, it's best to forget all about it.
> **Sarah:** I don't think I'll ever forget [48'24].

Emphatically placed at the end of part 3, just as the painting was fully shown for the first time at the end of part 2, the scene reinforces the effect of a *mise-en-abyme* between artefact and episode that the choice of shots throughout the episode had already hinted at several times, and asserts the ambition of the series to create a specific filmic/artistic space devoid of the voyeurism present in the painter's choice of nudity for Sarah, just as the plot ostentatiously avoided the easy line of an affair between painter and maid. Within the limits of studio costume drama, the episode does provide the maids with "a room of their own," in every sense of the word.

Notes

1. *Upstairs Downstairs* is a British TV series originally produced by London Weekend Television which ran from 1971 to 1975. Set in the Belgravia area of London between 1903 and 1930, it depicts the lives of the servants "downstairs" and those of their masters "upstairs." The focus on servants was originally the idea of two actresses, Jean Marsh and Eileen Atkins, who were supposed to feature in the series as the two lead female servant characters. Marsh played Rose, one of the two lead female servant roles, but as Atkins was unable to take on the role of the other because of stage commitments, Pauline Collins stepped in as Sarah.
2. "Good Morning America," ABC, 12 October 2013: http://abcnews.go.com/GMA/video/downton-abbey-cast-share-favorite-show-moments-21160330.
3. *Upstairs, Downstairs*, series 1, season 1, episode 2, "The Mistress and the Maids" (1971).
4. Helen Wheatley, "Rooms Within Rooms: *Upstairs Downstairs* and the Studio Costume Drama of the 1970s" in Catherine Johnson and Rob Turnock (eds.), *ITV Cultures: Independent Television Over Fifty Years*, Maidenhead: Open University Press, 2005, 143.
5. Richard Marson, *Inside Updown: The Story of Upstairs, Downstairs*, Dudley: Kaleidoscope Publishing, 2011 [2001].
6. Quoted in Marson, *Inside Updown: The Story of Upstairs, Downstairs*, 11.
7. *Ibid.*, 12.
8. *Ibid.*
9. *Ibid.*, 13.
10. Elizabeth Steere, *The Female Servant and Sensation Fiction: "Kitchen Literature,"* London: Palgrave Macmillan, 2013.
11. Marson, *Inside Updown: The Story of Upstairs, Downstairs*, 35.
12. *Ibid.*, 42.
13. SCONE: I want to paint you.
    SARAH: Paint me? You mean like Lady Marjorie?
    SCONE: That's right. [...]
    SARAH: Why? Would I be hung out on a wall for everybody to look at? [14'31–14'50].
14. Steven Fielding, "The New *Upstairs, Downstairs* Is More Period Than Drama," *The Guardian*, 27 December 2010, my emphasis.
15. Wheatley, "Rooms Within Rooms: *Upstairs Downstairs* and the Studio Costume Drama of the 1970s," 155.
16. *Ibid.*

About the Contributors

Ava **Baron** is a professor at Rider University (New Jersey) where she teaches sociology, legal studies and gender studies. She has published extensively on masculinity and work, the gendering of work, work organizations and technologies, women lawyers, and contemporary and historical issues related to women and employment law, including protective labor laws, theories of legal equality and sexual harassment.

Jonathan **Bignell** is a professor of television and film at the University of Reading (UK). He specializes in the history of television and is interested in comparative work, including relationships between factual and fictional television and the different ways that television developed in the UK, in continental Europe and in the U.S.

Richard **Butsch** is a professor of sociology and of film and media studies at Rider University (New Jersey). He has been a visiting researcher at the Centre for Contemporary Cultural Studies at the University of Birmingham (UK) and a Fulbright distinguished chair at the University of Eastern Piedmont (Italy).

Nicole **Cloarec** is an associate professor of English at the University of Rennes 1 (France). Her doctoral thesis was on Peter Greenaway and she has published a number of articles on British and North American cinema. Her research focuses on the cinema of the Quay brothers, Guy Maddin, Derek Jarman, questions of transmediality, adaption and documentary.

Renée **Dickason** is a professor at the University of Rennes 2 (France). Her research work focuses on the field of British cultural history, in particular the visual media and the representation of contemporary British society through television fictions, political communication and government advertising.

Wendy **Everett** is an honorary reader in film studies at the University of Bath (UK) and a research fellow at the Camargo Foundation. Her principal research interests are European cinema as well as color, identity, music and space, the fractal narratives of the postmodern, the nature of adaptation, and concepts of genre.

Georges **Fournier** is an associate professor in English civilization at the Department of Foreign Languages of the Jean Moulin University of Lyon 3 (France). His main research interest lies in British authored television. He has published many articles on political docudrama and is currently conducting research in factual programming.

David **Haigron** is an associate professor of English at the University of Rennes 2 (France). His doctoral thesis was entitled "The British Conservative Party's Televised Political Broadcasts (1974–1997): Mutations, Strategies, Images." His research focuses on political ideology and communication in the United Kingdom and in the Republic of Ireland.

Sabine **Hillen** teaches literature and social theory, adaptation in cinema and critical approaches to word and image at the University of Brussels (VUB) and the University of Antwerp (UA). She is the author of several essays on modern and contemporary literature, and her research focuses on the French reception of Anglophone culture.

T. Ann **Kennedy** is an associate professor at the University of Maine–Farmington. Her research and teaching areas include media and new media studies, feminist theory, race and ethnicity, gender and globalization, and twentieth-century and contemporary American literature and culture. She has presented papers at the annual conventions of the National Women's Studies Association, the American Culture/Popular Culture Association, and the Modern Language Association.

Delphine **Lemonnier-Texier** is an associate professor of Shakespearean and drama studies at the University of Rennes 2 (France). She has written a number of articles and has edited collections of essays on Shakespeare's plays as well as on the plays of Samuel Beckett. She also studies the notions of role and character in Shakespearean drama, among other Shakespearean topics.

Delphine **Letort** is an associate professor of English at the University of Maine (Le Mans, France). She is the author of *The Spike Lee Brand: A Study of Documentary Filmmaking* (State University of New York Press, 2015) and *Du film noir au néo-noir: mythes et stéréotypes de l'Amérique 1941–2008* (L'Harmattan, 2010) and editor of *Panorama mondial du film noir* for the *CinémAction* series (2014). She has published several articles on adaptation studies.

Carys **Lewis** has taught English over the past 30 years in France. Since 2011 she has been an associate professor at the University of Caen in the Applied Foreign Languages department and is a member of the Irish studies research group (GREI) at the University of Caen. She has previously published articles on Raymond Williams and the cultural studies movement in the UK and on the literature and culture of Wales.

Anne-Lise **Marin-Lamellet** is an associate professor of English studies at the University of Saint-Etienne (France). She works in the field of cultural studies in contemporary British cinema. Her doctoral dissertation was entitled "The Working-Class Hero through British Cinema Since 1956."

Penny **Starfield** is a professor of American studies and film studies at Caen University (France). She is vice-president of SERCIA, the international French-based society on English-speaking cinema and editor-in-chief of *Film Journal*, SERCIA's online review. She is a specialist of American New Wave and the representation of minorities.

Index

Numbers in **_bold italics_** indicate pages with photographs.

ABC **27**, 196–198, 234, 247n2
Absolutely Fabulous 34, 56
According to Jim 29
The Accused 230, 232
Ae Fond Kiss 171
affluent 1, 3, 26, 29, 30, 134; *see also* rich; wealthy
Agee, James 204, 205
Airport 60, 63
All in the Family 25
All My Children 68
Allen, Jim 106, 121, 124, 126, 129
Allen, Woody 224
Ally McBeal 189, 190, **191**, 196, 200n24
Almond, Paul 79, 88n5
Amalgamated Textile Workers' Union 219
American dream 2, 3, 13n6, 92
American Federation of Labor 218, 231
American Idol 69
America's Most Wanted 60
Anderson, Bill 134, 147
Anderson, Lindsay 134, 147
Ang, Ien 68, 72n24
The Angel's Share 171
The Angry Silence 134–138, 140, 142, 147, 147n1, 148n9, 148n12
Anstey, Edgar 122
Apted, Michael 16, 76–87, 88n5
The Archers 42
Are You Being Served? 34, 44, 56
aristocracy 4, 43, 142, 155
Asseyev, Tamara 224
Atkins, Eileen 12, 16, 235, 236, 245, 247
audience 3, 5, 14, 20, 21, 25, 28, 35, 36, 38, 39, 44, 50, 54, 54n2, 55n13, 58–61, 64–70, 79, 80, 82, 85–87, 92, 102, 105–106, 110–112, 113n19, 116, 119, 122, 123–128, 129n1, 138, 144, 148n9, 155, 158, 161, 208, 229, 232n21

Bachelor Father 29
Baillon, Jean-François 224, 232
Baker, Roy Ward 134, 147
The Ballad of John Axon 120
The Ballad of the Big Ships 121, 130n31

The Ballad of the Miners' Strike 121, 130n31
Barrett, Lezli-Ann 134, 147
BBC 4, 16, 51, 55n4, 64, 66, 77, 102–104, 109, 116, 119, 121–127, 129n19, 129n20, 130, 164, 172, 245
Benson 27
Biberman, Herbert J. 11, 16, 218, 221, 231
Bicycle Thieves 174
Biemann, Ursula 210, 216n16
Big Bang Theory 34
The Big Flame 106, 121, 171
Bignell, Jonathan 6, 58–73, 87, 88, 129n1, 131, 249
Billy Elliot 134, 138–139, 141, 146–147
Biograph Films 219
Bird, Antonia 134, 147
Black Jack 171
Bleasdale, Alan 7, 16, 101, 103, 104, 106, 112n6, 113n10
Blue Collar 220
Body of Proof 185, 190, 196
Boehner, John 2
Bones 190, 196, 200n22
Bonnie and Clyde 220, 230
Boston Legal 189, 190, 196, 200n24
Boulting, John 134, 135, 147
Boulting, Roy 137
Bourdieu, Pierre 2, 36, 41, 95, 100
Boys from the Blackstuff 7, 8, 101–114
The Brady Bunch 26
Brassed Off 134, 138, 139, 140, 141, 142, 143, 147, 148n11
Bread 39, 40, 52, 56, 122
Bread and Roses 16, 143, 172, 218, 219, 220, 221, 224, 225, 227, 228, 229, 230
Brecht, Berthold 8, 109, 110, 121
Britannia Hospital 134, 138, 139, 140, 141, 147, 149n23
Britcom 6, 34, 57
British Film Institute 54, 116, 127, 179n2
Broken Blossoms 219, 231
Brookside 106
Brownlow, Kevin 218, 231n1
Burns, Ed 205
Burns and Allen 24

251

Index

Bush administration 207
Business as Usual 134, 139, 140, 141, 142, 143, 144, 145, 147, 150*n*31, 150*n*32
Butterflies 52, 56

Cameron, David 1
Cannadine, David 13*n*16, 38, 150, 153
capitalism 3, 4, 11, 20, 107, 122, 151*n*38, 173, 174, 175, 187, 194, 205, 206, 207, 209, 120–215
Carla's Song 143, 171, 172
Carry On at Your Convenience 134, 135, 136, 138, 144, 145, 148
Cassidy, John 2
Castaway 60
Cathy Come Home 116, 119, 121, 122, 123, 124, 125, 128, 130*n*37, 171, 173
Caughie, John 70
Channel Five 63
Channel 4 59, 63, 64, 65, 66, 67, 106, 128, 171, 174
Chaplin, Charlie 3, 219, 231*n*9
chav 2, 5, 13*n*11, 77, 78
Chester, Riley 23
cinéma vérité 61
Citizen Smith 38, 39, 56
city 3, 6, 7, 19, 35, 42, 43, 85, 89–100, 105–108, 113*n*10, 118, 123, 127, 170, 172–176, 180*n*32, 205; see also urban areas
City of Angels 196
class distinction 34–57, 89, 192, 197
class identity 9, 13*n*16, 42, 108, 234
class struggle 3, 11, 76, 130*n*36, 144, 145, 153, 174, 104, 206, 207, 218, 227
Clegg, Nick 1
The Cleveland Show 31
Clinton, Hillary 2
The Closer 196
Cole, Nigel 134, 147
Comrades 9, 16, 153–166
Conservative Decade, government, Party 12*n*2, 138, 141, 174; see also Tory
Cops 60
Cornell, Paul 37
Coronation Street 62, 68, 113*n*16, 128
The Cosby Show 26, 30
countryside 81, 85, 130*n*39, 176; see also rural areas
Courtship of Eddie's Father 29
crime, criminality 60, 91, 173, 196, 206, 209, 213
Crimewatch 60
Crossing Jordan 196
cultural capital 2, 4, 36, 41, 47, 55
Curot, Frank 218
Cutting Edge 65

Daldry, Stephen 134, 147
Dallas 68
Dantas, Luisa 7, 89–100
Day, Martin 37
Days of Hope 117, 124, 129*n*10
The Defenders 196
deindustrialization 139, 206, 209
Desperate Housewives 200*n*24
The Devil Wears Prada 231
Dickason, Renée 6, 34–55, 119
Dickens, Charles 113*n*6, 204
Dirty Pretty Things 143
discrimination 83, 94, 98, 185, 186, 188, 190, 193, 199*n*11, 200*n*32, 222
Disraeli, Benjamin 153
Dittmar, Linda 221
Dixon of Dock Green 125
Dockers 134, 138, 139, 140, 141, 142, 143, 144, 145, 147
docudrama 7, 85, 115, 116, 119, 120, 122, 123, 126, 127, 128, 220
documentary 4, 7, 8, 11, 14, 58–70, 76–88, 89–100, 105, 112, 115–132, 167, 168, 174, 177, 178, 204, 210, 218–221
docusoap 60, 62–64, 69
domcom, domestic sitcom 5, 6, 21–23, 37, 38
Douglas, Bill 9, 154, 155, 161, 162*n*9, 162*n*17, 165*n*38
Dovey, Jon 70
Downton Abbey 234
Dragonfly Productions 63
dramedy 190, 196, 200*n*24
Drop the Dead Donkey 38, 42, 46, 56
Duguid, Marc 54
Dunn, Nell 121

EastEnders 68, 128
Eckert, Charles 219
Edge of the City 224
Edna, the Inebriate Woman 119, 121, 125
Education 7, 18, 19, 28, 36, 41, 47, 49, 177, 213, 215
Edzard, Christine 9, 158, 159, 161, 164*n*29
Eight Is Enough 30
11'09'01 172
Ellis, Gabriella 69
Emily Owens 196
employee 42, 43, 104, 120, 140, 144, 150*n*32, 185, 187, 189, 192
employer 55*n*3, 103, 140, 142, 144, 148*n*13, 149*n*17, 150*n*29, 185, 192, 195, 200*n*21, 237
equality 2, 34, 86, 98, 130*n*36, 156, 184, 185, 195, 222, 223, 230
ethnicity 11, 31, 65, 134, 143, 144, 150*n*30, 185, 192, 206, 220, 225, 226, 228, 231*n*1, 232, 250

Evans, Walker 204
Everybody Loves Raymond 28, 30

Fabian Society, Fabianism 123, 130n36
Face 134, 138, 139, 143, 147
factual television 6, 59, 61, 70
The Fall and Rise of Reginald Perrin 42, 51, 52, 56
The Family 62, 63
Family Guy 29, 30, 31
Family Life 171
Father Knows Best 24, 25, 26
Fawlty Towers 34, 47, 54, 56
Federal Arts projects 19
Fellowes, Julian 234
feminism 3, 10, 143, 145, 200n31, 207, 214, 216n9, 224, 245, 250
Firecracker Films 65
Fiske, John 7, 11, 102
Flaherty, Robert 116, 118, 220
Flame in the Streets 134, 136, 137, 140, 142, 147
The Flintstones 22, 24, 27, 28, 29, 31
The Fool 153–164
Forbes, Bryan 137
Ford, John 116
Forsyth, Bill 143
The Fosters 31, 54
Fox 16, *191*, 196–197, 224, **226**
Frank, Harriet 224
Frankel, David 231
Frears, Stephen 115, 126, 143
The Front 224, 231
Frost, Vicky 65
The Frost Report 36, 55n5

Galton, Ray 37
Galusca, Roxana 215
Garnett, Tony 116, 117, 124, 126, 127, 128, 129n8
Geer, Will 221
gentrification 90, 91, 95
Geordie Shore 67
George and Mildred 40, 50, 57
The George Burns and Gracie Allen Show 26
Gerbner, George 21
Gleason, Jackie 23
Gledhill, Christine 173
globalization 34, 206, 207
Goffman, Erving 81
The Goldbergs 23
Golden Boy 197
The Golden Vision 171
The Good Life 39, 40, 50, **51**, 52, 57
Good Wife 197
Gordon, Linda 221, 230
Granada 78, 79, 117

Grand Designs 59
The Grapes of Wrath 116
Great British Class Survey 2
Great Depression 19, 116
Green, Guy 134, 137, 147
Greengrass, Paul 128
Gregory's Two Girls 143
Grey's Anatomy 190, 192, 193, 197
Grierson, John 115, 117, 118
Griffith, David Wark 4, 219, 231
Group 3 115, 129n2
Growing Pains 26

Halsey, A.H. 35, 56
Hancock's Half Hour 34, 37, 57
Hanley, Linsey 39, 55n11
Happy Days 26, 27
Harlan County, U.S.A. 220, 231
Harlan County War 231
Harper, Sue 4, 14n25, 15
Hawkesworth, John 236
HBO 16, 164n29, 197–198, 204, 205, 216n1, 216n20, 217
Herman, Mark 134, 147
Hesford, Wendy 209, 216n14, 217
Hidden Agenda 172, 179n2, 179n4
hierarchy 10, 12, 18, 42, 43, 93, 154, 185, 194, 212, 218, 219, 230, 234, 235, 240, 245
Higgins, Colin 231
Hill, John 4, 14n23, 14n24, 14n26, 15, 147n6, 149n18, 151, 173, 179n4, 179n5, 179n23, 180n28, 180, 181
The Hills 69
Hollyoaks 68
Hollywood 3, 14n22, 15, 115, 116, 119, 179n7, 220, 221, 224, 227, 228, 231n2, 231n8, 231n11, 232n18, 233
Home Improvement 28, 30
homelessness 97, 123, 173
Homicide: Life on the Streets 197, 206
The Honeymooners 23
Hosein, Jason 89, 99n1
Housing Problems 122
How Clean Is Your House 59, 63
How I Met Your Mother 34
Hughes, Donna M. 211, 216n18, 216n19

I Love Lucy 24, 34
I Remember Mama 23, 24
I'm All Right, Jack 134–138, **135**, 140, 147, 148n7
The Immigrant (1917) 219
The Immigrant (2013) 231n6
immigration 14n20, 34, 89, 172, 207, 209, 219, 229
In Black and White (aka *Save the Children Fund Film*) 172, 179n3

254 Index

In Plain Sight 197
In Two Minds 171
Independent America: Rising from Ruins 89, 99n1
inequality 2, 9–11, 13n6, 13n8, 13n9, 20, 35, 91, 153, 154, 161, 177, 180n27, 185, 190, 192, 195, 216n20
internet 7, 55n4, 89, 93, 106
It's a Free World 150n29, 172
ITV 4, 16, 59, 113n11, 117, 124, 125, 128, 148n9, 247n4

JAG 197
Jarrico, Paul 221
The Jeffersons 26
Jimmy's Hall 172
Jones, Owen 2, 15, 77, 78, 87n1, 88
Judging Amy 184, 197

Kalish, Max 19
Kaplan, Jonathan 230, 232n19
Kazan, Elia 137, 231n6
Keeping Up Appearances 50, 57
Kelleter, Frank 205, 216n5, 217
Kennedy, Liam 216n5, 216n7, 216n8, 217
Kes 171
Keynes, John Maynard 134
The King of Queens 29, 30
Kino Production Group 122
Klein, James 221, 231
Kopple, Barbara 220, 231
Kosminsky, Peter 128, 131n53

L.A. Law 184, 188, 197
labor 4, 8, 12n2, 18–20, 22, 32, 55n15, 77, 84, 85, 109, 112n3, 113n10, 121, 130n36, 132, 134, 136, 138, 144, 145, 150, 154, 156, 158, 159, 163n24, 164n28, 174, 176, 179n14, , 181, 184–187, 195, 198n5, 199n12, 201n33, 205–207, 210–213, 215, 218, 221, 222, 230, 231
Labor's Reward 218, 219, 223, 231
Labour Party 1, 106, 123, 140, 148n10, 149, 180n25
Ladette to Lady 67
Ladybird, Ladybird 143, 171
Lambert, Stephen 66, 72n20
Land and Freedom 150n27, 171
Land of Opportunity 7, 16, 89–100
Larkin, Margaret 218
The Last of the Summer Wine 42, 57
Laverty, Paul 16, 229
Law & Order 185, 188, 197, 199n16, 200n23
Law & Order: SVU 184, 197
Lefebvre, Henri 169, 179n12, 181
Lerman, Robert 18, 32
Let Us Now Praise Famous Men 204

The Life of Riley 23
The Likely Lads 40, 48, 49, 57
Lime Pictures 67, 68, 70
Little, Daran 68, 72n23
Little Britain 4, 16, 77
Littlewood, Joan 121
Loach, Ken 4, 8–10, 16, 106, 116, 117, 119, 120, 123, 125–130, 143, 147n3, 150n27, 150n29, 167–181, **175**, 219, 220, 227, 229–232
Locke, Ollie 69
London Labour & the London Poor 158, 164n25, 164n26, 166
Longmire 190, 197
Looking for Eric 171
Looks and Smiles 171
Love Thy Neighbour 134–136, 138, 140, 144, 147, 149n20
Loveless, George 155–158, 162n7, 162n12, 162n15, 163n17, 163n20, 166
lower class 9, 167, 178n1; *see also* working class
lower-middle class 37, 39, 42, 55n21, 63
The Lumpfish 121

MacTaggart, James 124, 131n41, 132
Mad Men 194, 197, 216n1
Made in Chelsea 68, 69
Made in Dagenham 134, 143–148, 150n32, 150n37
Major, John 1, 12n2, 13n4, 15, 138
management 19, 22, 27, 30, 31, 35, 38, 42, 44–16, 51, 54n2, 64, 130n34, 136, 137, 139, 141, 148n13, 149n13, 149n23, 150n36, 187, 195, 209
Marsh, Jean 12, 16, 235–237, 245, **246**, 247n1
Marson, Richard 235–237, 247n5, 247n6, 247n11
Marxism, post-Marxism 1–3, 10, 77, 106, 130n36, 143, 145
masculinity 11, 107, 179n1, 190, 195, 200n31, 201, 205–207, 211–216, 224, 230
Mayhew, Henry 158, 159, 163n25, 164n26, 166
McCarthy, Joseph 11, 130n32, 224
melodrama 69, 70, 122, 218
Mercer, David 121, 126
meritocracy 1
Mersey Shore 67
The Middle 31
middle class 4, 22, 23, 26, 28, 30, 31, 39, 40, 45–47, 50–52, 77, 83, 86, 106, 122, 153
Milburn, Alan 1, 13n5, 16
miner 11, 78, 84, 121, 130n31, 138–140, 146, 149n16, 220–223, 230
minority 7, 9, 10, 85, 91, 96, 112, 143–145,

Index

150n30, 192, 198n2, 200n26, 219, 220, 228
Modern Family 30
The Molly Maguires 224, 231
Monitor 119
Moore, Charlotte 64–66, 71n16, 72n19
My Beautiful Laundrette 143
My Big Fat Gypsy Wedding 65, 66
My Name Is Joe 171
My Three Sons 25, 26
My Wife and Kids 30
Mykura, Hamish 63, 64, 71n13

naturalism 71, 129n6, 148n6, 207, 216, 218
The Navigators 171
NBC 196–198, 199n16, 206
neoliberalism 9, 96, 134, 138, 145, 146, 151, 213, 215, 216n7, 216n11
New Orleans 89–100
The New Statesman 38, 49, 50, 57
Newman, Sydney 117
Nichols, Bill 7, 14n29, 15, 60, 71n7, 73, 90, 96, 99n4, 99n14, 100, 117, 129n13, 132
Nichols, Mike 231
Night Mail 120
9 to 5 231
Nixon, Richard 209, 210, 212, 214
Norma Rae 11, 12, 16, 218–221, 224–233, **226**
Norman, Lear 25
nouveau riche 50

Obama, Barack 2, 13n8, 15
The Office 34, 42, 57
On the Buses 40, 45, 55n14, 57
On the Waterfront 137
One Born Every Minute 63, 64
One Foot in the Grave 41, 57
Only Fools and Horses 39–41, 52, 56n26, 57
The Only Way Is Essex 67–70
Operatunity 59
Orwell, George 35, 54n1
Oster, Corinne 224, 231n13, 232n15, 232n17, 233
Our Daily Bread 116

Palmer, Gareth 60, 61, 71n6, 71n8, 73
Panorama 119
Parker, Charles 119
The Passaic Textile Strike 218, 219, 221, 228, 231
Pattillo, Mary 89, 99n2, 99n7, 99n11, 100
Penn, Arthur 220, 230
period drama 234, 235, 245
The Phil Silvers Show 22, 34
Pickford, Mary 224
Piketty, Thomas 2, 13n13, 15

Play for Today 103, 119, 125, 131n47
The Ploughman's Lunch 143
Poor Cow 121, 171
poverty 4, 8, 11, 13n5, 36, 82–85, 91, 95–98, 117, 122–125, 128, 153, 156–161, 162n15, 164n26, 173–178, 180n27, 180n36, 185, 204, 206, 213–217, 219, 220, 230, 235
The Price of Coal 171
privilege 13n4, 23, 60, 68, 76, 159
Property Ladder 59
Public Service Broadcasting 58, 59, 65, 66, 103, 127

The Quatermass Experiment 119
Questions of Leadership 171, 174

race, racism 4, 10, 26, 65, 83, 89–100, 106, 143, 144, 185, 188, 189, 192, 194, 200n26, 200n28, 200n30, 200n32, 206, 207, 216n9, 225–228
radio ballads (genre) 8, 120, 121, 130n24
Radio Ballads (program) 119–121, 130n24, 130n26
The Rag Trade 45, 57
Raining Stones 168, 171, 174–178, **174**
Ramsay, Lynne 134, 147
The Rank and File 171
Ratcatcher 134, 147, 148n12, 149n19
Ravetch, Irving 16, 224
The Real World 60
reality TV 58–72
realism, social realism 4, 6, 8, 9, 11, 58, 62, 68–70, 71n2, 102, 105, 106, 110–112, 113n16, 116, 118, 125, 129n6, 146, 154, 167–170, 173, 178, 204–207, 212, 213, 225
Registrar General 35, 54n2
Reichart, Julia 221, 231
Reith, John 122, 126, 128, 130n34
rich 4, 24, 81–85, 124, 153, 156, 158, 163n24, 164n26, 174–176, 219, 245; *see also* affluent; wealthy
Riff Raff 150, 171, 179n4
Rising Damp 44, 47, 57
Ritt, Martin 16, 218, 224–226, 231, 232n15, 232n17
Robbins, John 134
Rose, Alex 224
Roseanne **27**, 31, 216n9
Rosenbaum, James 19, 32n4, 33
Ross, Steven J. 4, 14n22, 15, 218, 227, 231n2, 231n11, 232n18, 233
Rothaker Films 218, 231
Route Irish 171, 172
Royle Family 40, 41, 57
rural areas 6, 35, 42–44, 154; *see also* countryside
Russak, Sam 218, 231

256 Index

The Salon 59
Salt of the Earth 11, 16, 218–231
Sandford, Jeremy 107, 119, 121, 125
Sands Films 159, 164n29
Sanford and Son 27
satire 37, 51, 55n5, 136, 137, 141, 146, 149n23
Schrader, Paul 220
Screen on Line 54
7UP 7, 76–88, **79**
Seventh Heaven 30
sexual harassment 10, 145, 185, 203, 219, 228
sexuality 10, 186–196, 200n26, 200n29, 209, 212
Shanks, Michael 137, 148, 151
Shapiro, Stephen 205, 216n5, 216n7, 216n8, 216n11, 217
Silverman, Peter 231
Simon, David 11, 16, 198, 204–207, 217
Simpson, Alan 37
The Simpsons 22, 28
Sklar, Robert 3, 14n19, 14n21, 15
soap opera 34, 42, 58, 60, 62, 68, 69
social capital 36, 43
social mobility 1, 13n5, 76
The Song of Steel 121, 130n31
The Spirit of '45 168, 177, 178
Steinbeck, John 116
Step by Step 28, 29
Steptoe and Son 34, 48, 57
stereotype 3–6, 17, 18, 21, 23, 25, 27–29, 31, 44, 52, 65, 77, 87, 92, 93, 96, 97, 194, 200n26, 207, 213, 224
Stockman, Olivier 16, 159, 164n29
Strand, Paul 220
strike 9, 11, 12, 45, 78, 106, 124, 129n10, 134–152, 218–233
Supernanny 61, 66, 67, 69
Survivor 60
Sutton, Crystal Lee 219, 224
Sweet Sixteen 169, 171, 176

Terry and June 39, 57
Thatcher, Margaret 1, 2, 9, 13n3, 16, 34, 35, 38, 50, 56n22, 76–78, 83, 85, 106, 112n6, 113n10, 138, 146, 148n10, 148n11, 150n38, 151n40, 152, 161, 167, 174, 176–178
Thirty Years of Conflict 121, 130n31
This Wonderful World 115
Thomas, Gerald 134, 147
Thompson, Edward Palmer 7, 16, 101, 112n1, 114
3 Clear Sundays 119
Tickets 172
Till Death Us Do Part 34, 39, 41, 57
To the Manor Born 42, 43, 49, 56n26, 57
toff 1, 162n37
Tolpuddle Martyrs 154, 157, 162n15

Tonight 119
Took, Barry 38
Topping, Keith 37, 55n8, 56
Toryism 1, 12n2, 138, 149; see also Conservative
trade union 108, 126, 140, 142, 149n25, 158, 162n12, 174
Tuan, Yi-Fu 170, 179n15, 181
Two and Half Men 29, 30
Typically British 115
underclass 4, 5, 9, 13n11, 14n23, 65, 77, 167, 178n1
unemployment 27, 51, 53, 55n3, 55n15, 83, 85, 99n8, 103, 105–108, 111, 112n6, 113n10, 113n16, 128, 173, 174, 176, 177, 178n1, 180n33
Union for Mine Workers 220
Union Maids 220, 221, 231
Up the Junction 119, 121, 124–126, 171
upper class 4, 36, 39, 76, 81–83, 95, 126, 138, 155, 159, 165n36, 192,
upper-middle class 22, 24–26, 29, 42, 45, 81, 185
Upstairs, Downstairs (LWT, 1971–75) 4, 12, 16, 234–247, **239, 240, 242, 244, 246**
urban areas 6, 7, 35, 42, 43, 89–100, 123, 127, 170, 205; see also city

The Vicar of Dibley 42, 43, 57
Vidor, King 116, 129n5, 132

Waldman Report 117
Walker, Johnny 5, 14n27, 16
The Waltons 30
Watkins, Peter 119, 123, 130n33
Watson, George 153, 161n1, 166
Watson, Paul 62
Wayon, Damon 30
wealth, wealthy, 29, 36, 43, 44, 50, 55n4, 67, 68, 76, 82, 95, 99n5, 116, 159, 173, 176, 180n27, 211, 213, 214; see also affluent; rich
Weber, Henri 136, 147n2, 149n17, 152
The Wednesday Play 119, 125, 127, 128
Welfare State 34, 134, 177
What Not to Wear 67
Whatever Happened to the Likely Lads 48, 49, 57
Wheatley, Helen 234, 245, 247n4
Wife Swap 59, 63, 66
Wilkins, Jes 65, 71n17
Williams, Raymond 8, 71n2, 73, 109–111
Williams, Tennessee 220
Wilson, Harold 123
Wilson, Michael 16, 221
The Wind That Shakes the Barley 150n27, 172
Winter of Discontent 106, 141
The Wire 11, 16, 198, 204–217

Wood, Tony 69, 70
Woodhead, Leslie 117
Woods, Faye 68, 69, 71, 73
workcom 44
working class 2–12, 14n23, 20–31, 36, 39, 41, 43–45, 48, 50, 52, 54, 55n4, 55n14, 60, 62, 63, 66, 76–78, 83, 84, 97, 98, 101–114, 115–132, 134–152, 167, 175, 176, 185, 192, 199n7, 206–208, 210, 213, 215, 216, 218–220, 225, 229, 230; post-working class 9, 167, 178n1; *see also* lower class
Working Girl 231
workplace 6, 10, 11, 37, 45, 62, 128, 184–203, 207, 230

World in Action 78, 117
World War I 34, 124, 124n10, 131n42, 210
Wright, Basil 120
Writing Desire 210

The X Factor 68

Yes Minister 46, 54, 57
You Are What You Eat 67
The Young Ones 38, 56n25, 57
youth 2, 19, 67–69, 77–81, 87, 126, 142, 149n24, 176, 186, 214, 215, 224

Z-Cars 109, 125, 127

www.ingramcontent.com/pod-product-compliance
Lightning Source LLC
Chambersburg PA
CBHW051216300426
44116CB00006B/595